Paul Morphy

The Pride and Sorrow of Chess

Paul Morphy

The Pride and Sorrow of Chess

David Lawson

edited by Thomas Aiello

University of Louisiana at Lafayette Press
2010

COVER CREDITS: background courtesy iStockphoto.com; Morphy photography (front cover) by Matthew Brady, courtesy Dale Brandreth and www.chessbookstore.com; Morphy engraving (rear cover) by D. J. Pound, courtesy Dale Brandreth and www.chessbookstore.com.

All uncredited images within this volume are reproduced from the original edition of *Paul Morphy: The Pride and Sorrow of Chess*.

University of Louisiana at Lafayette Press
P.O. Box 40831
Lafayette, LA 70504-0831
http://ulpress.org

ISBN 13: 978-1-887366-97-7
ISBN 10: 1-887366-97-0

Library of Congress Cataloging-in-Publication Data

Lawson, David.
 Paul Morphy : the pride and sorrow of chess / David Lawson, edited by
Thomas Aiello.
   p. cm.
 Includes bibliographical references and index.
 ISBN-13: 978-1-887366-97-7 (hardcover : alk. paper)
 ISBN-10: 1-887366-97-0 (hardcover : alk. paper)
 1. Morphy, Paul Charles, 1837-1884. 2. Chess players--Louisiana--Biography. I. Aiello, Thomas, 1977- II. Title.
 GV1439.M7L36 2010
 794.1092--dc22
 [B]
                                2010023091

CONTENTS

AUTHOR'S ACKNOWLEDGMENTS

It is with appreciation and pleasure that acknowledgment is made for helpfulness with material for this biography by Dale Brandreth, G. H. Diggle, Robert Sinnott, and Mrs. Alice N. Loranth, head of the John G. White Department of the Cleveland Public Library. I wish particularly to express gratitude for the suggestions and generous help of James J. Barrett, with special reference to the selection, preparation, and proofreading of the games.

And to my wife, Rosalind, I owe much for help and patience in the preparation of the material for this biography of Paul Morphy. This is the culmination of some years of trial for her, what with the time I have spent engrossed with my Morphy material and in the search for more. I may add, her help in the reading and correcting of the manuscript has been invaluable.

EDITOR'S ACKNOWLEDGMENTS

The editor would like to thank Dale Brandreth and Edward Winter for their help and advice. Both were incredibly kind and patient, answering a barrage of questions with timely grace. This project could not have come about without their help. The U. S. Copyright Office was also incredibly helpful, answering a landslide of repetitious, elementary questions without frustration or insults. (Or, perhaps, answerers dutifully kept their frustration and insults to themselves. That, in itself, deserves the questioner's gratitude.) Karen Kukil of the Smith College Special Collections library was fundamentally helpful in the development of Lawson's biographical material, as was noted Lola Ridge scholar Elaine Sproat. Both of them volunteered invaluable advice and information. Finally, Jennifer Ritter provided interest, advice, and support when the editor needed it most.

Editor's Introduction

In 1846, Paul Morphy became a legitimate child prodigy.
In 1857, he became the United States chess champion.
In 1875, he went crazy.

Such are the plot points that common biographical sketches use to trace the portrait of an otherwise unassuming New Orleans lawyer. But the outlines of Morphy's rise to fame and his descent into madness miss the marrow that provides the bulk and heft of such a skeletal presentation. He was a wealthy urbanite with an overbearing, overprotective mother. He was a prisoner to the expectations of a family name in a place, Louisiana, where family names still provided the scope of both initial possibility and later reputation. He was a southerner in an age of Civil War (and might very well have been a Confederate spy). He was a propitious, quiet loner who was thrust into the spotlight of fame, even as he fought it at every turn. And he was, finally, a global phenomenon who usually saw himself as nothing more than a Louisiana gentleman.

Such are the plot points that any armchair psychologist could use to trace a crucible of frustration and discontent.

There are places in Morphy's biography that remain enigmatic, and most biographical treatments of the chess champion pick and choose from various elements of the dominant themes of his life. All treatments of Morphy published after 1976, however, have one commonality that binds each through varied arguments and emphases—David Lawson's *Paul Morphy: The Pride and Sorrow of Chess*. As William Caverlee has noted, the book "remains the chief text for Morphy devotees."[1] The breadth of Lawson's research and the care with which he applies his analysis present the fullest possible portrait of the nineteenth-century's most celebrated chess player.

Paul Morphy was born in June 1837 to a prominent New Orleans family. He learned to play chess by watching his relatives, all chess enthusiasts, play recreationally. It was in these formative stages that Morphy began practicing what would become his trademark strategy, early and rapid development. As a child, he played and defeated the American general and chess player Winfield Scott, providing him with his first measure of celebrity. He also defeated European chess master Eugène Rousseau, as well as Johann Lowenthal. But his years at Spring Hill College provide Lawson and his readers the first real inkling that Morphy's uniqueness went beyond his preternatural chess ability. Morphy abandoned chess during his college days, just as he would abandon it after his European conquest. As his friend Charles Maurian noted,

> Morphy was never so passionately fond, so inordinately devoted to chess as is generally believed. An intimate acquaintance and long observation enables us to state this positively. His only devotion to the game, if it may be so termed, lay in his ambition to meet and to defeat the best players and great masters of this country and of Europe. He felt his enormous strength, and never for a moment doubted the outcome. Indeed, before his first departure for Europe he privately and modestly, yet with perfect confidence, predicted to us his certain success, and when he returned he expressed the conviction that he had played poorly, rashly; that none of his opponents should have done so well as they did against him. But, this one ambition satisfied, he appeared to have lost nearly all interest in the game.

He was pushed in his early days by his Uncle Ernest Morphy, who rushed his young nephew into matches and publicized his successes. At the same time, his parents seemed reticent to allow him to play in stakes matches or other forms of professional play. Lawson notes that his closeness to his family and willingness to accede to their wishes dominated Morphy's life, and the contradictory messages he received from them would remain an overriding existential crisis.

Still, after college (and with a surely reticent family), Morphy embarked for New York to make his name in chess. He challenged all at the New York Chess Club at the odds of pawn and move. He began sending letters to Howard Staunton, England's acknowledged champion, requesting a match either in the U. S. or abroad. He also engaged in stakes matches (with or without his family's consent).

But when Morphy traveled to London to hunt Staunton ("I visited your country," he told an Englishman, "for the purpose of challenging Mr. Staunton.") his family disapproved of the stakes required to make such a match come about. Lawson quotes Maurian that "after consulting with the rest of the family [about the Staunton match], they had resolved not only not to help raising the amount wanted, but that moreover they should not allow him to play a money match either with his own money or anybody else's. That in the event of his being in anyway aided they were ready to send some responsible agent to London whose duty it would be to let Mr. Morphy know that he must either decline playing or continuing the match or that he will be brought home by force if necessary; that they were determined to prevent a money match by all means." But Lawson reminds us that "there had been no inkling of family disapproval when Morphy wanted to engage Staunton in the $5,000-a-side match in New Orleans. Surely the family knew all about it, for the letter and terms had been printed in New Orleans papers. It would seem that Paul's father had not previously taken the same severe position on money matches, for Ernest Morphy, Alonzo's brother, would not have endeavored to get Paul a match for $300 a side in 1856 if his brother had objected."

Lawson is also careful to note that family problems were ancillary to Morphy's broader chess life. He credits Morphy's depression after his return from his successful European trip to the continued attacks of Staunton and his followers after their proposed match fell through. It was at this time that Morphy demonstrated an antipathy towards chess that hadn't surfaced since his college days. On his tour of American cities after his voyage home, Morphy gave several variations on a stump speech that included a warning for those who might take the game too seriously:

> A word now on the game itself. Chess never has been and never can be aught but a recreation. It should not be indulged in to the detriment of other and more serious avocations—should not absorb the mind or engross the thoughts of those who worship at its shrine; but should be kept in the background and restrained within its proper province. As a mere game, a relaxation from the severer pursuits of life, it is deserving of high commendation. It is not only the most delightful and scientific, but the most moral of amusements. Unlike other games in which lucre is the end and aim of the contestants, it recommends itself to the wise by the fact that its mimic battles are fought for no prize but honor. It is eminently and emphatically the philosopher's game. Let the chess board supercede the card-table, and a great improvement will be visible in the morals of the community.

And so there was the strain of professionalism in chess. There was the strain of a demanding family. And then there was the strain of being a southerner in the mid-nineteenth century. "Without doubt," writes Lawson, Morphy "was torn between his loyalty to the Union and to the state of Louisiana." In his senior thesis at Spring Hill College, Morphy proscribed very narrow limits for possible justifications for war. His brother joined a New Orleans regiment, but Paul did not. But his sense of loyalty was still there, and in October 1861, he traveled to Richmond, where he kept the company of P. G. T. Beauregard and played chess with Richmond's high society.

"Undoubtedly," notes Lawson, "Morphy went to Richmond with some thought of being useful, perhaps influenced by other Southern youths who were responding to the call of the South. And it may be that he was on Beauregard's staff for a short while and that he had been seen at Manassas, as had been reported. It would seem that Beauregard sensed that Morphy had little or no enthusiasm for secession and that the general brought it home to Morphy that he was not war material, on or off the battlefield."

Soon Morphy decided to leave New Orleans and the South. In October 1862, he traveled to Paris to meet his family.

> We are all following with intense anxiety the fortunes of the tremendous conflict now raging beyond the Atlantic, for upon the issue depends our all in life. Under such circumstances you will readily understand that I should feel little disposed to engage in the objectless strife of the chess board. Besides you will remember that as far back as two years ago I stated to you in New York my firm determination to abandon chess altogether. I am more strongly confirmed than ever in the belief that the time devoted to chess is literally frittered away. It is, to be sure, a most exhilarating sport, but it is only a sport; and it is not to be wondered at that such as have been passionately addicted to the charming pastime, should one day ask themselves whether sober reason does not advise its utter dereliction. I have, for my own part, resolved not to be moved from my purpose of not engaging in chess hereafter.

His Civil War anxiety and his unwillingness to engage in his true talent were not cause and consequence, but the two were definitely entwined in his thinking. His contradictory feelings about war and the South's place in it continued to haunt him until the conflict's end.

But if family and chess and war weren't enough, there was also Morphy's failure at his chosen vocation. Morphy received his law degree after his bachelor's, and after his chess triumphs attempted to settle into his profession. One failure prior to the Civil War was matched by another at its conclusion. Lawson provides some interesting speculative analysis as to why this might be: Morphy was lazy, he was unpracticed, he was unwilling to talk about chess in a city that only wanted to talk to him about chess. But whatever the reasons for this most recent failure, it was failure nonetheless.

"It was in 1875," writes Lawson, "that Maurian first began to notice some strange talk by Morphy..."

> Soon after, Morphy's imbalance reached a climax when he suspected a barber of being in collusion with one of his friends, Mr. Binder, whom he attacked, actually trying to provoke a duel (Maurian said he was a good swordsman), believing the friend had wronged him. This raised the question of mental competence. As a consequence of the attack, thinking it might be the prelude to further violence against himself or others, his family considered putting him in an institution for care and treatment, the 'Louisiana Retreat,' run by an order of the Catholic Church. So one day all the family took a ride, and he was brought in. Upon realizing the situation, Morphy so expounded the law applying to his case that the nuns refused to accept him, and his mother and the others realized he needed no such constraint.
>
> It was this attack upon Mr. Binder that brought public attention to his condition and North, South and all of Europe took it up, of course exaggerating the whole incident. There were inquiries about Morphy's condition and Maurian answered some of them. It was frequently questioned whether the condition might not have resulted from Morphy's extraordinary (as it was thought) mental strain induced by his chess playing.

But Lawson's treatment of Morphy's paranoia, hallucinations, and persecution complex is far more nuanced than that of his friend Charles Maurian. Of course, Morphy's mental illness has been a subject of conversation equal to that of his chess ability, and Lawson not only describes the events of his mental devolution, but also provides analysis of the psychoanalytic speculations on Morphy's condition. As do many later twentieth-century analysts, Lawson finds the Oedipal, Freudian context for Morphy discussions to be overly simplistic and unhelpful.

When examining Lawson's life's work, however, (and this book was most certainly his life's work) one is drawn from the enigma of Morphy to the enigma that is his biographer. Lawson's author biography in his original publication states that he "has been interested in Paul Morphy for over thirty years. He has visited Morphy's home in New Orleans and has followed Morphy's trail to Paris and London, always in search of additional information. He has published many articles on Morphy and is considered to be the world's foremost authority on him as well as the greatest collector of Morphiana. Mr. Lawson is a consulting civil and industrial engineer."

He was born Charles Whipple in Glasgow, Scotland, in April 1886, to parents Hyson Paine Whipple and Helen Robertson Howie. He apparently moved to the United States in 1893. Whether he lived with a family named Lawson after moving to the United States or changed it on his own is unknown. But as of the early 1930s, his parents were living comfortably in Ware, Massachusetts.[2]

Lawson, for his part, settled in New York, and like many immigrants of the time became active in radical political causes. Among them was the Ferrer Association, an anarchist educational society created in 1910 by Emma Goldman and Alexander Berkman. The association was named for the Spanish anarchist and educational reformer Francisco Ferrer, who had been executed the previous year for his role in a massive anti-clerical workers' rebellion. His American namesake worked to publish his writings in English and create schools modeled on Ferrer's *Escuela Moderna*. Lawson's leftist politics and his devotion to research and learning made Ferrer a natural fit, but his membership in the association would soon lead to a different kind of education. Milling about amongst the utopian radicals, all eager for educational reform on Ferrer's anarchist model, was the poet Lola Ridge.[3]

Lola, born Rose Emily Ridge, was a native of Dublin, thirteen years Lawson's senior, and spent her formative years in New Zealand and Australia. In New Zealand, she met the manager of a local gold mine. In 1895, the two began an ill-fated marriage that ran its course by the early 1900s. After its dissolution, Ridge moved to New York at age thirty-four, hoping to become the poetic success she could never be on the islands. Like Lawson she was an immigrant. Like Lawson she was active in radical politics. And like Lawson, she drifted toward the anarchist utopian Ferrer Association, where she met her fellow immigrant, far younger but full of the same strident zeal. On October 22, 1919, she married him.[4]

Ridge was an activist and a feminist, and she emphasized both of these identities in her work. At the time of her marriage to Lawson, she had already published "The Ghetto," the poem that would make her name through the 1920s and 1930s. Meanwhile, Lawson, flush with the bloom of May, was preternaturally devoted to his December bride. As the late teens became the late twenties, that devotion hadn't swayed. Ridge was a sickly woman, constantly prone to illness. She often spent summers in Mastic or Yaddo, New York to recuperate and escape the brutal city summer. But wherever her travels took her, her husband continually looked after her needs, sending clothes and medicine and food when she was away.[5]

As Ridge fretted over her persistent illnesses and worked on her poetry, Lawson worked as an engineer for both New York and Jersey City. But he wasn't doing what he wanted. He hoped desperately to work on bridge and building projects, and worked diligently through the late 1920s and early 1930s to reach his goals. It was an age of increasing specialization and civil service exams, and the accreditation process could be grueling. In his time away from work, Lawson continued to take a variety of qualifying examinations to place him in a higher position. In 1929, he took exams to qualify as assistant engineer for structured steel design and civil engineering, as well as one for structural steel designer. As he worked, however, New York passed an ordinance requiring engineers to be licensed by the state, which required not only a twenty-five dollar fee, but yet another in a long line of exams. It was an intense, seemingly endless process, but Lawson remained diligent. He found a job with the New Jersey State Highway Commission and appears to have kept it through at least the bulk of the Depression-era 1930s.[6]

But Lawson's education didn't stop with his qualifying exams. Through the late 1920s and early 1930s, he earned college credit by taking night courses after work. Again he studied diligently. Again he demonstrated a preternatural devotion to his efforts. It was this course of study, particularly in 1932 and 1933, which gave him the grasp of French required to carry on his Morphy research. "My French examination is only ten days off now," he wrote his wife in August 1933, "but I feel pretty good about it." He passed, forging the linguistic base for what would become his life's work, whether he knew it at that point or not.[7]

The feat seems all the more stunning considering the time and economic conditions. Ridge's illnesses and need for the clear air of vacations kept the small family on the brink of poverty. The couple never seems to have hit extremely dire straights, but money remained a concern, particularly in the heart of the Depression.[8]

Still, some French courses and a civil engineering job across the Hudson River do not at first glance seem to provide the seedbed for a sprawling narrative biography forty years in the making. The seedbed, however, was there.

Lawson's marriage put him in heady literary circles. He and Ridge were intensely close to novelist Evelyn Scott. Scott, *née* Elsie Dunn, was a Tennessee native who spent five formative years in Brazil, where she married and took her pseudonym. She traveled for much of her life, but used New York as her home base, relying on the friendship of Ridge and Lawson to help manage her affairs while away. Scott's most prominent work was *The Wave* (1929), an experimental novel—the second in a trilogy—about the Civil War.[9] The pair was also inordinately friendly with William Rose Benét and his older sister Laura. Laura was a poet and novelist, and in the late 1920s and 1930s she was also an assistant editor for book reviews at the *New York Evening Post*, the *New York Evening Sun*, and the *New York Times*. Bill Benét founded and edited the *Saturday Review of Literature*. A poet in his own right, Benét would go on to win the Pulitzer Prize in 1942 for his poetry collection, *The Dust Which Is God*.[10] Unlike most New Jersey state employees, Lawson moved in high literary circles. The author and critic Joseph Wood Krutch[11] was a family friend, as were the editors Henry Seidel Canby and Amy Loveman, who along with Bill Benét helped found the *Saturday Review of Literature*. Author and critic Gerald Sykes.[12] Harriet Monroe, founder and editor of *Poetry* magazine. The Chicago composer Henrietta Glick. New York artist and photographer Mary Marquis. Robinson Jeffers. Harry Hazlitt. Gaston Lachaise. Lenore Marshall.[13] Idella Purnell, editor of *Palms*, an influential poetry magazine.[14] In his dealings with the literary and artistic lights of the time, Lawson found himself with virtually unfettered access to the craft and business of authorship.

Even without these friendships, however, Lawson's literary education would still have made tremendous strides in his Broadway home. He acted as a de facto agent and editor for his wife. Amongst the couple's vocal worries about the rise of Hitler, their infatuation with the 1932 solar eclipse, and their incessant reading schedule was an extended continuing discussion about the nature of poetry, and Ridge's in particular. Lawson pushed his wife to complete her work, provided criticism of everything from theme to punctuation, and even occasionally served as her typist.[15] This was literary education by any other name, and Lawson's work with Ridge, his close relationships with the editors and artists of the twenties and thirties, his voracious reading, and his slow but steady mastery of French all made *The Pride and Sorrow of Chess* possible.

He would begin his study of Paul Morphy in 1938. Ridge had recently returned from a Guggenheim fellowship in the American southwest, but her always tenuous health continued to fail her. By 1938, her best work was behind her. Ridge would die in May 1941 from pulmonary tuberculosis at age 67.[16] The much younger Lawson was left with time and sadness and a void where his literary outlet and his obsessive devotion once resided. Paul Morphy, a study in sadness himself, would fill that void.

Though his obsession with the chess master began in the late 1930s, the rigor of his investigation reached its full flower in the 1940s. Lawson became a member of the New York Academy of Chess and Checkers, drawing a simultaneous blindfold game with Newell W. Banks (Banks was the simultaneous blindfold player) in 1948. In February 1951, Lawson began an extended correspondence with the Jesuit Spring Hill College, Morphy's Mobile, Alabama, alma mater. He worked closely with Alumni Secretary and Publicity Director Cliff Worsham and librarian Robert J. Zietz to get all of the pictures, documents, and related papers in Spring Hill's collection. Officials provided suggestions and citations for possible newspaper sources. The school's priests took an active interest, as well. In return, he shared with Worsham some of his work on Morphy. Spring Hill was in the process of developing an exhibition on the player for its museum.[17]

The transaction was inherently complicated, as a massive fire in 1869 and another in 1909 devastated many of the school's records, including much of its Morphy material, among them the player's theses and grade reports. When other avenues proved futile, Lawson even tried to solicit the help of Spring Hill alumni in New Orleans to assist him with research. For their part, the Spring Hill staff worked diligently for Lawson, thrilled that someone was interested in the school's most famous student. "We have never," reported Zietz, "done this type of thing in the past."

Lawson's correspondence with the university lapsed after 1953, only to revive again in 1956, then again briefly in 1957. After further research, spanning the course of another decade, Lawson again corresponded with the school's public relations director. By that point, however, Alabama's primary sources had run their course, and the relationship changed to the reciprocal trading of articles and other secondary material.[18]

The Spring Hill letters, and Lawson's other correspondence of the period, demonstrate a new drive in the engineer-turned-author. Gone was the loving, pliant doting he demonstrated to his wife, replaced with a fervent persistence, irascible and demanding both in his pursuit of Morphy and in his protection of his own reputation as the guardian of Morphy's life and legacy. The changes in Lawson, however, were more than attitudinal.

In place of his wife's literary luminaries, Lawson began friendships with people such as Norman Tweed Whitaker, an eccentric chessplayer with a significant criminal record. While Lawson was dining with Evelyn Wood and Gaston Lachaise in the early 1930s, for example, Whitaker was serving eighteen months in prison for his role in the kidnapping of Charles Lindbergh's baby. Still, he was a master player who knew and competed with the best of his day.[19] Lawson kept correspondence with George Kol-

tanowski, editor of the *San Francisco Chronicle's* chess column and a renowned blindfold player.[20] His preparation for the book also put him in
contact with William E. Napier at the very end of the master's life, for
information on Napier's uncle, Harry Nelson Pillsbury.[21] His time at the
Manhattan Chess Club put him in close contact with Hermann Helms,
Jacques Mieses, Nancy Roos, and the widow of Frank James Marshall.[22]

His new connections and friendships paid off. By the 1950s, Lawson
had clearly established himself as the principal authority on Morphy. In
1959, for example, Francis Parkinson Keyes wrote requesting clarification
of several factual issues pertaining to her biographical novel *The Chess
Players*, still in progress at the time. Keyes was publishing at the same time
as Ridge and her contemporaries, but she never ran in those circles. This
was not the rekindling of an old friendship. This was an author turning to
an expert, an inherent acknowledgement of Lawson's prowess in Morphy
studies.[23]

But though Lawson clearly had a new obsession, a new life, a new authority—and though Ridge had long since passed away—Lawson was not
without a meaningful, close relationship with a talented, famous woman.
In the early 1950s, he started a friendship with chess master Mary Bain.
Like Ridge, she was an immigrant. She was a veritable celebrity in her field,
the first woman to represent the United States in a national chess championship. She traveled extensively. There were, of course, differences, as
well. Bain, born in 1902 in Hungary, was younger than Lawson. She didn't
move in literary circles. The relationship appears to have been completely platonic. Lawson, however, doted on her in much the same way he did
Ridge so many years before. He helped her prepare for her trips, asked her
for copies of her work and offered to help annotate it. He attended to her
affairs while she was away, sending parcels and packages and facilitating
her other correspondence. Bain would die in 1972, as Lawson was in the
last stages of his opus.[24]

Again a woman close to him had died. Again Lawson was left with
Morphy. At that point, however, Lawson had remarried, his wife Rosalind
helping correct his drafts and patiently enduring the inevitable marital ne-
glect that accompanies authorship. He would dedicate the book to her.[25]

In 1976, he published *Paul Morphy: The Pride and Sorrow of Chess* with
David McKay, when he was 89 years old. Two years after the publication
of his masterpiece, he sold his Morphy collection to chess publisher Dale
Brandreth. The decades of collecting, writing, haggling, traveling, and
purchasing had reached their crescendo. Ridge was gone. Bain was gone.

Now Morphy, too, had run his course. Lawson was soon to follow. He died in 1980.[26]

Much of the minutia of Lawson's biography remains unknown, but the single-minded passion with which Lawson pursued his subject indicates that he would want the focus of such an introduction on Morphy, anyway. And, most certainly, his biography traces a "satisfactory outline of the man."[27] Or, at least, the most satisfactory outline possible. His passion for his subject does not lead to blind hagiography. It gives us a nuanced account of a talented and troubled figure—a gifted man who remained haunted by his gift. Morphy is an important figure to chess history, to Sport History, to Louisiana History, to American History. His friend Oliver Wendell Holmes found perhaps the best brief summation of the argument for his necessity in 1859:

> His career is known to you all. There are many corners of our land which the truly royal game of kings and conquerors has not yet reached, where if an hour is given to pastime, it is only in an honest match of checquers played with red and white kernels of corn, probably enough upon the top of the housewife's bellows. But there is no gap in the forest, there is no fresh trodden waste in the prairie, which has not heard the name of the New Orleans boy, who left the nursery of his youth, like one of those fabulous heroes of whom our childhood loved to read, and came back bearing with him the spoils of giants whom he had slain, after overthrowing their castles and appropriating the allegiance of their queens.
>
> I need not therefore tell his story; it is so long that it takes a volume to tell it. It is so brief that one sentence may embrace it all. Honor went before him, and Victory followed after.

A NOTE ON THE TEXT

Lawson's biography develops its narrative in a unique style, particularly for someone with the author's literary background. While Lawson has much to say about the chess champion and his biography, he repeatedly employs the voices of correspondents and letters to tell Morphy's tale. Writers generally cringe at such amateur tactics. I did, as well. But as I spent more time with the manuscript, I realized that the talent and insight of the correspondents would have made omission of their language a robbery to us all. I have therefore made no effort to reduce the number of block quotations in the text. I have embraced them as integral to Lawson's story and his presentation. They are backed by an appendix that includes even more primary source material. I have at many points fixed grammatical mistakes and awkward word choice to make the book easier to read. I have added explanatory notes where appropriate. I have also added an annotated bibliography of selected biographical works on Morphy since the publication of Lawson's original manuscript.

But though I haven't omitted the block quotes, I have omitted and altered other of the book's original components. Lawson included myriad pictures throughout the text of his original manuscript. Some of those pictures have been retained, others have been omitted or replaced with new images. All have been moved to two distinct picture sections. Also included in Lawson's original publication was a Part II, a collection of sixty Morphy chess games. I have removed it from this volume. With the continual publication and analysis of Morphy games, Lawson's Part II provides nothing that cannot be just as conveniently (and in algebraic notation) found in myriad other Morphy books or outlets. Internet chess databases such as www.chessgames.com, for example, carry all of the games cited by Lawson and more, each with running contemporary commentary to make them far more understandable to modern players and enthusiasts.

Finally, some copies of *Paul Morphy: The Pride and Sorrow of Chess* included an errata list. Others did not. In a 1979 letter to Edward Winter, Lawson included a copy of the errata, concerned that many of the published copies did not include it.[28] Where appropriate, I have included Lawson's desired changes in the body of the text.

Thomas Aiello, 2010

NOTES
TO EDITOR'S INTRODUCTION

1. William Caverlee, "The Unenthusiastic Chess Champion of the World," *Oxford American* (The Sports Issue 2007): 70-71.

2. According to the 1930 United States Census, a David Lawson originally from Scotland was working as a ship fitter in a New York shipyard. This may or may not be Morphy's eventual biographer. As of September 1929, Lawson was working for the New Jersey State Highway Commission. Source material for Lawson's biography is scarce. He was a lifelong New York resident after moving to the United States. His Social Security Number was 113-20-0282. He was a nonsmoker. See "John Whipple or Charles M. Howie or Charles Whipple or David Lawson," http://genweb.whipple.org/d0220/I47887.html; Department of Commerce—Bureau of the Census, "Population Schedule," Fifteenth Census of the United States: 1930, sheet 77 B; and Lola Ridge Papers, 1900-1941, MS 131, Sophia Smith Collection, Smith College, Northampton, Massachusetts (hereinafter cited as Ridge Papers). Still, even after work with these sources, some of the best source material for this brief biographical sketch came from email correspondence with Dale Brandreth, in the possession of the author.

3. Ridge Papers; and Donna M. Allego, "Lola Ridge: Biography," Modern American Poetry, http://www.english.illinois.edu/maps/poets/m_r/ridge/bio.htm. For more on the Francisco Ferrer Association, see Modern School Collection, MC 1055, Special Collections and University Archives, Rutgers University, New Brunswick, New Jersey; and Paul Avrich, The Modern School Movement: Anarchism and Education in the United States (Oakland, CA: AK Press, 2006).

4. Allego, "Lola Ridge."

5. Allego, "Lola Ridge;" and Ridge Papers.

6. Ridge Papers.

7. Ibid.

8. Ibid.

9. Ridge Papers; and Robert C. Peterson, "Evelyn Scott, 1893-1963," *The Tennessee Encyclopedia of History and Culture* (Nashville: Tennessee Historical Society, 1998), http://tennesseeencyclopedia.net/imagegallery.php?EntryID=S014. For more on Evelyn Scott, see The Evelyn Scott Collection, MS 2015, Hoskins Library, University of Tennessee, Knoxville, Tennessee.

10. Ridge Papers. For more on the Bénets, see The Benet Family Papers, 1918-1960, Collection Number 4667, Carl A. Kroch Library, Cornell University, Ithaca, New York.

11. Ridge Papers. For more on Krutch, see Joseph Wood Krutch Papers, 1920-1971, mm74029009, Library of Congress, Washington, D.C.

12. Ridge Papers; and "Gerald Sykes, 80, Dies; Was Author and Critic," *New York Times*,

16 July 1984, B11.

13. Ridge Papers. For more on Marshall, see Lenore Marshall Papers, 1887-1980, MS Coll/Marshall, Rare Book and Manuscript Library of Butler Library, Columbia University, New York, New York.

14. Ridge Papers. For more on Purnell, see Idella Purnell Stone and Palms, TCRC98-A24, Harry Ransom Humanities Research Center, University of Texas at Austin.

15. Ridge Papers.

16. Michele Leggott, "The First Life: A Chronology of Lola Ridge's Australasian Years," *Bluff '06: A Poetry Symposium in Southland*, 21-23 April 2006, transcript provided at New Zealand Electronic Poetry Centre, http://www.nzepc.auckland.ac.nz/features/bluff06/leggott.asp.

17. "Banks Wins 27 of 34 Games," *New York Times*, 1 December 1948, 39; "Chess Letters and Documentation," David Lawson Collection, CPL Collection Development B802N, Cleveland Public Library, Cleveland, Ohio (hereinafter cited as Lawson Letters); and email correspondence with Dale Brandeth, in possession of the author.

18. Lawson Letters.

19. His correspondence with Whitaker, like most in this era, began with chess requests relating to Morphy. It began in 1950 and seems to have dwindled by 1951. "The Papers of Norman Tweed Whitaker," John G. White Collection, Cleveland Public Library, Cleveland, Ohio; Sam Sloan, "The Most Notorious International Chess Master in Chess History Was Probably Norman Tweed Whitaker," www.anusha.com/norman.htm, accessed 10 May 2009; Federal Bureau of Investigation, "FBI History: Famous Cases: The Lindbergh Kidnapping," www.fbi.gov/libref/historic/famcases/lindber/lindbernew.htm, accessed 10 May 2009; and Lawson Letters. See also, John Samuel Hilbert, *Shady Side: The Life and Crimes of Norman Tweed Whitaker* (New York: Cassia, 2000); and A. Scott Berg, *Lindbergh* (New York: G. P. Putnam's Sons, 1998).

20. "Koltanowski Letters," David Lawson Collection, CPL Collection Development B802N, Cleveland Public Library, Cleveland, Ohio; and "George Kotanowski, 1903-2000," *The Week In Chess Magazine*, The London Chess Center, www.chess-center.com/twic/kolt.html, accessed 10 May 2009.

21. "Collection of Harry Nelson Pillsbury Items," David Lawson Collection, CPL Collection Development B802N, Cleveland Public Library, Cleveland, Ohio (hereinafter cited as Pillsbury Papers).

22. For more on Marshall, see Frank Marshall, *My Fifty Years of Chess* (Kilkerran, Scotland: Hardinge Simpole, 2002, originally published 1942). Pillsbury Papers; and "Papers of Mary Bain," David Lawson Collection, CPL Collection Development B802N, Cleveland Public Library, Cleveland, Ohio (hereinafter cited as Bain Papers).

23. Frances Parkinson Keyes, "Letter: New Orleans, La., to David Lawson, Brook-

lyn, N.Y., 1959 Mar. 4," David Lawson Collection, CPL Collection Development B802N, Cleveland Public Library, Cleveland, Ohio.

24. Bain Papers.

25. Lawson's marriage to Rosalind was his third. He was married and divorced in between his relationship with Lola and his final marriage. For this and other clarification on Lawson's life, the author would like to thank Elaine Sproat, who interviewed Lawson on several occassioins and willingly shared her comments and analysis. Email correspondence in possession of the author.

26. Kurt Landsberger, "About the Letters," in *The Steinitz Papers: Letters and Documents of the First World Chess Champion, ed. Kurt Landsberger* (Jefferson, NC: McFarland & Co., 2002), 19; David Lawson, *The Pride and Sorrow of Chess* (New York: David McKay, 1976); and Edward Winter, "Chess Records," http://www.chesshistory. com/winter/extra/records.html.

27. Caverlee, "The Unenthusiastic Chess Champion of the World," 71.

28. Edward Winter, "5672. Errata list by David Lawson," Chess Notes, http://www. chesshistory.com/ winter/index.html.

David Lawson, from the dust jacket of the original 1976 edition of
Paul Morphy: Pride and Sorrow of Chess.

A young David Lawson.

Images courtesy of the
Special Collections,
Sophia Smith Collection,
William Allan Neilson Library,
Smith College,
Northhampton, Mass.

David Lawson with wife
Lola Ridge; photo at left is
dated 1925.

Images courtesy of the
Special Collections,
Sophia Smith Collection,
William Allan Neilson Library,
Smith College,
Northhampton, Mass.

Above, David Lawson at work in his study; below, David Lawson and Lola Ridge, on far ends, with Louise Adams Floyd, Ellen Kennen, and other unidentified friends.

Images courtesy of the Special Collections, Sophia Smith Collection, William Allan Neilson Library, Smith College, Northhampton, Mass.

AUTHOR'S INTRODUCTION

In the present resurgence of interest in chess in this country, the name of Paul Morphy has come to be associated with a most brilliant period in the game's history. It is true that Morphy's time at the chessboard was short; however, before the conclusion of that short time his "secret," as many have spoken of it, was revealed. But until that secret was revealed, all fell before him. His secret—rapid and consistent development—is now recognized as a basic law of chess, a law that revolutionized the game. As Al Horowitz put it, in his recent book, *The World Chess Championship*, "It is scarcely an exaggeration to say that without him [Morphy] chess as we know it would be unthinkable." Morphy's games were a major contribution to the world of chess, and a small selection of them is included in this volume to illustrate his varied virtuosity.*

Placide Canonge, who wrote the libretto for Thelcide Morphy's unfinished opera, *Louise de Lorraine*, cried out for a Creole to write Morphy's biography, and Frances Parkinson Keyes expressed the same wish in *The Chess Players*, "that a full-sized biography should be written and that its author should be a Creole."

Although this author is not a Creole, he has lived in New Orleans and knows well the Vieux Carré. At different times over the years he has visited the rooms of the old Morphy House at 417 Royal Street (number 89 when Morphy lived there), the house that already had a history when Louisiana became a state.

Practically all the books on Morphy and his games have been written by foreigners. Only two have been written in the English language. The other books were published in France, Germany, Holland, Russia, Sweden, Spain, Italy, Cuba, Mexico, Argentina, the Ukraine, and Yugoslavia, the last in 1971. Some of these have contained extensive collections of his games, Maróczy's over four hundred. In 1859, two little books of his games were published in New York, but now they have been unknown for a century and are not obtainable.*

---

* EDITOR'S NOTE: The collection of sixty games included in Lawson's original publication as Part II of *Paul Morphy: The Pride and Sorrow of Chess* are not included in this new edition. The largesse of Morphy and the influence of Lawson's original text have created widespread availability for the games the author included. They can be found in numerous studies, as well as in many online venues.

It is not surprising that when Philip W. Sergeant of London published *Morphy's Games of Chess* in 1916, the first new work on Morphy in English since 1860, J. H. Blake, an English reviewer, should comment in the *British Chess Magazine*, "Is it not a little singular that no prominent American player has thought it worth while to provide for his countryman in his native tongue a literary monument worthy of his fame."

With this biography, the author is hopeful that he has thrown some light and understanding upon Morphy's great, grievous, and solitary years. They were years of triumph and trial, years when under great stress from conditions beyond his control he acted strangely at times, yet always the gentleman, finding some solace for diversion in his latter days in his walks along palm-lined Canal Street or in the Vieux Carré.

---

* EDITOR'S NOTE: This situation has changed. Lawson's influence led to a Morphy renaissance. His oeuvre is published in its known totality in virtually every available format. There is also a body of Morphy biography that has appeared in the years since Lawson's volume. The author included in his original a comprehensive bibliography that is included in this updated volume. In addition, an updated annotated bibliography follows, noting the English-language biographical treatments that have appeared since 1976.

PAUL MORPHY! The name rings like a bell in the Halls of Chess. At first high, clear, impetuous with eagerness, his pawns were in the way, it becomes strong, vibrant, dominant with courtesy but to change soon to a muffled tolling.

CHAPTER 1

The New World Welcomes

Paul Morphy and his games are America's most dramatic contribution to the world of chess, and in international competition he has represented his country at its best. At one time or another over the years, he has been referred to as the Alexander, the Byron, and the Napoleon of chess. He combined some of the qualities of each and, like Napoleon, he too lived his last years a captive of circumstances.

At the age of twenty-two, Morphy was the first to be universally hailed "The World Chess Champion." In Paris, on April 4, 1859, at a farewell banquet for him, it was St. Amant who placed a laurel wreath upon the marble bust of Morphy by the sculptor Eugene Lequesne. In London, at a gathering ten days later, his health was toasted as "The Champion of the World." When Morphy arrived in New York, on May 29, 1859, John Van Buren, son of President Van Buren, concluded a testimonial presentation at the University of the City of New York (now New York University) by proclaiming: "Paul Morphy, The Chess Champion of the World." And in Boston soon thereafter, at an extraordinary banquet attended by Louis Agassiz, Henry Wadsworth Longfellow, the mayor of Boston, the president of Harvard, and other educators, poets, and scientists, it was Oliver Wendell Holmes who proposed "the health of Paul Morphy, The World Chess Champion." Yet unlike another at a later time, Morphy himself laid no claim to the title.

Morphy (baptized Paul Charles Morphy) was born June 22, 1837, in New Orleans, and it is now well-established that his paternal ancestors were of Irish origin, although not until recent years was documentary evidence discovered to prove the fact. Even Sergeant, in his first book on Morphy, was unaware that such was the case. Mention of it in the obituary of Ernest Morphy (Paul's uncle) in the Dubuque *Chess Journal* of 1874 had escaped his notice.

The Last Will and Testament of Paul Morphy's grandfather, Diego Morphy, filed in New Orleans in 1813, links Paul's father, Alonzo Morphy, with Paul's great-grandfather, Michael Morphy. This great-grandfather had changed his name from Murphy to Morphy when he arrived in Madrid from Ireland in 1753, in accommodation to the Castilian pronunciation.

The history of Paul Morphy's progenitors, going back to his great-grandfather, is marked by much activity in diplomacy and law, and great political involvement, at times dramatically so. And Paul, like his forebears, became a public figure known throughout his own country and abroad before his twenty-second year.

As early as 1793, Morphy's ancestors made their appearance in the annals of United States history, before any of them had touched the nation's shores. The first to be so distinguished was Michael Morphy, who was an officer in an Irish regiment prior to his immigration to Spain. His reasons for leaving Ireland, whether political or religious, can only be a matter for conjecture. In any case, in Spain he became a captain of the Royal Guard, serving his early years in Madrid. Later he moved to Malaga, where he engaged in the merchant trade and married Maria Porro. To them was born Paul's grandfather, Diego.

Records in the Washington National Archives show that although Michael was a Spanish citizen, he applied for and received an appointment as American consul to Malaga, as the following exchange of letters bears witness. They are (apart from their interest as they relate to this biography) of historical significance, since they pertain to the early, difficult years of the United States. It may be noted in passing that Michael signed his letters as Michael Morphy, but that Thomas Jefferson, in replying, addressed him as Michael Murphy.

> Malaga, 11th November 1791
> To the Honorable Members of Congress of the United States
> of North America. The address of Michael Morphy Resident at
> Malaga in the Kingdom of Spain.
>
> Sirs:
>
> I have the honor of presenting you with this address encouraged
> thereto by my well known Services to the trading Subjects of
> America to this Port as their Agent since the Independency of
> that Country and during this period I have procured that every
> protection should be shown to the Colors so as to make their
> Traffick here as free in every respect as that of other Nations.
> There has been from ten to fifteen American Vessels yearly that
> have brought Cargos and Loaded others at Malaga since the
> Peace and I have hitherto only acted as Agent for them in this
> Bussiness from an authority of their Consignees which merited
> a tacit acquiescence of the Spanish Government wherein I have
> not experienced any novelty, but having lately had knowledge

that Interest is now making with the American Minister at the Court of Madrid, William Carmichael Esqr. for his forwarding memorials to Congress from people here who without any merrit that I can learn want to superceed me in Soliciting for an appointment of Agent or Consul for this Port, I think it my duty to avail of the present moment to have the honor of making my case known to the Honorable Members and of being the person who without any other recompense or view of interest than a small Emolument voluntarily allowed me by the Masters of American Vessels has always served them with the greatest attention and procured them every condescension and favor that could be expected from the beginning of their Infancy as a new State in their Trade to this part of Spain. Which if considered by the Honorable Members to merrit a prior prefference for my having the honor to hold now, or at any other time such an appointment as they may deem most necessary to give for a representative at the Port of Malaga. They may be assured that I will be happy to continue in their Service and to do everything becoming a faithful Servant of that Country etc. & etc.

I have the honor to be with the greatest Respect
Your Most Obedient
Humble Servant
Michael Morphy

In due course (sixteen months later), Michael Morphy received the following letter from Thomas Jefferson, Secretary of State under President George Washington (Philadelphia was the capital of the United States at that time):

To Michael Murphy Esq.   Philadelphia, March 2nd, 1793

Sir.
The President of the United States desiring to avail the public of your services as Counsul for the Port of Malaga in the Kingdom of Spain, I have now the honor of inclosing you the Commission and a copy of the Laws of the United States, together with the copy of a circular letter written to our Consuls and Vice Consuls the 26th August 1790 to serve as their standing instructions.

I am with sentiments of proper esteem, Sir
Th. Jefferson
United States Secretary of State

Obviously, Thomas Jefferson had heard about Michael Morphy from others before he (Morphy) was commissioned to act as United States consul for Malaga. Additional correspondence pertaining to this appointment, together with other correspondence from and to Michael Morphy, is to be found in the National Archives and Records in Washington, D.C. As will be seen in Michael Morphy's letters to Jefferson and others (Jefferson did not continue long as secretary), Algerian pirates were causing much damage to American shipping and even taking American seamen into slavery.

Upon receipt of his commission as United States Consul for the Port of Malaga, Morphy replied as follows:

Malaga 30th, June 1793

Sir,

I have received the 20th instant by the Schooner Fredericksburg Packet of Philadelphia, Atkinson Anderson, Master, the honor of your letter dated the 2nd March, and also that of the Commission granted by the President and Senate as Consul of the United States of America at Malaga, and a copy of the Laws thereto appertaining which with that of a circular letter written to the Consuls and Vice Consuls the 26th August 1790, shall serve as my Standing Instructions. . . .

In the communications which you are pleased to direct shall be given by my office to your department every six months, which is also to comprehend the cargoes outward and inward—do you mean Sir, the quality of the goods only, or is it to be the contents—If it is to be the latter, I beg leave to offer, that it would be better for the Masters of Vessels to sign a report of these homeward cargoes before me to present to the custom house, for I cannot see what use it will be to furnish such intelligence at so late a period as six months.

I have the honor to be with great truth and regard:
Sir
Your Most Obedient
Humble Servant
Michael Morphy

Thomas Jefferson, Esq., etc.

Morphy dispatched another letter to Thomas Jefferson on July 30, 1793. This letter and the above June 30 letter will be found complete in the Appendix.

In this same year, 1793, Nathanial Cutting was appointed secretary to Col. David Humphreys, American minister to Portugal, and Cutting headed a committee to collect information on how best to protect American shipping and secure the release of American seamen held as slaves by the Algerians.

Cutting visited Morphy in Malaga in October 1793 for several days, as the former related in his journal:

> Thursday 17th Oct. 1793 . . . The guide took us to a cursed, blackguard Psado, alias Tavern, where we expected to be obliged to pass the night in the midst of noise, filth, stench, and fleas,—but fortunately we repaired immediately to the house of Mr. Morphy, the American Consul, who called at a lodging-house on the north side of the Public walk, where we found accommodations much better than where we left our baggage and servants. Without loss of time we had our baggage removed and took possession. Mr. Morphy drank tea and spent an hour or two with us.

> Friday 18th Oct. 1793 . . . At 2 p.m. Repaired to the house of Mr. M. Morphy to dine agreeably to appointment. We were introduced to Mrs. M. Morphy and three of her daughters—the other two and two sons, being absent!

> Saturday 19th Oct. 1793 . . . Our master of mules came about 11 o'clock and sent off our Baggage; we took an early dinner and mounted our mules about half past one p.m. Mr. Morphy has been very attentive to us, visited us twice this forenoon, and renewed his charge to the muleteers and Master Carrier to be very attentive to us and our baggage.

Two years later, Consul Morphy (he was now being addressed as "Morphy") was the first to forward dispatches notifying the United States through then Secretary of State Timothy Pickering that peace had been secured with the Dey of Algiers and that 102 American seamen held as slaves had been freed upon the payment of $600,000 in ransom money. When a few years later the Tripoli pirates ravaged American shipping, the growing United States Navy resolved the matter in a different fashion.

Evidently Michael Morphy met the requirements of his office well, for Colonel Humphreys, in a letter to President Washington dated February 3, 1794, commented that "without touching on Consular appointments in general, I will just say in passing, I think Mr. Morphy at Malaga a very good one." Thomas Jefferson had earlier written to one American consul that some consuls were "of no more account than the fifth wheel of a coach."

Michael Morphy continued on as American consul at Malaga until the end of the century; another was appointed in January 1800. It would appear that he died some months before this date, for nothing further is known of him after his exchange of letters with Timothy Pickering in 1799. His wife, Maria Porro, died some time after 1813, having borne Morphy two sons and five daughters. However, records exist of only one child, Diego, born in 1765 at Malaga. Little is known of him until we find him in the New World at Saint-Domingue—and at a troubled time. The year was 1793, a time simultaneous with Michael Morphy's becoming consul at Malaga. It was a time of insurrection, revolution having come to Saint-Domingue with its population of four hundred thousand slaves, under the leadership of Toussaint L'Ouverture.

Here in Saint-Domingue, Paul's grandfather Diego had married Mollie (Maria) Creagh in 1789. She was of a good Irish family and bore Diego a son, Diego, Jr., in 1790. At about this time, the presence of whites on the island was being threatened, and Diego devised a plan of escape for his family. He placed his infant son in a market basket and covered him with vegetables. Diego then sent him, along with his mother, who was disguised as a produce vendor, to board an English vessel at anchor in the harbor. Successfully passing the guards, Diego's wife stayed on the vessel bound for Philadelphia. Not long after, Don Diego escaped to Charleston, South Carolina, and soon rejoined his wife and son in Philadelphia. Certainly the Morphy family's entrance into the United States was as dramatic as Paul's later visit to Europe.

Probably because of his Spanish birth and the position of his father at Malaga, Don Diego became acquainted with, if he or his father had not already known, Don Joseph de Jaudenes, first Spanish minister to the United States, who appointed Don Diego Spanish consul to the states of North Carolina, South Carolina, and Georgia on January 31, 1795. He then took up residence at Charleston, South Carolina.

Don Diego had two more children, daughters, by Mollie Creagh, before she died in 1796. The following year Diego married Louisa Peire, and two sons and three daughters were born to them in Charleston. The elder son, christened Alonzo Michael, Paul Morphy's father, was born November 23, 1798, and the younger, Ernest, November 22, 1807.

In 1809 Don Diego moved to New Orleans, upon being appointed

Spanish consul for that port, and served in that post until his death, which occurred soon after his Will and Testament was filed on August 27, 1813. He was survived by his mother, Doña Maria Porro, his wife, Doña Louisa Peire, and all eight children by his two marriages.

Upon the death of Diego, Sr., Diego, Jr., who had served as vice consul under his father, was appointed Spanish consul for the Port of New Orleans, a post he held until 1818, when he was appointed vice consul to Natchez, Mississippi. He soon resigned and, being of an intellectual temperament, returned to New Orleans, where he devoted himself to teaching and the writing of books on the French and Spanish languages. Now the Morphys had broken their ties to the Old World. Years later Paul Morphy was to pay a fleeting visit to Spain, the land of his grandfather's birth.

CHAPTER 2

Three Encounters and a Problem

Alonzo Morphy, who was eleven years of age when the family moved to New Orleans, decided early to become a lawyer, and in due course entered the Collège d'Orléans for that purpose. Upon graduation, he presented himself before the Louisiana State Supreme Court for examination, and on January 7, 1819, he was granted the Louisiana Supreme Court Judges' Certificate, which stated that he was found, "after due and strict examination in open court . . . well and sufficiently qualified to practice as an Attorney and Counsellor at Law in the courts of this State."

The following month, according to the certificate granted him by the Louisiana District Court of the United States, "Alonzo Morphy, Esquire, was duly admitted to practice as Attorney and Counsellor Proctor and Advocate . . . and . . . thereupon he took the oath required by Law." He now established himself in practice at 61 Toulouse Street, New Orleans. A few years later he was elected to the state legislature and served in the House of Representatives from 1825 to 1829.

Apparently believing Alonzo Morphy well-qualified, Governor Derbigny appointed him Attorney General for Louisiana on January 20, 1829. Exactly one month later, on February 20, 1829, a marriage contract was drawn up and signed between

> Mr. Alonzo Michael Morphy, of legal age living in this city, born at Charleston, S.C., legitimate son of the late Mr. Diego Morphy and the late Lady Peire, on the one part. And the Damsel Louise Thérèse Felicitie Thelcide Le Carpentier, of legal age living in this city where she was born, legitimate daughter of Mr. Joseph Essau Le Carpentier and Lady Modest Blache, on the second part.

The next day, one bann having been published and the other two dispensed with, the pair were married in St. Louis Cathedral, the Reverend Abbé Moni performing the ceremony.

Alonzo now occupied the house at 1113 Chartres Street, known today as the Beauregard House because in later years it was the home of Confederate General Pierre G. T. Beauregard. Morphy soon became quite active in social, financial, and community affairs. Among other activities, he became regent of the New Orleans Public Schools, administrator of the Charity Hospital, and director of the Bank of Louisiana. On August 31, 1839, Governor A. B. Roman appointed him state supreme court justice, a post he filled into 1846. His brother Ernest Morphy, nine years his junior, became appraiser at the New Orleans Custom House.

The Morphy family remained at Chartres Street until 1841, when Alonzo bought the house at 89 (now 417) Royal Street. During extensive alterations, which took several months, the family lived in one of the Pontalba buildings on St. Peter Street. The Royal Street house already had a long history in 1841. William C. C. Claiborne, Louisiana's first governor, had established the Banque de la Louisiane there, soon after statehood was granted in 1813, and Andrew Jackson had often been entertained in the rooms above the bank, especially during his candidacy for the Presidency.* It remained the Morphy home until 1886, when Helena, Paul's youngest sister and last of the immediate family, died.

The house at 1113 Chartres Street, however, was the birthplace of all of Alonzo's children. Edward, the elder son, was born December 26, 1834, while Paul was born on June 22, 1837. Paul's sisters, Malvina and Helena, were born, respectively, on February 5, 1830, and October 21, 1839.

Alonzo Morphy had now become a distinguished jurist, while Paul's mother, Thelcide, more often known as Telcide, had acquired some distinction as a musician and composer. An accomplished pianist and harpist, she also had a fine mezzo-soprano voice and often entertained with musicales, frequently bringing in outside talent. On such occasions she might have introduced one of her own compositions, perhaps a trio for piano, violin, and cello, a number of which were published.

The game of chess was one of the Morphy family's chief recreations, a diversion often enjoyed on a quiet evening. It seems they all played. Of Alonzo's and Ernest's games we know a good deal, since Paul played many games with both, a few of which have come down to us. But Paul also played many games with his Grandfather Joseph Le Carpentier and his Uncle Charles Le Carpentier. His brother, Edward, gave promise of being a very strong player but, nettled by Paul's beating him badly, he gave the game up, saying he would never play again. Only years later did he engage in an occasional game, Paul giving him Knight odds. In this family setting, Paul grew up with a great fondness for music and an aptitude for chess.

---

* EDITOR'S NOTE: The Banque de la Louisiane was actually established in 1805, following American transfer rather than following statehood. Additionally, Louisiana became a state on April 30, 1812, not 1813.

Years later, Regina Morphy, daughter of brother Edward, reminiscned about the evenings of music, conversation, and chess in her forty-page booklet, *Life of Paul Morphy in the Vieux Carré of New Orleans and Abroad*, which she published in 1926. Regina also had a talent for music and composed many waltzes, her first composition being, "The Paul Morphy Waltz," published in 1893.

In her booklet Regina recounts how

> the Morphy home at 89, Royal Street was at all times, the centre of gayety and pleasure. Almost every week, Mrs. Morphy entertained large house parties, and her weekly "musicales" were highly artistic and enjoyable. Although Paul was not a musician in the true sense of the word, he was noted for his splendid ear for music, and once he heard a tune, he never forgot it and he thoroughly enjoyed these evenings devoted to classic music and brilliant conversation... He was exceedingly fond of grand opera and very seldom missed a performance at the old French Opera House on Bourbon Street. .... During intermissions he would call upon some of his lady friends who occupied boxes and invite them to a promenade in the "foyer" where refreshments were served.

Toward the end of her better years, Mrs. Morphy started a more ambitious work, the score for a five-act opera, *Louise de Lorraine*. The libretto was written by L. Placide Canonge, one-time impresario of the Théâtre de l'Opéra. But Thelcide got no further than the first four acts, her spirit burdened with increasing concern for Paul in his last years.

Little is known of Paul's earliest experiences with chess. Undoubtedly, like Capablanca, about whom a similar story is told, Paul first learned about chess by watching his relatives play. In Paul's case, the relatives were his father and Uncle Ernest. In fact, Ernest Morphy, writing in 1849 to Kieseritzky, editor of *La Régence*, said that Paul first learned the game that way, this contrary to the usual story that he was formally taught the moves of the game by his father when he was ten years of age.

Charles A. Maurian, who was almost the same age as Paul and who became Paul's life-long and closest friend, said in an interview years later in the New Orleans *Picayune* of January 17, 1909, that "it was a well known fact that Paul was a chess genius when he was barely nine years old."

The following is the earliest known incident about Paul as related by Maurian in the same *Picayune* article:

> On a balmy summer afternoon Judge Morphy and his brother

Ernest were seated on the back porch, which overlooked the long yard, playing chess. The game had been a particularly interesting one, and lasted several hours, with the result that both armies were sadly reduced, though apparently still of equal strength. The Judge's King seemed in an impregnable position, and Mr. Morphy, after vainly checking and checking, wiped his perspiring brow and remarked that the game was a certain draw. Judge Morphy smilingly agreed with him and the pieces were swept aside to be reset for another trial. Now, little Paul, hardly out of skirts, had been an interested spectator to the closing stages of the drawn battle, and while the men were being replaced he astonished his elders by saying: "Uncle, you should have won that game."

Judge Morphy and Ernest Morphy looked at the boy and the former asked, "What do you know about it, Paul?" Paul, with the assurance of a born genius, asked leave to set the pieces in the final position, and, just to humor him, his father consented. The boy faithfully and accurately arranged the men; and, then studying the board for only a moment, leaned forward and said: "Here it is: check with the Rook, now the King has to take it, and the rest is easy." And sure enough it was. The child had seen a mate in an apparently impossible position, and the Judge and his brother simply stared at him, hardly able to express themselves in words.

While it is not known just when the above incident took place, obviously it happened before Paul was ten years old. In her booklet, Regina Morphy says, "He was about ten when he won games from the older and more proficient players." But it is Paul Morphy himself who has given us the first definite date of his interest in the game and possibly the beginning of his serious play. While in New York attending the National Chess Congress of 1857, he told Charles H. Stanley, one of the participants, that he was taken to the Stanley–Rousseau chess match that was played in New Orleans in 1845. His Uncle Ernest had acted as Rousseau's second, and probably Paul had asked to be taken along.

It is likely that he had been watching his father playing even before he was six years old, for at eight and ten years of age he was engaging General Winfield Scott and Dr. Camille Rizzo successfully, as we shall see. Also, General Tillson has said that Paul composed his only chess problem when he was nine. (More about that later.) In a game with Dr. Rizzo, he foresaw a mate in four moves against him, which his opponent overlooked. This indicates that at age ten Paul knew a good deal more than just the "moves."

A biographical sketch of Morphy in the 1857 book *The First American Chess Congress* states that

> one peculiarity of Paul's play during the infantile stage of his Chess life [obviously before meeting General Scott and Dr. Rizzo] while his father, his grandfather, his uncle and his brother were his chief adversaries, used to create considerable merriment among the fireside circle of chess lovers with whom he was brought into contact. His pawns seemed to him to be only so many obstacles in his path, and his first work upon commencing a game was to exchange or sacrifice them all, giving free range to his pieces, after which, with his unimpeded Queen, Rooks, Bishops and Knights he began a fierce onslaught upon his opponent's forces, which was often valorously maintained until it resulted in mate.

Obviously, Paul soon saw the great advantage of rapid development of his pieces and soon learned the importance of Pawns against strong opponents, and rumors of his prowess became bruited about. When Winfield Scott was in New Orleans for five days in December 1846, on his way to Mexico to take command of the American Army, it was arranged that Paul should play him. General Scott had some reputation as an amateur. Also, he had played often with H. R. Agnel, author of *Chess for Winter Evenings*, and Col. J. Monroe, author of *The Science and Art of Chess*, who dedicated his book "To Lieutenant General Winfield Scott, himself skilled in the play of chess." The following account of the Scott–Morphy meeting appeared in a May 1904 issue of the *Evening Post*:

> The first game of chess played by Paul Morphy, under anything like public circumstances was with General Winfield Scott.... In those days [1846] a number of the leading citizens of New Orleans had a club on Royal Street just over the famous Sazerac Coffee House, and among the members of the coterie were Paul Morphy's father, Chief Justice Eustis of the State Supreme Court ... and others who are not important to this story.
>
> General Winfield Scott had many acquaintances there, some of them quite intimate, and knowing the habits of the members he repaired to their very comfortable rooms within a few hours after reaching the city. One of Scott's passions was for chess. It may be said to have been one of his vanities as well. He was in the front rank of amateurs in his day. After renewing old friendships and talking a little about the war, he turned to

Chief Justice Eustis and asked whether he could have a game of chess in the evening, explaining that he had been deprived of his favorite amusement for a year or two and was naturally keen to resume it. "I want to be put upon my mettle." . . . "Very well," said Justice Eustis, "We can arrange it. At eight o'clock tonight, if that will suit you."

At eight o'clock, dinner having been disposed of, the room was full. Gen. Scott, a towering giant, was asked to meet his competitor, a small boy of about ten years of age [eight and a half] and not by any means a prepossessing boy, dressed in velvet knickerbockers, with a lace shirt and a big spreading collar of the same material. . . .

At first Gen. Scott imagined it was a sorry jest, and his tremendous dignity arose in protest. It seemed to him that his old friends had committed an incredible and unpardonable impertinence. Then Justice Eustis assured him that his wish ha[d] been scrupulously consulted; that this boy was quite worthy of his notice. So the game began with Gen. Scott still angry and by no means satisfied. Paul won the move and advanced the Queen's rook's pawn [oddly, years later when Morphy met Anderssen in 1858, Anderssen played this same move against him three times during their match]. In response to the General's play he advanced the other pawn. Next he had two knights in the field; then another pawn opened the line for the Queen, and at the tenth move he had the General checkmated before he had even begun to develop his defense. There was only one more game. Paul Morphy, after the sixth move, marked the spot and announced the movement for the debacle—which occurred according to schedule—and the General arose trembling with amazement and indignation. Paul was taken home, silent as usual, and the incident reached the end.

The few survivors of that era still talk of Paul Morphy's first appearance in public, but only by hearsay. Gen. Scott lived to wonder that he should have ever played with the first chess genius of the century, or for that matter, of any other century.

Thereafter, Paul was sometimes taken to the Sazerac Coffee House and to the Exchange Reading Rooms on Exchange Place, where the chess players of New Orleans often gathered. That more was not heard of the Scott incident at the time was doubtless due to consideration for the general and the above account did not appear until some fifty years had passed. The case was likely the same with Paul's first meeting with Lowenthal in

1850 (to be discussed later), for the real story of that encounter did not come out until some six years later.

The following story in the New Orleans *Picayune* of January 17, 1909, tells of Paul's early games with his maternal grandfather:

> The Judge's father-in-law [Joseph Le Carpentier] heard of the skill of his grandson, and insisted upon playing him and Paul was taken to the gentleman's house. The two played, and grandfather, who lacked the skill of his sons, never had a chance with Paul. Finally the old man accepted odds, first of a pawn, then of a Bishop, and finally of a Rook, and still he was no match for Paul. The sight of Paul and grandfather playing the royal game is one that is indelibly stamped on the mind of Mr. Maurian. It was a funny sight, as he described it, to see little Paul sitting on books piled upon his chair so that he could reach the table, with the worried old gentleman opposite him, and the chessmen spread out between the two. Mr. Maurian was only a small boy at the time, but he can recall that picture today as he saw it sixty years ago.
>
> It is not on record that the grandfather ever won a single game from little Paul, but that was no disgrace, as few indeed could make headway against the juvenile prodigy. The Morphys, like most of the leading French and Spanish families of affluence in their day, had family reunions every Sunday. One Sunday they would gather at the Judge's house for dinner . . . the following week would find them at the grandfather's house, and so on in a continuous round. The gatherings were always the occasions of chess parties, and, as some think, little Paul took his first impressions of the game at these occasions.

About this time, Paul expressed himself in another direction in chess, as related by Ernest Morphy and General John Tillson. (Tillson and Ernest Morphy both lived for some years during the 1850s in Quincy, Illinois, and they were co-editors of the chess column of the Quincy *Whig* in 1859.) In a letter to Gustave Reichhelm, chess editor of the Philadelphia *Sunday Times*, General Tillson discusses a chess problem "that . . . was composed by Paul Morphy before he was ten years of age. This is a fact," which may account for its being a little problem.

This little chess problem, said to have been composed by Paul, is given by Philip W. Sergeant in his *Morphy's Games of Chess*; but Sergeant labels it "Morphy's Alleged Problem," noting that Alain C. White cast doubt upon its being authentic.

Apparently, Morphy did not tell everything to his close friend Charles
Maurian, for after Morphy's death, Maurian, then chess editor of the New
Orleans *Times-Democrat*, had the following to say in its issue of October
12, 1884, giving the problem as follows:

In answer to various inquiries addressed to us as to its authenticity, we can only say that while we have no proofs positive in
the matter, and never had any direct contraction of it from Mr.
Morphy, we have good reason to believe that he never composed it. Had he done so, we feel fully assured we would long
since have known the fact.

Unquestionably it is Morphy's chess problem and his only one. Ernest
Morphy sent it, together with a Morphy game (about which more later)
and a letter dated June 10, 1856, to the New York *Clipper*, and both were
published—the letter in the June 21, 1856, issue, and the problem and
game in the June 28, 1856, issue. Sam Loyd also published the problem in
the New York *Musical World* of April 30, 1859, together with Louis Pauls-
en's only chess problem.

Ernest Morphy has given us a picture of Paul as a young boy about
ten, in an incident with a Dr. Camille Rizzo who had some reputation in
New Orleans as a composer of chess problems and who also conducted the
"Académie des Èchecs" for the teaching of chess. Ernest describes the incident in the following letter in the Macon *Telegraph* of May 23, 1867. (The
account of the meeting first appeared in the Quincy *Whig* in 1859.)

Quincy, Adams Co. Ill., March 8, 1867
Mr. S. Boykin, Macon, Georgia
Dear Sir:—

Here is a little incident of Paul's early career, hardly known,
but of some interest. . . . About nineteen years ago, there lived
in New Orleans an Italian, Dr. Rizzo, who had acquired some

notoriety by the composition of some inverse problems. The Signor unfortunately extended that mania of the inverse even to the game itself; and maintained that he ought to be declared the victor who could obtain a preponderance of forces such as to force a sui-mate, or better still as he invariably termed it, "a sublime sui-mate." The feat, of course he could perform only against inferior opponents. But to our incident: Mr. Charles Le Carpentier, Paul's uncle, had declared to Rizzo that he had a little nephew, only ten years, who could beat him at the natural game; and the challenge having been accepted, the next day saw them at the Doctor's house, across the board, Charles Le Carpentier acting as umpire and the sole spectator.

The game went on for some twenty moves, when Lo! A fortuitous position happened, concealing a position of checkmate in four moves against Paul. While Rizzo was pondering on his move, Le Carpentier quietly looked at his nephew and saw a picture for a painter. There, motionless sat the chap, his little bosom heaving, and two large tears of vexation flowing along his cheeks. He also had seen the impending mate. But *mirabile dictu!* Rizzo moves at last, overlooking the mate, and obliged after ten moves to strike his colors. He could not be prevailed upon to fight a second time.

Very respectfully, yours, &c.
                                                    Ernest Morphy

In the following excerpt from the New Orleans *Times-Democrat* of December 30, 1894, another observer, S. Spencer, tells of seeing the young Paul Morphy at chess:

It was but three years after the Stanley–Rousseau match of 1845 that the wonderful feats of chess of a boy aged about eleven began to be bruited about. He had played with his relatives and friends, some of whom were able and experienced amateurs, and had vanquished them all. The veteran Rousseau had been pitted against him, and he in turn had gone down before the victorious child. All his school mates had heard of his prowess and there were few who did not look upon him with a species of awe. It was said that he had learned chess without a master by simply looking on at the games played at his father's house.

Such was the beginning of Paul Morphy's chess career. Well do we remember seeing him from the street playing chess with his grandfather, Mr. Le Carpentier, in the latter's counting room, situated in the lower story of his residence. The boy was small,

and the ledgers or other of grandpa's commercial books had to
be piled up under him to enable him to sit at the required height
to the table; and when we thus saw him we did not know, but
learned afterward, that the grandson was all the time giving
grandpa the odds of a rook and beating him like old Harry.

As the year 1849 approached, Paul was demonstrating the strength
of a master, and this without benefit of books as vouched for by Ernest
Morphy. He now began playing with the strongest of New Orleans players, in addition to Uncle Ernest. On his twelfth birthday, June 22, 1849,
Paul undertook a blindfold game against his Uncle Ernest and as he made
his twentieth move, he remarked that he must now win. Thereupon, Dr.
A. P. Ford, an old chess opponent of Ernest's, carried Paul into an adjoining room and presented him with an inlaid mother-of-pearl chessboard,
which is now possessed by the author.*

(It might be mentioned at this time that the game given by Sergeant
[GAME XCVII] in *Morphy's Games of Chess* as played between Paul Morphy and the above-mentioned Dr. A. P. Ford was not played by Paul Morphy, nor was it a blindfold game. Dr. Ford's opponent was Ernest Morphy,
and the game was played October 5, 1840. The game was sent by Ernest
Morphy himself as his game to the Cincinnati *Sunday Dispatch* and *Porter's
Spirit of the Times* in 1859. The author has the original score as recorded
by Ernest Morphy. Therefore, this game should not appear in any future
collection of Paul Morphy's games.)**

Among the best players of the New Orleans Chess Club in the late
1840s were Eugène Rousseau (undoubtedly the strongest), Ernest Morphy, Dr. A. P. Ford, Charles Le Carpentier, and James (later Judge) Mc-
Connell. Years later, at a Manhattan Chess Club dinner, Judge McConnell
related the following experience with Paul Morphy, as reported in the New
Orleans *Times-Democrat* of December 3, 1905:

> [Judge McConnell] declared that after an experience at chess
> that covered nearly if not quite a half century, and of personal

---

* EDITOR'S NOTE: In 1978, chess publisher Dale Brandreth purchased Lawson's collection of Morphy memorabilia. He donated the bulk of Lawson's letters and documents
to the Cleveland Public Library, but they are as yet uncatalogued and unavailable to
public researchers.

** EDITOR'S NOTE: Again, the whereabouts of this original score are unknown, but
the preponderance of evidence provided by Lawson throughout seems to back his contention.

play with practically every great master of the game, famous during that period, he had long since reached the conclusion that not one possessed the remarkable intuitive grasp of the possibilities of the game that Morphy displayed. While he undoubtedly possessed a memory of wonderful powers, and so practically never forgot whatever he deemed worth remembering in relation to the game, whether moves, openings, defenses, or even whole games, yet it was this faculty of instant appreciation of all, or practically all, that lay in a given position at chess that most markedly distinguished and differentiated the greatest American master. In illustration of this point, Mr. McConnell related an anecdote of his own first meeting with Morphy in the latter part of the 1840's, when the latter was a little lad only about twelve years old. Mr. McConnell was even at that time one of the leading players of the Crescent City, and having heard much from Ernest Morphy, Eugène Rousseau and other local chessists of the strength of the little Paul, he determined to take no risks in the game nor to treat his little adversary with any lightness.

After a long struggle, by a rather neat combination of his own, as he thought, Mr. McConnell had succeeded in winning a clear piece, when suddenly, in more minutely examining the position, he discovered that, by a most recondite line of play, some seven or eight moves deep, following a move with which he was obliged to conclude his combination, his youthful adversary might turn seeming defeat into victory. Somewhat disconcerted, he, however, succeeded in concealing his emotion over the discovery, and thinking that it was almost impossible that so young a player as his antagonist could have penetrated so deeply into the position, he proceeded, with seeming unconcern, to make his move. Imagine his consternation when, almost before his hand had quitted his piece, his young opponent not only instantly made the *coup juste* in reply, but followed it up with the whole series of winning moves without the slightest hesitation.

Out of the thirty games played with McConnell about that time, Paul lost but one. From the above account by Judge McConnell it is evident that Paul had been playing Rousseau before him. Eugène Rousseau was well known in European chess circles. In a series of one hundred games with Kieseritzky—best known as the editor of *La Régence* and for his games with Anderssen, and the Kieseritzky Gambit—Rousseau had barely lost the contest. He was well known in this country for his match with Stanley in 1845. During 1848–1849, out of over fifty games with Paul, he may have won five at most. Of all these games, the records of but two survive.

The following game with Rousseau is the first Paul Morphy game to be published, and it has become a part of chess history. Ernest Morphy sent it to Kieseritzky, together with a letter, and both were published in the January 1851 issue of *La Régence* as follows:

New Orleans, October 31, 1849

Dear Sir,

I send you herewith a game of chess played on the 28th instant between Mr. R. [Rousseau] and the young Paul Morphy, my nephew, who is only twelve. This child has never opened a work on chess; he has learnt the game himself by following the parties played between members of his family. In the openings he makes the right moves as if by inspiration; and it is astonishing to note the precision of his calculations in the middle and end game. When seated before the chessboard, his face betrays no agitation even in the most critical positions; in such cases he generally whistles an air through his teeth and patiently seeks for the combination to get him out of trouble. Further, he plays three or four severe enough games every Sunday (the only day on which his father allows him to play) without showing the least fatigue.

Your devoted friend
Ernest Morphy

Paul Morphy	E. Rousseau		
WHITE	BLACK	WHITE	BLACK
1. P–K4	P–K4	13. QxP ch	Q–Q3
2. N–KB3	N–QB3	14. QxQ ch	KxQ
3. B–B4	P–B4	15. N–B7 ch	K–K3
4. P–Q3	N–B3	16. NxR	PxP
5. O–O	P–Q5	17. PxP	K–B3
6. N–N5	P–Q4	18. P–QN4	B–K3
7. PxQP	NxP	19. R–K1	B–N1
8. N–QB3	QN–K2	20. B–N2 ch	K–N4
9. Q–B3	P–B3	21. R–K5 ch	K–R3
10. QN–K4	PxN	22. B–B1 ch	P–N4
11. Q–B7 ch	K–Q2	23. RxP	Resigns
12. Q–K6 ch	K–B2		

This is GAME CXLIV of Sergeant's collection, and with its publication, the second period of Paul's chess career may be said to have begun.

CHAPTER 3

A Surprise Encounter

We now come to the major highlight of Paul's early chess career. Exactly two months after the Morphy–Rousseau game mentioned in Chapter 2 was played, Johann J. Lowenthal, a political refugee from Hungary, arrived in New York, a total stranger to the land, although well known in European chess circles. He had come to the United States hoping to start a new life in the West.

One day soon after his arrival, in deep dejection, he picked up a copy of the New York *Albion*, and, although the language was strange to him, he chanced upon a chess problem in the newspaper's pages. Immediately he felt a welcoming to the land, and the next day, having called upon the editor, he was given an introduction to Charles H. Stanley, of whom he had heard in Europe. Through Stanley's introductions, Lowenthal met other American players across the country.

It may not be amiss to mention at this time, in view of what was to happen some months later, that during his short stay in New York, Lowenthal met successfully the city's best players over the chessboard. Journeying westward, he was similarly successful in Lexington, Cincinnati, and Louisville, frequently giving odds to the local players. After a short stay in Louisville, he departed for New Orleans, arriving there on May 18, 1850.

Maurian tells the following story of Lowenthal's visit in the New Orleans *Picayune* of January 17, 1909:

> It was while Paul was at the height of his early reputation that Lowenthal, the Hungarian master, considered one of the great players of the time, arrived in New Orleans. . . .
>
> Lowenthal's reputation was such that the chess players of New Orleans planned to give him a great reception, and at the little club in the Third District the foreigner was royally entertained. He contested a number of off-hand games in which he was successful against the city's strong players, and then it was that Mr. Ernest Morphy told him of Paul's skill and invited him to the Judge's house to meet the lad.
>
> Herr Lowenthal had heard of infant wonders before, and while he accepted the invitation to the Judge's house he did not expect

to find in Paul anything more than in the usual juvenile chess genius. The Judge welcomed his guest, and after dinner the gentlemen repaired to the drawing-room for a game of chess. Herr Lowenthal saw little Paul, patted him on the head patronizingly and smiled as he entered the lists against the youngster. Herr Lowenthal, not wishing to take advantage of the boy, offered to give him odds, but Judge Morphy and Mr. Ernest Morphy insisted that the visitor play Paul on equal terms, and then if the lad was found easy, he might be given a handicap for the next game.

The battle began, and Paul, in no wise disturbed at the reputation of his opponent, played with his usual skill and confidence. The contest had not gone a dozen moves before Herr Lownthal realized that he was up against the hardest proposition he had ever sought to solve. The first game was of no great length, and to the surprise of every one Paul won handily. Another game was played with similar result and a third also went to the school boy.

Henceforth his reputation extended beyond the circle of his relatives and friends; and if, prior to this encounter, there had been doubtful Thomases who had misgivings about his genius, they certainly disappeared now.

Such, indeed, was the confidence inspired by his victory over Lowenthal that certain gentlemen, with more enthusiasm than discretion, suggested to Judge Morphy the propriety of sending his son to the International Chess Congress announced to take place in London in 1851. The practical father, however, refused to consider such a proposition, and instead of going to England, Paul Morphy in December 1850 entered college.

In *Brentano's Chess Monthly* of November 1880, General Tillson gives Ernest Morphy's description of Lowenthal's encounter with the young Paul:

Paul, he says, was a little fellow and stood up to the table. Mr. Morphy and his brother, Judge Morphy, the father of Paul, [and Rousseau] were lookers-on. Lowenthal was one of the most noted and scientific players in the world, and a finished courteous gentleman. He at first supposed that the game would be a bagatelle, but Mr. Morphy told me that as he [Lowenthal] got into the game and felt Paul's force, his startled look and upraised brows after each move of Paul's was perfectly ludicrous[,] or as Mr. Morphy in his French vernacular expressed it, "comique."

While Charles Maurian was not present when these games with Lowenthal were played (he and Paul were only some months apart in age), he knew many of those who were present and later became quite intimate with them. As he said in an interview published in the New Orleans *Times-Democrat* of June 10, 1892, he knew Rousseau and Ernest and Judge Morphy very well. There are records of chess games he played with them, and with others of the unnamed people who were present at the Morphy–Lowenthal encounter. Maurian also says in the *Times-Democrat* article that he

> who for years lived with him [Paul Morphy] in daily companionship, who played chess with him almost daily, who talked chess with him almost constantly, heard from his own lips and many a time all the details of this self-same encounter with Lowenthal in 1850.

Maurian does not reveal in his *Picayune* account (and perhaps did not know) that only the first game was played on May 22, 1850. Lowenthal returned on May 25, undoubtedly expecting to do better, but he also lost the two games played that day. It is usually mentioned in Morphy collections that one of the games ended in a draw, as Ernest Morphy also stated. But more about that later.

Ernest Morphy was the first to disclose the story of Lowenthal's defeat by Paul in the 1850 encounter and then only after six years had passed. In 1856 he sent the following letter to a New York weekly, the *Clipper*, which had started a chess column, and the letter was published in its June 21, 1856, issue.

> Moscow, Clermont County, Ohio
> June 10, 1856
>
> N. Marache, Esq.
> Chess Editor of the New York Clipper
>
> Dear Sir:
>
> For years past Mr. Rousseau, on account of important and arduous duties, and myself as a votary of rural life, have both given up playing chess. My nephew, Paul Morphy, who is incontestably our superior, now holds the scepter of chess in New Orleans. In May, 1850, when only thirteen years of age, he played three games with the celebrated Hungarian player, Mr. Lowenthal. The first game was drawn, and the two others gloriously won by Master Paul.

You have herewith one of these games—unfortunately the only one recorded—and also a two-move enigma composed as far back as 1849.

Yours, most sincerely
Ernest Morphy

(A second game, a Sicilian Defense, Morphy later remembered for Fiske, who published it in the *Chess Monthly* in 1859.) The game with notes that Ernest Morphy enclosed with his letter was a Petroff Defense. The enigma or problem was a two-mover, Paul's only problem, which was discussed in Chapter 2. Both the game with Ernest Morphy's notes and the problem were published in the *Clipper* on June 28, 1856. In presenting the game, the chess editor commented as follows:

HONOR TO CHESS

We specially call the attention of our readers to the game published in this week's issue, played between Paul Morphy (now the leading player of New Orleans) and Herr Lowenthal, when a resident of the United States. We copy the game, with its notes, *verbatim*, from a score sent us by our esteemed correspondent, Ernest Morphy. Problem No. 10, also a pretty and classic contribution from the same youthful chess genius, is well worthy of attention.

GAME NO. 10

Played in 1850, between Master Paul Morphy, when thirteen years old, and Herr Lowenthal, the celebrated Hungarian player.

Morphy	Lowenthal		
WHITE	BLACK	WHITE	BLACK
1. P–K4	P–K4	13. QNxPa	BxNb
2. N–KB3	N–KB3	14. N–N6 dis ch	Q–K3
3. NxP	P–Q3	15. NxR	QxQ
4. N–KB3	NxP	16. BxQ	K–B1
5. Q–K2	Q–K2	17. P–QR3	B–Q3
6. P–Q3	N–KB3	18. B–Q3	K–N1
7. N–B3	B–K3	19. NxP	KxN
8. B–N5	P–KR3	20. P–KB3	P–QN4
9. BxN	QxB	21. B–K4	N–Q2
10. P–Q4	P–B3	22. QR–K1	N–B3
11. O–O–O	P–Q4	23. QR–K2	R–K1
12. N–K5	B–QN5	24. BxB ch	PxBc

WHITE	BLACK	WHITE	BLACK
25. RxR	NxR	41. RxP	N–K4 ch
26. P–KN3d	P–N4	42. K–N5	P–N6
27. K–Q2	N–N2	43. R–R7 ch	K–Q1
28. R–R1e	P–QR4	44. P–B4	PxP
29. K–Q3f	K–K3	45. PxP	N–Q6
30. P–QR4	P–QN5	46. K–B4	NxBP
31. P–QB4g	B–B2	47. R–R7	B–K4
32. R–K1 ch	K–Q3	48. RxP	BxP
33. R–K5	PxP ch	49. KxP	B–N2
34. KxP	N–K3	50. R–R7	B–K4
35. R–N5	N–B1	51. P–R5	NxPh
36. R–Q5 ch	K–K3	52. R–R5	BxP
37. R–QB5	K–Q3	53. RxN ch	K–B1
38. P–Q5	K–Q2	54. R–QN5	K–B2
39. R–B6	B–Q3	55. P–QR6	Abandons
40. R–R6	N–N3		

PETROFF'S DEFENSE

a. A feasible sacrifice of two minor Pieces for a Rook, two Pawns and the gain of several moves.

b. The best move.

c. Was it preferable to take with Knight?

d. A clever disposition of Pawns to annul the power of adverse Knight. Between superior players such minutiae generally decide the fate of the day.

e. Master Paul, now and hereafter, wields his Rook with considerable tact.

f. Honor to this industrious King!

g. Philidorian-like.

h. There is not a good move for black; his game is irretrievable.*

*This is as fine a specimen of Chess skill and ingenuity, especially in one so young, as it has been our lot to see for some time.

Chess Editor *Clipper.*

This Petroff game with Ernest Morphy's notes is given here complete because of a gross error in Lowenthal's edition of *Morphy's Games of Chess,* published in 1860. In Lowenthal's book, the Petroff game shown above to have been won by Morphy is altered beginning with move fifty-five so that it becomes a drawn game. Following Lowenthal—whose London book (the Bohn edition) became the accepted source for the many games it contained—this game has ever since been copied as a draw in all collections of Morphy's games in which it has appeared. It would appear that circumstances seemed to conspire to perpetuate this falsification.

The great interest in Paul Morphy and his games that developed during his first visit to Europe prompted Lowenthal to publish a collection of Morphy's games. Similarly, in Paris, Jean Prèti wished to bring out a collection of Morphy's games, and Morphy helped both in the selection of about one hundred of them. He helped Lowenthal during his last days in London before leaving for New York, although his time was much taken up with social affairs, exhibitions, and banquets.

Fiske, then editor of the *Chess Monthly*, mentioned the collection Lowenthal was working on in a letter to Prof. George Allen, dated August 12, 1859:

> I don't altogether understand the affair but it appears that he [Lowenthal] has sold it [the book of Morphy's games] both to Bohn [of London] and the Appletons [of New York] and the arrangement has reached Bohn's ear and he is furious. Morphy suspected something of the kind before he left London, and upon his arrival here made Appleton withdraw from their announcement the line which styled him the editor.

After completing the "Memoir" for the book and notes for 168 games (Prèti had kept his to just over 100), Lowenthal sent the manuscript to Appleton & Company of New York, and Morphy was looking over the galley proofs in early October. Appleton published *Morphy's Games of Chess* in December 1859. Lowenthal had not waited to add the five games Morphy played simultaneously on April 26 of that year against the five masters, Bird, Boden, Barnes, Lowenthal, and Rivière.

But no sooner had Lowenthal forwarded the manuscript to Appleton than he started to add additional games for Bohn, including among them the Petroff game between himself and Morphy, which had not been chosen for Appleton. However, he altered a few moves as mentioned above and ended the game as a draw, instead of ending it as it had in reality ended—"gloriously won by Master Paul."

Since the Bohn edition had more games than the Appleton edition (thirty-eight more), it was the more widely sought after. It appeared about two months after the Appleton edition and went through many printings until its last in 1913, while the Appleton edition never got beyond its first printing.

As quoted above in the Fiske letter, Morphy did no editing for the book; he merely helped for a few days on selection of games for the Appleton edition. He did even less than indicated by the notice "To the Reader," which appears in both editions, for, as Maurian wrote in his chess column in the New Orleans *Sunday Delta* of January 29, 1860:

> The notice "To the Reader" which prefaces the work and which is signed by Mr. Morphy, was not written by him; he merely affixed his name to it to recommend Mr. Lowenthal's book to his friends and to chess players.

However, the Bohn edition *was* the primary source of many Morphy games and it had many more games than any other collection of that time (1859-1860)—Lange's, Prèti's, and Staunton's notwithstanding. Moreover, it appeared to be authorized *in toto* by Morphy, who had agreed to Lowenthal's issuing a collection of his games, although in fact he (Morphy) knew nothing about the Bohn edition (and its additions), although Fiske says he had his suspicions, until he saw it in print. The London edition thus became the basis for all following collections of Morphy's games. And so this Petroff game, actually won by Paul, has come down to us as a draw, none having questioned Lowenthal's explanation as given on page 349 of the Bohn edition. (It is GAME CXLVI in Sergeant's *Morphy's Games of Chess*.)

It is probable that neither Sergeant nor other chess authors before him were aware of the early publication of the game as given by Ernest Morphy. Uncle Ernest had sent the game not only to the New York *Clipper* years before but also to Howard Staunton, chess editor of the *Illustrated London News*, who published it together with Ernest Morphy's letter, on November 22, 1856.

Of course Ernest Morphy knew that in sending it to Staunton it would be seen by Lowenthal, who had a similar chess column in the London *Era*, and he could expect the game score and letter to be challenged if at variance with the truth, especially as they publicized Lowenthal, a world master, being beaten two times out of three by a twelve-year-old boy.

Lowenthal did not denounce the game score at the time, nor did he suggest that the game had ended in a draw. On the contrary, it appears that Lowenthal, in replying to "Americanus" (evidently someone who had seen the game in Staunton's chess column the week before and had asked if it were true), conceded the defeat in his chess column in the *Era* of November 30, 1856.

> Americanus—Yes; it is quite true that in 1850 Herr Lowenthal lost one or two games with Master Paul Morphy, of New

Orleans, then a lad of thirteen. It is six years ago, and he has only an imperfect recollection of the circumstance, because the games were careless ones over the board, neither intended as specimens of Chess nor for publication. Players of the first order lose a game now and then to Rook players.

It might be taken from this reference to Rook players that Lowenthal's opponent had received the odds of a Rook or should have received such odds; but they had played even, as the two published games between them prove. In fact, Morphy never received odds from anyone; instead he started giving them as a child, although this question of odds arose many years later (see Chapter 26).

Lowenthal may well have wished to forget his having referred to Morphy in 1856 as a "Rook player," when two years later, in 1858, Morphy's true reputation became known in England during his European tour. It may be noted, on the other hand, that Staunton, remembering the letter and game that he had published in 1856, took pleasure in reminding the readers of his chess column on May 22, 1858, just before Morphy's arrival in England "that Mr. Morphy when a mere child beat Mr. Lowenthal two games out of three," the Petroff game being one of the two.

However, even if Lowenthal's reply to "Americanus" had never appeared, it is impossible that Lowenthal could have entirely missed Ernest Morphy's presentation of the game. In 1856 and 1857 the game appeared in the five following publications: in the United States, England, and Switzerland as it had been presented by Ernest in the New York *Clipper*; Staunton's *Illustrated London News*, *Frank Leslie's Illustrated Newspaper*, Porter's *Spirit of the Times*, and the *Schweizerische Schachzeitung*.

The following excerpt from the Bohn edition strongly suggests the probability that Lowenthal had seen the game in one or another of the above publications when looking for additional Morphy games. As he says on page viii of the "Preface":

> The book contains a far larger number of games than was at first contemplated. The editor feels, however, that in having yielded to the advice of his Chess friends, and inserted every instructive game played by Mr. Morphy, of which he could procure a copy, he has greatly enhanced the value of the volume, without doing any injury to Mr. Morphy's reputation. The additional games are not to be found in any other collection; they have been gathered from the various periodicals, English and Foreign, which devote their pages to the progress of chess.

Yet, when he later specifically mentions the Petroff game, Lowenthal writes as though the game had never been published before, simply ignoring the previous publications, and the reason for his reply to "Americanus" in his chess column of November 30, 1856.

In presenting the game as a draw, however, he must have felt the need for some explanation. Therefore, preceding the two known games played in 1850, which he was now adding for the Bohn edition, Lowenthal states (see page 349 of the Bohn edition):

> The two following games were played between Mr. Lowenthal and Mr. Morphy in the month of May 1850, during a visit of the former to the City of New Orleans. It is right to mention that at this time only two games were played between Messrs. Morphy and Lowenthal. Of the two games actually contested on the occasion, Mr. Morphy won the first and the second was drawn. The latter game the Petroff, we have by us accompanied by notes, in the M.S. of Mr. Ernest Morphy, who recorded it at the time it was played.

Lowenthal may even have been able to justify this explanation to himself. But it is obvious that if he had some manuscript, it was not Ernest Morphy's. Possibly, if the manuscript had no name on it and was in poor condition after ten years, Lowenthal's *wish* that it be Ernest Morphy's was father to his belief that it was.

In any event, Lowenthal's bringing Ernest Morphy's name into the explanation of the game forestalled any questioning. Even if one had seen the game before, one would imagine some previous error. And Lowenthal undoubtedly counted on the probability that most people would not remember a game they read about four years ago, concerning some unknown player. Ironically, this game, which Lowenthal (as quoted earlier) considered unworthy of publication when represented as a game *won* by Morphy, became of sufficient interest to include in his Bohn edition when represented as a *drawn* game.

During Morphy's visit to England, friendship developed between him and Lowenthal, and the latter became a staunch supporter of Morphy, apart from his work on the collection of Morphy games. It seems likely that it was out of consideration of Lowenthal's sensibilities that Morphy let Lowenthal's publication of the early Petroff game as a draw go unchallenged. In any case, it was a *fait accompli*, and any challenge would have precipitated a very disagreeable situation.

It would appear that Lowenthal attempted in every way to minimize his losses to Paul by saying in his "Memoir," which precedes the game section of his book (page 4 of the Bohn edition), that he (Lowenthal) "was at that time depressed in mind and suffering in body, and was also prostrated by the climate." Yet the fact remains that, while he played and lost two games to young Paul on May 25, 1850, the very next day, May 26, 1850, he played Eugène Rousseau, winning all five games that were played. He himself mentions in his narrative in *The First American Chess Congress* that "on the 26th [May, 1850] I played with Mr. Rousseau (not match games) and won five games—all we played." This he remembered well. Eugène Rousseau was considered the strongest player in New Orleans at that time.

Although Lowenthal was not certain whether there were two or three games played with Morphy in 1850, all other sources mention three games. Lowenthal had seen the *The First American Chess Congress* book. He had in fact been one of its contributors and had selected some games from it for his Bohn edition. The Congress book states that

> He [Lowenthal] visited New York and some of the western cities, and finally reached New Orleans in May, 1850. On the twenty-second and twenty-fifth of that month he played with Paul Morphy (at that time not yet thirteen years of age) in the presence of Mr. Rousseau, and Mr. Ernest Morphy and a large number of amateurs of New Orleans.
>
> The first game was a drawn one, but the second and third were won by the invincible young Philidor.

Yet about these 1850 games, Lowenthal's memory seems "deficient," and, as Maurian put it,

> It is singular that Lowenthal did not remember exactly how many games he played with Paul Morphy in 1850. In the very interesting account of his visit to America (*The First American Chess Congress* book, page 394) he says:
>
> "I do not remember whether we played in all two or three games; one was drawn, the other or others I lost." They played three games, as stated by D. W. Fiske, on the authority of Paul Morphy himself (*The First American Chess Congress* book, page 507) in the presence of Mr. Rousseau, Mr. Ernest Morphy and a large number of the amateurs of New Orleans. The facts are undisputed.

Maurian had something to say about the third game in the New Orleans *Times-Democrat* of January 10, 1892:

> Fortunately, I can say something about this third and unpublished game which has its importance. I have it from Morphy himself, and, although I am not aware that it was ever in print, I have often mentioned it in conversation with chess friends. Morphy, when spoken to about this game and asked why it had never been published, replied to the effect that it was simply unworthy of publication as Lowenthal had made an oversight at an early stage of the game, by which he suffered such heavy loss that he at once resigned. And eyewitnesses to the game, here supplemented Morphy's statement by adding that, as soon as the oversight was committed, the youthful player chivalrously insisted upon the master's retracting his move, whereupon Lowenthal smiled at the child's naïveté of his adversary but declined the offer.

There is thus seemingly an explanation for one of the three games having been called a draw. Since Lowenthal had refused to retract his move and Paul was unwilling to accept the game as a win, it is probable that it was agreed to call the game a draw for the record. This would coincide with Ernest Morphy's mention of a draw and two wins, and also Fiske's statement in the Book of the Congress.

Apparently Maurian never knew about any arrangement for the draw above mentioned, and Paul said nothing about it in talking about the early Lowenthal games, for he did not tell everything to even his closest friend—witness Maurian never knew about Paul's only chess problem, which likely had come up some time for discussion.

And so when Lowenthal published the Petroff game, Maurian may well have considered this the drawn game of the three, for very evidently he never knew that Ernest Morphy had sent the game to the New York *Clipper*. Marache had published both the game and the problem on the same page and date of the *Clipper*, and if Maurian had known about the publication of one he would have known about the other, and we know he never knew about the problem for he said so.

Ernest Morphy left New Orleans in 1852 and was living in Ohio when he sent Paul's game and problem to Marache, and very evidently he just never told his New Orleans friends and relatives that he had done so. Also, Ernest Morphy was too meticulous and rigidly honest a person to have given out two such different versions of the Petroff game, one as a draw, and the other as "gloriously won by Master Paul," as he demonstrated by his game score. The score of the third game mentioned by Maurian and Ernest Morphy, if recorded, is unknown.

It is quite clear that Lowenthal, notwithstanding the statement in his London edition of *Morphy's Games of Chess*, had played three games of chess with Paul Morphy in 1850, and accepting Ernest Morphy's version of the Petroff game, of which there is proof, rather than Lowenthal's version, which is based upon some hypothetical manuscript, this Petroff game should hereafter be shown as a win for Morphy in all future collections of his games, the position after fifty-four moves being as shown below, with White to make his fifty-fifth move.*

WHITE   BLACK
55. P–R6   Resigns

Ernest Morphy used the word "Abandons" instead of "Resigns."

Lowenthal

Morphy

White to make his fifty-fifth move. Resigns.
55. P–R6

* EDITOR'S NOTE: This is now the most common citation of the disputed game, owing entirely to Lawson's account.

CHAPTER 4

From School to the Mississippi

At the time of Lowenthal's visit to New Orleans, Paul was attending Jefferson Academy at 53 Bourbon Street. The Academy's advertisement circular stated, "School hours are from half-past Eight till Three, and from half-past Four to Six." Here he and Charles Maurian were classmates. Probably they had met before, since Maurian says the families were intimately acquainted. He tells a little about Paul and those school years in the following extract from a New Orleans *Picayune* article in the January 17, 1909, issue:

> A dreamy-eyed delicate boy, sitting at his little desk, his elbows on the boards, and his palms supporting chin, plunged in deep thought. Morphy was always thinking, thinking, thinking and there was a depth in his dark soulful eyes that it was hard to fathom.
>
> Every morning he would leave his father's fine home in Royal Street . . . and with his bundle of books hanging from a strap over his shoulder, would take his way up to the Jefferson Academy, in Bourbon Street, between Custom house and Bienville. Mr. J. G. Lord was the master of the school, and beside Paul, Edward Morphy, his brother, was also numbered among the pupils. . . . Nobody knows just when or how Paul learned the game of chess, and it is generally believed that he picked it up from watching his father and his uncle play on the broad back porch of the Morphy mansion. The game fascinated Paul as a little boy, and he would linger by the table watching his relatives moving the queens, the rooks and other pieces about, when other lads of his years were out at play. . . .
>
> Paul at school was always studious. . . . He preferred literature, but had a good head for mathematics [and] found enjoyment on sitting down with one of the classics.
>
> Often when the boys were at their rough games in the courtyard Paul, not physically strong enough to join the pastime, would sit watching them with just the suggestion of longing in his eyes. . . . Paul's delicate physique was an early concern of his father, and with the hope of developing the lad, Judge Morphy

engaged a famous maître d'arms to instruct him in the art of
fencing. Paul devoted himself to the exercise with the same application that he gave to everything else, and was soon quite a
swordsman, but in after years he dropped fencing entirely. Paul
was still taking his fencing lessons while a student at Spring
Hill College, Mobile.

In 1850 Paul completed his preparatory work at Jefferson Academy
and then registered at Spring Hill College in Mobile, Alabama, on December 3, 1850. His entry in the college records merely notes that he was the
brother of Edward Morphy, who had first entered Spring Hill two years
before. Once again, Paul and Maurian were classmates.

Throughout his college years it was periodically noted in the college
records that Paul's "conduct was excellent, application very earnest and un-
remitting and improvement very rapid." Existing college records, though
very incomplete (for Spring Hill College has suffered two disastrous fires
since Morphy's days there), show that he received many awards and pre-
miums for his studies in languages (Latin, Greek, French, and English),
mathematics, and all other subjects during his college years.

Apart from studies of a serious nature, Morphy took an active part
in dramatics and rhetoric. In his first year he was elected president of the
Thespian Society and throughout his years at college he took important
roles in the plays presented by the students.

At the Annual Commencement, October 14, 1851, he took the part
of Charles in the Comédie Française play *Grégoire*. At the following commencement he played Portia in *The Merchant of Venice*, his brother taking
the part of Shylock.

The diversity of his interests is indicated by his June 1853 "Latin
Analysis of Cicero's Oration pro Marcello," which, the Spring Hill College
records state, "evinced his ability to appreciate the merits of that beautiful Oration." Also discussed in the college records was his discourse as a
member of the Philomatic Society in February 1854, when he "delivered a
lecture on Astronomy & particularly the discovery of the Planet Le Verrier
[Neptune] & those of Sir Wm. Herschel among the Nebula."

Father Kenny, S.J., author of *The Torch on the Hill*, writes in reference
to Morphy's address at the 1854 Commencement, at which Paul received
the A.B. degree:

> War was the subject of his graduating thesis, and he brought
> within very narrow limits the conditions that make it justifi-
> able. The logic of his argument would exclude forcible seces-

sion, and whether in play or in life Morphy was severely logical, even to a fault. But such a course brought consequences that preyed upon his mind.

In passing, it is of interest to take note of Morphy's stand on war and secession, as revealed in the above passage. Perhaps it will help to explain the motives for his behavior during the Civil War, which was later to have such tragic effects on him, his career, his family, and his fortune.

Morphy stayed on at Spring Hill another year, and Maurian later noted that Paul graduated with the highest honors ever awarded by the institution and occupied himself almost exclusively with mathematics and philosophy. At the 1855 Commencement, at which he received his A.M. degree, Morphy took for the subject of his address, "The Political Creed of the Age."

During his years at Spring Hill, Morphy devoted himself to his studies and college activities, almost completely to the exclusion of chess. It would seem he had little interest in it at the time. In fact, Maurian says in his long obituary in the New Orleans *Times-Democrat* of July 13, 1884, that

> his [Morphy's] departure for Spring Hill in the autumn of the same year [1850] seems to have caused a prolonged interruption in the youthful prodigy's practice of the game, for excepting such play as he may have had at home during his brief vacations, they lasted from October 15 to December 1, he may be said to have virtually abandoned chess during his collegiate career.
>
> It was only in the summer of 1853, the year before his graduation, that, to oblige some college mates who had become enthusiastic over chess, he played with them a number of games and these at odds of Queen or of Rook and Knight combined.

Later in the same obituary, Maurian makes an even stronger statement concerning Paul's interest in the game:

> Speaking as knowing whereof we speak, we deem it but just to correct two generally received impressions as to the departed master. First, then, Paul Morphy was never so passionately fond, so inordinately devoted to chess as is generally believed. An intimate acquaintance and long observation enables us to state this positively. His only devotion to the game, if it may be so termed, lay in his ambition to meet and to defeat the best players and great masters of this country and of Europe. He felt his enormous strength, and never for a moment doubted the

outcome. Indeed, before his first departure for Europe he privately and modestly, yet with perfect confidence, predicted to us his certain success, and when he returned he expressed the conviction that he had played poorly, rashly; that none of his opponents should have done so well as they did against him. But, this one ambition satisfied, he appeared to have lost nearly all interest in the game.

In her *Life of Paul Morphy*, Regina Morphy-Voitier includes the following reminiscence of Maurian's:

> Paul and I [during their years at Spring Hill College] happened to be placed adjoining each other in the study rooms, in the class rooms and everywhere, and our previous acquaintance soon ripened into great intimacy. For a year or two I may say that I hardly lost sight of him except for about six weeks at vacation time, and during that whole time I never saw Paul play a single game of Chess. He never talked Chess to anyone nor probably gave it a thought. He had neither a Chess board nor even a Chess book. At Spring Hill he continued to be the close student he had been at Jefferson Academy in New-Orleans, and his intellectual superiority over his companion soon became manifest to all there as it had been in earlier days. I have heard one of his professors, a man of mature years and great experience, say that of the thousands and thousands of boys and youths that came under his observation in long years devoted to teaching the young, he had never met anyone that could compare with Paul Morphy in strength and capacity of intellect. Unfortunately, this could not be said of the physical man. While his mental faculties were being constantly enlarged and strengthened by constant study, his physical frame did not receive a corresponding development by that active exercise of the body so necessary at his prime of life, and there was not that equilibrium between the two so essential to the perfection of both.
>
> He never could vanquish his repugnance for the sports that are so attractive. He saw, however, the necessity of doing something, and for some months or perhaps a year, he took lessons in the art of fencing. He practiced a bit regularly, and it undoubtedly proved very beneficial to him. But it is to be regretted that he did not take this course earlier, and especially that it did not continue longer. It is my firm belief that later misfortune would have been thereby avoided.

About the year 1852 the first Chess board and men that I had
seen at Spring Hill made their appearance under the joint property of Raphael Carraquesde of the City of Mexico and Louis
Landry of Louisiana. These young gentlemen played frequently and initiated some of their companions into the mysteries
of the game. Paul seldom took any part in this play except as
referee, in cases where a point of Chess law was to be decided.
On very rare occasions, he played a few games with them at the
odds of Queen's rook and Knight, and I believe was uniformly
successful.

Sometime during the Spring of 1853 I happened to be in the
College Infirmary for some trifling indisposition and Paul was
also there for some similar complaint. Through strange chance,
the Chess board of Raphael and Landry happened to be there
also. Noticing the Chess board, the idea came into my head to
ask Morphy the very stupid question which since then has often been put to me (retaliation), "How is it possible that two
intelligent beings should sit for an hour or more moving little
figures of white and black wood, and find recreation therein?"

"If you knew the game," he answered, "you would change your
opinion." "Well," I replied, "suppose you teach me the moves
just to kill time, for I feel I shall never have the patience to play
a game through."

Paul taught me the moves. We then played several games for
study, he explaining the reasons for the moves. After that sitting I had changed my mind and opinion, in fact I had suddenly
jumped from one extreme to the other, and I could scarcely
conceive how a man that did not play Chess could be happy.
We remained two days in the Infirmary, and my first care in
coming out was to procure a Chess board of my own, and I had
all the book stores of Mobile and New-Orleans ransacked for
Chess books, and gave a great deal more time to its study than
I should. During the two years that we remained at college together, Morphy played a considerable number of games with
me at odds gradually diminishing as I improved. We seldom
played more than a game at a sitting, but few of them lasted less
than two or three hours. He did not play with any other adversary, except on a visit to Mobile with the professor of Spanish,
Mr. Sanchez, who made a pretty good fight at odds of a Rook.

Mr. Morphy had the following Chess books with him, the only
ones, as far as I know that he ever possessed until the New York
Chess Congress in 1857. Horwitz and Kling's *Chess Studies*,

which he pronounced a very good and useful book for students, although not free from error; the B. Vols composing the collection of Kieseritzky's *La Régence*, and Stuanton's *Chess Tournament*. I had a translation of Lewis' *Treatise* in French [and] Staunton's *Chess Player's Handbook and Companion*.

Paul never used books except for a few minutes at a time. But I believe that a great many of the games actually played that they contained were played by us, especially those by acknowledged first class players, such as Staunton, Anderssen and Kieseritsky. During the same year, he also played a considerable number of games with me at odds gradually diminishing as I improved.

Although Maurian very soon became too strong to receive the odds of Queen from Morphy, sixteen years were to pass before he became too strong to receive the odds of Queen's Knight. An apt pupil, Maurian reduced his odds slightly during the first year of his apprenticeship, as shown by an entry in one of his notebooks, which he made, it would appear, expecting others to see it some day:

Note to Readers.

The game on the following page was played by correspondence between Messrs. Torda and Maurian and it ended in a draw. The games that come after this are from a little match played between Mr. P. M. and Maurian. This match consisted of nine games, in 3 of them Mr. P. M. was to give the odds of the Rook and Knight, in the 3 next, the odds of Rook, Pawn and 2 moves and in 3 others, the odds of Rook, Pawn and move. It was begun on Thursday the 20th of January 1854.

Of this match of nine games, Morphy won two and drew one of the first three. He won one and lost two of the second three, and won two and lost one of the last three. Among the games recorded in this notebook is one in which Maurian received the odds of Queen from Morphy, probably the first game between them that was recorded. In another Maurian notebook we find the following:

Chess Game—Charles Maurian 1856

On the 23rd of October, Charles Maurian commenced the present Chess games merely for the sake of amusement and pastime. I, the above named am a passionate admirer of the game of Chess, and although I have not yet succeeded in seeing over

four or five moves, yet I do not despair of struggling one day
at very small odds with Paul Morphy, the chess King of New
Orleans. I will begin by a game played between us, at the time
that Paul removed back again to Mr. Alonzo Morphy's house
of Royal Street, on Sunday 12 October 1856, Mr. Paul Morphy
giving the odds of the Queen's Knight and move.

Then followed the game, which was unknown to the chess world until Maurian published it in the New Orleans *Times-Democrat* on April 15,
1894, and it is still in no Morphy collection.

One day at Spring Hill, Father Beaudequin, who sometimes played
chess with the students, happened to hear Paul remark that he thought
he could beat his fellow classmates playing blindfolded. It is probable that
the Father knew nothing of Paul's prowess at chess, and so offered to play
him. Paul played without sight of the board, and the Father was very much
surprised when he lost.

It may be recalled that Ernest Morphy, in his letter to Kieseritzky in
1849, told him that "this child has never opened a work on chess," and yet
he was playing like a master at twelve years of age. Apparently he had little
need of books or interest in having them. From what Maurian said, Paul
seems never to have had any books on the subject of chess until 1853, when,
probably due to Maurian's enthusiasm, he acquired a few. Frederick Milne
Edge, Morphy's secretary in Europe, relates the following in his book *The
Exploits and Triumphs in Europe of Paul Morphy*. (This book is the source of
all quotations from Edge that will subsequently appear in this biography,
unless a specific Edge letter is mentioned.)

> In answer to a gentleman in Paris as to whether he [Morphy]
> had not studied many works on chess, I heard him state that
> no author had been of much value to him, and that he was as-
> tonished at finding various positions and solutions given as
> novel—certain moves producing certain results, etc., for that
> he had made the same deductions himself, as necessary con-
> sequences.

However, at the end of 1853 he acquired a copy of Staunton's book
of the 1851 London tournament, which he soon gave to James McConnell. McConnell said that upon opening it he found that Paul had expressed himself concerning some of the games with marginal notes and
had amended the title page to read, "By H. Staunton, Esq., author of *The
Handbook of Chess, Chess-players Companion*, &c. &c. &c. 'and some devil-

ish bad games.'" In 1874 he was to give a more considered opinion of Howard Staunton as chess master.

During his last year at Spring Hill, Morphy's interest in chess, or shall we say chess activity, increased somewhat, probably as a consequence of Maurian's enthusiasm, and the two made several trips to Mobile, undoubtedly with chess in mind. Morphy knew Judge Meek, who sat in court there, and he made the acquaintance of others. Judge Meek has told that he played Morphy several games on March 1, 1855, all of which Meek lost. While there, Paul played Dr. Ayers with equal success. He may also have played with the editor of the Mobile *Weekly Register*, with whom he was acquainted. One of the *Register*'s reporters published the following account in the paper's October 13, 1855, issue, concerning the 1855 Spring Hill Commencement, at which Morphy delivered his graduation address, "The Political Creed of the Age":

> Spring Hill College—Mr. Editor, Four young men received the first Academical honor [yesterday]. I will mention only your friend, Mr. Paul Morphy of New Orleans, who, before being promoted to the Degree of A.M., delivered with an uncommon degree of earnestness a speech remarkable for solid argumentation and high philosophical principles.

In the Macon *Telegraph* of May 2, 1867, Miron Hazeltine, chess editor and chronicler of the Morphy era, related the following anecdote of another of Morphy's visits to Mobile:

> A good story passed current among the players and we believe got into print [*Frank Leslie's Illustrated Newspaper*, October 11, 1856], to the effect that, Paul Morphy being in town [Mobile], during a session of the Court over which our subject [Judge Meek] presided, the Judge concocted some pretext for an adjournment for the day, went over to the hotel, and buried the anxiety of clients and the wranglings of Counsel in the willing oblivion of his favorite pastime, *en lutte* with his favorite young master. On being rallied about it he used to adjust his spectacles, and with a merry twinkle of his eyes, remark that he thought they embellished that a little at his expense.

After the 1855 Commencement, Paul returned to New Orleans and lost no time in matriculating at the University of Louisiana in November 1855. Applying himself closely to his studies, he received his law degree on April 7, 1857, as mentioned in the New Orleans *Daily Creole* of April 8, 1857:

Commencement Exercise—Law School University of Louisiana—The session for the present year of the Law Department
of the Louisiana State University closed with appropriate exercises at Odd Fellow's Hall. This department of the University
is in most efficient organization, and has taken rank for sound
learning among the first schools of the kind in America. . . .
Christian Roselius, Professor of Civil Law and Dean of the Faculty, in some very appropriate and happily conceived remarks
. . . conferred the honorary degree of L.L.B. on the following
named gentlemen: Paul Morphy, ...

Blessed with an unusual memory, Morphy could easily recite by heart
nearly the entire Civil Code of Louisiana. However, Paul was not immediately admitted to practice at the bar. Restrictions required that one be
of legal age, and Morphy was obliged to wait more than a year before he
could begin practicing his profession. It will never be known for a certainty whether this long wait was a determining factor in the course of his
future life.

As previously noted, Paul had played but little chess during his college years, none for the first two and a half years, except perhaps at home
during vacation. One such vacation game is unusual because it ended with
Paul giving mate by simply castling.

Some months before Paul expected to receive his law degree, knowing
he would not be allowed to practice until the middle of the following year,
he began to consider playing chess on a larger field, undoubtedly urged
on by his Uncle Ernest, who was inordinately proud of him. Uncle Ernest,
who had sent the Lowenthal game to Marache and Staunton, had also sent
it to *Frank Leslie's Illustrated Newspaper,* which published it on August 23,
1856, together with the following notice:

We shall have more to say of this young chess genius next week.
He will play a match with Stanley (or, as the greater includes
the less, any other player in the United States) for $300 a side.
Those anxious to learn further particulars can apply to the
chess editor, who will give the readers of this column the desired information in the next issue, if the seal of privacy can be
removed from his letter. . . .

The next issue, August 30, 1856, contained the following item:

CHESS CHALLENGE EXTRAORDINARY.—Mr. Ernest
Morphy of Moscow, Claremount County, Ohio, a very strong

player and one of the most masterly analysts in this or any other country, has written a private letter to a friend in this city, stating that he is desirous to get up a match, between the 1st and the 31st of January next at New Orleans, between his nephew, Paul Morphy, (as he writes, incontestably the superior of himself or Rousseau, and who now holds the scepter of chess in New Orleans), and Mr. Stanley or Marache (and we presume any other player in the country) for $300 a side—$100 to go to the loser (if Paul wins) to pay the expenses of the journey to New Orleans. Mr. James McConnell, attorney at law, New Orleans, or Paul Morphy himself, may be written to in regard to it. The proposition emanates from Mr. Ernest Morphy, who subscribes $50 towards the purse.

However, according to the New York chess columns, there appeared to be great reluctance on the part of Stanley (considered to be American chess champion) and others to come forward, although only three of Morphy's games had been published as yet: the Rousseau game in 1851, and two games in the *Clipper* (the Petroff and a McConnell game).

But reports of Paul's genius had reached New York, and Lowenthal, in passing through on his way to London in 1851, had told Stanley something of his experience in meeting Paul in 1850.

However, about a month after Paul's challenge to the American chess players, tragedy struck the Morphy household. One September day, while Judge Morphy was conversing near the courthouse, he turned suddenly in response to a friend, and the large brim of a Panama hat cut across his eye. Although in pain, the Judge paid little attention to it until the next day, when the eye became inflamed, and a physician was called who had him confined to a dark room for some time. His health became impaired, and he died on November 22, 1856, of apoplexy or congestion of the brain, leaving an estate of $146,162.54.

This tragic event so affected the close-knit Morphy family that it very nearly prevented Paul's participation in the plans for the holding of the National Chess Congress in October of the next year, some eleven months later.

In the meantime, the January 1857 issue of the recently launched *Chess Monthly* magazine noted that

Mr. Paul Morphy, the most promising player of the day yields the chess scepter of New Orleans. His late challenge to any player in the United States has not yet been accepted.

Early in 1857, Daniel Willard Fiske, editor of the *Chess Monthly*, suggested the desirability of a national chess congress. At a special session of the New York Chess Club held March 26, 1857, a committee was appointed to issue a formal proposal for a general assemblage of American players, and to correspond with other clubs upon the feasibility of such an assemblage. Fiske acted as secretary of this committee.

A circular dated April 17, 1857, was widely circulated throughout the Union to chess clubs and well-known amateurs, and Fiske wrote the following letter to Charles Maurian (later published in the New Orleans *Times-Democrat* of January 6, 1895):

> June 29, 1857
>
> Charles A. Maurian
> Commercial Reading Rooms, New Orleans
>
> Dear Sir: I have written today to Mr. Morphy with reference to the coming National Tournament and to learn the opinions and wishes of the chessmen of New Orleans in reference to the undertaking. . . .
>
> Will you be good enough to confer with Mr. Morphy, to whom I have written at greater length? I have suggested to him that you send in immediately the names of three or four persons to act on the part of New Orleans as members of the managing committee. Beg Mr. Morphy to be one of that number, as his name attached to the committee would aid us everywhere more than that of any other man in the Union. The committee hope that your city, so famous a few years back as the seat of a fine chess contest [Stanley–Rousseau match, 1845] and so well known now, both here and in Europe, as the residence of Mr. Morphy, will not be lukewarm in the matter.
>
> Yours—Daniel W. Fiske

The *First American Chess Congress* book discussed Morphy's reply to this letter:

> Early in July [Fiske got a reply] from Mr. Morphy declining to accede to the request, the death of his father a few months before making him reluctant to take part in such a scene of festivity as a Chess Congress. A lengthy letter was then sent to Mr. Maurian, urging him and others of Mr. Morphy's friends in New Orleans, to press the matter for the sake of Chess and the Congress.

This second letter of Fiske's was also published in the New Orleans *Times-Democrat* of January 6, 1895:

September 3, 1857

Charles A. Maurian, New Orleans

Dear Sir:—Mr. Michinard sailed for New Orleans yesterday and will bring you the latest news in reference to the Great Congress. . . .

The great question here, as well as throughout the entire North, is will Paul Morphy come? In spite of the adverse belief of Mr. Michinard, we all hope that he will. The bare announcement that he might be certainly expected would help on our subscription in this part of the Union more than all other circumstances combined. Assure him that whether victor or loser, he would be the lion of the tournament. We are willing to make any arrangement that may be necessary to secure his attendance. It would increase our subscriptions, double the interest of the tournament and add largely to its respectability abroad.

Let me beg you to state all these things to Mr. Morphy, and convince him that no other person has it in his power to do so much good to American chess as he has, and that the entire community of chess players confidently expect it at his hands.

Mr. Hammond of Boston; Montgomery, Thomas, Elkin, Baldwin, and Doughtery of Philadelphia; Montgomery of Georgia; Cheney of Syracuse; Calthrop of Connecticut, besides Stanley and others, of New York, will play in the tournament. We were all much pleased with Mr. Michinard's visit. I only regret that I came in too late from the country to see much of him.

Yours,
Daniel W. Fiske

The *Prospectus* of the National Chess Congress had been prepared and distributed some time in advance of the Congress's actual commencement on October 6, 1857. It listed the Committee of Management and the Committee of Co-operation, on which every region of the country from Maine to California was represented. Paul Morphy was also listed (in anticipation) as a member of the Committee on the Chess Code, having been asked to serve by both the Committee of Management and Prof. George Allen of Philadelphia, chairman of the Committee on the Code.

It is evident from the above correspondence that Paul Morphy, practically an unknown, paradoxically began to dominate the American chess scene, even before arrangements for the National Congress of 1857 were completed. Early in September, however, Morphy replied to both Fiske and Allen, declining to participate:

New Orleans, September 5, 1857

Daniel W. Fiske, Esq.
My Dear Sir:

I find by the Prospectus of the National Chess Congress that I am of the "Committee on the Chess Code." Although a very flattering compliment, it is one which I must with great respect decline, as it will not be in my power to leave New Orleans this or the coming month. I therefore address you, as the Secretary of the New York Managing Committee, to beg that you tender the "Committee" my sincere thanks for the honor conferred upon me, and the assurance of my regret at being compelled to decline it.

Yours in chess
Paul Morphy

New Orleans, September 7, 1857

Dear Sir [Prof. George Allen]:

Your very flattering letter has come to hand, and it is with great regret, I assure you, that I find myself unable to return such an answer as I could desire. Honored as I feel in being one of the Committee on the Chess Code and eager as I would be to render my respected colleagues all the assistance in my power, I am yet compelled most respectfully to decline the honor of serving on the "Committee." It will be impossible for me to travel North in October next, and participate either in the Tournament or discussion which will precede it. Under these circumstances, I have only to thank you for the highly flattering tenor of your communication, and to tender members of the "Committee" the expression of my hearty wishes for the success of their labors.

With high regard
Paul Morphy

However, Judge Meek, a close family friend, brought a good deal of persuasive pressure to bear upon Paul's family in this matter, and finally Maurian was given permission to send a telegram on September 19, 1857, which was delivered two days later.

> Paul Morphy starts for N. York on Wednesday 23rd. –Chas
> Maurian.

Shortly before Morphy left for New York, he was elected president of the New Orleans Chess Club. The *Times-Democrat* reported that on September 23, 1857,

> at 5 o'clock in the afternoon Mr. Morphy took passage [via the
> Mississippi] on board the steamer Benjamin Franklin bound
> for Cincinnati, and eight [eleven] days thereafter he landed in
> New York.

Immediately upon receiving the telegram that Morphy would be present, the New York Committee of Management issued the following circular, which was sent to all chess clubs and prominent amateurs of the country:

> September 23, 1857
> The Committee of Management of the National Chess Con-
> gress, take great pleasure in announcing that all the arrange-
> ments for the first great assemblage of Chess Players of this
> country, are at length complete. Nearly every one of the leading
> amateurs in the United States will be present. Mr. Paul Morphy
> of New Orleans will positively attend. . . .
> Charles D. Mead, President

It will be noted in the above circular that much emphasis was placed upon the attendance of Morphy, although not one person expected or who later attended the Congress, with the sole exception of Judge Meek, had ever met him. Yet this Congress was destined to be remembered down through the years as "The Morphy Congress."

The *Prospectus* of the Congress laid down conditions and procedure for the Grand Tournament, the Minor Tournament, and the Problem Tourney. Problems for the Tourney were

> to be addressed to Eugene B. Cook, *Hoboken, New Jersey,* before
> the first day of November 1857. This late date has been chosen
> in order to enable the composers of England, Germany, and
> France [meaning all Europe] to compete with their brethren of
> America for these prizes.

The Problem Tourney was open to all, and was ultimately won by Rudolph Willmers of Vienna.

The following "Rules, Regulations and Proceedings" in the *Prospectus* are of special interest when considered in contrast to present-day tournament conditions:

> 4. The combatants in the Grand Tournament are to meet at the New York Club on Monday, the fifth of October at three p.m. when they will be paired off by lot. The playing will be commenced on the following day.
> 6. The games are to be played in accordance with the Code of Chess Rules, published in Staunton's Chess Player's Hand Book, and all disputed points referred to a Special Committee appointed by the Committee of Management, whose decision must be considered final. Drawn games are not to be counted.
> 7. The hours of play will be from 9 a.m. until 12 p.m.
> 10. One game at least is to be played at a sitting. After four hours, however, at the request of either party, a game may be adjourned for one hour. All play will cease at 12 o'clock, p.m. or as near that time as both parties in a game shall have played an equal number of moves.
> 11. In cases of unreasonable delay, the Committee of Management reserve to themselves the right to limit the time to be consumed on any move, to thirty minutes.
> 12. As the Committee of Management guarantee to every subscriber of five dollars and upwards, a correct and detailed account of the Congress, all the games played, and all the problems competing for prizes, are to be regarded as their property, and no one will be allowed to publish any of such games or problems, without their express sanction.

The "Programme of Proceedings" in the *Prospectus* stated that the features of the Congress were to be

> sessions for debate in which the interests of American Chess and the present condition of the Chess Code will be fully discussed. . . . A Grand Tournament composed of acknowledged first-class players, receiving no odds from any other players, or from each other, is intended to form the second feature. . . . The method of play will be as follows: The contestants shall meet on Monday, the fifth of October, at three p.m. Should the number of entrances amount to any even and easily divisible number, say 32 [sixteen was the actual number entered] they shall then be paired off by lot and commence their games si-

multaneously.

The eight players winning three out of five games, are to be declared victors in this *first section* of the Tournament, and the eight losers excluded from further share in the contest. The eight winners are then to be paired off by lot as before, the four couples beginning their matches simultaneously. The four winners of the first three games are to be declared victors in this *second section* of the Tournament, and entitled to the four prizes.

To determine the order in which the prizes shall be distributed, the four prize-bearers will then be paired off against each other as before, each couple to play the best of five games. The two winners in this *third section* of the Tournament shall then play a match for the two highest prizes, and the player winning the first five games shall be entitled to the first prize—the second prize going to the loser. The two losers in this *third section* of the Tournament, shall also contend for the third and fourth prizes. The winner of the first three games shall receive the third prize—the fourth going to the loser.

It will be noted that no official time limit was set on moves in the "Rules," nor was there any provision for the sealing of moves at adjournment. Game scores were not to be freely available for publication. Rule 11 was never invoked, although it might well have been in the match between Morphy and Paulsen, for its application could have affected the score of the players. But more about this in the following chapters.

CHAPTER 5

The National Chess Congress

As was noticed in Chapter 4, Morphy came to the Congress by way of the Mississippi to Cincinnati. Thence, by railroad, he arrived in New York on Sunday, October 4, registering at the St. Nicholas Hotel. Now present to participate in the Grand Tournament were:

W. S. Allison—	Hastings, Minn.
Hiram Kennicott—	Chicago, Ill.
T. Lichtenhein—	New York City
N. Marache—	New York City
Hon. A. B. Meek—	Mobile, Ala.
Hubert Knott—	Brooklyn, N.Y.
Paul Morphy—	New Orleans, La.
Louis Paulsen—	Dubuque, Iowa
Frederick Perrin—	New York City
Dr. B. I. Raphael—	Louisville, Ky.
Charles H. Stanley—	New York City
James Thompson—	New York City

And others were expected.

At the appointed time the next day, October 5, at 3 p.m., those mentioned above, together with W. J. A. Fuller and Denis Julien, met and requested Colonel Charles D. Mead to act as their chairman, and Daniel W. Fiske as secretary for the first feature of the Congress—discussion of pertinent matters.

Uppermost for consideration was some means of avoiding the unfortunate pairing of players that might result from the method described in the *Prospectus*. Under this "knock-out" system, used at the London 1851 Tournament, the strongest players might be eliminated, even in the first round. Should Morphy and Paulsen, generally considered the two strongest players, be drawn against each other in the first round, under this plan one of them would be excluded from all further participation in the tournament.

Several other methods of pairing were discussed. It was (as recorded in *The First American Chess Congress*)

49

remembered that considerable disappointment had been felt in the London tournament, from the fact that some of the very best players had been drawn against each other in the first round or section. Several, who would otherwise have probably taken prizes, had been thus thrown out at the very first stage. . . . After a lengthy discussion it was determined to reject other propositions, and to carry out the method of play adopted and published in the Prospectus. Several other questions of minor importance were debated, and so much time was consumed in these preliminary arrangements that it was resolved to postpone the drawing until the afternoon of the next day.

And so the pairings were left entirely to chance. There was much activity and excitement that first night, for, as *The First American Chess Congress* book describes:

In the evening [October 5] the rooms of the club were thronged with spectators to witness some passages-at-arms between Mr. Paul Morphy and Mr. Charles H. Stanley, considered American Champion.

Actually, Frederick Perrin was the first to engage Morphy in New York. In his book *The Exploits and Triumphs in Europe of Paul Morphy*, Frederick M. Edge tells something of that first evening at the New York Chess Club:

Who that was present that evening does not remember Paul Morphy's first appearance at the New York City Chess Club? The secretary, Mr. Frederick Perrin, valorously offered to be his first antagonist, and presented about the same resistance as a mosquito to an avalanche. Then who should enter the room but the warrior, Stanley. . . . Loud cries were made for Stanley! Stanley! And Mr. Perrin [now on the second game] resigned his seat to the newcomer, in deference to so general a request. Thus commenced a contest, or rather a succession of contests, in which Mr. Stanley was indeed astonished. "Mate" followed upon "Mate," until he arose from his chair in bewildered defeat.

Of the four games played, Stanley lost all. There must have been much wondering on the part of all those in attendance that night.

Judge Meek, Alabama's strongest player, had arrived a little early at the Congress and had told everyone what to expect when Morphy came. But, as Hazeltine later told it in the Macon *Telegraph* of May 2, 1867:

When our subject [Judge Meek] visited New York in 1857 it was to introduce the conqueror of us all, Paul Morphy—and that as our conqueror. "Oh! yes," was the credulous answer, "he beats you and Dr. Ayers, and his uncle and Rousseau, rusty with inaction; but wait until he gets here." Nobody boasted in Judge Meek's presence, but the inference was plain enough. Then, one who ever saw him will remember the light that would fill those pleasant eyes, the smile that overspread those noble features, and that peculiar manner in which he would adjust his glasses, and with quiet confidence agree that they would see. Did ever the event more thoroughly justify the judgment of expectation? Morphy arrived. At once it was evident that the tenderest ties of honor and friendship existed between them. No father could watch with more tender anxiety, or glory with more exultant pride in the triumphs of a favored son, than this great man, in the victorious career of his protégé. And the youthful hero in turn, reverenced his noble friend as a father could not more have been reverenced.

The December 1857 *Chess Monthly* also carried an account of Morphy's arrival at the Congress:

It was with the prestige acquired by his victories over Lowenthal, Rousseau, Ernest Morphy, Ayers, Meek and McConnell that Paul Morphy arrived in New York on the fifth [fourth] of October to take part in the first Congress of the American Chess Association. Notwithstanding his high reputation, there were many, who from his youth and the small number of his published games, manifested much incredulity concerning his Chess strength.

But on the evening of his arrival all doubts were removed in the minds of those who witnessed his passages-at-arms with Mr. Stanley and Mr. Perrin at the rooms of the New York Club, and the first prize was universally conceded to him, even before the entries for the Grand Tournament had been completed.

The next morning, October 6, at 11 a.m., all those participating in the National Chess Congress met to formally organize, choosing Judge Meek as president and Daniel W. Fiske as secretary. Frederick M. Edge was elected an assistant secretary.

Originally, it had been expected that the rooms of the New York Chess Club would suffice, but interest in the meeting had been underestimated. When it became evident that the larger quarters would be required, the

Committee of Management secured commodious quarters at 764 Broadway, known as Descombes' Rooms.

In addition to the above twelve entries for the Grand Tournament, the names of W. J. A. Fuller, Denis Julien, H. P. Montgomery, and Daniel W. Fiske were added, for a total of sixteen entrants. S. R. Calthrop arrived later, and since it was agreeable to the other players, Denis Julien retired in his favor. The players now received their certificates for the Congress.

The drawing for pairing followed the 1851 London Tournament play (to be found in Staunton's *Chess Tournament* 1851):

> Eight white tickets and eight yellow ones numbered respectively, 1, 2, 3, 4, 5, 6, 7 and 8 were put into the ballot-box: The white tickets being further marked "Choice of Chess-men and first move." Whoever drew No. 1 of the white tickets had to play with the party who drew No. 1 of the yellow; whoever drew No. 2 of the white had to play with No. 2 of the yellow; and so on throughout. The drawers of the white had the choice as to the color of the chessmen, i.e., whether they would play with the white or the black pieces and the privilege of moving first in the opening game.

As it happened, Morphy drew Thompson for the first round, while Paulsen drew Calthrop. In like manner the other players were paired. That afternoon, Morphy sent the following telegram to his brother, Edward:

> N.Y. 6th
> Arrived last Sunday—playing begins today—
> Am pitted against James Thompson.

Thompson was a chess veteran who was well known in Paris and London before he came to New York. He was a strong player and was accustomed to giving odds to others. Play began at 1:40 p.m., but Thompson resigned at 2:30 p.m. Nevertheless, the second game began twenty minutes later and ended at 5:40 p.m., Thompson again resigning.

On the second day, October 7, Morphy and Thompson did not play. The latter perhaps wished to gather strength, since the score stood Morphy two, Thompson zero. In these two days, Paulsen had won his three games and so advanced to the second section. However, Morphy did not remain idle, for he played several side games with George Hammond of Boston and Colonel Mead of New York.

On Thursday, October 8, Thompson resigned his third game with

Morphy after forty-six moves, and two hours and thirty minutes of play. Now Morphy advanced to the second section. Later that day he played side games with H. P. Montgomery, Louis Paulsen, and James Thompson, winning all games.

Morphy and Paulsen, being victors in the first section and obliged to wait for others to win the necessary three games, were now free for side games or other activity. Paulsen created a sensation on Friday by announcing that on Saturday, October 10, he would play four games simultaneously and without sight of the boards, and invited Morphy to take one of the boards against him. Morphy accepted on the condition that he also play blindfold. They then engaged in a private game that day, which ended in a draw six hours later.

The next day, October 10, before a large audience in Descombes' Rooms, Morphy and Paulsen sat back-to-back on a raised platform. Play began at 4:30 p.m., Paulsen and Morphy calling out their moves with neither seeing any boards. At 10:30 p.m., Morphy announced checkmate in five moves upon Paulsen, calling out his twenty-third move against him.

Howard Staunton made a generous comment on Morphy's manner of play, when he later published in his chess column in the *Illustrated London News* of February 1, 1862, this first blindfold game Morphy played with Paulsen:

> In the faculty of imparting vitality to a position Mr. Morphy is hardly second to La Bourdonnais. It is very rare, indeed, to find a game of his which is not in some part enlivened by a stroke of vigor or a flash of inspiration. The advance of the Pawn here [Morphy's move 16] operates a change in the aspect of affairs which is almost magical.

By midnight Paulsen had won his game against C. H. Schultz, but adjourned his two remaining games until Monday. Paulsen's exhibition of four simultaneous blindfold games was almost unparalleled in chess history.

The pairing for the second section took place on Monday, October 12, Paulsen drawing Montgomery, while Morphy drew Meek. That evening Paulsen concluded his adjourned blindfold games, winning from Fuller and drawing with Julien. Although he had not won a complete victory (of the four games, he won two, drew one, and lost one), the feat was considered extraordinary for the quality of the games. Only once before had such an attempt been made. However, Paulsen went one better, for on October 21, he undertook the playing of five blindfold games, *never* before attempted. Of the five blindfold games played on that occasion, Paulsen won four and drew the fifth.

In the Grand Tournament, Judge Meek had been the victor in the first section against Fuller, but not until Fuller had won two games. Upon winning his third game from Fuller on October 14, he immediately began his series of games with Paul, having previously drawn to play him in the event of his (the Judge's) winning from Fuller.

Morphy won his first game from Meek in less than an hour. It was told in the Macon *Telegraph* of May 9, 1867, that

> During the brief contests with Morphy he [Judge Meek] made a playful threat that caused a good deal of amusement. He told the little hero, thus striding over them all so triumphantly, that if he didn't stop beating him so all the time, and, at least, once in a while give him some kind of a chance, he would pick him up, put him in his pocket and carry him off—a threat which, considering the immense disparity in their physical proportions seemed not at all impossible of execution.

Morphy's two additional wins over the Judge followed rapidly, and he was declared a victor in the second section. In the meantime, Paulsen had won two games of Montgomery and was granted the third by default, Montgomery having been obliged to return to Philadelphia.

On Saturday evening, October 17, the Congress adjourned temporarily for dinner to the St. Denis Hotel, of which Denis Julien was the proprietor. *The First American Chess Congress* describes a most unique "Bill of Fare," with various dishes named after past and present chess personalities: Bilguer,* M'Donnell,** Benjamin Franklin (his *Morals of Chess* being well known), and others. Paulsen's name was also on the menu. However,

---

* EDITOR'S NOTE: Paul Rudolf von Bilguer was a German chess master who died at age 25 in 1840. His *Handbuch des Schachspiels* (*Handbook of Chess*) had made his name.

** EDITOR'S NOTE: Alexander McDonnell died in 1835 of kidney disease. The Irish player was best known for competing with Frenchman Louis-Charles Mahé de La Bourdonnais in the World Chess Championship of 1834. The discrepancy in Lawson's spelling is not a technique of convenience. It is, rather, a function of McDonnell's various spellings of his last name, and thus a profusion of different choices for chess historians in later years. "M'Donnell" is one of the recognized spellings, as is "MacDonnell." But "McDonnell" is probably the most common twenty-first century spelling. For a thorough discussion of the McDonnell name debate, see Edward Winter, "Alexander McDonnell," http://www.chesshistory.com/winter/extra/mcdonnell.html (2004).

Julien had not forgotten Morphy, for on his tentative list he had the "Arc de Triomphe en pâté de gouyana, à la Morphy, orné de guirlandes de pensées en pastillage, et surmonté de la Déesse Caïssa Couronnant la Victoire." It is understandable that Morphy, innately modest, would demure, and therefore his name did not appear on the "Bill of Fare."

> The dining-hall was most appropriately decorated, emblems of the game, and the names of its leading ornaments meeting the sight at every turn. The table itself was weighty with chess adornments. In glittering confectionery appeared a temple of Caïssa, and a monument to the memory of Philidor. There were statues of Franklin in ice, Kings, Queens and Knights in jelly, Bishops, Castles and Pawns in cream, and huge cakes in the shape of chessboards. The bill of fare was certainly unique. It was neatly printed, headed by an elegant representation of a board and men, and containing such curious dishes as "Filets de boeuf à la Meek-mead," "Dindonneaux au Congress," "Bastion de Gibier à la Palamède," "Chartreuse de Perdrix à l'Échiquier," "Vol-au-Vent de Cervelles à la Paulsen," "Pommes de Terre à la M'Donnell," "Gâteaux à la Julien," "Pudding à la Franklin," and a hundred similar singular specimens of culinary chess. It is needless to state how much better the "Côtelettes d'Agneau à la Bilguer" tasted than simple lambchops.

As *The First American Chess Congress* notes, Judge Meek presided over the dinner, and, toward the end of his remarks, said:

> Our players have evinced in the Tournament that they possess skill and science equal to the masters of the Old World; and ere long, beside the classic names of Staunton, and Anderssen, and Der Lasa, and St. Amant, and Lowenthal, the Muse of Caïssa will delight to register those of Morphy, and Paulsen, and Stanley, and Montgomery, and Lichtenhein, and Mead, and Hammond, and others who have nobly won green chaplets by their "doughty deeds" in the embattled lists of chess, and on the mosaic pavement which she so proudly treads.

He then proposed a toast to the New York Chess Club to which Colonel Mead responded. In closing, as stated in *The First American Chess Congress*, the colonel proposed "the health of Paul Morphy, the refined gentleman, the accomplished scholar, and the master chess-player." To which Morphy responded:

Mr. President and Gentlemen of the Congress,—I sincerely thank you. To one, to all I tender the expression of my warm and heartfelt acknowledgements. Much, however, as I feel honored, I must be permitted to see in this gathering of chess celebrities something more than a tribute to merit whether real or supposed. Gentlemen, we have come together for a noble purpose; we meet at this festive board to rejoice at the success of a grand undertaking. Great, truly great, is the occasion. For the first time in the annals of American Chess, a Congress is being held which bids fair to mark an era in the history of our noble game. Chess, hitherto viewed by our countrymen in the light of a mere amusement, assumes at last its appropriate place among the sciences which at once adorn and exalt the intellect. We have met this night to hail the dawn of a true appreciation of its manifold claims to regard. And, gentlemen, may we not cherish the hope that this, the first great national gathering of the votaries of Caïssa, may prove but the forerunner of many yet to come? Should time realize this fond anticipation, to you, the gentlemen of the New York Club, will belong the praise of having taken the lead in the glorious cause. You have, in the political phrase, set the ball in motion. From the New York Club—from the altar where you worship—has gone forth the first note of praise, destined soon to swell into a mighty anthem to the achievements of our kingly pastime. I exhult to think that the Chess warriors of the Crescent City will catch a spark of the enthusiasm of the New York amateurs; that gallant Southern spears, too long idle will again be couched, and jousts as brilliant as that of '45 [Stanley–Rousseau] be witnessed once more.

But, gentlemen of the Chess Congress, I perceive that I too far tax your patience. I avail myself of the opportunity presented to tender to each and every one of you the assurance of my deep indebtedness for the more than kind manner in which I have been welcomed to New York. I propose, in conclusion.

The Chess Editors of New York, Their labors have materially contributed to the spread of our noble and intellectual game.

To this, W. J. A. Fuller, chess editor of *Frank Leslie's Illustrated Newspaper*, responded at length, finally remarking (as quoted in *The First American Chess Congress* book):

But what shall I say of the crowning excellence and glory of the Congress—the wonderful playing of our young Philidor? No, I am wrong; for though I believe I was the first to give him that appellation, yet it is a misnomer. Philidor but shadowed forth the mightier chess genius which it was reserved for America to produce, in the person of our young friend, Paul Morphy, in whom we all take such national pride. He verifies the truth of the poet's line: "Westward the star of Empire takes its way." He charms us no less by his quiet, unobtrusive deportment, modest and refined nature, gentlemanly courtesy, elegant manners, and genial companionship, than by his wondrous skill at our noble game.

Thoroughly conversant with all the openings and endings, he shows that he had laid every writer under contribution to increase his stock of "book knowledge," but it is his own matchless genius which embraces and enlarges them all, that wins the victory, and that enables us, as we intend to do, to challenge the world to produce his peer. He reminds us of the noble river on whose banks he lives, which gathering in its course the contributions of various tributary streams, pours at last its own current into the ocean, deep, clear and irresistible.

The First American Chess Congress states that after other speeches and the singing of songs composed by Judge Meek and Denis Julien, Thomas Frère spoke, concluding with a salute to "The Brotherhood of Chess, as its origin is untraceable, may its existence be everlasting," and

Mr. Marache . . . paid some handsome compliments to the chess players of the South, and concluded his remarks by toasting Mr. Rousseau, of New Orleans, which remarks were happily responded to by Mr. Morphy, and thus ended this gala American chess event.

On October 19, the Congress voted for a permanent organization to be called the American Chess Association. Paul Morphy put the name of Colonel Charles D. Mead in nomination for the presidency and he was unanimously elected. The articles of the Association provided for the election of Honorary Members who must all be foreigners, and the following were duly elected:

Mr. J. Lowenthal	London
Mr. H. Staunton	London
Mr. T. von Heyderbrandt und der Lasa	Berlin
Mr. Charles St. Amant	Paris
Mr. C. F. Jaenisch	St. Petersburg
Mr. A. Anderssen	Breslau
Mr. George Walker	London

Mr. Perrin, the secretary of the New York Chess Club, informed the Congress (see *The First American Chess Congress*) that he had received two letters from Mr. Lowenthal of London, "the first suggesting the advisableness of always giving the first move in public games, to the player of the white pieces, and the second, giving a new analysis of the Pawn and Move opening."

The pairing of the third section of the Grand Tournament took place on October 22. The draw set Morphy against Lichtenhein, and Paulsen against Dr. Raphael. Morphy won the first and second games of Lichtenhein, but the third game ended in a draw, due to one of Morphy's rare oversights. The game actually went to fifty-five moves, although only thirty-one were published. Oddly enough, Paulsen was also obliged to concede a draw in this section to Dr. Raphael.

On October 26, both Morphy and Paulsen won the third games of their respective opponents and so advanced to the final test for the First Prize.

Now, the two most formidable players of the Congress were to face each other. Paulsen and Morphy were in most striking contrast—physically, mentally, and temperamentally. Paulsen was a blond Nordic, large in frame, cautious, and phlegmatic; Morphy dark-haired and dark-eyed, short in stature, and quick in reactions, combinations, and play. But they were much alike in modesty and courtesy, and each had stirred the Congress to heights of enthusiasm and expectation—Morphy, with his half-revealed mastery of the chessboard, and Paulsen, with his "clairvoyant" power (to use his own word in speaking of his blindfold chess playing). Both were eager for the final contest. Stanley, in witnessing Paulsen's and Morphy's blindfold playing, gave it as his opinion (in the New York *Porter's Spirit of the Times,* June 19, 1858), that

> if there be any truth in clairvoyance, there is the explanation. We believe that either Morphy or Paulsen can see the entire boiling of chess boards whereon they direct their play, half a mile off, in a dark room.

At last the match that chance had created and the Congress had hoped and waited for was about to start. The winner of the first five games would become American champion and would be entitled to the First Prize. Morphy and Paulsen had identical tournament scores, each with nine wins, no losses, and one draw.

On Thursday, October 29, play began, ending after five hours and thirty minutes with Morphy winning. That same evening, they started the second game at 7:30 p.m., but adjourned it at midnight to resume at 11:30 a.m. the following day. After an adjournment for dinner on Friday, they played until midnight. On Saturday, after fifteen hours of play, a draw was agreed to.

Fiske, in a letter to Professor George Allen about Morphy, dated November 8, 1857, has an explanation for this lengthy second game ending in a draw:

> Nothing can be more pleasing or graceful than the elegance of his [Morphy's] play—I mean his manner of touching the pieces and moving them and so forth. I have never seen him impatient but once. In his second game with Paulsen, after the German had taken repeatedly thirty, forty-five and fifty minutes (and in some instances over one hour) upon his moves, Morphy became so thoroughly worn out that in his haste he made what should have been his second move first and was only able to draw a won game (a splendid piece of chess that it had been up to that moment). He was so depressed at the failure to score so fine a game (although no one but me knew its effect upon his mind) that he played weakly the two following contests and lost one of them.

Undoubtedly, slow playing on the part of Paulsen was the reason for time records being kept during his games with Morphy. Moves over five minutes during the second game and portions of others were recorded. During the entire second game, Morphy's total time for moves over five minutes was only twenty-five minutes, while Paulsen consumed eleven hours for the same.

Steinitz, in his opening statement on Morphy in the January 1885 issue of the *International Chess Magazine*, distorts the truth when he writes to disclaim "the superhuman accuracy which has been ascribed to Morphy." If Steinitz's first example is considered (this second match game with Paulsen), it becomes evident that Steinitz was unaware of the circumstances of the game that Fiske's letter reveals.

As Reinfeld says of this second game with Paulsen in *The Human Side of Chess*, "Morphy had responded a little impatiently, thereby transposing two moves and changing a win to a draw." But for someone of Morphy's temperament, those long waits on moves must have been very trying, since he sat immobile at the chessboard as was his custom, not allowing himself to show signs of impatience. On one such occasion, Edge says, "Morphy sat calmly looking on, without the slightest evidence of impatience" as Paulsen took two hours to make his move.

In this second game he reversed what should have been his twenty-third and twenty-fourth moves by touching his Queen for move twenty-three, fifteen seconds after Paulsen had pondered for thirty-five minutes over his twenty-third move. Morphy had the following to say about this twenty-third move in his notes on the game for the *Congress* book:

> A most unfortunate slip. As soon as the second player [Morphy] had touched the Queen he remarked that had he taken the Knight the contest should not have been prolonged a dozen moves. And that he had the winning combination in his mind, he proved . . . after the close of the game.

As Fiske mentioned, Morphy lost the next game and drew the fourth on November 2. The fifth game commenced immediately after the fourth and was won by Morphy.

The sixth—the famous Queen Sacrifice game—was played on November 3, Paulsen having the move. In this game, as in most of the others, the elapsed time was recorded for some moves only. On his sixteenth move, Paulsen deliberated for thirty-eight minutes before moving. Morphy replied in less than five minutes, threatening mate in two moves. On his seventeenth move, Morphy took twelve minutes before offering his Queen for a Bishop (Morphy's longest time on any move during the tournament), but Paulsen looked at Morphy's Queen a long time before accepting it. *Frank Leslie's Illustrated Newspaper* of November 28, 1857, gives the following account of this moment in the game:

> Mr. Stanley, one of the bystanders, remarked of Mr. Morphy, on making this seemingly rash move, that he should be confined in a lunatic Asylum. Not one present could fathom the meaning of this bold play, until move after move showed to the wonderstruck spectators how accurate had been Mr. Morphy's calculation . . . seeing into a dozen moves ahead with all the attendant variations!

W. J. A. Fuller's remarks about this game (given in the *Steinitz-Zukertort Chess Match Programme*) are also of interest:

> Steinitz confirmed me in my opinion that Morphy played some of his best moves by intuition, as it was impossible that human

brain could have thoroughly analyzed the result. Take, by way of illustration, the 30th move in his 4th game of the match with Harrwitz, where the simple advance of a Pawn was followed up with such ingenuity and accuracy; or the game in his match with Paulsen . . . where he [Morphy] gave up his Queen for a Bishop. Just before this game Morphy went down to the restaurant with me and took a glass of sherry and a biscuit. His patience was worn out by the great length of time Paulsen took for each move. His usually equable temper was so disturbed, that he clenched his fist and said[,] "Paulsen shall never win another game of me while he lives[,]" and he never did.

When he made the move referred to, we all thought that he had made a mistake; especially as he had taken so little time for the move. Paulsen, with his usual caution, deliberated long—over an hour—before he took the Queen. He doubtless thought of Virgil's line *Timeo Danaos, et dona ferentes.* Meanwhile the rest of us had set up the position, and our joint analysis failed to discover Morphy's subsequent moves.

William Steinitz, analyzing this game in his *Modern Chess Instructor,* published in 1889, comments:

White cannot be blamed for not seeing the most wonderful combination that the opponent had prepared . . . One of the most charming poetical chess compositions that has ever been devised in practical play. . . . Full justice has not been done to Morphy's extraordinary position judgment.

Black—Morphy

White—Paulsen

The moves
17. R–R2
Black to make his seventeenth move
17. ... Q–B

And Steinitz adorned the front cover of the *Modern Chess Instructor* with this game printed in gold, showing the position after Morphy's dramatic seventeenth move, Queen takes Bishop. The diagram on the previous page shows the position as the Black Queen is about to capture the White Bishop.

Oddly, Steinitz, in his short list of brilliant games in the January 1885 issue of the *International Chess Magazine*, was not aware that this game was a Paulsen match game, for which there was little excuse, since the game was published as such in *The First American Chess Congress*. Calling it a casual game, he refused to accord it merit for brilliance, although he obviously changed his mind later.

In the February 1885 issue of the *International Chess Magazine*, when discussing Morphy's chess activities, Steinitz states: "Morphy found his principal opponents unprepared and rusty." This remark calls for comment. It might be asked which opponents Steinitz had in mind—Paulsen, Lowenthal, Harrwitz, or Anderssen? All certainly were principal opponents at one time or another. Paulsen had certainly been more active than Morphy prior to the Congress. While Morphy was yet a college student, playing but a few games of chess here and there, Paulsen had been active in the western United States for some time, playing numerous blindfold and casual games with many strong players. And Staunton, in commenting in *Chess Praxis* about the Morphy–Lowenthal match, mentioned that Lowenthal had had "all the advantage of incessant practice, a life, in fact, devoted to the game." As for Harrwitz, who was the professional in residence at La Régence, need anything be added? Concerning Anderssen, more later. In any case, the "rust" of which Steiniz speaks in reference to Morphy's opponents is far from apparent.

The seventh match game, played on November 6, was won by Morphy in twenty-six moves, and the match ended on November 10 when Morphy won the eighth game and First Prize.

After the match, Fiske described Morphy's and Paulsen's different styles of play in the *Chess Monthly* of December 1857:

> Mr. Morphy is bold and attacking, resembling in this particular the lamented M'Donnell; Mr. Paulsen is cautious and defensive to a fault. Mr. Morphy always met Pawn to King's fourth with Pawn to King's fourth; Mr. Paulsen, when his adversary had the move, invariably played Pawn to Queen's Bishop fourth. Mr. Morphy is rapid in his moves and quick in his combinations, his time on any move never having reached a quarter of an hour [12

minutes] and that only once. Mr. Paulsen is exceedingly slow, some of his moves having occupied more than an hour and several in succession having exceeded thirty minutes.

G. A. MacDonnell, in his book *Chess Life-Pictures*, described Morphy and his manner of playing, having witnessed many of his games when in England:

> His smile was delightful; it seemed to kindle up the brain-fuel that fed his eyes with light, and it made them shoot forth most brilliant rays. . . . He moved very fast, but never hurriedly. He never put his hand near a piece until he was going to move it, nor placed any of them inexactly on the board, so as to leave his antagonist doubtful as to its position, never swooped down upon a piece he was going to capture nor described an atmospheric arc with his arm previous to making the coup that was to strike the spectators with wonder, or ensure for him the victory. . . . Morphy generally kept his eyes fixed intently upon the board whilst he was playing, yet, like that gentleman [Henry T. Buckle] he always looked up from it as soon as he had a winning game, but never with an exulting or triumphant gaze. He seldom—in fact, in my presence never—expended more than a minute or two over his best and deepest combinations.

> He never seemed to exert himself, much less to cudgel his brains, but played with consummate ease, as though his moves were the result of inspiration. I fancy he always discerned the right move at a glance, and only paused before making it partly out of respect for his antagonist and partly to certify himself of its correctness, to make assurance doubly sure, and to accustom himself to sobriety of demeanor in all circumstances. . . . I fully agree with Mr. Boden's opinion, that he possessed a truly gigantic capacity for chess that was never fully called forth, because even its partial development sufficed to enable him to triumph over all opponents.

CHAPTER 6

First Prize and Congress Aftermath

After Morphy won his eighth match game of Paulsen on November 10, the Committee of Management made immediate plans for the formal presentation of prizes to all winners on the following day, November 11, the Minor Tournament having also been concluded. Because of the great public interest in the National Chess Congress, it was decided to open the doors of Descombes' Rooms to all chess lovers and (as related in *The First American Chess Congress*),

> a large audience having assembled, Col. Mead, President of the American Chess Association, took the chair at eight o'clock. After expressing his regret that the Honorable A. B. Meek, the able presiding officer of the Congress, was not present to award the prizes, Col. Mead said that the sessions of the National Chess Congress would this evening terminate.
>
> The President then proceeded to read the following list of prize-bearers:

GRAND TOURNAMENT

First Prize	Mr. PAUL MORPHY	New Orleans, La.
Second Prize	Mr. LOUIS PAULSEN	Dubuque, Iowa
Third Prize	Mr. T. LICHTENHEIN	New York City
Fourth Prize	Dr. B. I. RAPHAEL	Louisville, Ky.

MINOR TOURNAMENT

First Prize	Mr. WILLIAM HORNER	Brooklyn, N.Y.
Second Prize	Mr. MOSES SOLOMONS	New York City
Third Prize	Mr. WILLIAM SEEBACH	New York City
Fourth Prize	Mr. MARTIN MANTIN	New York City

> Then turning to Mr. Morphy the President said:
>
> "In delivering to Mr. Morphy, the chief victor in the Grand Tournament, the first prize, consisting of a service of silver plate, I discharge a duty which I know meets with the cordial approbation of every member of this Congress. To none, I truly

believe, is this act more gratifying than to those whom he has so gallantly vanquished. To none is it more agreeable than to myself to be the means of conveying to him that to which he has proven himself, by his superiority as a chess-player, to be justly entitled."

The remaining prizes were awarded, the President stating that the prizes for problems would be delivered as soon as the Committee who had the competing positions in charge, had finished their labors.

The service of plate, which formed the first prize, was then exhibited. It was manufactured to the order of the Committee by Ball, Black & Co. of New York, and consisted of a silver pitcher, four goblets, and a salver. The latter bore the following inscription:

This Service of Plate
is presented to
PAUL MORPHY
The Victor in the Grand Tournament
at the First Congress
of the
American National Chess Association
New York, 1857

Above this inscription was an admirable representation of Mr. Morphy and Mr. Paulsen seated at a chess-table playing. Both of the likenesses were excellent, having been copied from a photograph by Brady. The pitcher and goblets bore the initials P.M.

On the same table lay an elegant testimonial purchased for Mr. Paulsen, by a number of the members, as a token of the gratification with which they had witnessed his blindfold games. It was a medal of gold in the form of an American shield, having on the obverse a design representing Mr. Paulsen playing five simultaneous games without sight of the boards. The reverse bore this inscription:

Presented to
LOUIS PAULSEN
by
Members of the National Chess Association
October, 1857

After the distribution of the prizes Mr. Morphy who had been requested by the subscribers to perform this duty, proceeded to present this elegant medal to Mr. Paulsen. Upon doing so, Mr. Morphy said:

"Mr. Paulsen, in behalf of several members of the first National Chess Congress, I present you with this testimonial. If measured by the admiration it is meant to convey of our estimation of your wonderful blindfold play it will not be deemed of little value. Sir, I claim you for the United States. Although not a native of America, you have done more for the honor of American chess than her most gifted sons. Old Europe may boast of her Stauntons and Anderssens, her Harrwitzes and Lowenthals, her Der Lasas and Petroffs; it is the greater boast of America that the blindfold chess of Paulsen has not yet been equalled. What if Labourdonnais played two, Philidor three and Kieseritzky four games at one time? We have in our midst one whose amusement it is to play five, and who will soon fulfil his promise of playing seven blindfold games of chess simultaneously. We fling proud defiance across the waters. Come one, come all!

"Let the superhuman feats of our Paulsen be performed with equal success by the much-vaunted European chess Knights! Let the much and deservedly extolled Harrwitz enter the lists! We challenge him—we challenge all the magnates of the Old World. But, Sir, your achievements need no commendation at my hands—they speak for themselves. And now, with a reiteration of our thanks for the many highly interesting entertainments you have so kindly given us, we beg you to accept this slight token of our admiration and gratitude."

Mr. Paulsen received the gift from the hands of Mr. Morphy and replied as follows:

"The honor which you have deigned to confer on me, in presenting to me such a beautiful and valuable present, is so great, that I only regret not being able to return my thanks in words sufficiently expressive of the feelings of gratitude, appreciation, and pleasure, which move my heart at this moment. The pleasure which I have enjoyed at our recent campaign in fighting many a peaceful battle, and in making the acquaintance of the noble champion of our Congress, as well as of other worthy and esteemed friends of Caïssa—this pleasure is so great that I do not hesitate a moment to mark these days as among the very happiest of my life. And ever afterward, when far from you, in the West of this broad country, where Providence has

secured me a home, the remembrance of these days will be to
me a source of joy and pleasure. Once more, Sir, let me express
to you my sincere and heartfelt gratitude."

Colonel Mead, after reminding the members of the necessity of
supporting the American Chess Association, then pronounced
the first National Chess Congress finally adjourned.

That Morphy's prize was in the form of an elegant set of silver valued
at $300 (the First Prize amount) was undoubtedly due to his having let it
be known that he would not wish the prize in the form of money. All the
other prizes were cash awards. Morphy never wished, in fact, refused, to
profit monetarily from chess, but money stakes were usually necessary to
complete arrangements for a match and so always presented a problem to
him.

As noted above, Morphy's success at the Congress had been expected
from the first day. Even Paulsen had foretold it, and public expression of
this anticipation was found in *Frank Leslie's Illustrated Newspaper* of October 31, 1857:

It is tactically understood that the final contest in the tournament will be between Paul Morphy and Paulsen. . . . He [Mor-
phy] is considered by the leading players in the Congress to
be the most brilliant and successful amateur living, and as he
proposes shortly to visit Europe [this is the first intimation of a
trip abroad] we fully expect to hear of his treating all the great
Chess magnates there as he has done those of the New World.

Both Lowenthal and Staunton of London were following closely the
progress of the National Congress in the *Chess Monthly*, to which Lowenthal contributed. They both kept up a running correspondence with D. W.
Fiske and Eugene B. Cook, and examined various American publications
that reported different aspects of the Congress. As will be seen by the extract from the following letter to Cook, Staunton took particular note of
the above reference to Morphy's possible visit to Europe in *Frank Leslie's
Illustrated Newspaper*, and, in view of the strained relations that later developed between Staunton and Morphy, the letter has special interest:

Leigham Avenue
Streatham, Surrey, Nov. 17, 1857

My dear Sir.

The packet came safely to hand. . . . I see from one of your journals Mr. Morphy meditates a visit to Europe: I wish you would use your influence with him to delay the journey until the time of the gathering of the Chess Association at Birmingham next Spring or Summer; and further that you would ascertain whether Mr. Paulsen's avocations would permit him to visit us at the same time. I should be delighted as would most of our amateurs to see them both on that occasion, and my gratification at seeing them, would be doubly enhanced *were you to accompany them.* Pray do what you can to bring this about: it might lead to an interchange of visits between the chief players of the two countries and be productive of incalculable benefit to the game. I should always have real pleasure in showing them the hospitality my house can provide.

> Faithfully,
> H. Staunton

Apparently convinced of his strength if need be, after his triumph in New York, Morphy soon began to think of invading Europe, and talked about it to Fiske, with whom he had developed a close friendship. As Morphy left New York on December 17, a month after the date of Staunton's letter, he probably knew about Staunton's invitation before leaving. And it seems he showed it to Fiske, who mentioned it in a letter to George Allen dated December 20, 1857:

> By the way, Staunton, in the epistle alluded to above, having heard that Morphy intends to visit Europe, very handsomely proffers him the hospitality of his house during his stay in England. This part of his communication I have seen since Cook copied it out and enclosed it to Morphy.

But back to Morphy's activities during the period of the Congress. When he was not engaged in tournament play, Morphy played many casual games, for as Edge wrote much later, when discussing Morphy's European games, "Morphy was easily approached by anybody, no matter what their strength. . . . As he invariably refused to play for any stakes, this pleased them the more."

As well as the Grand and Minor Tournaments, the Committee of Management had made plans for other games for the diversion of members of the Congress, and about the middle of October it announced that a grand consultation game was planned between Northern and Southern players. The North was to be represented by Colonel C. D. Mead, H. P. Montgom-

ery, and Louis Paulsen; the South by Judge A. B. Meek, Paul Morphy, and
Dr. B. I. Raphael. However, the early departure of Judge Meek caused the
plan to be abandoned.

Other games and diversions were arranged for players excluded from
tournament play, and for others. On October 20, on an excursion to High
Bridge, Morphy and Paulsen played two blindfold games simultaneously, no boards or men being used. Morphy won one; the other was unfinished.

As *The First American Chess Congress* states:

> Also among the amusements of the members were a number of
> so-called *alternation games,* as many as twenty players taking
> part in one of these practical chess jests. Nor did Mr. Morphy
> and Mr. Paulsen, after completing their daily game, hesitate
> to while away an hour in the evening by participating in one
> of these laughable battles. The blunders committed in these
> conjunctions of strong and weak players were a source of great
> merriment.

As the Congress drew to a close, Morphy was determined to test his
powers further, and in the following letter to Maurian, he shows himself
eager for combat across the board:

> St. Denis Hotel
> New York, November 16, 1857
>
> My dear Charles,
>
> Your very kind letters have reached their destination and I am
> happy to state in reply that with the exception of Walker's "One
> Thousand Games" I shall procure you all the chess books you
> wish to have.
>
> You must be appraised of the final result of the match between
> Paulsen and myself: the score at the termination of the contest,
> stood as follows: Morphy 5, Paulsen 1, drawn 2. I would have
> a good deal to write about, but prefer postponing all I might
> tell you until my return to New Orleans. Some statements will
> surprise you. I shall probably leave next week, unless detained
> (and it is very likely I will be detained) by some match with
> one of the first class New York players at the odds of Pawn and
> move.
>
> For reasons which it would be too long to enumerate in a letter,
> but which I will explain to your satisfaction when I will return
> home, I see fit to challenge any New York player to a match at

pawn and move. If the challenge is accepted, as I have no doubt it will be, I hope that the New Orleans players will be prepared to back me. I shall also (and for equally good reasons) challenge all the members of the New York Club to play a consultation match with me.

Do not however, hastily infer that there exists the smallest degree of ill feeling between myself and most of the New York players. The truth is that my challenge is addressed solely to Thompson who possesses no small amount of chess vanity.

After losing eight games out of eight on even terms, he is unwilling (with what justice and show of reason I appeal to every chess player to say) to take the odds of pawn and move which I give to Marache, fully his equal as you know. The result of his conceit is that at present we never play together. With Marache at the above mentioned odds, I have played five games winning three and drawing two. Out of six games contested with Perrin at pawn and two I have won four and lost two. Mr. Thompson seems to fancy that it is beneath his dignity to accept odds of a player who has won every game contested with him, but enough of him. My impression is that I can give him the odds and make even games. We shall see.

Truly yours,
Paul Morphy

P.S.
Do not forget to see Rousseau, my uncle Charles LeCarpentier, (and every New Orleans player willing to stake anything on the result) in reference to this match.

P.M.

Morphy's challenge to play against all the members of the New York Chess Club in consultation was not taken up by the club. As reported in the *Chess Monthly* of December 1857, Morphy then

manifested a desire to play one or two games against the three or five strongest New Yorkers in consultation, and arrangements were made for that purpose, but the unwillingness of the New Yorkers finally defeated the design.

On the same date that he wrote the above letter to Maurian, *The First American Chess Congress* states that Morphy

addressed a courteous note to the Secretary of the New York Club, in which he stated that he was desirous, before leaving for the South, of testing his actual strength and with that in view he ventured to proffer the odds of Pawn and move, in a match, to any of the leading members of the Club. The challenge was accepted on behalf of the Club, by Mr. Charles H. Stanley. Mr. T. J. Bryan, a gentleman whose countenance is a familiar one both in the Chess circles of Paris and New York, arranged the preliminaries on the part of Mr. Morphy [Mr. Bryan had acted in a limited way for Mr. Staunton in his 1843 match with St. Amant], while Mr. Bailey acted as the second of Mr. Stanley.

The first winner of seven games was to be considered the winner of the match at one hundred dollars a side, but after playing five games, the score standing Morphy four, Stanley none and Drawn one, Mr. Stanley, through his second, resigned.

Sergeant, in his book *Morphy's Games of Chess*, gives one of these games, which was played November 30, and notes that it

is the only game of which the score has been preserved in the match wherein Morphy gave odds of Pawn and move to C. H. Stanley, after the finish of the Congress. It was the fifth and last game of the match.

Recent research has discovered the scores of two additional games, the first and second of the match, both to be seen later. The first game of the match was played on November 28, ending in a draw. Fiske wrote to George Allen the next day: "Morphy began his match at Pawn & Move with Stanley last evening. With a forced mate in five moves, he played too hastily and only drew the game." James J. Barrett, formerly chess editor of the Buffalo *Courier-Express*, confirms Fiske's statement, as will be seen in his notes to the game. Barrett discusses how Morphy, in his haste, allowed great carelessness to deprive him of a very unusual mate, which should have been his due after the beginning of a beautiful combination.*

The fifth and last game between Stanley and Morphy was played on November 30. Several days later, Stanley sent word that he was resigning the match.

In a letter to Professor Allen dated December 20, 1857, Fiske tells what

---

* EDITOR'S NOTE: Lawson published the game in his Part II, which is not included in this edition. With its publication in Lawson's original, however, it has become part of Morphy's chess oeuvre and is available through a variety of other outlets.

happened to the Morphy–Stanley match stakes:

> The score standing Stanley none, Morphy four and one drawn
> game (drawn through Morphy's carelessness) Stanley resigned
> the match. Loving Morphy as I do it is a pleasant thing for me to
> tell that, before leaving New York, he sent the stakes, accompa-
> nied by a kind note, to Mrs. Stanley, who, poor lady, sadly needs
> them. Stanley would have drunk it all up, but now his wife and
> children will be benefited by the money. When the world shall
> have lost the glorious Paul (which God send, may not happen
> for half-a-century) and someone shall write his biography I
> hope this and some other incidents I wrote of, will find a place
> in the narrative. They will show that his heart is as great as his
> intellect is astute. But he will not let me speak of them now.

In December, Mrs. Stanley gave birth to a daughter, and Stanley named
her Pauline, in honor of Paul Morphy.

Morphy, now released from tournament play, contested many other
games, more than those recorded or even mentioned, for as Edge said, he
was easily approached. Now, however, almost all games were at the large
odds of Queen's Rook or Knight. A notable exception to games at odds
were those played with John W. Schulten, who had at times past played
with St. Amant and Labourdonnais and possessed, as the *Chess Monthly* of
January 1858 said,

> a far spread reputation as a chess player. A multitude of his
> games, contested on even terms, with the leading players of Eu-
> rope have been published in the Chess periodicals of the last
> fifteen years.

Altogether, Morphy and Schulten played twenty-four games during
the last two days of November and into December, Schulten being in New
York those few days for the express purpose of meeting Morphy. Morphy
won twenty-three games, and undoubtedly, the monotony induced by so
many wins accounts for his lapse of a single loss. This lost game speaks
for itself and hardly merits discussion (see GAME 4 in Sergeant's *Morphy
Gleanings*).

In reporting on one of these games for the *Clipper* (GAME CLXIX in
Sergeant's game collection), Marache quotes Schulten as saying, "It is a
real delight to lose such a game as that. Beautiful, Beautiful."

Later, a lady present at one of those Schulten sittings described the scene in an article in the Philadelphia *Item* of May 1859:

PAUL MORPHY SEEN THROUGH
A LADY'S EYE GLASS

Everybody is talking about Paul Morphy and his coming ovation [May 25, 1859], and are we, ladies, to hold our peace? When
all the rest of the world is expressing so decided an opinion,
too? Certainly not. It's what we never did and never could—
a course of conduct utterly at variance with all our feminine
instincts; and, therefore, if our readers will go back a year or so
with us we will take them into the rooms of the New York Chess
Club, and give them a peep at the illustrious American who has
created such a furor among the devotees of Caïssa abroad.

Our abode is a dense atmosphere of blue cigar smoke, wreath-
ing and curling about the room. Chess players seem to derive
immense satisfaction from smoking; but, by degrees, as our
eyes become accustomed to the misty illusion, we distinguish,
perhaps, a dozen groups, scattered about over as many chess
boards. A solemn silence prevails, unbroken, save by whispers.
As we enter, people glance indifferently up, and then down
again. If Queen Victoria herself [she was fond of chess] was to
stand on the threshold of the New York Chess Club, nobody
would be astonished, and "checkmate" would be the only observation elicited. In the adjoining room, however, a crowd is
collected, all striving to catch a glimpse at some object of engrossing interest in the center. Here our bonnets and ribbons
stand us in good account, and we are courteously accomodated
[*sic*] with a chair beside the chess board.

Paul Morphy himself, a slender, boyish looking youth, with
smooth cheek, long chestnut hair, thrown back from his broad
white forehead, and a truly American fragility of figure; if you
met him in the street you would take him for a boy of fifteen.
The large violet eyes, however, are the most noticeable feature
in his face, with their long black lashes, and luminous iris, that
seem to dilate, and grow larger and larger with every second.
How his white, slender fore-finger hovers over the pieces—
how the quick eye, charged with electric fire, detects every
advantage—how the faint flush stains his cheek, as the game
becomes complicated!

There—his veteran adversary has compassed a coup d'état
that would seem fatal to any eyes but those of Paul Morphy. He
leans back in his chair, surveying the board with a gaze that has

all the intense abstraction of the clairvoyant. The other players leave their half-fought battles and cluster eagerly around the
young Napoleon. You might hear the fall of a pin, so breathless
is the hush. In an instant he resumes the game, with a brilliant
series of daring and hazardous moves, throwing away his strongest pieces with a recklessness and audacity which call a gleam
of triumph to the brow of his antagonist. The white-haired veteran is just about to overwhelm young Morphy, when his plans
are stopped short by a softly spoken checkmate, scarcely above
a whisper, from the lips of the boy.

The spectators, unable longer to suppress their excitement,
burst into enthusiastic plaudits, but the youthful conqueror
only smiles quietly and in silence, as if rather annoyed than
otherwise by praises. The defeated player eagerly pleads for
"yet another battle," saying, with admiring frankness, "It is a
pleasure to be vanquished by you." And the lists are once more
entered afresh. There is no shadow of weariness on the smooth
young brow. No—Paul Morphy could play on all night.

Morphy played no other games with Thompson during this stay in
New York, since Thompson declined to accept the odds of Pawn and
move. About a year later he accepted the greater odds of Queen's Knight
and lost the match of nine games. As regards Paulsen, the New York *Albion*
reported that it was "not generally known that Morphy and Paulsen played
ten or eleven off-hand games presumably even, all of which Morphy won,"
but of these extra games we have no record. Nor have we any record of
games in which Paulsen accepted the odds of pawn and move, although
the chess press at the time reported that such games had taken place.

At that time, publicity was usually withheld if a player expressed the
wish that his games be kept private. "The irritating custom of suppressing
the players' names," as Sergeant says in *A Century of British Chess*, "or at
best veiling them, has to be borne with; amateurs were very shy of their
names appearing in print."

In fact, often out of consideration for the loser, his name would be
withheld if the games were published. The names of a number of Morphy's
opponents were not known until years later in some cases, and others will
never be known. Maurian, in his chess column in the New Orleans *Sunday
Delta*, frequently referred to Morphy's opponents as "Amateurs," as, for example, when he published the game in which Paul checkmated his father
by castling on his eighteenth move. Maurian published the game in 1858,
but not until 1884 was the name of Paul's opponent known.

After Morphy's death, Maurian wrote in the New Orleans *Times-Democrat* of July 27, 1884:

> The subjoined curious little *partie* at odds [Queen's Rook], which is given in the various collections of Morphy's games simply as between Mr. Morphy and an Amateur, will acquire renewed interest for the Chess world when it is stated that the Amateur in question was in fact Morphy's father, Judge Alonzo Morphy, and the game was played about the year 1850, when the great master was hardly thirteen years old.

Sergeant was never aware of this relationship of the opponents in *Morphy's Games of Chess*, in which the game appears as GAME CCXCVII.

While in New York, Morphy made no attempt to emulate Paulsen in blindfold playing. Apart from his blindfold games with Paulsen, only one other such game is known during the time of his (Morphy's) stay in New York. On November 19, he played Lichtenhein successfully without sight of the board.

With T. J. Bryan, Morphy contested ten games at odds of Pawn and three moves, and later some seventy at Knight odds. Of all these games with Bryan, some eighty, only one has come down to us.

On Sunday, December 6, he visited Eugene B. Cook in Hoboken, New Jersey, accompanied by Frederick Perrin, W. J. A. Fuller, and D. W. Fiske. While there, the three visitors played a consultation game against Morphy, which they won. Cook, a brilliant problematist, was an invalid confined to his house most of the time. When *The First American Chess Congress* was published, the frontispiece was a chess problem composed by him and "Dedicated with the highest Esteem and Admiration to Paul Morphy, the Only."

Cook later composed six chess problems in the form of the six letters M O R P H Y. Over the years, others have dedicated problems to Morphy, among them Alexander Petroff, Frank Healey, Ilya Schumov, G. F. Ansidei, and S. N. Carvalho. Petroff's and Healey's problems were published in the *Chess Monthly* of July 1859, Petroff's appearing together with a letter from him to Morphy.

Morphy was now about to extend his chess activity, due to having met Fiske. The *Chess Monthly* was started as a joint venture by Daniel W. Fiske and Miron J. Hazeltine acting as editors and publishers. The first issue appeared in January 1857. However, Fiske observed the rising star of Morphy's reputation during the Congress in October and wished him to join the magazine as co-editor. Since Fiske was apparently the principle party of the venture, it seems he eased Hazeltine out. Within a month after Morphy's arrival in New York, Fiske was expressing the hope that Morphy would be editing with him, beginning in the new year. Before the middle of December the matter was settled, and the printer notified that Morphy and Fiske would be co-editors beginning January 1858.

It may be remembered that at the Congress dinner, W. J. A. Fuller had said, "*We intend to* . . . challenge the world to produce his peer." About the middle of November 1857, enthusiasm over Morphy led to the following statement in the December issue of the *Chess Monthly*:

> It is expected that the American Chess Association will shortly publish a challenge to Europe, which we shall probably lay before our readers next month. It will propose a match at Chess between Mr. Morphy and any living European player to take place in New York during the year 1858 for any sum from two to five thousand dollars. New York seems the most desirable place for such an encounter as it is almost equidistant, in time, from both London and New Orleans. Such players present at the Congress as had witnessed the play of the chief European amateurs have no fears as to the result. Mr. Morphy's play is certainly not excelled in the published games of any living cultivator of Chess.

Although Morphy would have preferred any such challenge to be issued by the American Chess Association, differences of opinion on conditions and arrangements for the challenge prevented the Association from acting before Morphy returned to New Orleans.

During the time of the Congress, Matthew Brady, the well-known photographer, took several pictures of Morphy, singly and with other members of the Congress, and it was announced in the *Chess Monthly* of July 1858 that there would be published

> a lithographic Picture embracing Likenesses of about Twenty of the most eminent Chess Players in the United States—the same being an exact Copy of the group as arranged and Photographed by Mr. Brady of New York.

> In the foreground is represented the figures of Messrs. Morphy and Paulsen in the act of playing their memorable Match, with Judge Meek of Alabama as Arbitrator and the rear is made up of leading Chess Players watching with intense interest the progress of the Game.

The lithograph is a fine item of great historical chess interest, but there are few copies extant.

Although it is now known to be incomplete, the January 1858 issue of the *Chess Monthly* printed the following list of games played by Morphy (including tournament games) during his stay in New York:

Paul Morphy's Game Score in New York 1857

GAMES WON—LOST—DRAWN

EVEN GAMES					GAMES AT ODDS			
Win	Lose	Draw	Opponent	Odds	Win	Lose	Draw	Opponent
1	0	0	S. R. Calthrop	P.M.	3	0	2	N. Marache
1	0	0	L. Elkin	P.M.	4	0	1	C. H. Stanley
3	0	0	D. W. Fiske					
2	0	0	W. J. A. Fuller	P2	8	2	0	F. Perrin
7	1	0	G. Hammond	P2	3	1	0	H. Richardson
1	0	0	H. Kennicott					
4	0	3	T. Lichtenhein	P3	8	2	0	T. J. Bryan
3	0	0	N. Marache					
1	0	0	C. D. Mead	QN	30	18	7	T. J. Bryan
5	0	0	A. B. Meek	QN	10	3	3	D. Julien
1	0	0	H. P. Montgomery	QN	2	0	0	A. King
1	0	0	D. Parry	QN	1	0	1	M. Mantin
8	1	3	L. Paulsen	QN	17	9	3	F. Perrin
1	0	2	F. Perrin	QN	7	1	1	A. Reif
1	0	0	B. I. Raphael	QN	0	0	1	M. Solomons
23	1	0	J. W. Schulten					
2	0	0	M. Solomons	QR	1	0	0	T. M. Brown
12	1	0	C. H. Stanley	QR	1	0	0	M. Mantin
8	0	0	J. Thompson	QR	9	0	0	A. Perrin
85	4	8			104	36	19	

Blindfold—Morphy 2, Paulsen 0
Blindfold—Morphy 1, Lichtenhein 0
Consultation—Morphy 0—Fiske, Fuller & Perrin 1

Passing references to Morphy's style of play during his New York stay are to be found in the December 1857 issue of the *Chess Monthly*:

> Physically Mr. Morphy is of short stature and slight build. He has the dark eye and hair of the South and much of the light hearted nature of his Gallic descent. His genial disposition, his unaffected modesty and gentlemanly courtesy have endeared

him to all his acquaintances. The most noteworthy features of his chess character are the remarkable rapidity of his combinations, his masterly knowledge of the openings and ends of games, and the wonderful faculty which he possesses of recalling games played months before. No player ever made more of a slight attack than he does. Blindfold[ed] he plays two games at once with about the same strength and quickness as over the board. His peculiar style is as well adopted for giving odds as was that of M'Donnell.

At last, Morphy's prolonged stay in New York was coming to an end. He was expected home before the New Year. Fiske writes of his last evening in New York in a letter to Professor Allen dated December 20, 1857:

> Something more than a score of us New Yorkers gave Paul a dinner on Wednesday the 16th, the evening before his departure. We had a fine time. It was less formal and far pleasanter than our Congressional banquet. Mr. Thompson presided. Morphy made a capital speech, which I could not persuade him to write out for me. It was much longer and altogether a far better display of the man's character than the remarks he made at the St. Denis dinner—Frère's toast was[,] "The Game of Chess: thank God, it has no Mason and Dixon's line!"

Then, as *The First American Chess Congress* relates:

> On the seventeenth of December, 1857, Mr. Morphy left New York, where he had spent nearly three months and a half, on his way to his Southern home. . . . Near the close of the year he reached New Orleans, by way of the Mississippi, and met with a cordial reception from his friends and the chess-players of that city, by whom he was serenaded soon after his arrival.

CHAPTER 7

The Challenge

Morphy reached New Orleans just before the New Year. In his first letter to Fiske, given below, he mentioned the "Creole" reception that he received. The *Chess Monthly*, of which he was now co-editor with Fiske, appeared some days before the first of each month. Since the January number announced that, "It is understood, unless otherwise stated that all Notes to Games and Analysis are written by Mr. Morphy," it is evident that he had prepared several games with notes before leaving New York. Of these games, four were his own, including the Queen Sacrifice game. It is evident that Morphy took his editorial duties very seriously, annotating six games each for the January and February issues with comprehensive notes.

The January *Chess Monthly* carried the following announcement:

> Mr. Morphy extends the challenge sent to the New York Club so as to comprise all the leading practitioners of the United States. He proffers any American player the odds of the Pawn and Move and will always be glad to arrange a match upon those terms.

The New Orleans *Sunday Delta*, of which Charles A. Maurian became chess editor in March, published some of the games Morphy played while awaiting an answer to his challenge, as well as happenings at the New Orleans Chess Club, of which Morphy was now president. Morphy's letters to Fiske in the months from January to May are the chief source of information about his activities during that time:

New Orleans January 25th, 1858
Daniel W. Fiske, Esq.

My dear Daniel,

From the moment of my arrival up to the present hour I have had, as you may well imagine, but little leisure at my disposal. Even today so much of my time is taken up that I can only hastily drop a line or two. The New Orleans Chess Club is more flourishing than ever. It numbers while I write more than thirty members, and ere another month will have passed away, the number will have swollen to fifty or sixty. The Club now meets at the rooms of the Mercantile Library Association, corner of Exchange Alley and Canal Street—the very heart of New Orleans. I one night played two and on another occasion three blindfold games simultaneously, all of which I won. The rooms were literally crowded, and the spectators much pleased and interested.

I pass the very flattering, or to speak more truly, the "Creole" reception which greeted me here. It was one of those things that are felt deeply and long remembered, but not described.

Do not be surprised at the comparatively meager notes appended to the games. Some games, as you know, require but few comments. Hereafter, I shall make it an inflexible rule to be very full in my remarks and criticisms.

Present my regards to all the members of your club, as also to such gentlemen, not chess players, as I have had the honor of knowing while in New York.

Your best friend,
Paul Morphy

P.S. I hope the *Monthly* is doing well. I shall exert myself to the utmost to procure subscribers. Let me hear from you at your earliest convenience; I shall probably write again this week and at greater length.

Still unable to practice his profession, Morphy set about developing his blindfold chess skill, as indicated in the above letter. He entertained his chess club with blindfold exhibitions, increasing from two simultaneous games in January, to seven or eight in April. We have no record of any games of these latter exhibitions, but it was reported that he won six and lost one of the seven games of the exhibition he played on March 31, and it was announced at that time that he would play eight blindfold games the week of May 2.

His challenge to any American player, offering the odds of Pawn and move in a match for one hundred dollars a side, received no response.

The enthusiasm of his friends and the New Orleans Chess Club now knew no bounds, and the club decided it would issue a challenge on his behalf to the Old World. It addressed the following letter and terms for a match to Howard Staunton of London, which was later published in the *Chess Monthly* of April 1858:

New Orleans, Feb. 4, 1858
Howard Staunton, Esq.

Sir,—On behalf of the New Orleans Chess Club, and in compliance with the instructions of that body, we, the undersigned committee, have the honor to invite you to visit our city, and there meet Mr. Paul Morphy in a chess match. In transmitting this invitation permit us to observe, that we are prompted no less by the desire to become personally acquainted with one whom we have so long admired, than by the very natural anxiety to ascertain the strength of our American players by the decisive criterion of actual conflict over the board.

We can see no valid reason why an exercise so intellectual and ennobling as chess, should be excluded from the generous rivalry which exists between the Old and the New World, in all branches of human knowledge and industry. That the spirit of emulation from which this rivalry arises has not, hitherto, been made to embrace our chivalrous game, may be mainly ascribed to the fact that, although the general attention paid to chess in the United States during the last fifteen years has produced a number of fine players, yet their relative force remained undetermined, and none could assert an indisputable right to preeminence. The last Chess Congress has, however, removed this obstacle, by finally settling the claims of the several aspirants to the championship; and it must now be a matter of general desire to fix, by actual contest with the best European amateurs, the rank which American players shall hold in the hierarchy of chess.

For this purpose it was suggested that Mr. Morphy, the winner at the late Congress, and the present American champion, should cross the ocean, and boldly encounter the distinguished magnates of the transatlantic chess circles; but it unfortunately happens that serious family reasons forbid Mr. Morphy, for the present, to entertain the thought of visiting Europe. It therefore becomes necessary to arrange, if possible, a meeting between the latter and the acknowledged European champion, in regard to whom there can be no scope for choice or hesitation—the common voice of the chess world pronounces your name; and to us it is a subject of congratulation that the scepter of transatlantic chess is wielded by one who, with respect to regularity of communication between the two countries, and for other reasons, enjoys facilities for accepting our invitation possessed by no other European player.

We take the liberty herewith to enclose a series of proposed "terms of the match" which has been drawn up, not for the purpose of imposing conditions, but with a view to obviate the necessity of repeated correspondence. We have been studious to make these terms as equitable as possible, and to include all matters upon which contestation was likely to arise. You are respectfully invited to suggest any alterations which you may deem advisable, not only in the minor points embraced, but also as to the amount of the stakes, the time fixed for the commencement of the match, &c., &c.

Fully subscribing to the wisdom of the proposal made by you, in the introduction to the "Book of the Tournament," we beg leave to express our entire willingness to insert a clause providing that "one-half at least" (or even *all*) "of the games shall be *open* ones."

In conclusion, Sir, receive the assurance that it will afford us extreme pleasure to welcome among us a gentleman, who is as greatly admired for his powers in play as he is esteemed for his many and valuable contributions to the literature of chess.

Hoping soon to receive a favorable answer, we remain, with distinguished regard your obedient servants,

E. W. Halsey	Chas. A. Maurian, Jr.
Francis Michinard	P. E. Bonford
E. Pandely	

TERMS OF THE MATCH

1. The amount of the stakes, on each side, to be five thousand dollars, and the winner of the first eleven games to be declared the victor, and entitled to the stakes.

2. The match to be played in the city of New Orleans.

3. Should the English player lose the match, the sum of one thousand dollars ($1000) to be paid to him out of the stakes, in reimbursement of the expenses incurred by him in accepting the challenge.

4. The games to be conducted in accordance with the rules laid down in Mr. Staunton's Chess Player's Handbook.

5. The parties to play with Staunton chessmen of the usual club-size, and on a board of corresponding dimensions.

6. The match to be commenced on or about the first of May 1858, (or on any day other during the present year most agreeable to Mr. Staunton), and to be continued at not less than four sittings each week.

7. In order that the stay of the English player in New Orleans be not unnecessarily prolonged, he shall have the right to fix the hours of play at from ten o'clock a.m., to two p.m., and from six to ten o'clock, p.m.

8. The time occupied in deliberating on any move, shall not exceed thirty minutes.

9. The right to publish the games is reserved exclusively to the contestants subject only to such private arrangements as they may agree upon.

10. The stakes on the part of Mr. Staunton to be deposited prior to the commencement of the match in the hands of . . . ; and those on the part of Mr. Morphy, in the hands of Eugene Rousseau, Esq., cashier of the Citizen's Bank of Louisiana.

Staunton was singled out for this challenge because, in the opinion of the committee, he was the most outstanding figure in English chess. Not only had he defeated St. Amant of France in 1843, at which time Staunton was probably the strongest chess master in Europe, but Staunton had also published many authoritative books on chess. He was the author of the *Handbook of Chess, Chess-Player's Companion,* and *Chess Tournament, 1851.* He was editor of *The Chess Player's Chronicle* for thirteen years and chess editor of the *Illustrated London News.* In short, the general impression prevailed in the United States that he was *the* English chess champion. However, this opinion was strongly challenged abroad.

Upon reading of the challenge to Staunton, Samuel Boden, chess editor of the London *Field,* voiced the following opinion:

America vs. Europe—Our cousins on the other side of the Atlantic, having apparently made up their minds to resign for the present the contest for the lead of the Turf, have turned their attention to Chess, and in consequence the New Orleans Club have forwarded a challenge to Mr. Staunton whom they profess to consider "the acknowledged European Champion" of this noble game.

Now, we can see no possible objection to the acceptance of this challenge by Mr. Staunton, as a private individual, if he thinks proper, and we have no doubt that it is made in good faith by the New Orleans Chess Club; but, though we do not devote any space to the record of chess games, yet we cannot avoid entering our protest against this selection on the part of our rivals of a champion for our side, whose defeat, if it takes place, will be chronicled as that of all Europe.

The editor of the chess department in the *Illustrated News*, and of the "Manual of Chess" which bears his name, is no doubt a high authority on the rules of the game; but that he is now the champion, even of London, alone, over the board, we unhesitatingly deny—and this fact is notorious enough in this country, while on the Continent the idea of his being considered the champion of Europe would be ridiculed as the height of absurdity. If, as it is alleged, Mr. Morphy cannot attend the Congress at Birmingham, in June next, to which he has been invited, let the challenge be forwarded through some public channel to any or all of the principle clubs in England, France, and Germany; and then, if it is taken up, the reputation of the respective countries will be at stake, or, if declined without some valid reason, they will suffer accordingly.

Staunton replied to the New Orleans challenge in his chess column of April 3 and in the following letter to the New Orleans Chess Club of the same date:

London, April 3, 1858

Gentlemen:

In reply to your very courteous proposal for me to visit New Orleans for the purpose of encountering Mr. Paul Morphy at Chess, permit me to mention that for many years professional duties have compelled me to abandon the practice of the game almost entirely except in the most desultory manner, and that at the present time these duties are so exacting that it is with difficulty I am enabled to snatch one day out of seven for exercise and relaxation.

Under such circumstances you will at once perceive that a long and arduous chess contest, even in this Metropolis, would be an enterprise too formidable for me to embark in without ample opportunity for the recovery of my old strength in play, together with such arrangements as would prevent the sacrifice of my professional engagements for the sake of a match at chess, and that the idea of my undertaking one in a foreign country, many thousand miles from here, is admissible only in a dream.

With friendly greeting to my proposed antagonist, whose talent and enthusiasm no one can more highly estimate, and with compliments to you for the honor implied in your selection of me as the opponent of such a champion, I beg to subscribe myself, with every consideration.

Yours obediently
H. Staunton

To Messrs. Halsey, Maurian
Bonford, Michinard and Pandely. New Orleans.

Staunton's reply did not reach New Orleans until the end of April. In the meantime, Morphy continued to delight the members of his club with games and blindfold exhibitions. Apparently, he was very active at the club, for he played many games, mostly at large odds of Queen's Rook or Knight.

On April 21 he played two games, giving the odds of Pawn and two moves in each game to four of the strongest New Orleans players in consultation. April also brought two visitors. W. W. Montgomery of Georgia arrived just before April, staying a week. He and Morphy played their first four games even, Morphy winning all. Morphy then played him at odds of Pawn and two moves, and under these conditions Montgomery won one but lost two. At Knight odds, Morphy won nine out of ten games, the tenth being a draw.

The other visitor in April was T. H. Worrall of Mexico, who paid a flying call. Yet in those few short days he played fifteen games with Morphy at odds of Queen's Knight, of which the latter won eight. Morphy did much better with him a year later in London. Others with whom he contested at this time at large odds were John Tanner, James McConnell (now giving him a Knight), Maurian, and Dr. Beattie. Also, Morphy was providing Fiske with annotated games for the *Chess Monthly*, although he found little time for it. And of course he was thinking all this time of Staunton.

Apparently after being prodded by Fiske for games for the *Chess Monthly*, he sent the following letter:

New Orleans, March 9, 1858
Daniel W. Fiske, Esq.

My dear Fiske,

Do not get too excited about the delay this month; it has not been in my power to forward the games sooner. Thenceforward, depend upon it, the games will reach you in good time. I only send four, requesting you to insert whatever others you may see fit, as I really am at a loss to select among those I have here.

The New Orleans Chess Club has challenged Mr. Staunton for a stake of 5000 dollars. I will send you tomorrow a copy of the letter addressed to that gentleman, together with the proposed "terms of the match"—I have received a very flattering communication from Belton Bill Co., Texas, informing me that a chess club has been established there under the name the "Morphy Chess Club." I understand that another "Morphy Chess Club" has been started in Maine.

Present my regards to each and every member of your club and believe me

Ever your best friend
Paul Morphy

Upon receipt of Staunton's reply to the challenge of the New Orleans Chess Club, Morphy's plans began to take shape in his mind. He would accept, with his family's permission, the invitation to attend the Birmingham Chess Meeting set for June, and would then accept whatever fate decreed. It would seem that Paul's was a somewhat secretive nature, for he never mentioned Birmingham in his letters to Fiske, nor certain important matters to Maurian (these to be discussed in Chapter 9).

In his statement in the *Illustrated London News*, Staunton noted "that the combat shall take place in New Orleans appears to us utterly fatal to the match." His declining to come all the way to New Orleans simply for the purpose of playing a match with Morphy cannot be considered unreasonable. But in his letter to the New Orleans Chess Club, Staunton also added two necessary conditions to be met for the match, if held in London, namely, "ample opportunity for the recovery of my old strength in play, together with such arrangements as would prevent the sacrifice of my professional engagements."

As Morphy was quite ready to accede to both conditions, he had no doubt that the match would be arranged were he to go to London. With unbounded confidence in his superiority and undoubtedly encouraged by others, he made plans to go abroad, much against his family's wishes. He was most willing and eager to meet all comers.

His family was not enthusiastic about the trip for several reasons. They were concerned about interference with his professional career, for Paul would come of age in June and would then be able to establish himself in practice. Reluctantly, and only after setting down certain conditions, the family yielded to great pressure from the New Orleans Chess Club Committee's prominent members, and from Ernest Morphy and Judge Meek. Very likely, Morphy's family believed the trip could hardly last longer than three or four months at most. Presumably, the family knew of his invitation to attend the Birmingham meeting, which was to commence June 22, and saw no great objections to his participation. At that time, only Morphy knew his true intentions; but as he was later to reveal, his primary motive in going abroad was to challenge Staunton.

On May 30, shortly before his departure for Europe, Morphy sent a letter to Fiske, which by the great courtesy of James J. Barrett of Buffalo, New York,* we are enabled to reproduce here. It is an excellent specimen of Morphy's writing and his estimate of his blindfold play. It concludes with his proclaiming his determination to voyage to Europe and there offer his challenge to the celebrated players of that continent and the British Isles.

New Orleans, May the 30th, 1858
Daniel W. Fiske, Esq.

My dear Fiske,

I send you five games for the July issue of the "Monthly"; they are all short and lively specimens of games at large odds. Two out of the five were contested in New York, the remaining three were played in this city. I should thank you for publishing four of my blindfold games in the August number (three Evans gambits and one King's gambit). These have all been inserted in the N.O. Sunday Delta, as also in Frank Leslie's; but I much desire that they should appear in the "Monthly," as I rank them among the best and prettiest I ever played. By the way, and entre nous, I have seen no blindfold game of Paulsen's that justifies the somewhat ridiculous praises that are bestowed upon him; and while I admit that he may be able to play more games at one

---

* EDITOR'S NOTE: James J. Barrett was the chess columnist at the *Buffalo Courier Express*, as well as a collector of chess memorabilia. Lawson thanks him in his acknowledgements not only for supplying such letters, but also for helping with "the selection, preparation, and proofreading of the games." See *The Steinitz Papers: Letters and Documents of the First World Chess Champion*, ed. Kurt Landsberger (Jefferson, NC: McFarland & Co., 2002), 20.

time than I can, I claim that an impartial comparison between the specimens of blindfold play we have both given to the public will lead every true chess man to the conclusion that Paulsen is *not the American blindfold player.* I have no time to annotate the games and do not regret it; Fuller or yourself may for once, as I am sure you will with pleasure, perform that task and do that justice to the games which I could not. All I ask is a fair trial; I am firmly convinced that hitherto justice has not been done to my blindfold play outside of New Orleans. I would suggest that together with the four games alluded to, you publish some of the very best of Paulsen's; I will then await with perfect confidence the decision of every competent judge.

> Yours in haste
> Paul Morphy

P.S. I shall leave tomorrow evening on my way to New York. I have made up my mind to cross the Atlantic and throw the gauntlet to all comers.

> P.M.

CHAPTER 8

London and Lowenthal

In London, Staunton was keeping his readers informed about Morphy. Almost every weekly issue of the *Illustrated London News* had some mention of Morphy or one of his games. Obviously, London had heard much about Morphy, as Staunton's comments suggest:

> April 10—Annual Meeting of the Chess Association. It was noticed in our column last week that this event, the Chess-players' Derby Day, was fixed to commence on the 22nd of June. The arrangements of the local committee are, of course, not yet complete, but it is whispered that they have succeeded in insuring the presence of the American chess phenomenon, Paul Morphy, an attraction, of itself, sufficient to secure the largest attendance which had been known for years.

> May 22—No official intimation as to the postponement of the Birmingham Meeting has been given, the committee being unable to take any step until a reply to their invitation to Mr. Morphy has been secured . . . and remember that Mr. Morphy, when a mere child, beat Mr. Lowenthal two games out of three.

> June 19—Visit of Mr. Morphy, the American Chess Champion. A communication which has just reached us by the *Fulton*, from New York, conveys the gratifying intelligence that Mr. Paul Morphy has definitely settled to visit England and attend the meeting of the British Association at Birmingham now postponed to August.

> June 26—Arrival of Mr. Morphy. The communication addressed to this gentleman announcing the postponement of the Chess Association meeting from June 21 to August 24th having miscarried, he unexpectedly made his appearance in Birmingham on Monday [June 21], prepared to do battle *a l'outrance* for the honor of the Stars and Stripes. Fortunately his intention was to make some considerable stay in Europe; he has therefore consented to take part in the gathering of August, which will probably be one of the most brilliant chess assemblages known.

As had been the case prior to his arrival at the New York Chess Congress, Morphy was a well-known personality in English chess circles, even before his arrival in England. Soon after his arrival, Ernest Falkbeer, chess editor of the London *Sunday Times*, made the following remarks in his chess column after mentioning some other chess masters:

> As to the rest, Morphy's presence in London is the all-absorbing topic of the Chess World, and detracts even from the interest of the meeting at Birmingham. This is, at least, a chess player from head to foot. Since Philidor and Labourdonnais we do not remember a similar apparition.

Had Morphy decided not to accept the Birmingham invitation and had he planned to leave for England a short time later than he did, chess history might well have taken a vastly different course. Charles H. Stanley had received a letter from Staunton, to whom he had written upon learning about the New Orleans Chess Club challenge. Instead of imparting the interesting information he received in his letter from Staunton to a chess editor, and having no chess column of his own at the time, he sent the following letter to the New York *Spirit of the Times*. It was published July 10, 1858.

> Dear "Spirit"—Having no longer any regular channel through which to gossip with the vast brotherhood of Caïssa's worshippers, a vent must be somewhere found. . . .
>
> Well, our young friend Paul Morphy has gone to England. I shall hear of his doings very shortly, when we will speak further on the subject. In what other manner can we account for the gigantic strides with which the spirit of chess has measured this vast country, if we fail to attribute it to the publicity given to its merits.
>
> What I did mean especially to refer to was a communication lately received from my old friend, Mr. Howard Staunton, on the subject of Mr. Morphy's challenge; being in reply to my letter wherein I urged Mr. Staunton (knowing that it would be out of the question from himself to abandon all his engagements for such purpose) to stir up some other first-rate player upon whose time were less calls, and parade him, making, if possible, New York the battleground.
>
> In reply, Mr. Staunton informs me that the *pecuniaries* would be insurmountable for so expensive a contest; but at the same time makes a suggestion which, had not Mr. Morphy taken

his departure, I think we might have brought to bear. What *do* you think it was? It was simply to play a match, Staunton vs. Morphy, for 500 pounds a side, by the *Electric Telegraph!* Just fancy—Morphy seated at our own club rooms in Bondstreet, and Staunton at the London Club in St. James street, blazing away at one another at a distance of some three thousand miles! If ever I fight a duel, I shall select small swords at that distance. At such a game, however, Staunton would have had master Paul at some advantage as to time, at least; as his (Staunton's) moves would arrive here some hours *before they were sent;* whereas Morphy's would not reach London until *some time after!* So much for that matter.

Your old friend and contributor
C. H. Stanley

The suggestion of a transatlantic Electric Telegraph Chess Match at that time was startling news indeed, especially a match between Morphy and Staunton. Telegraph chess matches were rather common, telegraph companies offering free service, but these occurred only between neighboring cities. Baltimore and Washington in 1844 were the first to use the new medium, followed by London and Portsmouth in 1845. Thereafter, there were many such telegraph matches—for example, those between New York and Philadelphia in 1856–57.

Some forty years were to elapse from that time before an English-American cable match materialized. In 1897, following a match the year before, a Parliamentary Cable Chess Match took place between the British House of Commons and the United States House of Representatives, which ended in an even score.

Of course, Staunton was not aware of Morphy's real strength at the time he suggested the telegraph match. Few of Morphy's games had been published in England, nor had he played against such masters as Europe possessed, with the exception of his childhood games with Rousseau and Lowenthal. Although Morphy dominated the American Chess Congress, no players there, except Paulsen (also unknown in Europe) compared with European players. Morphy's skill was therefore totally underestimated in Europe.

In any case, the telegraph match never took place, since Morphy left for Europe before news of Staunton's suggestion became known in the United States. Morphy had planned his journey in order to reach Birmingham a day or so before the announced date for the meeting—June 22, 1858. However, the Managing Committee had decided at the last min-

ute to postpone the meeting until August 24, and news to that effect had
not reached America until the day after Morphy left New York, as Staunton had mentioned in the *Illustrated London News*. Had he been aware of
the postponement and of Staunton's challenge for a cable match, Morphy
might well have deferred his trip to Europe. For, as he later revealed in a
letter to Lord Lyttelton written October 26, 1858, "I visited your country
for the purpose of challenging Mr. Staunton."

On the morning of June 20, 1858, Morphy arrived in Liverpool. He
was not a good sailor, and the twelve-day voyage had affected him adversely. No doubt, as expressed in the English and German press, his debilitated
physical condition affected his playing for some time.

After his arrival in Liverpool, he entrained at once for Birmingham. In
an article in the New Orleans *Times-Democrat* of June 18, 1899, Alderman
Thomas Avery, president of the Birmingham Chess Club, tells of meeting
him at the Curzon Street Station:

> I was never more astonished by the appearance of anyone. Hav-
> ing formed my opinion of the man by the strength of his chess,
> I expected to see a tall broad-shouldered individual, with a big
> beard and a ferocious expression. And there he turned out to
> be a slight, beardless stripling youth in a broad-brimmed straw
> hat, a black tie and a meek and mild manner. I took him at once
> to the photographer, and had the portrait taken which is now
> in the Birmingham Chess Club. He was a very gentlemanly
> young fellow; no talker, and as it seemed to me, a player who
> performed all his wonderful feats by instinct and without any
> visible effort.

Advised by Avery of the postponement of the meeting, Morphy proceeded to London the next morning and arrived there that afternoon,
June 21. Edge, Morphy's companion in Europe, writes of Morphy being
ill in Birmingham and of his getting up from a sickbed to go to London.
In London, he registered at Lowe's Hotel, owned by Edward Lowe, an accomplished chess player. And so it happened that Lowe, with whom he
played the next day, became Morphy's first opponent in England. Morphy
won all six games they played. Following this experience, Lowe rushed to
the Grand Chess Divan to tell of Morphy's arrival and what could be expected of him.

The following day, June 23, Morphy visited the Grand Divan and the
St. George's Chess Club. At the latter, he met Thomas Hampton, secretary
of the club, who was the first to engage him there. Just how soon Mor-

phy met Staunton is not known, but evidently it was on the twenty-third or twenty-fourth of June, because he enjoyed Staunton's hospitality at his country home at Streatham that weekend, as Edge mentions in one of his letters.

After friendly greetings, Morphy renewed the challenge of the New Orleans Chess Club, which Staunton conditionally accepted, requesting, as Edge states, a month "to brush up on his chess openings and endings." To this month's delay, Morphy readily assented, adding, as he wrote to Lord Lyttelton, "that my stakes [will] be forthcoming the moment . . . desired." This matter of the stakes should be kept in mind for future reference.

About Morphy's first meeting with Staunton, Edge writes:

> On Mr. Staunton's arrival, Paul Morphy asked him if he had any objection to play an off-hand game. Now it is Morphy's almost invariable custom to wait to be asked; the solitary exceptions to this rule (to my knowledge) being in the cases of Messrs. Staunton and Harrwitz. Mr. Staunton declined the offer on the ground of an engagement preventing, and notwithstanding that they met frequently at the St. George's, he would never consent to a contest of the most friendly description.

While at Streatham, Staunton proposed some consultation games, Thomas W. Barnes and the Reverend John Owen also having been invited to Staunton's country estate. Morphy and Barnes were paired against Staunton and Owen, and the former pair won the first game. A second game between the same partners was adjourned and not resumed until nine days later at the St. George's Club. In the meantime, the game was well analyzed by Barnes, Owen, and others, all agreeing it could end only in a draw. However, when resumed, it was won by Morphy and Barnes.

Whether any games took place between Morphy and Staunton that weekend other than those in consultation with Barnes and Owen has remained a subject for speculation for many years. W. P. Turnbull, author of *Chess in Action*, told Philip W. Sergeant that he had heard that Morphy and Staunton did play private games together at that time. As Sergeant suggests, it was undoubtedly Staunton who stipulated that there be no publicity, and therefore nothing was divulged concerning them while Staunton was alive. Both Barnes and Staunton died in 1874. However, Owen lived on until 1901, and evidently Turnbull's information came from him. Without doubt, chess was what brought the four of them together that weekend, and it is most reasonable to believe that more than one game of chess was played while they were there.

Barnes and Boden were the first strong players Morphy met in England. He met Boden at the Divan, and of the first two games played, Morphy won one and drew the other. Edge says that thereafter they played in a private room, Boden being sensitive about this chess playing. The final score between them stood Morphy six, Boden one, and three drawn, not counting another game played months later when Morphy played Boden and four other masters simultaneously. Boden was one of the first to recognize Morphy's strength, as the following comment he made in the London *Field* of July 1858 suggests:

> Let us do Mr. Morphy full justice; he is beyond question, one of the finest players living; and we may fairly question whether he will meet with his superior. He possesses singular coolness along with great concentrative power, is deliberate but not by any means slow, and to great depth of insight he unites a rapidity and faculty in combination which we have not seen surpassed. His memory is remarkably tenacious, and the unerring truth and force with which he pursues an advantage once obtained have excited the admiration of the best players in London. His style of play is attacking and brilliant, occasionally rather over hazardous, but he possesses a steadiness which when we consider his youth, is marvelous. We heartily congratulate our chess brethren in America upon the skill and chivalry of their young champion. . . . He possesses a truly gigantic capacity for chess which was never fully called forth, because even its partial development sufficed to enable him to triumph over all opponents.

With Barnes, Morphy played a series of twenty-six games. Surprisingly, at the beginning, each scored every other game of the first ten played. Edge describes their encounter as follows:

> His [Morphy's] next antagonist was Mr. Barnes and the result of their play was, at first, most surprising. During several successive days they scored alternate games, and the London chess world consequently measured Morphy's powers by this antagonist. Ultimately the former recovered from the effects of his voyage, and the proportion was established of Morphy 19 to 7 for Barnes, the last ten or twelve games being scored almost without a break.

Barnes thus made the best showing of all Morphy's opponents because their games took place just after the latter's arrival. Lowenthal made the following comment on Morphy's play during his first days in London, in the *Era* of July 18, 1858:

> Our report of last week shows that after recovering from the fa-
> tigue of a voyage across the Atlantic, and the excitement natu-
> ral on finding himself among strangers, his play has been simi-
> lar to that exhibited in America. . . . A slight illness probably
> induced by the same cause, compelled him, to defer his match
> with Herr Lowenthal for a few days.

Morphy made it a point to visit all the London chess clubs, among which there was some rivalry (Sergeant says they were divided into cliques). He did not show special preference to any one of them in particular, although he played much of the time at the Divan. After having met many of the strong English players, he came to recognize Boden as the strongest of them all. His only known over-the-board meeting with Ernest Falkbeer was at the Philidorian Rooms, according to Falkbeer in his book *Paul Morphy* (the English translation of Max Lange's *Paul Morphy Skizze aus der Schachwelt*). There, Falkbeer says, he "took part with Mr. Mucklow against Messrs. Brien and Falkbeer. The game resulted in favor of the latter parties; but being a mere experiment, was never noticed by any publication."

Although Morphy and Staunton met frequently at the St. George's, they never sat down together. Morphy, having made the first move, now awaited Staunton's approach. It would appear that the reason for their having no friendly game in public was that Staunton desired first to observe Morphy's strength and manner of play against other opponents. He was unwilling to risk losing to Morphy, although he could not have been much impressed by Morphy's early performance in London, for as Edge remarked of the first twelve or fifteen games Morphy played with Barnes:

> Judging from these parties, Paul Morphy was little, if anything,
> superior to that gentleman, but time had not been allowed him
> to recover from the fatigues of his voyage, and I have always
> remarked that traveling, even by rail, seriously deteriorates
> Morphy's game.

Probably the strongest member of the St. George's Chess Club after Staunton was the Reverend John Owen. Owen, Staunton's closest friend, preferred playing under the alias of "Alter," and all his games appeared under that pseudonym in Staunton's chess column. Morphy contested several games with him on July 3. Of the three games played that day, Owen won the first and Morphy won the last two. Later, they played two more games, Morphy winning both.

Yet it was Staunton with whom Morphy most desired to play. However, very soon after their first meeting, Staunton asked that their match be postponed until after the Birmingham meeting in August. Morphy agreed to this second postponement, and Staunton affirmed the agreement in the *Illustrated London News*:

> July 10—Mr. Morphy has proffered to play Mr. Staunton a match of 21 games for a stake of 500 pounds a side, and the latter has accepted the challenge, conditionally that the terms of play are such as he can agree to without infraction of his present literary engagements. As there appears every disposition on the part of his opponent to meet his wishes in this respect the match will probably take place in London shortly after the Birmingham Chess Meeting.

Edge, in writing to Fiske on July 6, was quite certain that the Morphy-Staunton match would occur in a matter of a few weeks:

> I am glad to inform you *subrosa*, that a match is about being arranged between these two [Morphy and Staunton] and I can assure you that, my own feelings apart, the belief is here that Staunton will be defeated. This match will come off in about a month's time, as Staunton says he requires a certain period to rub up his openings &c. Meanwhile, he shows no disposition to try an off-hand game with the "American," as he will probably speak of him, before long, in the *Illustrated*.
>
> This week Morphy plays a short match of the *first seven games for 50 pounds a side*, with Lowenthal, of which you shall have full particulars next week. This match is, of course, looked upon as a test of his strength, and I am much afraid that Staunton will want to pay forfeit after the licking which Lowenthal will receive.

Evidently, Edge had not been told by Morphy that Staunton had postponed their match until after the Birmingham Meeting, which meant it would not occur until well into September. He thus knew nothing of the matter until he saw it in Staunton's chess column.

Morphy had met Lowenthal during his first week in London, when the latter was still smarting from Staunton's publicity in May about his defeat in 1850 by a boy not yet thirteen. Lowenthal thus lost no time in proposing a match to clear the score between them. He doubtless thought the chances of winning were in his favor, after having observed Morphy play during his first week or so in England. Morphy had not yet recovered completely from the effects of the voyage. In fact, the match was delayed a few days on account of it, and then further delayed when Lowenthal's friends asked that the stakes and number of games be increased.

Apparently, these friends of Lowenthal's, confident that he would win, persuaded him to double the stakes to £100 a side and to increase the number of games necessary to win to nine. Half of Lowenthal's stakes were found by members of the St. George's Club. Evidently Morphy provided his own stakes, not having accepted anything up to this point from the New Orleans Chess Club. The club had offered expense money for the trip, and had agreed to provide stake money up to $5,000 for the Staunton match, as indicated in their challenge.

Lowenthal's chess strength had increased since his encounter with Paul in 1850. Even Staunton, who was not on the best of terms with Lowenthal, conceded in his book *Chess Pràxis* Lowenthal's great knowledge of chess theory and the fact that he had "all the advantage of incessant practice, a life, in fact, devoted to the game." He was superior to Barnes, as he was soon to demonstrate at Birmingham in August.

In his chess column in the London *Era* of July 18, Lowenthal supplied the following information about the terms of his match with Morphy:

> We last week informed our readers that a match at chess was in course of arrangement between the American champion, Mr. Paul Morphy, and Herr Lowenthal. The arrangements have been brought to a most satisfactory conclusion, and the match will be duly commenced on Monday next [July 19]. The winner of the first nine games is to be the victor.
>
> The stake is £100 a side, and the play is to take place on four days each week, viz., Monday, Tuesday, Thursday and Friday. One game will be played at each sitting, unless adjourned by mutual consent. Half the games to be played at the St. George's and half at the London Chess Club. The games [are] to be exclusively the property of the players. . . . The seconds of Mr. Morphy are Lord Arthur Hay and the Rev. J. Owen, and those of Mr. Lowenthal, Messrs. Barnes and Oldham. Mr. Staunton has been named umpire, and Mr. Lewis stakeholder.
>
> The stipulations in this match are exceedingly simple and fair for both parties. They are as follows:
>
> 1. The Winner of the first nine games shall be entitled to the stakes.

2. The first move shall be decided by lot, in the first game, and shall subsequently belong to each player alternately, drawn games notwithstanding.

3. One half of the games shall be played at the St. George's Chess Club, the other half at the London Chess Club.

4. The play shall take place on the following days in each week: Mondays, Tuesdays, Thursdays and Fridays. On Monday and Tuesday, at the London Chess Club, at two p.m.: Thursday and Friday at noon, at the St. George's Chess Club, unless otherwise agreed.

5. Either party failing to appear within half an hour of the appointed time shall incur a penalty of one pound, one shilling; within an hour, 2 pounds, 2 shillings; within an hour and a half, 5 pounds, 5 shillings; the fines in each case being payable to the opposite party.

6. No game shall be protracted beyond one sitting, unless adjourned by mutual consent.

7. After five hours' play, either party shall be at liberty to demand an adjournment for an hour.

8. The games shall be the joint property of the players.

As Edge wrote to Maurian, Morphy acceded to Lowenthal's request that "no stipulation as to the time of each move be made," which may have been a mistake. Had Morphy known that Lowenthal might take up to an hour on a move, which did, in fact, happen (game eight of the match being a good example), he might have hesitated. In Lowenthal's match with Harrwitz a few years earlier, one of the conditions was a time limit of twenty minutes for any move.

The match started on July 19 at the St. George's Club, but after six hours it was adjourned for refreshments. After another two hours that evening, it ended in a draw. The next day the second game was played at the London Chess Club, ending in a win for Morphy. The third game, also won by Morphy, was a very long one of eighty moves, and probably lasted much longer than the first, which was seven hours, thirty minutes long. The fourth game, which Lowenthal resigned at his thirty-first move, was pronounced by the German critics as the most brilliant of the series. By August 6, ten games had been played, of which Morphy had won seven and lost two. The other was a draw.

Needless to say, Staunton was one of those most interested in the progress of the match. There now seemed to be a discernible change in his attitude toward Morphy, and there was much talk at the clubs on this subject.

On August 6, Edge began a letter to Fiske concerning the Lowenthal match:

> At the commencement, before in fact the match had begun, Morphy bet Lowe that Lowenthal would not score 5 games, and it now stands M.7—L.2—Drawn 1. leaving two games for Morphy to gain to pocket the 100 Spondulicks. I need not send you the games inasmuch as you will find them in the *Illustrated London News*, accompanied by those mean, sneaking notes, which have constituted Staunton the "Chess Pariah" of the London world. . . . After the second game, which Morphy won, the first being a "draw," the Rev. John Owen, alias "Alter" who is one of Morphy's seconds, came up to Lowenthal and said to him in my hearing[,] "Never mind, one swallow don't make a summer." This reverend gent . . . is more inimical to Morphy than any man in London. God knows how he became Morphy's second; Morphy did not choose him. After each game Lowenthal lost, he would come to Morphy and tell him that he had won by L.'s oversight, and that he played much below his strength, or he would not beat him. Morphy has become so disgusted by his ungentlemanly conduct, and thickheaded observations on the games, that he has challenged him to a match, giving him the odds of Pawn & Move, and this may probably come off, before the match with Staunton. . . .

> But Owen states that he does not look upon the result of the match with Lowenthal as conclusive of Morphy's superiority, nor does he think that Morphy having gained of himself 4 out of 5 offhand games, in which Owen took an average of 1/4 hour to a move prove anything, and that he wishes to play two matches simultaneously with him, one at even, one at Pawn and Move—alternate games. . . .

> Staunton has shown his willingness to play after the Birmingham meeting by allowing a committee to form in his favor at the St. George's, to raise funds to back him &c. but if Owen can make a match with Morphy at even, Staunton will be justified in saying: "I have made every preparation to play, but Mr. Morphy's procedure has prevented my doing so. Mr. Morphy plays Mr. Owen even,—I give Mr. Owen Pawn and Move. Mr. Morphy playing Mr. Owen even, must also accept Pawn and Move

from me." Paul Morphy very properly will not consent to play him [Owen], therefore, even, and Lord Arthur Hay backs him up in such determination. This nobleman, a splendid looking officer in the Queen's Guards, and a member of St. George's[,] is much taken with Morphy and always comes to his assistance when such jealous devils as Owen & Co, are besetting him. You may rely upon the match coming off with Staunton in September.

The same letter continues as follows, under the date of August 13:

The Rev. John Owen (alias "Alter") consented to play the match at Pawn and Move on Tuesday last [August 10]; the terms being the winner of the first five games (5) for a set of Ivory Staunton Men. If Owen won, Morphy to play him afterwards even; if the contrary, Morphy to give him Pawn and two. Staunton gives Owen Pawn and one, and loses the majority of games, and the impression was at the St. George's that no man living could give him these odds in a match. The first game Morphy won in 18 moves, time 1 1/2 hours, whereof Owen took 2 hours. The second game was drawn, after 6 hours play; the 3rd and 4th were both won by Morphy, leaving Owen at Zero. This is considered Morphy's greatest performance since his arrival in Europe, and the folks at the St. George's believe now that Alter will not get a game. The match is resumed tomorrow [August 14]; when it will probably be finished [it was].

Morphy has not played with anyone during the continuance of his match with the Hungarian [up to August 6]. We have been constantly together, and have seen most of the sights in London. I look particularly after his health, which I am happy to say is capitally good: his nerve is excellent, and I think he is at least a pawn and move stronger than when he played here at first, for he was then somewhat fatigued from his voyage.

On August 6, Lowenthal visited Morphy at Lowe's Hotel. He wished to explain a very unfavorable and inaccurate paragraph in the *Era*. It had been printed without his knowledge, since he had turned over the editing of his chess column to another for the duration of his match with Morphy. Lowenthal was visibly ill, and Morphy insisted on postponing the match games until he recovered, which took a week. This interval (August 10 through 14) provided time for Morphy's match game with "Alter," of which Edge spoke in the above letter to Fiske.

In his Morphy book, Edge tells of the following boast made by Owen prior to the match:

> Now Alter had been playing for months past at those odds [Pawn and move] with Mr. Staunton, holding his own against that gentleman, and he considered that if he [Mr. Staunton] could not beat him, certainly Morphy could not. So confident was he of the result, that he told the young American: "Were it not for my position [as a clergyman] I would willingly play for £1000."

It was well for "Alter" that his "cloth" had saved him from the higher stakes, for, as Edge relates, of the seven games played with Morphy at the odds of Pawn and move, "Alter" won none, Morphy won five, and the other two were drawn. Although Owen had agreed to play a second match at greater odds if he lost this first match, the second match never took place.

Edge, again in his Morphy book, mentions Morphy's confidence about these and other matches:

> Before the contest [with Owen] commenced, he said to me: "Alter may win two games, but he will not win more," and I would here notice his [Morphy's] power of estimating an opponent's strength. When the preliminaries were settled with Herr Lowenthal, he stated to me: "If I cared about betting, I would bet that Lowenthal does not win five games. Of course there will be plenty of draws, but he will not get more than four." On our way to Paris, he said: "Well, now I am going to play Harrwitz, and I would bet the same as about Lowenthal," and when he was preparing to meet Anderssen, he awarded four games to the Prussian champion. In every instance he overrated his opponents, or, perhaps I should rather say, underrated himself.

As has been noted, English players were not initially impressed by Morphy's play, Staunton apparently less so than others. But with Morphy's gathering strength, demonstrated by his growing majorities over England's strongest players, opinion soon changed in his favor. Boden and Lowenthal were the first to recognize and admit his superiority. However, at the beginning of his match with Morphy, Lowenthal had confidence in his ability to hold his own. As Edge quotes Lowenthal:

> I felt chagrined at the result of the first one or two games, because I thought that I ought to have won them; but now I feel no longer dissatisfied, for I am convinced that I was vanquished by superior strength. . . . After the first game I went home saying

to myself, Well, Morphy is not so terrible after all! The second *partie* failed to change my opinion; but in the third, I saw all my combinations twisted and turned against me, and I felt myself in a grasp against which it was almost vain to struggle.

As Morphy's victories over Lowenthal increased, together with his extraordinary match victory over Owen, the main topic of conversation at the London clubs was the likelihood of the Morphy–Staunton match. Edge mentions hearing such remarks as, "Mr. Staunton now knows too well what antagonist he will have to deal with." As early as July 24, Edge wrote in a letter to Maurian of doubts expressed at the clubs as to whether the match would ever be held. These caused Morphy much concern, as Edge mentioned in this same letter to Maurian:

Morphy crossed the ocean, and threw down his gauntlet in the very sanctum of his adversary—the den of the dragon—the St. George's Club. No way now for Staunton to refuse. Accept he must[,] but play, will he? And men are now betting odds of 5 to 4 at the St. George's, the London and the Divan, that Staunton will find some pretext for not playing. He does not like the present appearance of things, for during the past fortnight although Morphy has been playing right and left, with men of all shades of strength, he has not lost a game, more especially in view of the match now progressing between Morphy and Lowenthal. Lowenthal was the proposer of this match, which was offered by him in the most friendly spirit, with an eye, also to wiping out his former defeat by a boy of 13 years old, which you of course remember.

Although doubts expressed about the match with Staunton caused Morphy much concern, Edge was not at all worried:

On myself, however, I can conscientiously declare that it [the clubs' gossip] had no effect. I did not believe it possible that any man having so publicly accepted a challenge, would attempt to avoid a contest, and expressed this opinion to Mr. Morphy, "It will be well not to accept all that one hears. Mr. Staunton has numerous enemies; do not allow yourself to be prejudiced by them, but look upon his acceptance of the challenge as a certainty that the match will come off."

In his composite August 6 and 13 letter to Fiske, Edge reaffirms his own confidence that the match would occur:

You may rely upon the match coming off with Staunton in September, and Morphy is too much a diplomatist to commit any
faux pas, which may give Staunton a loop-hole to escape. . . .

You can state positively that the match between Staunton and
Morphy for £500 a side will commence the first week in September; the scorer of the first eleven games to be winner.

Lowenthal resumed match play on August 12, winning the eleventh
game, and the match continued until August 21, when Morphy won his
ninth game and the match. The final score was Morphy nine, Lowenthal
three, and two games drawn. Morphy was awarded £100 for winning the
match, but he immediately presented Lowenthal with a set of furniture
valued at £120, for a new apartment the latter had just acquired.

CHAPTER 9

Staunton and Stakes

As the Lowenthal match progressed, Staunton showed increasing signs of unfriendliness toward Morphy. At about this time, Edge wrote Fiske that "Morphy wants me to say for the hundredth time, 'on no account to take anything relating to him from the *Illustrated London News.*'"

On August 7, Staunton's chess column gave the following reply to a real or imaginary correspondent:

> I.D.W.—Mr. Morphy came to this country unattended by seconds or bottle-holder but we are glad to learn by the annexed paragraph, which is copied from *Leslie's Illustrated Newspaper* that his friends in New York are likely to rally round him pretty strongly at the Birmingham Tournament.

At this time there was every expectation that Morphy and Staunton would participate in the August meeting. On July 3, Staunton said in his chess column, "Mr. Staunton, Mr. Paul Morphy (who is now in England), and several other players of distinguished excellence, have already signified their intention to take part in the grand tournament."

On August 14, Morphy penned the following letter to Staunton, ignoring the questions implicit in the latter's August 7 column:

August 14, 1858

Mr. Howard Staunton
Dear Sir,

> As we are now approaching the Birmingham meeting, at the termination of which you have fixed our match to commence, I think it would be advisable to settle the preliminaries during this week. Would you be good enough to state some early period when your seconds can meet mine, so that a contest which I have so much at heart, and which from your eminent position excites so much interest in the chess world, may be looked upon as a *fait accompli*.
>
> I am dear sir, yours very respectfully,
Paul Morphy

It should be noted in the above letter to Staunton that Morphy is the first to ask for a meeting of their seconds to arrange the preliminaries, including the posting of stake funds. This should be kept in mind in reference to Staunton's chess column of August 28, to be given later.

While Morphy awaited a reply to his letter of August 14, H. E. Bird, one of England's strongest players, returned to London, and the result of his encounter with Morphy was most dramatic. Of twelve games played, Morphy won ten, lost one, and drew one.

To his letter of August 14, Morphy received a somewhat lengthy reply from Staunton, its main thrust being that the latter still required a few weeks for preparation. Not considering this a satisfactory reply, Morphy wrote again a few days later:

> August 21, 1858
> Dear Sir.—I must first apologize for not replying to your previous communication. As you observe, my numerous contests must be the excuse for my remissness.
>
> It is certainly a high compliment to so young a player as myself that you, whose reputation in the chess arena has been unapproached during so many long years, should require any preparation for our match. Immediately on my arrival in England, some two months since, I spoke to you in reference to our contest, and, in accepting the challenge, you stated that you should require some time to prepare, and you proposed a period for commencing which I accepted.
>
> I am well aware that your many engagements in the literary world must put you to some inconvenience in meeting me, and I am therefore desirous to consult your wishes in every respect. Would you please state the earliest opportunity when those engagements will permit the match coming off, such time being consistent with your previous preparation.
>
> The few weeks referred to in your favor seem to be rather vague, and I shall feel highly gratified by your fixing a definite period for the contest. *I leave the terms entirely to yourself.* I remain dear sir,
>
> > Yours very respectfully,
> > Paul Morphy

Staunton left London for Birmingham without deigning to reply, leaving Morphy's many questions about the match unanswered. As for the tournament, Edge states that "before leaving London [Staunton] assured his young opponent that he should not enter the lists, but should confine himself to simple consultation games," or games at odds, as he had done since 1853. Morphy now became more uncertain and had second thoughts about entering the tournament himself. As Edge said:

> He [Morphy] was well aware that his decision must necessarily produce considerable disappointment, but he was conscious that a tournament triumph is by no means an accurate test of strength. If chess can ever become a game of chance, it is under such circumstances; and the only sure criterion of the respective strengths of two opponents is by actual hand-to-hand encounter.

There has been some talk that Morphy was unduly influenced by Edge, especially on the matter of the Staunton match, but we have seen that Edge was more confident than Morphy that the match would ultimately take place. In any case, Morphy was a self-willed person, and he made his own decisions. Edge always played a subordinate role in Morphy's affairs, and chess historians are greatly beholden to Frederick Milne Edge for his factual accounts of the events which occurred while he was with Morphy, which was practically all the time Morphy was abroad. This writer would agree with Philip W. Sergeant, who states in his book *A Century of British Chess*, "that my own reading of Edge did not lead me to think him a liar."

Edge was in effect Morphy's shadow, acting as his secretary and companion. It is very evident from his letters to Fiske and from his books that Edge was ever solicitous of Morphy, attending him in health and sickness, helping him with his correspondence, and even serving as his valet, carrying his underlinen to him, etc.

The following quotations from Edge reveal his unquestionably unselfish devotion and loyalty to Morphy. The first is taken from *The Exploits and Triumphs in Europe of Paul Morphy*; the second from a letter to Fiske written February 10, 1859; and the third from another letter to Fiske written March 25, 1859:

> I was constantly with Morphy after his arrival in London, and a frequent subject of conversation between us was the match with Staunton. That, too, was the first, the principal topic at all the London Clubs we visited, and everything but the date was looked upon as decided.

> Since his [Morphy's] arrival in Europe I have forsaken everything for him, damaging myself, in consequence with my wife and family.

> I can say, never did man more devotedly serve another. I neglected my wife for him, accompanied him to Paris and left her till broken-hearted she came to fetch me back. I put a coldness between myself and all my family which only years will heal.

Although Morphy did not intend to enter the tournament, he planned to be present a portion of the time and announced that he would give a blindfold exhibition against eight players simultaneously. This created much excitement, for Europe had never witnessed such an event.

As for Staunton and the tournament, upon arriving at Birmingham he decided to enter and signed to play. Edge intimates that Staunton changed his mind because he knew Morphy would not be present. Over the years Staunton had always held himself above others and had maintained an attitude of superiority by playing games only when his offer of odds was accepted, or in consultation games.

Apparently, up until the last moment, the tournament committee expected neither to play. But when Staunton entered his name for the tournament, repeated telegrams were sent to Morphy urging that he also enter. In expressing his decision not to enter, Edge remarks that Morphy said, "he did not regard such a contest as any true test of skill."

The Birmingham tournament was run on the knock-out principle, as the London 1851 tournament had been. Pairings were to be chosen by lot, which meant that Staunton and Morphy might or might not have been paired together at any time. Staunton's attitude toward Morphy had become such (note Staunton's remarks below, a few days later in the *Illustrated London News* of August 28, 1858), that Morphy now wished to avoid chess contact with him until their match. This was probably the principal reason why he did not want to enter the tournament for, as Edge noted,

> whether he won or lost in that contest, it might be equally to the prejudice of the challenge. Mr. Staunton might say, "I have beaten Morphy; what is the use of further contest?" or "He has beaten me, I am consequently out of play. It would be madness to attempt a set match."

Therefore Morphy decided he should not arrive at Birmingham until it was too late to enter, for were he to arrive before, he would find it very difficult to resist the great pressure that would surely have been brought to bear to secure his entry. However, the Birmingham meeting would provide an excellent opportunity to ask Staunton directly, in the presence of witnesses, to name some definite date for the match.

Morphy had not planned for a stay of many months in Europe. He was expected home by Christmas at the latest, and so was most anxious for a definite date to be set. He must also have been uncomfortably aware of his family's attitude toward such matches, about which more later.

Accompanied by Edge, Morphy left London Thursday, August 26, by the mid-day train and, upon arriving in Birmingham, was enthusiastically received. Mr. Avery, president of the Birmingham Chess Club, introduced him to the members of the Association, and, as Edge relates:

> The cheers with which he was received were such as seldom came from others than Englishmen. Morphy advanced up the room without the slightest embarrassment, although his reception was as unlooked-for as it was flattering, St. Amant, who was present, wrote a brilliant account of the meeting to the Paris journal *Le Sport*. . . . "His walk is that of a king, and he advances through the crowd of strangers like a monarch receiving homage from his court."

That evening Mr. Avery arranged a little contest for him with J. S. Kipping, who offered the Evans Gambit to Morphy and lost. Morphy in his turn offered the gambit to Mr. Kipping and again won. These were the only games which he played at Birmingham, apart from the blindfold games planned for the next day.

The meeting was being held in the rooms of Queen's College, and a number of eminent players were attending, among them Staunton, Falkbeer, Lowenthal, St. Amant, Owen, Bird, and Kipping.

The Grand Tournament had started on August 24. In the hope that Morphy might arrive in time to compete, his name had been entered and paired with Mr. Smith. When Morphy failed to arrive, Mr. Smith was given the point. Of the players worthy of special note, Staunton, Lowenthal, Falkbeer, and St. Amant all won in the first round. Pairing for the second round brought Staunton against Lowenthal, and Falkbeer against St. Amant. Lowenthal knocked out Staunton, the latter neither winning nor drawing a game, while Falkbeer won of St. Amant. The remainder of the tournament play was to be held in London, the Grand Tournament being suspended the next day for Morphy's blindfold exhibition. The long-delayed final result of the tournament did not come until September 23, when Lowenthal, by defeating Falkbeer, won First Prize. It was a fine recovery, considering that he had suffered defeat by Morphy only three days before the tournament. The prize money was greatly increased, since Morphy had declined the seventy pounds that had been offered him to come to England.

Morphy lost no time in encountering Staunton at Birmingham. As Edge tells it:

> The meeting of the Association afforded an admirable opportunity to obtain from Mr. Staunton the naming of the day on which the match should commence. Part of the proceedings of the anniversary was a public soirée, and Paul Morphy resolved that he would then ask his antagonist, in the face of all present, to fix the date. I had the pleasure of accompanying our hero to Birmingham, and I witnessed the disagreeable *contre temps* which upset this admirable intention.
>
> Crossing the courtyard of the college on the morning of the soirée [August 27], we met Lord Lyttelton, Mr. Staunton, Mr. Avery, and, I think Mr. Wills. Now I do not know whether Mr. Staunton had got wind of what was to occur, but his action certainly frustrated Morphy's plan, and, for the moment, gave him the advantage. In all such rencontres the man who gets the first word has the attack and Mr. Staunton instantly availed himself of it. He opened fire by declaring that he was entirely out of the play—that he had long since been engaged on a great work—that he was under bonds to his publishers accordingly—that he might subject them to a loss of many thousands in playing at the present time, and so forth. But he never stated aught that appeared to intimate the possibility of the match not coming off eventually, his plea being that he required further time, in order to put sufficient matter into the hands of the printers, and to prepare himself subsequently for the contest. It was now Morphy's turn, and the attack changed hands.
>
> The question was put: "Mr. Staunton, will you play in October, in November, or December? Choose your own time, but let the arrangement be final." The answer was: "Well, Mr. Morphy, if you will consent to the postponement, I will play you at the beginning of November. I will see my publishers, and let you know the exact date within a few days."
>
> The Association now looked upon the affair as decided, and Morphy left Birmingham, firmly believing that the match would come off after all.

But Morphy was to see something very disturbing the next day (August 28) in Staunton's chess column, which, of course, had been prepared days before for publication. However, unaware of what the morrow would bring, Morphy and Edge went on in good spirits after their interview with Staunton, apparently satisfied that something had been accomplished, and proceeded to the rooms of Queen's College, where Morphy was to give his exhibition.

When they arrived at the rooms, they found that the tournament had been suspended, and, as Edge informs,

> Mr. Avery asked Morphy what eight antagonists he would select; when the latter replied it was immaterial to him, but that he should prefer all strong players. There were then in the room Messrs. Staunton, St. Amant, Lowenthal, Boden, Falkbeer, Brien, and others of not much inferior strength, and Morphy was in hopes that many, if not all of these gentlemen would offer themselves as opponents. But he was mistaken and great difficulty was experienced by the Committee of Management in making up the required eight.

Later, in *Brentano's Chess Monthly* of June 1881, Falkbeer told how Morphy had "urgently" pressed him to take one of the boards, "but I refused, preferring to watch the progress of the games and take notes." The Birmingham *Journal* of August 28, 1858, described the scene that afternoon:

> His opponents were Lord Lyttelton, President of the Association; the Rev. G. Salmon, the best player Ireland affords; Mr. J. S. Kipping, the Secretary of the Manchester Club and a very strong player; Mr. Thomas Avery, President of the Birmingham Club; Mr. Carr, Secretary of the Lexington Club; Dr. Jabez Freeman, lately President of the Birmingham Club; Mr. Rhodes, a leading member of the Leeds Club and Mr. W. R. Wills, Honorary Secretary of the British Association.
>
> The play commenced at one o'clock, and terminated about a quarter past six, and resulted in Mr. Morphy winning six games, losing one [to Mr. Kipping] and drawing one [with Mr. Avery]. The *modus operandi* was very simple. Mr. Morphy sat at one end of the library hall; at a table at the other end sat his eight opponents, with their eight boards before them. Mr. Morphy gazing at the lozenged window above him, with his arm thrown carelessly over the chair on which he sat, attacked each board

in succession. Move and countermove were audibly announced by a friend, and when the tables had been traversed one move at a time, the process was recommenced. It was a most interesting scene. Mr. Morphy had the whole eight games so thoroughly in his head that, when a piece was accidentally shifted on one of the boards, and a move was made in which it was involved, he, at once, detected something was wrong, and exclaimed that it was an "impossible move." Such it was acknowledged to be. In the same game Mr. Morphy left a piece *en prise*, the taking of which involved a mate in a few moves, and accordingly on his adversary taking the piece, unconscious of the snare laid for him, the game became Mr. Morphy's immediately.

His play was very rapid. Each game lasted on the average about thirty moves, so that he had to bear in mind at least 240 moves, and the position of every board throughout from beginning to end. The feat was evidently regarded by those present as an effort of genius not to be accomplished by more than one or two individuals in a century.

At this time blindfold play on several boards was in its infancy, and many were the dire warnings Morphy received about playing such exhibitions. When he later proposed to play twenty such games after his Paris blindfold, warnings from all directions dissuaded him from the attempt. The *London Press*, upon hearing that he was going to play eight such games at Birmingham, stated in its August 21, 1858, issue, "Sure we are that not even Mr. Morphy's brains can repeatedly endure such a strain without injury." Even before that, Lowenthal had written Fiske "that such exhibitions tax too heavily the Chess powers of any player and [expressed] regret . . . for the sake of his health, that he [Morphy] should indulge in it to such an extent."

And in New York, Marache, in his October 2, 1858, chess column in *Porter's Spirit of the Times,* warned:

In the course of his rapid and brilliant career, we cannot but censure the impropriety of allowing Mr. Morphy to play blindfold. Where are his friends? Where are his advisors to have permitted him to play eight simultaneous blindfold games—a task of such magnitude, when on the eve of his encountering Mr. Staunton. . . . Mr. Morphy's friends should bear in mind that, with our Chess prodigy, the *mental* strongly predominates over the physical. Let them take warning.

Morphy thought little of his success with blindfold play, dismissing it with the remark that, "It proves nothing." However, in *Brentano's Chess Monthly* of June 1881, Falkbeer expressed the opinion

> that memory is the main factor of success in playing blind games. And, of Morphy's gigantic memory, I had indubitable proof from my own observation at the time he was playing his celebrated match with Lowenthal. Both opponents had agreed to regard the games as their intellectual private property, not to be published.
>
> I was at the time editing the Chess Column of the London *Sunday Times*, and anxious to reproduce them there. In order to obtain the requisite information, I had to apply to one of the contesting parties. I first went to Morphy, who received me most cordially, and declared his entire willingness to dictate for me the last *partie*, played the day before. I begged him to repeat the game on the board, as I would in this manner, be better able to follow the progress of the contest. Morphy consented, and, at the 10th move of black (Lowenthal), I asked him to stop a moment, since it seemed to me that at this particular point, a better move might have been made. "Oh, you probably mean the move which you yourself made in one of your contests with Dufresne?" answered Morphy in his simple, artless way of speaking. I was startled. The partie mentioned had been played in Berlin in 1851, seven years before, and I had totally forgotten all its details. On observing this, Morphy called for a second board, and began, without the least hesitation, to repeat that game from the first to the last move without making a single mistake. I was speechless from surprise. Here was a man, whose attention was constantly distracted by countless demands on his memory, and yet he had perfectly retained for seven years all the details of a game insignificant in itself, and, moreover, printed in a language and description unknown to him. (The game was published in the Berliner *Schachzeitung* of 1851!)

Following Morphy's blindfold performance at Birmingham, a splendid soirée took place with Lord Lyttelton presiding. As Edge states, in his concluding remarks, Lyttelton

> paid a tribute to the extraordinary merit of Mr. Morphy as a Chess player, and characterized his feat of playing eight antagonists at one time, as the most wonderful thing he had ever beheld. He trusted that Mr. Morphy would be successful in all

his games but one, while absent from his native land; and that one his Lordship, amidst much laughter, trusted would be won by the veteran English player, Staunton. . . . Mr. Morphy then expressed his deep sense of gratitude for the cordial wishes of the President, as well as for his reception by the Association. In conclusion, speeches were delivered by Messrs. Avery, Staunton, Salmon and other gentlemen.

It would appear that the general impression at Birmingham, implied by Lord Lyttelton's hope that Morphy "would be successful in all his games but one," was that the Staunton match was just a matter of time. The same was also indicated by the activity of Staunton's friends at the St. George's Club in raising funds for the match. And had not Staunton replied to Morphy, in the presence of Lord Lyttelton and others, that "if you will consent to the postponement, I will see my publishers, and let you know the exact date within a few days"?

Staunton had now publicly committed himself, although "the exact date" had not yet been set. Morphy therefore decided he now had time to visit Paris. But upon his return to London the next day, August 28, he read the following statement in Staunton's chess column, presumably in reply to a correspondent. It was said that Staunton often used imaginary correspondents in his column, and "Anti-book" and others were thought to be such. In *Morphy Gleanings*, Sergeant states it was "a favorite device of Staunton's. Another was the publication of letters supporting his side of the case, without the writer's real signature."

> August 28—Anti-book. As you surmise, "knowing the authority," the slang of the sporting pages in question regarding the proposed encounter between Mr. Staunton and the young American is "bunkum." In matches of importance it is the invariable practice in this country, before anything definite is settled, for each party to be provided with representatives to arrange the terms and money for the stakes. Mr. Morphy has come here unfurnished in both respects; and, although both will no doubt be forthcoming in due time, it is clearly impossible, until they are, that any determinate arrangement can be made.
>
> 2. The statement of another contemporary that the reduction in the amount of stakes from £1000 a side to £500 was made at the suggestion of the English amateur is equally devoid of truth; the proposal to reduce the amount having been made by Mr. Morphy.

On reading the above, Edge asked Morphy to demand an immediate retraction, but Morphy refused to do so. He merely said to Edge, "When a man resorts to such means as these, he will not stop until he has committed himself irremediably. Let him go on." Morphy took no public notice of the "Anti-book" statement at this time for another reason also; he was determined not to do anything that might adversely affect the Staunton match. Instead, he patiently awaited Staunton's naming "the exact date" of the match, as promised.

It is singular that Staunton should remark that "Mr. Morphy has come here unfurnished . . . with representatives to arrange the terms and money for the stakes," for Morphy, in his letter of August 14, had asked Staunton "to settle the preliminaries during this week" and "to be good enough to state some early period when your seconds can meet mine." Also, upon meeting Staunton and renewing the challenge of the New Orleans Chess Club, Morphy had told Staunton that his "stakes would be forthcoming the moment he [Staunton] desired." Of course the readers of Staunton's chess column knew nothing of these previous oral and written statements by Morphy.

In regard to Staunton's remark about the reduction in the amount of stakes, Edge says:

> I was perfectly astonished when I read this statement: "Mr. Morphy had caused the stakes to be reduced from £1000 to £500 a side." Without mentioning Englishmen, there were Americans in London and Paris who asserted that Morphy could be backed against Mr. Staunton for £10,000 *and the money be raised within twenty-four hours*. I mentioned this fact to a noble lady in Paris, in order to show the confidence in which the young American was held, and she replied, "Oh, as regards that, you may tell Mr. Morphy from me, that for £10,000 against Mr. Staunton or any player in Europe, he must not go further than my house."

Extracts of two letters of a London publisher, Charles N. Skeet, probably to Fiske, are also of interest:

> July 6, 1858, London
> Dear Sir. . . .

> Your American Chess Champion Mr. Morphy called upon me last week and we conversed on the subject of his contemplated match with Mr. Staunton. I find that funds to any amount will be supplied to back him and therefore the thousand pounds

which was mentioned by Mr. Staunton as his mark will be no obstacle to the match. Morphy is a wonder for his age but the old fox will be too much for him.

Truly yours
Chas. N. Skeet

The intent of Morphy's visit and Skeet's remark that "I find that funds to any amount will be supplied" are unknown. It should also be noted that Skeet must have confused the £1,000 offer of Staunton's with the New Orleans Chess Club's offer of that amount to Staunton.

After witnessing Staunton's ultimate treatment of Morphy four months later, Skeet had this to say:

November 9, 1858, London
Dear Sir....

Mr. Morphy has won golden opinions here for his chivalrous conduct and Mr. Staunton has terribly sank in our estimation for the manner he has adopted. When Mr. Morphy first landed he must have been off his play to some extent which must account for the opinion that I passed on him in relation to Staunton. Now it is considered that nobody can approach him in excellence.

Truly yours
Chas. N. Skeet

If there be any further question that Staunton's "Anti-book" statement was a gross misrepresentation of the facts, the following statement about Morphy, which appeared in George Walker's *Bell's Life in London* of July 4, 1858, should lay them to rest:

The celebrated American chess player, Mr. Morphy has arrived in London, and requests us to announce in all courtesy and respect that he is prepared to play any man living a match of chess for any sum from one hundred to one thousand pounds. The match to consist of twenty-one games, exclusive of draws; to be begun directly, and the money posted down. Mr. Morphy would like to commence at once, as he intends visiting Birmingham, end of August, to play at the great chess gathering then and there to be holden. We believe Mr. Morphy's views as to details to be gentlemanlike and chess-like in every respect. He would object to playing in a private room, preferring to have his play looked over; he would leave the selection of the arena, we believe, to his opponent, but we do not bind ourselves to state more than an outline of his views. He would like to play daily, say from noon till the game was ended; but would object to leave games unfinished, and would, we hope, insist on some plan of regulating the time, without limiting the period really required by his opponent for calculating his move, would prevent all shoddy recourse to delay, such as sitting for hours over a single move when the King is in check and has but one square to go to. Mr. Morphy means chess and nothing but chess. He has come from New Orleans purposely to challenge Europe, and his chivalrous offer should be responded to as it deserves.

It is evident that Morphy made the request that Walker mentions, within a week after meeting Staunton, apparently hoping to have a match with someone while waiting for Staunton. Note that he asked for play to begin "directly" with "the money posted down," and note also that he suggested that the stakes be anywhere from £100 to £1,000. Obviously Morphy was unconcerned about the amount of the stakes.

Unfortunately for Morphy, money stakes were generally a necessary ingredient for a chess match, and it becomes evident that in less than two weeks after his arrival in London, Morphy wrote to Fiske about the chess match with Staunton. On July 10, Staunton had publicly acknowledged in the *Illustrated London News* that he had accepted Morphy's challenge "conditionally that the terms of play are such as he can agree to without infraction of his present literary engagements."

Morphy and Staunton probably met about five or six days before the announcement in the *Illustrated London News* and had agreed on the £500-a-side stakes. The challenge having been accepted, Morphy immediately wrote to Fiske that the match was in way of being arranged and that stakes in amount of £500 would be needed. Because of Staunton's conditions, a month's time "to brush up on his openings and endings," etc., Morphy was uncertain how soon it might start.

Money stakes were something that Morphy himself disliked in principle, and he now knew, as will be soon seen, that his family was strongly against them and opposed to any Morphy money being used for such a purpose. And so was he, preferring that others provide them if they wished to see a match, as indeed the New Orleans Chess Club had offered to do for a Morphy-Staunton match.

We now come to a revelation that threatened Morphy's chess career. Fiske, on receiving Morphy's letter and knowing the length of time required for communicating with London, telegraphed Maurian, who replied:

New Orleans, 27 July, 1858

D. W. Fiske, Esq.
Dear Sir.

I have received your telegraphic dispatch a few days ago. I have
not given you an immediate answer because circumstances for
which I was unprepared have complicated matters to such an
extent, that not being able to give you at length all the necessary explanations in a telegram the whole matter would have
been unintelligible to you. I will relate things as they actually
happened.

I had hardly received your message than I hastened to Mr. Le
Carpentier, Paul's uncle and lately his tutor. I thought it my duty
to see him first of all, he being at the same time a chess player
and deeply interested in all chess matters. I accordingly gave
him the letter and after a hasty perusal of its contents, he told
me, that he could in a half hour raise ten time[s] the amount
wanted, but would not do so, as it had been *expressly agreed* by
Paul and his family that he should *under no circumstances challenge another or accept himself a challenge to play a money match.*

He added however that he would consult with some other
members of the family and that he would give me an answer to-
day. This reception somewhat surprised me. I was quite unprepared for it. I had thought that he would have gladly attended
to the affair and worked with the rest of us to raise for Paul the
required amount.

The agreement by which Paul pledged himself not to play a
money match under any circumstances was quite new to me.

This morning I went to see Mr. Le Carpentier. Fully compre-
hending the difficulty of Paul's position, I explained to him to
what extremity his nephew would be reduced in the event of his
not being supported after having gone so far. I gave him to understand that even if he would not meddle with the affair Paul
had friends enough both here and elsewhere who were prepared to back him. (Laboring all the time under the impression
that he only disapproved the match). He answered that after
consulting with the rest of the family, they had *resolved* not only
not to help raising the amount wanted, but that moreover they
should not allow him to play a money match either with his
own money or anybody else's. That in the event of his being in
anyway aided they were ready to send some responsible agent
to London whose duty it would be to let Mr. Morphy know that
he must either decline playing or continuing the match or that

he will be brought home *by force* if necessary; that they were determined to prevent a money match by all means. It is pretty clear that they have no right to act thus [Paul was no longer a minor].

But I am afraid they would be as good as their word; and if they were to carry their desperate resolution into effect it would reduce Paul to the very painful alternative of discontinuing the match or of resisting the parental orders. In either case a heavy responsibility rests on the shoulders of his backers.

I need not tell you my dear sir how much I am grieved at seeing these things. My own position is one of extreme difficulty being on terms of intimacy both with Paul and with his family. I have laid the matter before several members of the Club and finally have resolved to write to you and explain the whole matter. I have given you these particulars but of course on account of Paul would not desire them to be known. I rely entirely upon your judgment and discretion. I would ask you in particular not to mention Mr. Le Carpentier's name and avoid as much as possible using mine. I am trying in all this to do what is best. If you should have any suggestion to make[,] a few words from you would be most acceptable. In conclusion I would beg you to believe that were it not for this unexpected difficulty the £500 would be very soon raised and forwarded. Please write to Paul as soon as possible, if I knew his address I would gladly do so myself.

Yours truly
Chas. A. Maurian

It is true that Morphy had disregarded his family's wishes in accepting Lowenthal's challenge at one hundred pounds a side. (Le Carpentier says he *"expressly agreed"* not to challenge or accept a money challenge.) But since he did not intend to keep the stakes if he won, Morphy probably did not consider it a real money match. He had accepted Lowenthal's challenge and provided his own stake money, as none had yet arrived from New Orleans. Confident that he would win, he would return the winnings in some form.

As for Staunton, immediately upon arriving in England Morphy had challenged him, saying that his stakes would be ready as soon as arrangements could be made for the match. He was determined, regardless of obstacles, to meet any who challenged his supremacy and did not intend to let the question of stakes get in his way. Doubtless he had mental reservations when he promised his family not to play matches for money stakes.

But all this must have weighed heavily on him while abroad. In all probability, he never mentioned his family's attitude to Edge; we have seen that he had not even told Maurian.

It is difficult to reconcile Maurian's startling disclosure of the family attitude on money matches with Morphy's past chess history. There had been no inkling of family disapproval when Morphy wanted to engage Staunton in the $5,000-a-side match in New Orleans. Surely the family knew all about it, for the letter and terms had been printed in New Orleans papers. It would seem that Paul's father had not previously taken the same severe position on money matches, for Ernest Morphy, Alonzo's brother, would not have endeavored to get Paul a match for $300 a side in 1856 (as reported earlier) if his brother had objected. Also, there appears to have been no family disapproval of Paul's match with Stanley at $100 a side. At that time Paul was a minor and subject to the family's wishes. In fact, Paul expected family support in the Stanley match, for in his letter to Maurian of November 16, 1857, quoted in Chapter 6, he had added the following postscript:

> P.S. Do not forget to see Rousseau, my uncle Charles Le Carpentier (and every New Orleans player willing to stake anything on the result) in reference to this match.

Evidently he had expected and received family approval.

Also, as co-editor of the *Chess Monthly*, Morphy announced in the January 1858 issue that he was extending the same challenge and terms to "all the leading practitioners of the United States." Again, nothing was heard of family disapproval. All together, this change in the family's attitude is difficult to understand.

Morphy's mistake was in not taking Maurian into his confidence when he left New Orleans. Morphy was inclined to be secretive and at times even devious. Apparently he told Maurian that he was going only to Birmingham and expected to meet strong European players there. He suggested to Maurian that he confine his remarks in the *Sunday Delta* (of which Maurian was then chess editor) to such generalities, without reference to any special match. This Maurian did, never mentioning the Staunton match.

Had Maurian known the family attitude, he would have consulted with members of the New Orleans Chess Club, and the club would have forwarded the required stake funds without bringing the family into it. This Morphy had hoped would occur when he wrote to Fiske, requesting that he act for him in the matter. However, it should be mentioned that as of June 1858 Morphy had reached his majority and was no longer *legally* subject to his family's wishes.

In any case, the New Orleans Chess Club acted quickly, and Maurian was able to send the following letter to Fiske:

New Orleans, 29 July, 1858

D. W. Fiske
Dear Sir:

I have yesterday mailed a letter to your address in which I gave you an account of the views of the Morphy family with respect to the proposed match. Since that time the Club has met and decided that they must help our friend by all means, that whatever the family might think on the subject was a private matter with which they had nothing to do. This I believe is quite right and makes me happy. As to the threat of somebody going to London, I hope it will not be carried into effect by the family. It would be useless if not worse. The amount is raised, you must have been appraised of it by telegraph.

Yours truly,
Chas. A. Maurian

The New Orleans Chess Club forwarded the £500 requested to the House of Heywood & Company, bankers of London, where it remained to the account of Paul Morphy until August 1859.

Morphy, having now finally received a public commitment from Staunton—"I will play you at the beginning of November"—and with nothing further to keep him in London, felt free to visit Paris, although with some misgivings.

CHAPTER 10

Harrwitz and "Letters of Gold"

On the morning of August 31, Edge awakened Morphy early as they expected to take the first Folkstone train, destination Paris, but due to Morphy's dilatoriness they arrived too late. They therefore took the 1:30 p.m. train for Dover and there boarded the channel steamer for Calais.

Although taken with a bad case of sea-sickness, Morphy was thinking of what lay ahead and said to Edge, "Well, now I am going to meet Harrwitz! I shall beat him in the same proportion as I beat Lowenthal, although he is a better match-player than Lowenthal. But I shall play better with Harrwitz."

Upon arrival at Calais they had a lengthy and expensive visit at the custom house, where Morphy was relieved of a quantity of underlinen and told it was customary. When they learned that the Paris train would not leave until 8 p.m. and would not reach the city until 6 a.m., Morphy proposed they stay overnight and take the morning train. They then registered at the Hotel Dessin and strolled about after dinner.

At 7:45 a.m. the next day they entrained for Paris and arrived after what Edge described as "the long, dreary ride of ten mortal hours." Edge said he wanted to dine, but "Morphy is never betrayed into rhapsody, and what he felt he didn't speak."

After putting up at Meurice's Hotel, they dined at the Restaurant des Trois Frères Provencaux. Then, without a word, Edge led Morphy to the Café de la Régence, of chess history, named after the Regent Duke of Orleans, where Voltaire, Jean Jacques Rousseau, Benjamin Franklin, Robespierre, and Napoleon had moved about the chessmen.

Without making themselves known that evening, they watched some play and heard that Harrwitz was expected back on Saturday to meet Mr. Morphy. The Cercle des Échecs had its room over the café, but the general public used the café rooms, where tables and chessmen were always available.

The next day, Thursday, Morphy announced himself and met Lécrivain, Journoud, and others. He then played Lécrivain, giving the odds of Pawn and two moves, winning seven out of nine games played. At the conclusion of this match, Rivière arrived, and his one game with Morphy ended in a draw. Later, Journoud played several games with Morphy, all of which the latter won. Thus ended Paul Morphy's first day at La Régence, everyone looking forward to the arrival of Harrwitz.

On Saturday, Harrwitz appeared at La Régence. David Harrwitz was a chess professional installed at the café, who devoted his life to chess playing. In his match with Lowenthal five years before, with the score standing nine to two against him, he went on to win the match eleven to ten. Staunton had arranged the match hoping and expecting Lowenthal would win. He never forgave Lowenthal's "betrayal" and thereafter was always spiteful toward him. Harrwitz had also won matches against Horwitz, Mayet, and Rivière, and came even with Anderssen in their match, all this before meeting Morphy. He could be found at La Régence almost daily from 1853 until about two years after he met Morphy. It would seem that Steinitz had little reason to consider him "rusty with inaction."

On September 4, the thirty-five-year-old Harrwitz and the twenty-one-year-old Morphy met. They shook hands, and Morphy, making for him an unusual advance, asked Harrwitz if he would be willing to play a match. Harrwitz replied so evasively that Morphy, probably wary since his difficulties with Staunton, said in an aside to Edge, "He won't play a match." Harrwitz's conduct was such that it quite possibly affected the results of Morphy's first games with him. However, when a crowd had gathered around them, Harrwitz said he would be willing to play an offhand game.

They sat down together, and Harrwitz asked Morphy to accept the King's Gambit. Harrwitz won this first game and, immensely pleased with himself, agreed to play a match. In view of Harrwitz's initial reaction to Morphy's request, one wonders whether Harrwitz would have so readily agreed to a match had the first game gone against him.

The two met the next day to arrange the match. Harrwitz's attitude about seconds was most peculiar; in fact, he said "if there were any seconds, there would be no match." Morphy had already asked Rivière and Journoud to act as his seconds, but when Harrwitz voiced his objection they withdrew, eager to see the match come off. Harrwitz then said that although his friends wished to back him, his stakes were not as yet made up. According to Edge, Morphy replied that this did not matter, "as he would accept any bets that might be offered during the match and they could therefore begin at once."

Eugene Lequesne, the French sculptor and a strong chess player active in tournaments, arrived, and he, Morphy, Harrwitz, and Edge met in a private room to settle the preliminaries for the match. Harrwitz objected to any seconds or umpires. It was agreed that the winner of the first seven games be the victor, that play should take place on four days of the week, and that Morphy was to accept all bets offered. Harrwitz also specified that play was to take place at La Régence public café. Once everything was settled, they immediately started the match. As it turned out, they were playing for a stake of 295 francs a side.

So on September 5, Morphy's match with Harrwitz began. Harrwitz won the first game, and, as Edge reported, in a manner bordering on insolence, to the disgust of all those about, Harrwitz took Morphy's hand and, feeling his pulse, called out to the crowd: "Well it is astonishing! His pulse does not beat any faster than if he had won the game." Harrwitz was now becoming very sure of himself. The second game went the same way as the first, with Harrwitz rollicking in his seat. Now he was sure he was master of the situation, and acted, as Edge put it, "as much as to say, 'Oh, it takes very little trouble to beat this fellow.' Many leading players in the café, especially Rivière and Journoud, were very savage at such conduct, but I told them—'Mark my words, Mr. Harrwitz will be quiet as a lamb before the end of the next week.'"

Edge (not privy to Morphy's thoughts) was certain the late hours Morphy was keeping, seeing the sights of Paris, were responsible for the lost games. Concerning the second game of the match, Steinitz remarked, as mentioned in Sergeant's *Morphy's Games of Chess*, that "no satisfactory explanation is given" of how Morphy lost it. It is an explanation only Morphy could have given; all one can say is that he showed no concern over losing, nor did he outwardly express disdain at Harrwitz's disgraceful antics. But, as Rivière said to Morphy while walking him and Edge back to the Hotel Breteuil, to which they had moved after the first few days, others at La Régence were uneasy, having placed bets on Morphy to win. Edge reports that Morphy only laughed and said, "How astonished all these men are going to be. Harrwitz will not win another game." Such was his plan and self-assurance.

The next day Morphy and Edge dined at the residence of G. E. Doazan, a friend of Deschapelles and Labourdonnais. Harrwitz was also of the company and acted in his most domineering manner, which caused Edge to say, "I am sorry, Mr. Harrwitz, you have not found Mr. Morphy in good fighting trim: The fact is, he has been preparing to meet you by not going to bed until common men are about to rise, but he has promised to retire early in future, and you will then find him a very different antagonist."

Morphy won the next two games. Of the fourth game of the match

Staunton said in the *Illustrated London News* of September 25, 1858, "Morphy carries all before him by the spirit and impetuosity of his attack, and finishes the battle in a style which would have commanded admiration from Labourdonnais." At this point, Harrwitz abandoned his overbearing manner. Morphy won the fifth game on September 13, and Harrwitz now became visibly unnerved, saying to a friend that his opponent was "very much stronger than any he had ever met."

In a letter to Morphy, Harrwitz now pleaded "ill health" and asked for a respite of about ten days. Morphy agreed, with the condition that thereafter they play daily, Sundays excepted, for the remainder of the match. Staunton discussed the matter in his chess column, and it might be noted that in several respects his remarks were equally pertinent to the situation between himself and Morphy:

> October 2, 1858—Match between Messrs. Morphy and Harrwitz. This conflict having now entered what may be called the "sick phase," an indispensable condition, apparently, in all modern chess matches whenever one of the combatants gets two or three games ahead, how long before the public will have to wait before hostilities recommence it is hard to say. Mr. Harrwitz, the indisposed, who, it is consolatory to know, is not so prostrate but that he is enabled to enjoy his daily chess in the Café de la Régence with opponents less troublesome than Mr. Morphy, had demanded a truce of eight or ten days. This his antagonist has at once agreed to, conditionally that, at the expiration of that time, a game shall be played daily until the victory is determined. The American's stipulation is so reasonable, considering he is only a sojourner in Paris, and he has shown such readiness in all cases to conform to the wishes of his adversary, that it is incumbent upon the members of the French Chess *Cercle*, not to allow of any further delay.

As Staunton pointed out, Harrwitz, after losing three games straight and being granted his ten days "sick leave," still continued his daily chess with others at La Régence. Often he played until midnight, usually at a franc a game.

The match was resumed on September 23, and again Harrwitz lost. The score now stood Morphy four, Harrwitz two, and, again, in spite of his agreement to play daily, Harrwitz adjourned the match for several days.

In response to general request, while waiting for Harrwitz to resume play, Morphy announced that on the coming Monday, September 27, he would play eight blindfold games simultaneously. The news created great excitement, for nothing like it had ever been attempted on the Continent. Earlier, Harrwitz had proposed to Morphy that together they do something of the sort, for which a five-franc admission could be charged, but Morphy would have none of it. And now, in offering the blindfold exhibition, Morphy specified that there must be free admission to one and all.

Such was the interest in France that telegrams went out to the poet Méry, the Duke of Brunswick, and others, bringing them back to Paris from their watering-places on the Rhine. But Morphy was not well. Although he had quickly recovered from his channel crossing, he was suffering from more than a physical indisposition. The slighting remarks and innuendoes that had been directed at him, in both England and France, had found a lodging place in him. Edge said that

> since the outset of the match with Harrwitz he [Morphy] had been ailing, but he preferred playing to making excuses. His own expression was, "Je ne suis pas homme aux excuses"— (I am no man to make excuses), and he was always ready for Harrwitz, although obliged to ride to the cafe. . . . At breakfast, on the morning fixed for this blindfold exhibition [to start at noon], he said to me, "I don't know how I shall get through my work to-day. I am afraid I shall be obliged to leave the room, and some evil-minded persons may think I am examining positions outside."

Edge blamed Paris water for Morphy's condition, and it may have had something to do with his illness, but it is likely that more than that was the cause of it. For the first several weeks, after his Atlantic crossing illness had worn off, England had agreed with him famously. (Perhaps English roast beef and puddings were responsible.) George Walker remarked in *Bell's Life in London* of August 21, 1858, that "Mr. Morphy is in excellent health and spirits, certainly stouter in form than when he landed on our shores," and Edge reported to Maurian that as of August 13 Morphy's health was "capitally good."

Soon thereafter, however, he was the subject of unpleasant statements; references to "bottleholder," "bunkum," "unfurnished with funds," etc., had their effect on his sensitive nature. He had actually led a sheltered life before leaving New Orleans and undoubtedly left England somewhat disillusioned and hurt. Nor did Harrwitz's outrageous conduct help to alleviate this feeling. An undemonstrative person, Morphy kept his emotions to himself, and bitterness no doubt festered within him. Edge evidently knew nothing of what was working inside Morphy.

However, the exhibition at La Régence was not delayed. Edge had arranged tables and a roped-off area for Morphy, and at 12:30 p.m., on September 27, Morphy called out Pawn to King's fourth on all boards. Play went on for ten hours, and Morphy remained practically immobile all that time, taking nothing, not even a drink of water. Dr. Johnston, Paris correspondent of the New York *Times*, gave the following account of the exhibition in that paper on October 19, 1858:

> The astounding performances of young Paul Morphy have brought the excitement in the chess-playing world of this city up to white heat. On Monday last he played against, and beat, blindfolded, eight of the best players of Paris at one time! The Café de la Régence, at which this extraordinary feat occurred, has two large rooms on the ground floor. In the first room, which is full of marble tables, were seated the eight adversaries of Mr. Morphy. In the second room, in which are two billiard tables, was seated the single player. A large portion of this room, including the billiard tables, was shut off from the crowd by a cord, and behind the tables, in a large arm-chair, sat Mr. Morphy, with his back nearly directly to the crowd. Two gentlemen, reporting for the press, kept the games, and two other gentlemen, Messrs. Journoud and Arnous de Rivi[è]re, cried out the moves, or rather carried them from one room to the other. The adversaries of Mr. Morphy were Messrs. Baucher, Bierwith, Borneman, Guibert, Lequesne, (the distinguished sculptor), Potier, Prèti, and Seguin.

> They were all either old or middle-aged men, and superior players, while Mr. Morphy is but twenty-one years of age. The boards of the eight players were numbered 1, 2, 3, etc., in the order in which I have given the names of the gentlemen. At 12 ½ o'clock the games commenced, Mr. Morphy playing the first, and calling out the same move for all the eight boards, K.P.2. The games were conducted in French, Mr. Morphy speaking French perfectly. At 7 o'clock No. 7 was beaten with an unlooked-for check-mate. Soon after 8 o'clock, No. 6 abandoned the game as hopeless, and half an hour later, Mr. Lequesne, No. 5 played for and gained a draw game. Nos. 1, 2, and 3 were soon after beaten. At 10 o'clock, No. 4 made the blind player accept a draw game, but it was 10 ½ o'clock before M. Seguin, No. 8, a very old gentleman, who contended with great desperation, was beaten. Thus he beat six, while two, who acted on the defensive and only sought a drawn game, effected their purpose, but a drawn game, under such circumstances, ought to be considered equivalent to a beat.

During the entire game, which lasted just ten hours, Mr. Morphy sat with his knees and eyes against the bare wall, never once rising or looking toward the audience, nor even taking a particle of drink or other refreshment. His only movements were those of crossing his legs from side to side, and, occasionally, thumping a tune with his fingers on the arms of the *fauteuil*. He cried out his moves without turning his head. Against 1, 2, 3, and 6 and 7, who were not up to the standard of the other three players, he frequently made his moves simultaneously after receiving theirs. He was calm throughout, and never made a mistake, nor did he call a move twice.

It must be recollected, moreover, that Mr. Morphy played "against the field"—in other words, that around each of the eight boards there was a large collection of excellent chess players, who gave their advice freely, and who had eight times longer to study their play in than the single player. He played certainly against fifty men, and they never ceased for a moment making supposed moves and studying their game most thoroughly during the long intervals that necessarily fell to each board. And yet Morphy, who was out of sight of these eight boards, saw the game plainer on each than those who surrounded them! I could scarcely have thought the thing possible if I had not seen it. At the end of the games there was a shout from the three hundred throats present, which made one believe he was back again in old Tammany Hall! The fact is there were a considerable number of Englishmen and Americans present (among the latter was Prof. Morse, who took a deep interest in these extraordinary games), but much the larger number were French. Morphy did not seem at all fatigued, and appeared so modest that the frenzy and admiration of the French knew no bounds.

He was shaken by the hand and complimented till he hung down his head in confusion. One gray-haired old man, an octogenarian chess-player, stroked his hair with his hands, as he would a child of his own, and showered him with terms of endearment. Morphy has no beard yet, and looks more like a schoolboy than a world's champion. He escaped from the excited crowd as soon as possible, and left with some friends, to get something to eat. It is not necessary to point out to chess-players the immensity of the intellectual feat; every one will admit that it borders upon the miraculous, and, as was remarked by one of his antagonists, M. Lequesne, such a mind never did exist, and, perhaps, never will again.

Finally Morphy was able to extricate himself from the crowd, with

Thomas Bryan on one side, Rivière on the other, and Edge trailing along behind. Morphy was able to escape only because huge "Père" Morel sprearheaded them to the street in football formation. Then the four of them—Morphy, Bryan, Rivière, and Edge—made for the Palais Royal and upstairs to a private room of the Restaurant Foy. They escaped hours later by a back door to avoid the crowd that had assembled outside. Edge says that

> Next morning, Morphy actually awakened me at seven o'clock, and told me, if I would get up, he would dictate to me the moves of yesterday's games. I never saw him in better spirits, or less fatigued, than on that occasion, as he showed me, for two long hours, the hundreds of variations depending on the play of the previous day, with such rapidity that I found it hard to follow the thread of his combinations.

George Walker, writing in *Bell's Life in London* on October 3, 1858, said, "The first [game], won of M. Baucher, is a gem of excellence, worthy of being written in letters of gold on the walls of the London Chess Club."

The next day Morphy caught a cold, after having taken a nap near an open window, and the following morning he was feverish, but Edge could not prevent him from meeting Harrwitz, who was now willing to play the seventh game. He said to Edge, "I would sooner lose the game, than that anybody should think I had exhausted myself by a *tour de force*, as some will do if I am absent at the proper hour."

Morphy arrived at La Régence at the agreed time but Harrwitz was not there. Some time later a message came from him objecting to playing in the public café and insisting on the private room of the chess club upstairs. This aroused great resentment among those present, especially Harrwitz's backers, for it had been agreed, Harrwitz had even insisted, that all games be played in the public café. Finally, when it seemed the match would go no further, the club room was opened to them, and Morphy went upstairs.

Harrwitz had the opening move but soon lost the attack. By the forty-first move it was obvious that Morphy could easily win the game. Edge says:

> But, in process of administering the *coup de grace*, Morphy's feverish state told upon him, and he committed an oversight which lost him a rook, when within a move or two of winning. It was so stupid a mistake, that he immediately burst out laughing at himself. Harrwitz picked off the unfortunate rook with the utmost nonchalance, as though it were the result of his own combinations, and actually told me afterwards, "Oh, the game

was a drawn one throughout."

Again, some days passed before Harrwitz would sit down with Morphy, although the former was still playing daily with others until past midnight. It was October 4 before Harrwitz would resume play, and again Morphy won. The score now stood Morphy five, Harrwitz two, and one game drawn. The next day, Morphy—not willing to grant another "sick leave" of fifteen days—received the following message: "Mr. Harrwitz resigned the match, on account of ill health."

The terms of the match called for seven games to be won, and Harrwitz's backers were furious that he should have terminated the match in this way, without even mentioning his intention to them. Harrwitz also told the stakeholder to hand over the stake money, and so Lequesne called at Morphy's hotel for that purpose. Morphy declined to accept the stakes, considering the unusual circumstances, although in any case he would have refused the money.

However, such turmoil developed between Harrwitz and his backers that he finally agreed to resume the match. Edge reports that Morphy now refused, saying, "Mr. Harrwitz having resigned the contest, there was an end of the matter but that he [Morphy] was ready to commence a second match immediately." Harrwitz declined the offer. However, the matter of the stakes had to be resolved. Morphy did not wish to accept them, but letters and protests poured in, complaining that a decision about the match and stakes was necessary for the settlement of all the bets placed on the match. Morphy finally agreed to accept the title of winner of the match and the stakes of 295 francs.

Morphy immediately deposited the amount with M. Delannoy, proprietor of La Régence, and had a notice posted that any of the subscribers to the stakes were at liberty to withdraw the amount of their subscriptions, the balance to be forwarded to Adolf Anderssen, to defray expenses for his expected trip to Paris and his contest with Mr. Morphy.

The news of Morphy's victory over Harrwitz, the renowned professional, was received with enthusiasm in New York, and Augustus B. Sage, well known for his historical tokens in bronze, had a medal struck for him. The American medalist George H. Lovett was the designer. The obverse side of the coin had a likeness of Morphy, while the reverse read: "He has beaten Harrwitz in chess playing and Staunton in courtesy."

Morphy continued to frequent La Régence for some time after the Harrwitz match, meeting any and all, regardless of strength. He tried on numerous occasions to induce Harrwitz to play another match or even casual games, but to no avail.

But Morphy's success—his winning almost every game at La Régence, whether even or at odds—prompted Monsieur Laroche, the strongest of French players, to suggest that Morphy offer odds to all players, himself included. Laroche had come to Paris, as had other old-time players, especially to meet Morphy.

He had previously hesitated, but now, encouraged by Laroche, Morphy had Edge inform Delannoy, proprietor of La Régence, that in the future, he (Morphy) would play no one without giving odds. As the *Chess Monthly* of January 1859 reported, "The chess world had not listened to such language since the days of Deschapelles and Labourdonnais." However, Morphy was willing to make an exception with Harrwitz, hoping in vain to get him to play.

In December, Harrwitz, wishing to show that he was as capable as Morphy, undertook to play eight blindfold games, for which he said he had practiced. Adolf Anderssen, who had just arrived in Paris, was present (Morphy was too ill to attend, had he wished to do so) and reported, as Edge quotes him, that "many of the players left pieces *en prise*, as though designedly." Edge remarked that "the strangest affair in connection with this display is, that although Harrwitz edited a chess column in the *Monde Illustré*, he never gave a single one of his blindfold games, nor would he permit any to be made public."

Harrwitz, who for years had been installed as the professional at La Régence after Kieseritzky, lost favor with the proprietor because of his poor sportsmanship and disgraceful conduct and, obliged to leave, went to London.

CHAPTER 11

The Staunton Miscarriage

All throughout the Harrwitz match, Staunton had hovered in Morphy's mind. November approached, and there was still no word from him. Rankling over Staunton's unblushing "Anti-book" statement—that it was his (Morphy's) lack of seconds and funds that was holding up their match—Morphy addressed another letter to him. Skeptical that the letter would go further than Staunton and desiring that his position in the matter be made known to the public, which knew only the "Anti-book" version, Morphy sent copies of the letter with a short note to the chess editors of the *Era*, *Bell's Life in London*, the *Field*, and the *Sunday Times*. The letter and note appeared as given below in all those papers on October 10, 1858. Morphy also sent a copy of the letter to the editor-in-chief of the *Illustrated London News*, as advised by an American friend.

> To the Editor of the *Era*:
> > Café de la Régence, Paris, October 6, 1858
> Sir:
> > May I request you to add to the great kindness shown me by your paper since my arrival in Europe, by publishing in your forthcoming number the accompanying copy of a letter to Howard Staunton, Esq. I shall esteem it a favor, as I am most desirous that my true position with reference to that gentleman should at length be put in its proper light before the public.
> > > I have the honor to remain, sir,
> > > > Your very obedient servant
> > > > Paul Morphy

> > Café de la Régence, Paris, October 6, 1858
> Howard Staunton, Esq.
> > Sir,—On my arrival in England, three months since, I renewed the challenge to you personally which the New Orleans Chess Club had given some months previously. You immediately accepted, but demanded a month's delay, in order to prepare yourself for the contest. Subsequently, you proposed that the time should be postponed until after the Birmingham meeting, to which I assented. On the approach of the period you had fixed, I addressed you a communication, requesting that the necessary preliminaries might be immediately settled,

but you left London without replying to it.

I went to Birmingham for the express purpose of asking you to put a stop to further delay, by fixing a date for the opening of our match; but before the opportunity presented itself, you came to me, and, in the presence of Lord Lyttelton, Mr. Avery, and other gentlemen, you stated that your time was much occupied in editing a new edition of Shakespeare, and that you were under heavy bonds to your publishers accordingly. But you reiterated your intention to play me, and said that if I would consent to a further postponement until the first week in November, you would, within a few days, communicate with me and fix the exact date. I have not heard further from you, either privately, by letter, or through the columns of the *Illustrated London News*.

A statement appeared in the Chess department of that Journal a few weeks since [August 28, "Anti-book"], that "Mr. Morphy had come to Europe unprovided with backers or seconds;" the inference being obvious that my want of funds was the reason of our match not taking place. As you are the editor of that department of the *Illustrated London News*, I felt hurt that a gentleman who had always received me at his club, and elsewhere, with great kindness and courtesy, should allow so prejudicial a statement to be made in reference to me—one, too, which is not strictly in accordance with fact.

Permit me to repeat what I have invariably declared in every Chess community I have had the honor of entering, that I am not a professional player—that I never wished to make any skill I possess the means of pecuniary advancement—and that my earnest desire is never to play for any stake but honor. My friends in New Orleans, however, subscribed a certain sum, without any countenance from me, and that sum has been ready for you to meet a considerable time past. Since my arrival in Paris I have been assured by numerous gentlemen, that the value of those stakes can be immediately increased to any amount; but, for myself, personally, reputation is the only incentive I recognize.

The matter of seconds cannot, certainly, offer any difficulty. I had the pleasure of being first received in London by the St. George's Chess Club, of which you are so distinguished a member; and of those gentlemen I request the honor of appointing my seconds, to whom I give full authority in settling all preliminaries.

In conclusion, I beg leave to state that I have addressed a copy of this letter to several editors, being most desirous that our true position should no longer be misunderstood by the community at large.

Again requesting you to fix the date for commencing our match.

I have the honor to remain, Sir,
Your very humble servant,
Paul Morphy

Only Staunton found no room for Morphy's letter in his chess column that weekend.

Morphy also addressed the following letter:

Café de la Régence, October 8, 1858

T. Hampton, Esq.,
Secretary of the St. George's Chess Club:

Sir,—I beg respectfully to inform you that the New Orleans Chess Club has deposited £500 at the Banking House of Messrs. Heywood & Co., London: that sum being my proportion of the stakes in the approaching match with Mr. Staunton.

I shall esteem it a great honor if the St. George's Chess Club will do me the favor of appointing my seconds in that contest. To such gentlemen as they may appoint I leave the settling of all preliminaries.

May I request you to lay this communication before the members of the Club, and to oblige me with an early answer?

I have the honor to remain, Sir,
Your very humble and obed't serv't,
Paul Morphy

Although Staunton did not give Morphy's letter publicity that weekend, he replied at once by private letter:

London, October 9, 1858

Sir,—In reply to your letter, I have to observe that you must be perfectly conscious that the difficulty in the way of my engaging in a chess-match is one over which I have no control. You were distinctly appraised, in answer to the extraordinary proposal of your friends that I should leave my home, family, and avocations, to proceed to New Orleans for the purpose of playing chess with you, that a long and arduous contest, even in London, would be an undertaking too formidable for me to embark in without ample opportunity for the recovery of my old strength in play, together with such arrangements as would prevent the sacrifice of my professional engagements. Upon your unexpected arrival here, the same thing was repeated to you, and my acceptance of your challenge was entirely conditional on my being able to gain time for practice.

The experience, however, of some weeks, during which I have labored unceasingly, to the serious injury of my health, shows that not only is it impracticable for me to save time for that purpose, but that by no means short of giving up a great work on which I am engaged, subjecting the publishers to the loss of thousands, and myself to an action for breach of contract, could I obtain time even for the match itself. Such a sacrifice is, of course, out of all question.

A match at chess or cricket may be a good thing in its way, but none but a madman would for either forfeit his engagements and imperil his professional reputation. Under these circumstances, I waited only the termination of your late struggle with Mr. Harrwitz, to explain that, fettered as I am at this moment, it is impossible for me to undertake any enterprise which would have the effect of withdrawing me from duties I am pledged to fulfil.

The result is not, perhaps, what either you or I desired, as it will occasion disappointment to many; but it is unavoidable, and the less to be regretted, since a contest, wherein one of the combatants must fight under disadvantages so manifest as those I should have to contend against, after many years retirement from practical chess, with my attention absorbed and my brain overtaxed by more important pursuits, could never be accounted a fair trial of skill.

> I have the honor to be,
> Yours, &c. H. Staunton

Paul Morphy, Esq.

P.S. I may add that, although denied the satisfaction of a set encounter with you at this period, I shall have much pleasure, if you will again become my guest, in playing you a few games *sans façon*.

Morphy was now determined that all communications concerning the match be public and aboveboard, and did not even acknowledge receipt of the letter. The following week, on October 16, Staunton placed the following notice in the correspondence section of his chess column:

> P.M., Paris—Mr. Morphy's games this week exclude both his letter and Mr. Staunton's reply. If we can spare space for them, they shall be given in the next number.

October 23 came and the *Illustrated London News* carried Morphy's letter and Staunton's reply. But while Staunton's reply was given in full, two important paragraphs of Morphy's letter had been deleted, one of which quoted from Staunton's damaging "Anti-book" statement. And so the readers of Staunton's chess column, the most widely read of all, saw only Morphy's abbreviated letter. Even some American papers got only Staunton's version. Without doubt, he thought the matter would go no further, at least from Morphy, and he judged Morphy well.

Heretofore, public discussion of Morphy's doings and his prospective chess match with Staunton had been confined to editors of the press. But now anonymous letters appeared, attacking Morphy for again asking Staunton to fix "the exact date" for their match. Suspicions were voiced that the anonymous writers were perhaps Staunton himself, but in any case it was surprising that Morphy's letter could generate such derogatory invectives as "young adventurer," "Morphy's jeremiads sound ineffably absurd," "vanity of an antagonist," and "does not speak much for that man's sense of honor."

All but one of the papers, apart from the *Illustrated London News*, refused to print them. *Bell's Life in London* published two of them on October 17, one signed "M.A." and the other "Fair Play." (These letters will be found in the Appendix, together with two letters in Morphy's defense—one from Edge and one signed "Pawn and Two.") After giving the "M.A." and "Fair Play" letters, the chess editor of *Bell's Life in London*, George Walker, appended the following:

> We regret these lucubrations are anonymous, as not showing how far they really represent the opinions of Mr. Staunton himself and his friends on the subject. Regarding their style and phraseology Mr. Staunton may perhaps ask to be saved from his friends, but that is matter of taste. . . . Inferiority once admitted, no matter from what cause, if Mr. Staunton takes the ground indicated in the above epistles, Mr. Morphy has but

cheerfully and quietly to drop the subject, and will certainly as a gentleman never challenge Mr. Staunton again. Morphy's friends may still reasonably inquire why all this was not said in June last, instead of giving apparent acceptance to the young American's challenge.

Morphy refused to be drawn into any newspaper discussion, but several friends would not let the "M.A." and "Fair Play" letters go unanswered, and four of their replies appeared in the October 24 issue of *Bell's Life in London*. The first of the four letters was by Edge, who summed up the whole matter as follows:

1. Mr. Morphy came to Europe to play Mr. Staunton.

2. Mr. Staunton made everybody believe he had accepted the challenge from Mr. Morphy.

3. Mr. Staunton allowed the St. George's Chess Club to raise the money to back him.

4. Mr. Staunton asked for a delay of one month, in order to brush up his openings and endings.

5. Mr. Staunton requested a postponement until after the Birmingham meeting.

6. Mr. Staunton fixed the beginning of November for the commencement of the match.

If all this do[es] not mean "I will play," then is there no meaning in language. I beg to subscribe myself, Mr. Editor, most respectfully yours.

Frederick Milne Edge

Hotel Breteuil, Paris, Oct. 20, 1858

It was true that Staunton, by publishing his October 23 reply to Morphy's letter, had now publicly stated that he would not contest him in a match. But Morphy was concerned that Staunton might later find that he could arrange to play a match at a time when it might be impossible for Morphy to alter his departure plans. Staunton had added in his postscript that he could not play "at this period" of time, but might he find some way to transfer the failure of the match to materialize to Morphy?

It would seem that Staunton's final attitude toward Morphy was foreshadowed by earlier comments in his chess column, when he said, "Mr. Morphy came to this country unattended by seconds or bottleholder" on August 7, and later when he said Morphy was "unfurnished in both respects," i.e., seconds and funds. Had Morphy taken public notice of the first remark perhaps the second would not have been made. However, Morphy had chosen to ignore all such remarks.

But now, with the bold deletion of the most telling part of Morphy's letter (about which Lord Lyttelton later said in his letter to Morphy of November 3, 1858, "I cannot see how it is possible to justify or excuse it"), Morphy finally agreed (after much urging from Edge) that it should be put on record that the match had failed to materialize through no fault or deficiency on his part. He therefore addressed the following letter (actually written by Edge) to Lord Lyttelton, president of the British Chess Association:

> Café de la Régence, Paris, Oct. 26, 1858
> My Lord,
>
> On the 4th of last February the Chess Club of New Orleans gave a challenge to your countryman, Mr. Howard Staunton, to visit that city and engage in a match at chess with me. On the 3d of April Mr. Staunton replied to this *defi* in the *Illustrated London News*, characterizing the terms of the cartel as "being distinguished by extreme courtesy," but objecting to so long a journey for such a purpose, and engaging me "to anticipate by a few months an intended voyage to Europe." Believing that "a journey of many thousand miles" was the only obstacle in the way of our meeting, I made immediate preparation, and, within two months, I had the pleasure of repeating the challenge personally in the rooms of the St. George's Chess Club.
>
> I need scarcely assure you, my Lord, that Mr. Staunton enjoys a reputation in the United States unsurpassed by that of any player in Europe since the death of Labourdonnais, and I felt highly honored when he accepted my challenge, merely requesting a lapse of one month for the purpose of preparing himself for the encounter. Within a short period subsequently, Mr. Staunton obtained my consent to a postponement until after the annual meeting of the British Chess Association. A week prior to that event I addressed him in the following terms:—
>
> "Dear Sir,—As we are now approaching the Birmingham meeting, at the termination of which you have fixed our match to

commence, I think it would be advisable to settle the preliminaries during this week. Would you be good enough to state some early period when your seconds can meet mine so that a contest which I have so much at heart, and which from your eminent position excites so much interest in the chess world, may be looked upon as a *fait accompli*. I am, dear sir, yours very respectfully, Paul Morphy."

Not receiving a satisfactory reply to this communication, I again wrote Mr. Staunton as follows:

"Dear Sir,—I must first apologize for not replying to your previous communication. As you observe, my numerous contests must be the excuse for my remissness.

"It is certainly a high compliment to so young a player as myself that you, whose reputation in the chess arena has been unapproached during so many long years, should require any preparation for our match. Immediately on my arrival in England, some two months since, I spoke to you in reference to our contest, and, in accepting the challenge, you stated that you should require some time to prepare, and you proposed a period for commencing, which I accepted.

"I am well aware that your many engagements in the literary world must put you to some inconvenience in meeting me, and I am therefore desirous to consult your wishes in every respect. Would you please state the earliest opportunity when those engagements will permit the match coming off, such time being consistent with your previous preparation?

"The 'few weeks' referred to in your favor seem to be rather vague, and I shall feel highly gratified by your fixing a definite period for the contest. *I leave the terms entirely to yourself.*—I remain, dear sir, yours very respectfully,

Paul Morphy"

Mr. Staunton left London for Birmingham without deigning to reply.

I attended the annual meeting of the Association for the express purpose of requesting a definite period for commencing the match. In the presence of your lordship and other gentlemen, Mr. Staunton fixed that commencement for the forepart of November, promising that he would inform me of the precise date within a few days. I heard nothing further from him on the subject. Your lordship will have remarked from the above that Mr. Staunton has thus obtained three separate and distinct postponements.

The approach of November induced me to again address Mr. Staunton, which I did on the 6th of the present month. As my letter was published in numerous London journals, and was also sent to the editor-in-chief of the *Illustrated London News*, I had a right to expect a public answer, particularly as I had complained of a false and damaging statement in the chess department of that paper. On the 16th Mr. Staunton stated editorially that—

"Mr. Morphy's games this week exclude both his letter and Mr. Staunton's reply. If we can spare space for them they shall be given in the next number."

On the 9th inst., within a short time of receiving my letter, Mr. Staunton replied to me *privately*. As my communication was a public one, I was somewhat surprised at the course pursued by a gentleman holding such a position as Mr. Staunton, and did not, therefore, even acknowledge receipt, fearing that I might thereby be induced unintentionally to commit myself. Having promised my letter and his reply, Mr. Staunton published what he represents as such in the *Illustrated London News* of the 23rd inst. He has thereby transferred the question from the chess arena to the bar of public opinion, and as a stranger in a foreign land—a land which has ever been the foremost in hospitality—I claim justice from Englishmen.

The most important portion of my letter Mr. Staunton has dared to suppress. I refer to the following paragraph, published by various journals, but omitted by the *Illustrated London News*, although sent to the editor of that paper as well as to Mr. Staunton himself:

"A statement appeared in the chess department of that journal a few weeks since [Aug. 28], that 'Mr. Morphy had come to Europe unprovided with backers or seconds,' the inference being obvious—that my want of funds was the reason of our match not taking place. As you are the editor of that department of the *Illustrated London News*, I felt hurt that a gentleman who had always received me at his club and elsewhere with great kindness and courtesy, should allow so prejudicial a statement to be made in reference to me; one, too, which is not strictly in accordance with fact."

On my first arriving England, I informed Mr. Staunton that

my stakes would be forthcoming the moment he desired, and I was therefore utterly at a loss to account for so unwarrantable a statement being made in reference to me, unless with the intention of compromising my position before the public. And I would ask your lordship's attention to the terms of the suppressed paragraph, such language as to avoid all insinuation of animus, and affording Mr. Staunton the amplest opportunity for explaining away the difficulty. The course pursued by that gentleman cannot do otherwise than justify me in ascribing to him the very worst of motives in publishing what he knew to be incorrect, in denying me common justice, and in giving as the whole of my letter, *what he knew to be only a part of it.*

From Mr. Staunton I now appeal to the great body of English chess players, I appeal to the British Chess Association, I appeal to yourself, my lord, as the *Maecenas* of English chess; and, as I visited your country for the purpose of challenging Mr. Staunton, which challenge he has repeatedly accepted, I now demand of you that you shall declare to the world it is through no fault of mine that this match has not taken place.

I have the honor to remain, my lord,

Yours very respectfully

Paul Morphy

Lord Lyttelton replied as follows:

Bodmin, Cornwall, 3d November, 1858

Paul Morphy, Esq.

Dear Sir:—I much regret that I have been unable till to-day to reply to your letter of the 26th October, which only reached me on the 1st inst.

With regard to the appeal which you have made to the British Chess Association, I may perhaps be allowed to say, as its President, that I fear nothing can be done about the matter in question by that body. It is one of recent and rather imperfect organization; its influence is not yet fully established. It is practically impossible to procure any effective meeting of its members at present, and it is doubtful whether it could take any step in the matter if it were to meet. I must therefore be understood as writing in my private character alone, but, at the same time, you are welcome, should you think it worth while (which I can hardly think it can be), to make further use of this letter, in any manner you may wish.

Your letter has but one professed object; that we should declare that it is not your fault that the match between yourself and Mr. Staunton has not taken place. To this the reply might be made in two words. I cannot conceive it possible that any one should impute that failure to you, nor am I aware that any one has done so. But, in the circumstances, I shall not perhaps be blamed, if I go somewhat further into the matter. In the general circumstances of the case, I conceive that Mr. Staunton was quite justified in declining the match. The fact is understood that he has for years been engaged in labors which must, whatever arrangements might be made, greatly interfere with his entering into a serious contest with a player of the highest force and in constant practice, and so far the failure of the match is the less to be regretted. Nor can I doubt the correctness of his recent statement, that the time barely necessary for the match itself could not be spared, without serious loss and inconvenience both to others and to himself.

But I cannot but think that in all fairness and considerateness, Mr. Staunton might have told you of this long before he did. I know no reason why he might not have ascertained it and informed you of it in answer to your first letter from America. Instead of this, it seems to me plain, both as to the interview at which I myself was present, and as to all the other communications which have passed, that Mr. Staunton gave you every reason to suppose that he would be ready to play the match within no long time. I am not aware, indeed (nor do I perceive that you said it), that you left America *solely* with the view of playing Mr. Staunton. It would, no doubt, make the case stronger, but it seems to me as unlikely as that you should have come, as has been already stated (anonymously, and certainly not with Mr. Staunton's concurrence), in order to attend the Birmingham Tournament.

With regard to the suppression of part of your last letter, I must observe, that I am not aware how far Mr. Staunton is responsible for what appears in the *Illustrated London News*. But whoever is responsible for that suppression, I must say, that I cannot see how it is possible to justify or excuse it.

I greatly regret the failure of a contest which would have been of much interest, and the only one, as I believe, which could have taken place with you, with any chance of its redounding to the credit of this country.

I still more regret that any annoyance or disappointment should have been undergone by one, who—as a foreigner—from his age, his ability, and his conduct and character, is eminently entitled to the utmost consideration in the European countries which he may visit.

I am, dear sir, yours truly
Lyttelton

In a letter to Fiske dated April 3, 1859, Edge related the long struggle he had had to get Morphy to sign his name to the final letter to Lord Lyttelton:

> And when Staunton published Morphy's letter, suppressing that important paragraph, I said that the latter (Morphy) must now address the British Chess Association and claim justice, *Morphy laughed in my face*, and replied: "the matter need go no further." I immediately sat down, boiling with rage, and penned the letter to Lord Lyttelton. I took it right away and submitted it to Mr. Bryan (Staunton's old second) who returned to the hotel with me and induced Morphy to sign it. . . . When Lord Lyttelton sent his capital reply, Morphy declared that it should not be published: seeing it was vain to hope for his consent, I waited until he was out of the way, and then sent it to the London papers.

Lord Lyttelton's letter almost but not quite closed the public discussion of the Morphy Staunton match, the match for which England, Europe, and America had been waiting for Staunton to set the date. It would appear that Lord Lyttelton had expressed the general sentiment in the country, as did the following resolution of the Manchester Chess Club:

> November 17, 1858; Resolved: That this meeting, while recognizing Mr. Staunton's right to decline any chess challenge which he might find inconvenient and incompatible with his other engagements, deems it proper (inasmuch as Lord Lyttelton has only felt himself at liberty to answer, in his private capacity, Mr. Morphy's appeal to him as President of the British Chess Association) to declare its full concurrence in the opinion expressed by Lord Lyttelton in his letter to Mr. Morphy, of the 3d inst., that in all fairness and considerateness Mr. Staunton should have told Mr. Morphy, long before he did, that he declined the proposed match.
>
> That copies of this resolution be sent to Mr. Morphy, Mr. Staunton, and the editor of the *Illustrated London News*.

Of all the English clubs, only one accepted and approved Staunton's tactics and explanations:

> November 26, 1858—Resolved: That the Cambridge University Chess Club, recognizing the important services rendered by Mr. Staunton to the cause of chess, and seeing with regret the ungenerous attacks which have for some time past been directed against him by a certain section of the press, notorious for its anti-English tendencies, are of opinion
>
> 1. That under the peculiar circumstances in which Mr. Staunton found himself placed, it was scarcely possible for him to do otherwise than decline the proposed match with Mr. Morphy.
>
> 2. That his allowing the challenge to remain open so long as there appeared the slightest hope of his being able to play, was, beyond all question, the proper course to be adopted by one really anxious for the encounter.

The *Era* of December 12, 1858, took strong exception to the Cambridge resolutions:

> The intention, of course, was to justify Mr. Staunton in taking the course he has adopted, but it does not do so. It says he was right in allowing the challenge to remain open till the last moment. If, indeed, Mr. Staunton had kept the challenge open as long as possible, no one would have blamed him, but that was precisely what he did not do. He accepted the challenge, and thereby closed with it, and his friends subscribed funds for the stakes. What Mr. Staunton did allow to remain open was the day; and after repeated promises to name it, that has been postponed to—never.

Also, a very long letter appeared in the *Field* (see Appendix) from a former warm friend of Staunton's, strongly supporting Morphy. Although the letter was signed "Pawn and Two," the writer had revealed his identity to Mr. Boden, the editor. On December 4, 1858, Staunton took notice of the letter in his chess column, asserting that "the writer labours under an egregious mistake in supposing Mr. Staunton declines a match at chess with Mr. Morphy from any apprehension of his prowess."

Finally, Lord Lyttelton's letter drew a response from Staunton in the *Illustrated London News* of November 20, 1858, although not in his chess column:

(To the Editor of the *Illustrated London News*) Nov. 15, 1858

Sir,—My attention has this moment been directed to a passage in a letter of Lord Lyttelton to Mr. Morphy wherein allusion is made to the "suppression" of a portion of Mr. Morphy's letter to me, which you published, together with my answer, in your Paper for Oct. 23. I have not seen the epistle to which Lord Lyttelton's is a reply; but I plead guilty at once to having omitted, when sending you Mr. Morphy's jeremiade and my answer, a couple of paragraphs from the former.

My reasons for omitting them were, in the first place, because they appeared to be irrelevant to the main point between Mr. Morphy and me; secondly, because I knew if the letters extended very much beyond the limited space you apportion to chess they were pretty certain of being omitted, or, as Mr. Morphy phrases it "*suppressed*" altogether; and, thirdly, because I had already written to a friend in Paris with whom, through my introduction, Mr. Morphy was living upon intimate terms, an explanation touching the notice Mr. Morphy professes to be so concerned at; and from my friend's reply, which intimated that Mr. Morphy was about to write to me in an amicable spirit, I, of course, supposed there was an end of the matter, and I should be permitted to pursue my work, and this young gentleman his play, without further misunderstanding.

That, after this, and in the face of my endeavors through your Journal to set his blindfold and other chess exploits before the public in the most advantageous light—in the face of every civility which to the extent of my opportunities I have endeavored to show him from the first moment of his arrival in the country—he could reconcile it to his sense of honor and honesty to impute to me a willful suppression of any portion of his letter, does, indeed, amaze me, and I only account for it by supposing he is under the influence of very ill advisors, or that his idea of what is honorable and honest is very different from what I had hoped and believed it to be.

I am, Sir, yours, &c.
H. Staunton

P.S. That you may judge with what likelihood and with what propriety Mr. Morphy attributes the omission of the *excerpta* to sinister motives, I enclose them, and shall be obliged by your giving them the additional publicity he craves as soon as your space permits:—

"A statement appeared in the chess department of that Journal (the *Illustrated London News*) a few weeks since that 'Mr. Morphy had come to Europe unprovided with backers or seconds'—the inference being obvious, that my want of funds was the reason of our match not taking place. As you are the editor of that department of the *Illustrated London News*, I felt much hurt that a gentleman who had always received me at his club and elsewhere with great kindness and courtesy should allow so prejudicial a statement to be made in reference to me; one, too, which is not strictly consonant with fact.

"In conclusion, I beg leave to state that I have addressed a copy of this letter to the editors of the *Illustrated London News*, *Bell's Life in London*, the *Era*, the *Field*, and the *Sunday Times*; being most desirous that our true position should no longer be misunderstood by the community at large. I again request you to fix the date for our commencing the match."

It would seem that Staunton, in endeavoring to justify his deletion of a portion of Morphy's letter, was again guilty of another misstatement in saying in the above letter

I had already written to a friend in Paris with whom, through my introduction, Mr. Morphy was living upon intimate terms, an explanation touching the notice Mr. Morphy professes to be so concerned at; and from my friend's reply, which intimated that Mr. Morphy was about to write to me in an amicable spirit, I, of course, supposed there was an end of the matter. . . .

Morphy denied having received any such introduction as Staunton mentioned, as will be seen in the following, which appeared a week later in the London *Field* of November 27, together with Mr. Boden's comments on Staunton's letter, which had appeared in the *Illustrated London News* of November 20:

After perusing the above letter, we had intended observing, among other things, that, although we accord to Mr. Staunton all the good-will and sympathy which he is entitled to, as a retiring chess-player and author of great eminence, yet he does not touch upon the two chief points at issue. The two are, the *contents* of the omitted paragraphs of Mr. Morphy's letter, and the reasons why the public and Mr. Morphy were kept in suspense and delusion for more than two months. We wish that Mr. Staunton had said he regretted his mistake in saying that

Mr. Morphy had come over unprovided with seconds, &c., and that during the two months which elapsed between his accepting and declining Mr. Morphy's challenge he was endeavoring strenuously, though unsuccessfully to gain time enough to play. Such, we trust, is the case, though not expressed in Mr. Staunton's letter. Any further comments of our own, however, are prevented by our having just received the following notice from Mr. Morphy anent Mr. Staunton's letter above.

MR. MORPHY'S STATEMENT

Mr. Morphy begs to state, in reply to Mr. Staunton's late letter to the editor of the *Illustrated London News*, that it was not merely because Mr. Staunton had published many of his (Mr. Morphy's) games in that paper, but also from the eminent services rendered by that gentleman to the interests of chess, that he worded the suppressed paragraph so as to afford the amplest opportunity for a satisfactory explanation. Mr. Staunton's *private* reply was published *verbatim* in a subsequent number of the *Illustrated News*, and did not contain the slightest reference to the statement complained of.

To the other assertion in Mr. Staunton's letter Mr. Morphy desires to give the most emphatic denial. He had no introduction whatever from Mr. Staunton to any friend of his in Paris or France. He is totally ignorant that Mr. Staunton ever made any explanation, directly or indirectly, and he certainly never led anybody to suppose that he was intending further correspondence with Mr. Staunton on the subject, being at length satisfied that he could not obtain justice from him. Mr. Morphy hopes that that gentleman will now correct the mis-statement to which the suppressed paragraph refers.

As regards the friend commissioned by Mr. Staunton to explain away the difficulty relating to backers, &c., Mr. Morphy is desirous that it should be understood this is the first he has heard of him.

The Morphy–Staunton match affair had aroused the English chess world and general interest to an extent not since equaled, because English pride was involved. Boden had a final word on the subject in the London *Field* on December 4, 1858, on the same day that Staunton unfortunately muddied the water still more:

Now it cannot be denied that the English, as a nation, are too fond of finding fault with their descendents, on the score of a deficiency in honorable conduct in their transactions between man and man. For this reason, we cannot but deplore the humiliating position into which English Chess-players have been plunged by the proceedings of their champion, Mr. Staunton, towards his American rival, Mr. Morphy.

This gentleman crossed the Atlantic in the most chivalrous manner, with the determination of "trying a fall" with the European masters of the game, and, immediately on his landing, threw down his glove to Mr. Staunton in particular (to whom he allowed his own terms), and, in the meantime, was ready to play all comers. Nothing could be more straight-forward than Mr. Morphy's conduct throughout the long period of time in which he has been kept in suspense, and during which time he has displayed an amount of patience and good temper, only to be equaled by himself when finally engaged over the board.

On the other hand, we are driven to the contemplation of the shifts to which Mr. Staunton has been induced to resort, and which are so ably detailed by our correspondent, "Pawn and Two," whose condemnation of them is shared by nearly all the leading players in Paris and London. National pride would lead us to support our own side, if we could do so without compromising our national honor; but since it appears that in the present contest, the former is doomed to succumb, let us guard the latter all the more carefully, and while we pity the feelings of the individual, let us show, that as a nation, we do not sympathize with his actions.

For him the excuse may possibly be made that he could not afford to risk his position as the acknowledged head of English Chess; but no apology can atone for the attitude which he has assumed towards Mr. Morphy, from the moment that he found there was a certainty of being compelled to come to a definite conclusion; and so far from his maneuvers being successful, they have had quite an opposite effect. We cordially agree, therefore, with our correspondent, that a new champion must be sought for; but we can hardly expect to meet with a player of Mr. Morphy's strength in our hour of need, and we are afraid that Europe, as well as England, must bow the neck to America, and acknowledge themselves.

At the same time, let us co-operate with "Pawn and Two" who himself stands high among the metropolitan players in the

laudable attempt to remove everything which tends to the disparagement of this noble game, and, above all, let us do homage
to such talent as is exhibited by Mr. Morphy, without considering whether he is English or American.

But Staunton has had his defenders. Notably, H. J. R. Murray, in the
British Chess Magazine of November-December 1908, presented him favorably as a man and as a chess player, but he was nevertheless very critical
of Staunton as a chess editor. With regard to the New Orleans challenge,
he considers Staunton's reply to have been a courteous refusal to play. As
to the controversy that broke out over the match, Murray remarks that "on
the whole, Morphy was the better served." However, Murray also said that
Staunton "misused his editorial position again and again" and "right down
to the end he indulged in ill-natured statements in the columns of the *Illustrated London News*. . . . He hit out at his enemies, real or supposed, under
the cover of answers to correspondents. There were people who refused
to credit the existence of these correspondents." Murray also said that "he
would have stood no chance against Morphy in 1858, even if he had retained his chess strength of 1843."

Another stout defender of Staunton was B. Goulding Brown, of whom
Sergeant took notice. Brown, in the *British Chess Magazine* of June 1916,
said:

> The most serious point against Staunton is the paragraph of
> *August 28* ["Anti-book"] alleging that Morphy had come to
> England unprovided with seconds or money for the stakes.
> This was ungenerous, but was it untrue? Staunton solemnly
> repeated his statement on December 4th. "Mr. Morphy may in-
> fer what he chooses from the paragraph in question. All we are
> concerned about is its truth, and since he persists in complain-
> ing that it was not 'consonant with fact,' we shall be obliged
> with his showing in what particular. We asserted that he came
> to England without representatives to arrange the terms, and
> without money for the stakes." Morphy let some weeks elapse
> before taxing Staunton on his letter of October 6th with the
> original paragraph. And his letter to the St. George's Club, an-
> nouncing the deposit of his stakes at Heywood's Bank is dated
> October 8th. Is it not likely that the money had arrived *in the
> interval*?

Knowing no more than he did, Brown's assumption that the stakes arrived "in the interval" seems reasonable. But as shown earlier, the New

Orleans Chess Club had forwarded the stake funds to Morphy on July 29, and they probably had arrived August 14. In any case, Morphy had his own funds, which he would have used in the interim, as he did with Lowenthal.

But Staunton had said more on December 4 than Mr. Brown quoted of him. He had also said, "We assert, too, that in not appearing at the Birmingham Tournament to compete with Mr. Staunton, and in not accepting his offer to play a few games at his residence, Mr. Morphy plainly shows that 'reputation' is not 'the only incentive' he recognizes." As for Morphy's refusal of Staunton's October 9 invitation to have some "friendly" games at his residence, he must have known that with the existing very strained relations between them, the invitation was a meaningless gesture. Sergeant made the following comment in *A Century of British Chess* about Staunton's insinuation:

> The allusion, in the words about reputation not being the only incentive, to the paragraph which he had himself suppressed in Morphy's letter of October 6, when he published it in the *Illustrated London News* was an unjustifiable sneer. What, then, did he mean to suggest was Morphy's incentive? Is not the implication that it was not one to his credit?

Sergeant also took up Staunton's reference to seconds in the same book:

> In an answer to real or imaginary Correspondent, on August 7th, Staunton had said: "Mr. Morphy came to this country unattended by seconds or bottleholder." Passing over the elegance of the last expression, we are entitled to ask whether Morphy was expected to bring seconds with him from America. Staunton knew that in his match against Lowenthal in July and August, in which he himself was umpire, Morphy had as his seconds Lord Arthur Hay and the Rev. John Owen. Were these gentlemen not respectable enough? From what hierarchy, on either side of the Atlantic, were Morphy's seconds to be produced?

What manner of man was Staunton? G. A. MacDonnell, in his book *Chess Life-Pictures*, describes him at the time of his meeting Morphy as an impressive personality: "Tall, erect, and broad-shouldered, he was military in his air, and graceful in every movement. It was summertime, yet he wore, as was his custom, a lavender zephyr outside his frock-coat. His apparel was slightly gaudy, his vest being an embroidered satin."

At one time, before, and perhaps during, his meetings with Morphy, Edge notes that "he [Staunton] actually wore shirts with kings, rooks, pawns, etc. printed over the bosoms and tails." For the benefit of the chess public, Staunton described these shirts in the May 1847 *Chess Players Chronicle*. "The patterns of the Chess shirts consist of the several Chess pieces prettily arranged and linked together."

Staunton's contributions to chess were great in terms of games, books, magazines, and even in terms of his chess column, although he often abused his editorial privileges. He must also be credited with organizing the first international chess tournament, a giant step in chess history. Nor were his interests limited to chess, for he edited a new edition of Shakespeare. But he is mainly remembered for his chess activity and doubtless was the world chess champion of the 1840s.

But Staunton's disposition was not the best. MacDonnell says that his "manner was very quiet, and his voice always gentle." His voice was gentle, except editorially. Even Murray said he "would fain ignore" his petty personalities, likes and dislikes if he could, and that, "His most faithful friends were those who rarely met him in the flesh. Personal intercourse inevitably ended before long in a breach."

In the *British Chess Magazine* of February 1891, Charles Tomlinson told of Henry T. Buckle, the historian and a very strong chess player, being asked whether he had ever played a match with Staunton and his replying, "No. I was always careful to maintain friendly relations with him."

Years later, in 1874, Paul Morphy, in an offhand conversation (*Dubuque Chess Journal*, December 1874), expressed the following opinion of Mr. Staunton as a chess master:

> Mr. Staunton's knowledge of the theory of the game was no doubt complete; his powers as an analyst were of the very highest order, his *coup d'oeil* and judgment of position and his general experience of the chess board, great; but all these qualities which are essential to make a GREAT chess player do not make him a player of GENIUS. These must be supplemented by imagination and by a certain inventive or creative power, which *conceives* positions and brings them about. Of this faculty (*he said*) he saw no evidence in the published games of Mr. Staunton.
>
> In a given position, where there is something to be done, no matter how recondite or difficult the idea, Mr. Staunton will

detect it, and carry out the combination in as finished a style as any great player that ever lived, but he will have had no agency in bringing about the position.

Therefore in his best day, Mr. Staunton in his opinion could not have made a successful fight against a man who had the same qualities as himself and who, besides, was possessed of the creative power above mentioned, such as were Anderssen of Germany, M'Donnell of England, and La Bourdonnais of France.

To all that had been said concerning Mr. Staunton personally, his brilliant conversational powers, etc. (he said) he could himself bear witness, and he had had frequent occasions to meet Mr. Staunton in social intercourse.

As a chess author, *he thought*, as everybody does, that Mr. Staunton's ability was of the very highest order, and that he had done more for the diffusion and propagation of chess than almost anybody else. As a commentator on games actually played, aside from the personalities, he was at times too prone to indulge in, he stood absolutely without a rival.

As a player he was entitled to a very high rank indeed, and perhaps he was, as is claimed for him, the ablest player of his day; at the same time he was not prepared to admit that Mr. Staunton possessed to any very great degree GENIUS FOR CHESS, as he understands the term.

In summing up the Staunton affair, we might do well to quote Philip W. Sergeant in his book, *Morphy's Games of Chess*, who, after referring to Murray's defense of Staunton, concludes that

It is not shown: (1) that Staunton had a genuine desire for the match; (2) that, if he had, he treated Morphy fairly in the interval between his letter of April 3 and that of October 9, when he refused any longer to entertain the idea of the match; (3) that if he had not, his apparent (though conditional) readiness to play can be justified; and (4) that he had any right to use his chess column, as he did, to depreciate and sneer at Morphy.

Morphy's case is clear. He came to Europe above all to play Staunton, whom he complimented by regarding as the leading master in Europe. He, possibly erroneously, but at least in good faith, took Staunton's statement in his chess column on April 3 as meaning that he would find him ready to play him in London

[More clearly stated in Staunton's letter to the New Orleans Chess Club as given earlier.]; but, in that case, it was easy for Staunton to correct his wrong impression as soon as they met at the St. George's. So far from doing this, right up to October 9 Staunton let Morphy think that a match could be played *in 1858*, if he would only wait until Staunton could find a date. And finally Morphy, being himself a chivalrous gentleman, had a title to be treated chivalrously by anyone who claimed also to be a gentleman. The chivalry of ridiculing your opponent as an adventurer without backing, or hinting furtively that he is a professional, is not apparent. Morphy sickened of chess tactics—off the board.

And, as Sergeant concluded, "So ends what can only be regarded as a melancholy chapter in English chess history."

CHAPTER 12

La Régence and Society

Morphy's last letter to Staunton was written as his match with Harrwitz drew to its abrupt close. When he received Staunton's reply that the match would be "impossible, fettered as I am at this moment," Morphy knew there was no need for a quick return to London.

While he could no more get Harrwitz to play additional games at La Régence than he had been successful with Staunton at the St. George's Club, there were other players at La Régence, many the strongest France had to offer, eager to measure their strength against him even at odds.

But even after offering odds to Prèti, Journoud, Lequesne, Laroche, Delannoy, and the well-known Budzinsky of Poland, the results were hardly different than when meeting them on even terms. After winning all games at Pawn and two moves against Delannoy, with whom Rivière, the most promising French player, had not been successful, Morphy offered Delannoy the odds of Queen's Knight. Before commencing, Delannoy called all to witness, as recorded in the New Orleans *Sunday Delta* of March 13, 1859, that "Mr. Morphy would not win a game" at Knight odds. However, the first series ended Morphy thirteen, Delannoy four.

Almost a quarter century later, Delannoy wrote of Morphy in *Brentano's Chess Monthly* of May 1881:

> Erudite, endowed with an amiable temper, charming, possessing first-rate manners, great, generous and magnanimous, he drew everybody towards him on his first appearance, and the sympathies of all players. The superiority of his play, the distinction of his language, and the elevation of his mind soon compelled the enthusiasm and the admiration of these same players.
>
> His name, during his sojourn in Paris, made a great noise; it even fills it now. In his presence, the triumphs and glory of his predecessors were almost forgotten, and the shades of Philidor, Deschapelles and Labourdonnais started at the bottom of their graves.

With Rivière, a friend, Morphy continued to play without odds. Eugène Rousseau was in Paris for some time and gloried in Paul's triumphs. Morphy now became the cynosure of high society. As of September 16, 1858, Edge had written to Fiske:

> I can assure you they treat him here like a God. The other night at the *Théâtre Français* nearly the entire orchestra stood up to look at him, he perfectly unconscious until we pointed it out to him. Everybody tries to get introduced to him, and the old players of the time of Labourdonnais treat him with the greatest reverence, telling him his games are worthy of that great master.

Among Morphy's first social invitations was one from the Duchess de la Trémoille. The Duchess told Morphy she had been playing chess since a child and had wanted to meet such an eminent practitioner of the game. Of the five games played the evening of their meeting, each won two, the fifth being drawn. The Princess Murat was also present and contested a game with Morphy. Rivière mentioned in his chess column in *L'Illustration* that other "grande dames" received the odds of a Queen.

Others with whom Morphy passed many pleasant evenings were Mme. Regnault de Saint Jean D'Angély and the Baronne de L. The latter was famous for her soirées and her salon was the weekly resort of the most celebrated artists and writers of France. On one occasion she persuaded the famous baritone Graziani (recently taking lessons from Prèti) to play with Morphy at Queen odds by playfully promising that Mr. Morphy would sing a duo with him afterwards. Perhaps there was a grain of truth in what she said about Morphy in expressing her liking for him: "Because he is another lazy Creole like myself."

The Duke of Brunswick, with whom Morphy first dined on September 19, was a confirmed chess player, hardly to be seen otherwise than at chess. Edge says they were frequent visitors to the Duke's box at the Italian Opera and even there the Duke played chess. On their first visit in October, they played chess throughout the entire performance of Norma. Edge mentions Morphy's discomfiture when he was the Duke's guest, since he was obliged to sit with his back to the stage, while facing the Duke and Count Isouard consulting against him.

On the second of November they heard the *Barber of Seville*, during which Morphy played his most famous game, the Duke again consulting with Count Isouard. In his games with Morphy, the Duke always had a partner, sometimes two, Counts Isouard and Casabianca consulting against him.

Count Casabianca gave a large soirée in Morphy's honor on one of the former's Friday "at home" days, October 29, at which many noblewomen and celebrated men were present. Morphy was introduced to all present as "The Napoleon of Chess." A number of Morphy's consultation games with the Duke of Brunswick, Count Isouard, and Count Casabianca took place on these "at home" days.

On other occasions he was entertained at Prince Murat's chateau, where the Princess would sometimes be joined by Count Casabianca in games against him.

Morphy sometimes declined invitations when he thought he would be expected to play chess, although very rarely did chess-playing interfere with his evening. On February 14 (as published in the New Orleans *Sunday Delta*, March 27, 1859), at a fête given

> by the Duke Decazes . . . [Morphy] played two games blind-fold against M. Prefect Lacoste and General Busserolles, both fine players, winning both. The moves were transmitted by Mr. Lequesne . . . and during the whole of the performance, Mr. Morphy sustained an animated conversation with Mme Decazes and several ladies and gentlemen.

As Edge recalled, one evening at the hotel, as Morphy and he sat talking (they had adjoining rooms), a stranger announced himself:

> "I am Prince Galitzin; I wish to see Mr. Morphy." Morphy looked up from an armchair and replied, "I am he." The Prince answered, "It is not possible! you're too young," and then he seated himself by Morphy's side and told him, "I first heard of your wonderful deeds on the frontiers of Siberia. One of my suite had a copy of the chess paper published in Berlin, the *Schachzeitung,* and ever since that time I have been wanting to see you." And he told our hero that he must pay a visit to St. Petersburg; for the chess club in the Imperial Palace would receive him with enthusiasm.

Among the first to recognize Morphy's significance in the chess arena was Eugène Lequesne, the well-known French sculptor. Morphy had been in France less than two weeks when Lequesne asked him to sit for his bust in marble. Morphy obliged with a first sitting on September 15. The bust was exhibited at the *Exposition des Beaux Arts* in 1859. Maurian mentions in the New Orleans *Sunday Delta* of February 6, 1859, that small replicas (three-fifths the actual size) had arrived in New Orleans by January 1859, and described the bust as "a perfect likeness." It received special attention the day before Morphy left Paris some months later. Lequesne also took a plaster cast of Morphy's right hand, now possessed by the author.*

About the first of November, Edge received a letter from Lowenthal asking information about one of the blindfold games Morphy had played at Birmingham. The Reverend George Salmon had taken board two against Morphy, and the game had gone to forty-nine moves, but since the score had not been clear, Staunton had published only the first twenty-four moves. As Edge remarked:

> Herr Lowenthal wrote me to request that I would forward him the remaining moves, as there was a desire to have the *partie* complete. It was nearly midnight, and Morphy had gone into his bedroom after dictating me some games played during the day, and, mindful of Herr Lowenthal's request, I called to him, asking whether he was coming back, when he replied that he was already in bed. I said I should be obliged if he would let me bring him a board and light, in order that he might dictate me the required moves, when he answered, "There's no necessity for that: read me over what Staunton published, and I'll give you the remainder." He called over the omitted moves as fast as I could write them down.

The American Minister (Ambassador) to France, the Honorable Mr. Mason, took a great interest in Morphy and was frequently to be seen sitting at the board when Morphy was playing. He was one of those present at Morphy's Paris blindfold exhibition. Edge wrote to Fiske on November 12 that the Minister "has requested permission to introduce Morphy to the Emperor, who has the reputation of being a very tolerable knight player."

It seems that something of Ambassador Mason's plans for Morphy had become known to New York papers before Edge wrote, for *Porter's Spirit of the Times* of November 6, 1858, had the following announcement:

> The fame of the youthful chess champion of the New World has penetrated the Imperial cloisters of the Tuileries, and his

---

* EDITOR'S NOTE: How Lawson came into the possession of the Lequesne sculpture is unknown, but, op cit page 18, his collection was sold in 1978 to chess publisher Dale Brandreth.

Majesty, Napoleon III, has invited Mr. Morphy to give a specimen of his blindfold playing before the Empress and ladies of
her court. His Imperial Majesty desires himself to engage Mr.
Morphy in a game, and, in acknowledgment of the pre-emi-
nence of the young American sovereign with whom he will thus
contend, he has consented to try to equalize his chances, by the
acceptance of a Rook at the commencement of the game.

Twelve days later, on November 18, Edge wrote the following letter to
Fiske:

> 1 Rue du Dauphin; Paris
> 18th November 1858
>
> My dear Fiske.
>
> Will you have the goodness to forward the following immedi-
> ately to Mons. Jean Prèti
>   Café de la Régence
>   Paris
> 2 Complete sets of the *Chess Monthly* for 1858.
>
> [The next paragraph concerns subscriptions.]
>
> There is nothing new. Morphy stays until Spring, and Ander-
> ssen comes here to play a match on 18th Dec. The universal
> stated opinion of all Europe now is, that Morphy is superior not
> merely to all living players, but to Labourdonnais etc. even. At
> the Régence, the old friends of Labourdonnais openly declare
> this; they say that P.M. is equally brilliant and much more *sol-
> ide*, and that he has reduced chess to "une science exacte." You
> will recollect that Paulsen said the same thing last year.
>
> Morphy has this week announced publicly that he will play
> none in France even except Harrwitz; but Harrwitz has had too
> much already. The statement in last *Illustrated London News*
> that Harrwitz was about to challenge Morphy to another con-
> test is a lie. Harrwitz won't even play an off-hand game. Fancy
> Morphy giving all France Pawn and move.
>
> The American Ambassador has become a warm friend of Mor-
> phy's and without his knowledge, has proposed and got him
> elected a member of the Cercle Imperial, to which only the
> Emperor, Princes Imperials, the highest noblesse, ministers
> and foreign ambassadors belong. Morphy was received by them
> with most distinguished honor. Mr. Mason is going also to

present him to the Emperor. "Honors crowd thick upon him," but they do not affect him.

Why do you not write us an epistle, and tell us about the N.Y. Club, Thompson, Mead[,] etc.? You ought to, and Morphy is expecting it of you.

I remain

Yours most truly

Fred. M. Edge

P.S. Address as above, but write soon.

Edge studiously avoids mention of the above matter about the Emperor in his book. Undoubtedly Morphy prohibited it, wishing to avoid any suggestion that he had "cashed in" prestigewise on a meeting with Napoleon III, a meeting he would have considered a very personal honor. Edge's only mention of Ambassador Mason in his book is that "the Hon. Mr. Mason took a warm interest in his countryman."

But for Edge's letters, nothing would have been known about the American Minister's requesting permission to present Morphy to the Emperor and his being received by members of the Cercle Impérial. Some news leaked into American papers, such as the New Orleans *Sunday Delta*, *Porter's Spirit*, etc., before Maurian and Fiske realized that Morphy wanted no publicity. However, the news that Morphy had been elected a member of the Cercle Impérial never became public. Even Fiske never mentioned it.

It is most likely that Morphy was received by the Emperor, even though there was no public announcement. Napoleon III had some interest in chess, as evidenced by his donation of a valuable Sèvres vase as a trophy to the First Prize winner of the 1867 Tournament, held in Paris. This tournament was won by Ignatz Kolisch, who later sought to arrange a match with Morphy. Harrwitz had been privileged to play before Prince Napoleon the year before, as reported in the New York *Tribune* of October 12, 1857, and most certainly Morphy constituted a far greater attraction to the court.

Morphy had played with everyone at La Régence, regardless of their strength, and had admittedly outclassed them all. Edge says he now began to show

> an antipathy to chess, and I experienced the greatest difficulty in inducing him to go to the Régence at all. When I would ask him at breakfast what he was going to do with himself during the day, his immediate reply would be, "I am not going to the Régence."

Perhaps in addition to being bored with chess, Morphy was also physically unwell. Edge says he had "been an invalid since his arrival in the French capital," and that "nothing proves so satisfactorily . . . Morphy's wondrous powers in chess, as his contests in France, laboring as he constantly did, under positive bodily suffering."

CHAPTER 13

"Morphy Won't Let Me"

When Morphy realized that the Staunton match was out of the question, the possibility of a match with Adolf Anderssen began to loom large in his mind. Unaware that plans for the Staunton match had been aborted, Fiske published the following announcement in the October 1858 *Chess Monthly*:

> Mr. Morphy will, most likely, go to Breslau and play him [Anderssen] a long match of twenty-one games. Staunton has formally accepted Mr. Morphy's challenge for five-hundred pounds. The contest is expected to commence the first week in November.

It is clear that Morphy had expected to go to Germany. Edge, in a letter to Fiske dated September 16, 1858, wrote: "After beating Harrwitz (St. Amant will not play) we shall go on to Berlin and Breslau. Anderssen, Lange and Mayet have got to bite the dust." Even as late as February 1859, Fiske noted in the *Chess Monthly* that

> Mr. Morphy hopes, before returning to this country, to have the pleasure of contending against Mr. Max Lange, the well-known player and critic, who now presides with so much ability over the pages of the venerable *Schachzeitung* of Berlin. Should he meet with the same success against Mr. Lange, that has heretofore attended him in the Old World he will, doubtless, publish a challenge to all Europe, proffering to any player the odds of Pawn and move.

Thoughts of a match with Anderssen had begun to take shape in early October, if not before, but confusion was added by the most unfortunate Staunton affair, which dragged on even after Morphy's October correspondence with Staunton and Lord Lyttelton. Such was Morphy's distraction that Edge mentions that the amateurs of La Régence, through Rivière, wrote to Anderssen, inviting him to come to Paris for a match with Morphy, who had told them he did not feel well enough for the trip to Breslau. Morphy also addressed the following letter to the Breslau Chess Club:

Hotel Breteuil, October 8, 1858
The Secretary
Breslau Chess Club
Dear Sir,

I have received lately two letters, one from the Chess Club of
Leipsic, and the other from Breslau, inviting me to their cities
in order to engage in a match with Mr. Anderssen. It is not possible to accept these propositions, but I wish to give you from
the amateurs of the Régence the 295 francs that have remained
from my parties with Mr. Harrwitz to help defray the cost of
travel for Mr. Anderssen in accepting the invitation to Paris.

Please accept the assurance of my high regard.
                                                        Paul Morphy

Anderssen replied at once that it would be impossible for him to leave
Breslau before mid-December, during his vacation. Dr. Schutze, secretary
of the Brelsau Chess Club, also wrote on behalf of Anderssen, offering in
turn to have the match in Breslau for a stake of fifty pounds, and an additional twenty-five pounds to be set aside for Morphy's travel expenses. The
latter offer Morphy refused:

Hotel Breteuil, Oct. 14, 1858
Dr. Schutze, Secretary
Breslau Chess Club
Dear Sir,

I regret that you do not understand my position: I have never and never will play as a professional and I am in a position
that allows me to travel at my own expense. The offer you have
made is very kind but should not be addressed to me.

It will not be possible for me to go to Breslau to contest with
Mr. Anderssen. I had hoped he could accept the invitation of
the French players, but the dispatch received Saturday deprives
me of hope that I will be able to measure myself with the German champion.
                           Please accept assurance of my high regards.
                                                        Paul Morphy

And so it appeared there would be no Morphy–Anderssen match, because Morphy, on hearing that Anderssen could not make the trip to Paris
before December, said, as Edge quotes him, "that he should be deprived of

the pleasure of crossing swords with the victor in the International Tournament [1851], inasmuch as he must be at home before Christmas." He was much more concerned about getting home than he was about meeting Anderssen. This suggests that his interest in chess was limited, for Anderssen's name was the greatest in European chess, and surely a match with Anderssen would have meant much to Morphy's worldwide chess standing. As Edge said:

> His voyage to Europe was useless, if he did not play Anderssen. All was of no effect. Morphy did not appear to have the slightest ambition, say what I would to him. He "must be at home in December; he had promised to be there, and home he would go."

Thinking only of Morphy and how much it would mean to him and his place in chess history, Edge determined to bring Morphy and Anderssen together. He quietly set to work, writing to the leading chess clubs of Europe and principal amateurs, telling of Morphy's decision to return home before he could engage Anderssen, hoping to enlist their support in encouraging Morphy to remain longer.

The following letter was sent to the Breslau Chess Club, reprinted from E. Falkbeer's *Paul Morphy*. Other letters by Edge to chess clubs and amateurs were similar:

> Hotel Breteuil, Oct. 30, 1858
>
> Breslau Chess Club
> Dr. Schutze
> Dear Sir:
>
> You have heard without doubt, with regret that the fine American chess player Mr. Paul Morphy is ready at this time to leave Europe in about fifteen days and also that he is not likely to return for several years. Nothing could be worse for all true chess amateurs; but although several strong players are willing to come to Paris to measure with him their strength, the early departure of Mr. Morphy will deprive us of great games that would be played between him and these illustrious champions. Mr. Morphy is the first to truly regret the obligations calling him to return to the Untied States and would prefer I am sure, to pass the winter in Europe. But he fears the dissatisfaction of his family with a too long prolongation of his sojourn with us.
>
> In this matter all the chess amateurs of Paris have decided to write to him one letter to get him to stay in the interest of

Chess. Also several clubs of London and Paris are themselves
following the same example and are themselves writing to him
in the same way. And if your circle would address him during
this week (!) it would without doubt show Mr. Morphy that it
is the unanimous wish that he stay longer and serve to present
to his family the reason why Mr. Morphy should delay his departure. I have had the pleasure of traveling with Mr. Morphy
since his arrival in Europe and I am convinced that he would
yield to such an important and unanimous wish.

With high regards, &c.

Fred. M. Edge

Europe was interested in a Morphy–Anderssen match much more
than it had been in the Morphy–Staunton encounter, and soon Morphy
received letters urging that he meet Anderssen. Anderssen himself wrote
to Morphy saying, "he did not think it possible he could leave without
playing him."

Morphy still insisted that he must leave, but when requests from his
friends were also reinforced by his doctor's statement that in his condition
he should not risk a winter crossing of the Atlantic (Edge sent the doctor's certificate on to the family in New Orleans), Morphy capitulated and
agreed to pass the winter in Paris. Edge then sent the following letter:

Hotel Breteuil, Nov. 17, 1858

Breslau Chess Club
Dr. Schutze, Secretary
Sir,

I have the honor to inform you that Mr. Paul Morphy has at last
given in to the pressing solicitations of European chess circles
and has resolved to pass the winter in Europe. He has expressed
the hope that the match between Mr. Anderssen and himself
will take place in Paris about the middle of next month and he
has promised to have the pleasure of writing to your celebrated
champion by to-morrow's post.

Please receive my regards

Fred. M. Edge

During the first week of December, Rivière received a letter from Anderssen about his approaching visit to Paris, and a few days later Morphy
got a telegram from him saying he would arrive on December 15 or there-
abouts. Since the beginning of December, Morphy had been confined to

bed with intestinal influenza and, as was the practice at that time, he was well leeched. He lost a lot of good blood as a result, which did not help his condition. To quote Edge:

> He was leeched, and lost a great quantity of blood—I told him three or four pints; to which he replied, "Then there's only a quart left." He was very low during a fortnight, and having to lift him out of bed only four days before the match with the great Prussian master, I found him too weak to stand upon his legs, although in bed he did not feel so helpless.

The day before Anderssen arrived, Edge received a letter from Carl Mayet saying Anderssen had left Breslau. On hearing the news, Edge relates:

> Morphy said to me, "I have a positive chess fever coming over me. Give me the board and pieces, and I'll show you some of Anderssen's games." And with astounding memory, he gave me battle after battle with different adversaries, variations and all. How he dilated on a certain game between him and Dufresne ["Evergreen" game, then unnamed]. . . . "There," said Morphy, "that shows the master."

The next day, Wednesday morning at ten o'clock, Edge found Anderssen in Morphy's bedroom, dismayed at finding him ill, and very reluctant to start a match until Morphy had recovered. However, Morphy, knowing Anderssen's time in Paris was very limited, assured him he would be quite well enough by the coming Monday. They settled the few necessary details about the match, agreeing that the first winner of seven games was to be the victor, and that the match was to be played for honor only, with no money stakes.

Since this was Anderssen's first visit to Paris, Edge offered to show him around, and after visiting the Louvre and other sites, they ended up at La Régence, where they found Harrwitz. Anderssen and Harrwitz had met before. Although the latter claimed to have won the majority of their games together, Anderssen disputed the fact and wished to settle the matter. He proposed they have some games and the result of a total of six games between them was that Anderssen won three, Harrwitz one, and two were drawn.

Morphy told his doctor that he must get him well enough to start the match with Anderssen the coming Monday, December 20. He feared only that a hard battle might exhaust him to such a degree that he might not be able to continue the next day. He agreed not to leave the hotel and that only a few onlookers should be present at the match.

"On Monday morning," Edge relates, "I got Morphy out of bed for almost the first time in nearly a fortnight[,] and at about noon assisted him into the room where the match was to come off."

In a letter to Professor Allen of January 20, 1859, Fiske writes as follows about Morphy's physical condition during the encounter:

> Morphy had an inflammation in the bowels (thank God it was not the *brain*) and arose from his bed, with the reluctant consent of his physician, who was present during the first two sittings, to meet Anderssen.

Dr. Johnston, Paris correspondent of the New York *Times*, describes the opening of the match in his firsthand account, dated Paris, December 23 (published January 11, 1859):

> For the last two years all the lions of Paris have been American. Young Morphy, the chess-player, is the last in the list. The great match between this gentleman and Professor Anderssen, of Breslau, commenced on Monday morning at 12 o'clock. M. Anderssen arrived in Paris the Wednesday previous, but Mr. Morphy was confined to bed with an attack of the influenza. In the meantime Mr. Anderssen played with several gentlemen at the Café de la Régence—among others, with Mr. Harrwitz. Six games were played between these two gentlemen, three of which were won by Anderssen, one by Harrwitz, and two were drawn. M. Anderssen also played with Mr. Schulten, of New York, a few games, which resulted in favor of the former.
>
> The great match between the champions of the Old and the New World commenced, as I said, on Monday, at Mr. Morphy's hotel [Breteuil], No. 1 Rue du Dauphin. The greatest excitement prevailed, and an arrangement was made by which the game was kept on three boards at the Café de la Régence (only a few blocks distant), a domestic carrying the moves every half hour. Thus the large crowd collected at the Café were enabled to follow the progress of the game. The game was commenced in the presence of Messrs. Lequesne, of the Institute, De Saint-Amant, Arnous de Riviere, Journoud, Prèti, Carlini, F. Edge, Jas. Mortimer, and your correspondent, all invited especially by Messrs. Morphy and Anderssen as witnesses of the game.
>
> Prof. Anderssen arrived at precisely 12 o'clock, in the company

of Messrs. Prèti and Carlini. Mr. Morphy, who had not yet risen from bed after his late indisposition, did not appear for half an hour, and when he did join the party, looked so pale and feeble that, it seemed as if he was risking too much in undertaking the task he had before him. However, he declared his head all right, and rapidly shaking hands with his adversary and the party present, he stepped at once to the board, seized a black and a white pawn, changed them under the table, and held out his hand for the Professor to make a choice. Mr. Morphy won the move, and the game commenced at once with Evans' Gambit.

It had been agreed on, in previous interviews, that the winner of the first seven games should be the victor. No money was staked by the contestants, and but little by the friends of the parties, for it was generally conceded that Mr. Morphy was sure to win the match. His friends, however, were offering in the clubs of Paris and London ten to one without takers.

The first game lasted seven hours, and was won by Prof. Anderssen. During the course of his game, which was conducted in the most brilliant manner, and in which were displayed an immense number of the most ingenious combinations on both sides, I had a good opportunity of studying the contestants. Nothing could be more unlike than the physique of the two players. Mr. Morphy is a frail, small boy, with a fine face and head, and a modest, almost timid air. Prof. Anderssen, on the contrary, is a tall man, slim, about fifty [forty] years of age, with a small, bald head, a slight stoop in the shoulders, lively black eyes, a clean-shaven face and a decidedly German cast of features. He is a quiet, gentlemanly man, with a sympathetic expression of the face, which immediately predisposes in his favor.

During this first game M. Anderssen moved much more rapidly than Mr. Morphy. Not a word was spoken by either player during the whole seven hours. No demonstrations or false moves were made by either party, to indicate to the other his plans. There seemed to be more originality, more genius, more of the *imprévu* in Mr. Morphy's moves, and more of study and experience in those of M. Anderssen. The two men are evidently more nearly matched than they ever were before.

On Tuesday the game commenced at 12 o'clock, and at the close was a draw. On Wednesday Mr. Morphy beat M. Anderssen two games in rapid succession—the first one in a few moves. The young giant is getting roused up.

M. Lequesne, the sculptor, has executed in marble a very fine bust of Mr. Morphy, which has been placed alongside of those of Labourdonnais and Philidor, at the Chess Club over the Café de la Régence. Small duplicates of this are on sale about town.

George Walker, in *Bell's Life in London* of January 2, 1859, spoke in a somewhat different tone of the Morphy-Anderssen encounter:

Anderssen's great soul seems occasionally broken by the prospect of almost certain defeat, and he plays with comparative difficulty and "don't careishness," but as a whole, he himself considers the games a fair average of his strength, and honorably admits he should not expect better results from a second match. . . .

In the course of one of the games between Messrs. Morphy and Anderssen, a move of the former excited much surprise among the bystanders. He had declined to take a piece, which, although apparently an exchange of knights, would have resulted, it was thought, conclusively in his favor. The game proceeded, nevertheless, without verbal comment, and was rapidly won by Mr. Morphy. No sooner did he deliver the "checkmate" than one of the most intense of the lookers-on, breathless with pent-up emotion, exclaimed, "for the love of heaven tell me why you did not take the knight." "Because," said Morphy, all alive to the nature of his friend's concern, "it was a stale-mate. Mr. Anderssen saw the game was desperate, and he planned this snare for me." So saying, he replaced the pieces as they had been at the critical moment, and demonstrated the result by a series of moves which would have been inevitable had he taken the Knight. "Was I not right, Mr. Anderssen?" "Precisely," ejaculated the bewildered gentleman.

After winning four games, Morphy went on to win the match. The score stood Morphy seven, Anderssen two, and two drawn. Morphy won the ninth game in thirty minutes and seventeen moves; it is a game that Steinitz labeled "brilliant" in his *International Chess Magazine* of January 1885. After the loss and draw of the first two games, Morphy won the next five. Sergeant remarks in *Morphy's Games of Chess* that Anderssen's "loss of the third game (Ruy Lopez) had the remarkable effect on Anderssen of deterring him henceforth from answering Morphy's P–K4 with P–K4, truly a compliment from an analyst like Anderssen!"

After each game Anderssen would walk over to the Café de la Régence to expedite the transmission of the moves to Berlin and Leipzig, for interest was intense in Germany. One may be sure there was much rejoicing in Germany after the first game.

Morphy had ventured the Evans Gambit against Anderssen—"that most beautiful of openings," as he called it—and lost after seventy-two moves. Perhaps his illness had something to do with the result, but Morphy told Edge afterward that the game "proved to him that the Evans is indubitably a lost game for the first player, if the defense be carefully played; inasmuch as the former can never recover the gambit pawn, and the position supposed to be acquired at the outset, cannot be maintained." Yet of all the Evans Gambits Morphy played (some eighty on record), he lost only two in even games, one other to Rivière, and a few when giving odds of Knight or Rook. Whether he offered or was offered the Evans Gambit, he almost invariably won, regardless of odds.

Reinfeld's analysis of the Morphy–Anderssen match games in *The Human Side of Chess* calls for some comment. Of course, post mortems have their value, but if one believes Reinfeld, Morphy was indeed lucky. Reinfeld's remarks on the third game are of special interest. He says:

> Morphy had White and played a Ruy Lopez. Morphy followed a variation recommended by Max Lange in his *Schachpartien* to the 12th move. Anderssen, on the other hand, had seen neither the book nor the variation. The line was extremely unfavorable for Anderssen, leaving him with a hopeless game, even at so early a stage.

Did Reinfeld really know that Morphy had seen Max Lange's *Schachpartien* and had profited by his variation? Did he really know that Anderssen had *not* seen *Schachpartien* (a book his partner and co-editor of *Schachzeitung* had published just the year before), and so knew nothing of Lange's important variation, which he says was the cause of Anderssen's downfall?

One must also question Reinfeld's judgment of Morphy (and Steinitz) as expressed elsewhere in *The Human Side of Chess*:

> But at bottom both of these geniuses were actuated by the same feeling: pride, the pride that comes from being unsure of oneself. In Morphy this lack of self-confidence paralyzed his abilities.

If either Morphy or Steinitz lacked self-confidence, it was not apparent. Probably no other two players were more sure of themselves. Reinfeld also maintains that "Morphy caved in at the first great rebuff." His first great rebuff was delivered by Staunton, but almost immediately thereafter he achieved his greatest successes in his matches with Harrwitz and Anderssen.

Reinfeld is frequently in error in his facts and assessments, as when he cites the incident when Morphy told Fuller, "Paulsen shall never win a game of me while he lives." And Reinfeld makes the point that "facts are stubborn things, and the fact is that Morphy lost his next game with Paulsen!" But Reinfeld places the incident after the second game, when it actually occurred before the sixth game. Morphy did not lose another game to Paulsen.

It is undoubtedly true, as Reinfeld says, that he had no thought of "diminishing any of the glory which rightfully belongs to Morphy," but nothing could be further from the truth than his statement, "In a *telling phrase* [italics added] Morphy later admitted that the desire for fame, the ultimate infirmity of noble minds, was the spur that goaded him on to victory." And Reinfeld also mentions "vaulting ambition," but neglects to quote or give sources for his statements.

One may ask where or when did Morphy admit that "desire for fame . . . goaded him on to victory." One may dismiss Morphy's statement in his letter to Staunton, dated October 6, 1858, that "reputation is the only incentive I recognize," as making the point that he had no professional or monetary interest in chess. One has only to consider Morphy's attitude and correspondence prior to the Morphy–Anderssen match. Certainly this match was the most momentous incident in Morphy's chess career and of the greatest significance to him and his position in the chess world, yet ambition had no part whatsoever in the match materializing. As Edge had put it to him strongly, "His voyage to Europe was useless, if he did not play Anderssen. All was of no effect. Morphy did not appear to have the slightest ambition."

Morphy had hoped to meet Anderssen, but when he learned that Anderssen could not come to Paris before mid-December, he dismissed the matter in his letter of October 14, 1858, to the Breslau Chess Club, given above, with a finality and lack of concern in line with his attitude to Edge about the match.

It is apparent that the "desire for fame" and "vaulting ambition" played no part in arrangements for the match, and it becomes evident from all the above that but for Edge and his scheming, there would have been no Morphy–Anderssen match, which came to pass in spite of Morphy and his intended plans.

And certainly Anderssen did not share Reinfeld's opinion that Morphy was fortunate in having won their match. At La Régence, Anderssen always found friends to tell him he should have won, to which he replied several times, "Tell that to Mr. Morphy." Edge also remarks that to another who said, "You are not playing anything like as well as with Dufresne," Anderssen replied, "No, Mr. Morphy won't let me." He then added, "It is no use struggling against him; he is like a piece of machinery which is sure to come to a certain conclusion." And as Falkbeer mentions in *Paul Morphy*, "at dinner before the last game was played, Anderssen said, jokingly and in good temper, 'He was glad to have already two sheep in safety.'"

The Paris correspondent of the New York *Express* said in his January 20 dispatch, referring to Anderssen:

> On the morning previous to his departure he said in my hearing—"I consider Mr. Morphy the finest chess player who ever existed. He is far superior to any now living, and would doubtless have beaten Labourdonnais himself. In all his games with me, he has not only played, in every instance, the exact move, but the most exact. He never makes a mistake (Morphy, present, here quietly smiled); but, if his adversary commits the slightest error, he is lost."

Edge notes that in reply to a question of Rivière's, Anderssen said, "It is impossible to play better than Mr. Morphy; if there be any difference in strength between him and Labourdonnais, it is in his favor."

The match ended on December 28 when Morphy won the eleventh game after four hours of play. The next day, while photographers were arranging for the group picture that appeared as the frontispiece in Max Lange's *Paul Morphy, Skizze aus der Schachwelt* (Part Two), which was published a few months later in 1859, Morphy and Anderssen played six offhand games in three hours, of which Morphy won five. As he was quoted in *Bell's Life in London* of January 2, 1859, after these games Anderssen said, "Morphy is too strong for any living player to hope to win more than a game here and there."

Morphy's match and association with Anderssen appears to have benefited him. He was thereafter in much better health, although he continued to shun La Régence. On the evening before Anderssen left (New Year's Day), he, Morphy, Edge, and probably others dined together, such was the friendship that had grown between the two opponents. Edge remarks:

> I have never seen a nobler-hearted gentleman than Herr An-
> derssen. He would sit at the board, examining the frightful
> positions into which Morphy had forced him, until his whole
> face was radiant with admiration of his antagonist's strategy,
> and, positively laughing outright, he would commence reset-
> ting the pieces for another game, without a remark. I never
> heard him make a single observation to Morphy complimen-
> tary of his skill; but, to others he was loud in admiration of the
> young American. He said to me,—"I win my games in seventy
> moves but Mr. Morphy wins his in twenty, but that is only natu-
> ral. . . ."
>
> As he wished us good-bye, he said slyly to Morphy, "They won't
> be pleased with me in Berlin, but I shall tell them[,] 'Mr. Mor-
> phy will come here himself.'"

In his dispatch of January 5, 1859, to the New York *Herald*, Edge reported that "Anderssen particularly requested Morphy to visit Berlin,
to close the mouths of the Berliners," and added that "Mr. Morphy may
shortly pay a flying visit to Berlin for the purpose of playing a few games
with Lange, Dufresne and Mayet."

Max Lange, co-editor with Anderssen of the *Schachzeitung*, was very
critical of Anderssen—considered the strongest European player—for
making advances to Morphy and going to Paris to meet him, instead of
obliging Morphy, "a young and rising player," to come to him. As Lange
said in his Paul Morphy book:

> It was clear that the American champion would be compelled to
> encounter the far-renowned German master ere he could boast
> of the championship of the world. His chivalrous mind would
> have doubtlessly led him to that final and decisive combat.

What Lange did not know was that Morphy was becoming disillusioned with chess playing. He had seldom gone to La Régence after failing
to get Harrwitz to try some more games. In fact, as Edge had said, "For two
months he had had an antipathy to chess, and I experienced the greatest
difficulty in inducing him to go to the Régence at all."

Anderssen did offer a reason to Lange for losing to Morphy as he did,
which may or may not have had much substance. As Falkbeer tells it in
Paul Morphy, Anderssen excused his loss by saying, "It is, however, impossible to keep one's excellence in a little glass casket, like a jewel, to take it
out whenever wanted; on the contrary, it can only be conserved by continuous and good practice." Much has been said about Anderssen's lack

of practice, yet he seemed in good practice for his first game with Morphy, and in his games with Harrwitz, winning against such an antagonist does not indicate that he was too "rusty" for combat. And it is true that there had been no tournaments for Anderssen or anyone after 1851, until the Manchester tournament of 1857, in which twelve strong players participated. Nevertheless, before meeting Morphy he had many encounters with strong players such as Lange, Mayet, and Dufresne. Gottschall says Anderssen often went to Leipzig and Berlin, and the former selected for his book on Anderssen over one hundred games he played in those cities, of which about forty were with the above-mentioned masters. One was the famous "Evergreen" game played with Dufresne in 1853.

Also, as co-editor of *Schachzeitung* with Lange, Anderssen was well acquainted with the games of other masters and with new developments. He also had seen many of Morphy's games in other publications, as well as some thirty that were published in the *Schachzeitung* in 1858.

In Anderssen's first game with Morphy, none of the "rust" that Steinitz mentioned (see Chapter 5) is apparent, nor any "intimidation" or signs of "lack of practice" that Reinfeld spoke of. Often considered the best of the match, this game was won by Anderssen, who appeared to be in full command of himself and the game throughout. In fact, Morphy wrote to Fiske during the match that Anderssen "is both bolder and stronger than any of his other opponents, and that his style and strength of play are fully up to the standard of 1851."

Anderssen accepted his defeat most graciously. He left Paris for Breslau on January 2, charmed with the city. Even under his heavy disappointment, he vowed to return soon. In a letter written a year after the match, Anderssen wrote very candidly about Morphy, expressing his great admiration of the latter's extraordinary chess capacity. (The letter is here translated from the German by Dr. A. Buschke.)

Breslau, December 31, 1859

Mr. Von Hyderbrandt V. der Lasa
Minister Resident [Rio de Janeiro, Brazil]
Dear Sir:

My most deepfelt thanks for sending me your latest work, with which you again presented me in such a friendly way. Even without your intention of dropping on the unsteady scales of public recognition which now so decisively tends in the direction of the transatlantic master, a counter-weight in favor of German chess mastery, your "Erinnerungen" [Lasa on historical chess, published 1859] will produce this effect since the games recorded therein are preferable to the Morphy games, in which faultless accuracy can, after all, be found only on the side of one of the players, on account of their being correctly played by both parties. I fully agree with your opinion on Morphy as well as with your disapproving of German chess vanity. You are perfectly right: the Berlin Club should have acted with the dignity of a chess academy whose duty it would have been to bring forward the talent and to support it, rather than to behave nobly and to show coldness and lack of esteem. If the necessary steps had been taken at the right time, Morphy very likely could have been induced to travel to Berlin. Later, however, when there was already talk about arranging a meeting between him and myself in Paris, he declined an invitation actually extended by the Leipzic (and Breslau) Club under the pretense ["because of" is probably the intended meaning here] his having to return home in the near future.

Whether you yourself who for years have kept aloof of all chess activities, could have fought the American victoriously without further preparations, may of course be doubtful. Notwithstanding, your strong self criticism cannot possibly refer to your proper and true strength which, in order to be revived, needs only some exercise. In any case you have evaluated correctly the miraculous talent of the foreign master. I not only believe that deeper combinations and brighter sparks of genius are at Morphy's disposition than were at Labourdonnais', but that in infallible calculation and soundness, he even surpasses the latter. He who plays with Morphy must not only renounce every hope of concealing even the subtlest traps, but he must also start with the idea that Morphy will clearly see through all, and that there can be no question of a misstep. On the contrary, if you see Morphy make a move that, at first glance, seems to yield you a chance to get some advantage, examine it carefully, because you will find that it is correct and that trying to take advantage of it will lead to disaster. But most fatal, when opposed to him, is overconfidence on account of a better position and strong attacking game. I cannot describe better the impression that Morphy made on me than by saying that he treats chess with the earnestness and conscientiousness of an artist. With us, the exertion that a game requires is only a matter of distraction, and lasts only as long as the game gives us pleasure; with him, it is a sacred duty. Never is a game of chess a mere pastime for him, but always a problem worthy of his steel, always a work of vocation, always as if an act by which he fulfills part of his mission.

To the fight with me he gave also outwardly such a strict appearance of solemnity, that it took away from it entirely the character of a gay occupation, and it had as far as I am concerned something oppressing, I would almost say strangling. The onlookers were forced to abstain even from the slightest whispering—something unusual which was to me all the stranger, as I am not aware of having been ever disturbed, during a game, by those surrounding me by any act of conversation (except barking of dogs and crying of children).

It goes without saying that he himself likewise during a game does not utter any sound other than Schach, to wit, really Schach, not Scheck, as the English players say. His figuring is, in general, not of remarkable or even tiring duration; he always takes as much time as such a tireless and experienced thinker requires depending on the position, but he never makes the impression of useless and tormented pressure or stress—an impression I occasionally had with Staunton. And in addition, he sits there with a face so lamb-pious as if he wanted to convey the impression that he could not do any harm to a child; but when he executes a move with an expression so really harmless and pretending tiredness, one can always presume that he is just preparing the greatest meanness.

Altogether, he is not only a great chess player but also a great diplomat and all maneuvers which he inaugurated in reference to me since his arrival in England, had no other purpose than to lure me to Paris and to burden me with the inconvenience of the trip. Likewise, I admired from the very beginning as a very tactful diplomatic maneuver that he took to his bed when I arrived in Paris, and I have never changed my mind about that. For that much I can assure you of: he did respect both of us, you as well as me, and not a trifle at that. If I say did, i.e., *Parfait defini; perfection praeteritum*, this of course applies only to myself, for my defeat can all the less have influenced his judgment about you as he knows, even in regard to myself, what the bell has tolled. Incidentally, I am not sorry about my trip to Paris, in fact I have already announced my return visit there during the Easter vacations and have fixed irrevocably time and hour of my arrival. Let us hope that then, when passing through Berlin, I shall have the pleasure, to meet you, dear Sir, in person, and then I could add quite a lot which can better be said than written, to my short communication about Morphy.

Very truly yours
Your obedient
A. Anderssen

In the above letter, written a year after the match, Anderssen is expressing a well-considered opinion of Morphy as chess master. It may be suggested that if Anderssen was strangling during the match, it was due to Morphy's moves and not to any imposed conditions of silence. Morphy never requested such conditions at La Régence—where the match would have been played but for Morphy's illness (instead of in his apartment). If such conditions prevailed, it was not at Morphy's request.

It is evident from what Lange says in his Morphy book that Morphy had promised Anderssen he would visit Germany that coming March—in fact, Morphy wrote to Fiske that "he [did] not intend to leave Europe without meeting Lange." But it is evident that Morphy had to forego the visit, due to his physical condition and pressure from his family for his quick return.

Regardless of Lange's hurt Germanic pride about Anderssen's being "made" to go to Paris (he thought Edge had schemed it), Lange was extremely enthusiastic about Morphy and more than once referred to him as "our hero."

Some thirty years later, Lange discussed Morphy and genius in the *Schachzeitung* of July 1891:

> Genius, as a capacity for opening new ways in any department, lies, with regard to our game, not in the advancement of theoretical innovations, whose intrinsic value is yet to be tested, and which are frequently surpassed and cancelled by subsequent innovations, nor is the discovery of new principles which have yet to stand the ordeal of time and practice. On the contrary, genius manifests itself more prominently by the successful originality with which it carries on the actual game. In this latter sense, it is the whole play of a master in its harmonious richness of characteristic combinations, which acts as pathfinder and model for the spirit of his time and of posterity.

> With Paul Morphy this capacity and art originated in the natural disposition of his brain, i.e., in the co-operation of all intellectual faculties given by nature, which find their main employment and creative activity particularly in application to chess where they reach their highest state of development.

> In this sense, Paul Morphy is and will remain the practical chess master par excellence. It is my unalterable opinion, and that of experienced chess-masters, that the American chess expert would have found his way against any kind of play of his time,

and if he was living today and in the full strength of his chess capacity, he would though, perhaps, momentarily embarrassed, after a short period of reflection discover the correct treatment of any style of play and be able to avail himself of it to his advantage in actual play, by reason of his extraordinary talent for chess. Those who advance the plea that he owed his fame mainly to the incorrectness of his adversaries, fail to consider that he had, in the first place, no other task than to overcome the style of play practiced by his actual opponents, and it would be clearly nonsensical to argue that, though he accomplished that task, he could not overcome an apparently more correct style of play. The mere reference to the so-called "modern school," so long as it is not better substantiated for this comparison, is little more than vain phraseology, and the conclusion that a style of play because modern, for this sole reason, be better than the old, passes criticism; for such a bare assertion cannot stand as a deduction before the tribunal of common sense.

Lange then quotes from Anderssen's letter to von der Lasa (the second paragraph given above), with which he expresses himself to be in complete agreement.

The Saturday previous to Morphy's match with Anderssen, Harrwitz had given his blindfold exhibition, in an attempt to emulate Morphy, but with the poor results mentioned earlier. As the *Era* of January 9, 1859, states, Morphy's immediate reaction was to declare that he would play twenty simultaneous blindfold games "against that number of as strong men as Paris can produce," after the conclusion of his match with Anderssen. This incredible proposal caused much concern among Morphy's friends, and he was finally persuaded not to attempt it. However, not until February 12, in the New York *Saturday Press*, of which Fiske was chess editor, was it indicated he might not do so:

> Our latest private letters from Mr. Morphy inform us that he has not yet authorized the publication that he intends to play twenty simultaneous blindfold games, and we hope that he will be dissuaded from the attempt to perform such a gigantic mental task.

Forty years later it was attempted by H. N. Pillsbury.

According to C. A. Gilberg, in his *Fifth American Chess Congress*, Morphy later wanted

to demonstrate how slightly he esteemed the task of conduct-
ing eight or ten games at the same time and without sight of the
boards. Mr. Morphy expressed his willingness, soon after his
return to New Orleans [1859], to undertake twenty games in
that manner [blindfold]. Prudent friends, however, dissuaded
him from an experiment which seemed to them to involve a
rash purpose to transgress the bounds of human capability.

Fiske had written to Professor Allen in January that Morphy was
"about to offer Harrwitz a match at Pawn and Move and will make the
same offer to any English player upon his return to London." Until the
Anderssen match, Morphy had exempted Harrwitz from his "odds-to-all"
rule from France, but now decided to silence the latter's pretensions. In
the presence of witnesses, Morphy authorized a fellow American, probably
James Mortimer, to propose to Harrwitz on his behalf a second match, on
the following terms: Harrwitz to receive the odds of Pawn and move; the
winner of the first five or seven games to be the victor, and the stake to be
five hundred francs, more or less, as Harrwitz might choose.

The challenge was duly presented to Harrwitz on January 3, but he
declined on the grounds that Morphy had treated him badly. However,
as the Era commented: "Considering the courtesy that Mr. Morphy had
extended to each and all of his antagonists since he visited Europe, this is
perhaps the most ludicrous excuse that could have been made for declining the challenge so boldly proposed."

Edge says that "Morphy felt so much desire to play this proposed
match, that he even offered to find stakes to back his antagonist, but all to
no purpose." As he is quoted in the New York Herald of January 30, 1859,
St. Amant said he believed Morphy could "give pawn and move to any living player" and had hoped to witness such a contest between Morphy and
Harrwitz. It was the general opinion that Harrwitz lacked the courage to
accept Morphy's challenge. When he received Harrwitz's refusal, Morphy
seemed to lose all interest in playing at La Régence, and to have taken a
positive aversion to chess.

Harrwitz now made an attempt to give La Régence players the same
odds as had Morphy, but without success. Morphy had given Budzinsky—
a very strong Polish player, probably as strong as Laroche—the odds of
Pawn and move, winning five games to Budzinsky's one. Harrwitz offered
him the same odds but the results were Harrwitz one, Budzinsky three.

In January 1859, the Chess Monthly carried the following announcement:

Mr. George Walker publicly states that in his opinion, Mr. Morphy can give any player in England the same odds [as those offered Harrwitz] and urges Mr. Morphy to issue a challenge to that effect upon his return to the shores of Albion.

On January 7, 1859, Dr. Johnston, the Paris correspondent of the New York *Times*, reported that

Mr. Morphy offers now to play Mr. Staunton, and give him a Pawn and a move; but, of course, no player of Mr. Staunton's caliber would accept such an offer. Mr. Morphy, however, is justified, after the course of Mr. Staunton, in making such an offer, and he says to his friends, that he is sure he can beat him with that advantage.

Porter's Spirit of the Times of January 15, 1859, also carried the news of Morphy's challenge: "To silence all cavil in regard to the English Champion [Staunton], Morphy now offers to give him pawn and move, and play him for any sum he pleases."

George Walker, in *Bell's Life in London* of July 17, 1859, may have expressed the ultimate vote of confidence in Morphy:

It is something for America to be able to say with truth, "we have Paul Morphy, a boy of twenty-two, who can give Pawn and Move to every other player in the world." And large as the world is, this, we, *Bell's Life in London*, honestly believe the BOY can do.

And so at the age of twenty-two, Morphy was internationally regarded as the strongest player in the world.

Edge, in his long dispatch of January 5, 1859, to the New York *Herald*, was the first to announce that "Paul Morphy had declared that he will play no more matches with anyone unless accepting Pawn and move from him." And perhaps he was not too presumptuous.

Undated daguerreotype of a young Paul Morphy.

Courtesy of The Historic New Orleans Collection, accession no. 1996.75.

Alonzo Morphy,
Paul's father (above);
Ernest Morphy, Paul's uncle
who introduced him to
chess (at right).

Alonzo Morphy image courtesy
of the Louisiana State Supreme
Court Law Library.

Paul Morphy (clockwise from top left): as he arrived in New York in 1857;
in New York, 1859; miniature by J. E. Saintin, 1859; and in New York, 1859.

The First American Chess Congress
held at New York City in November, 1857.

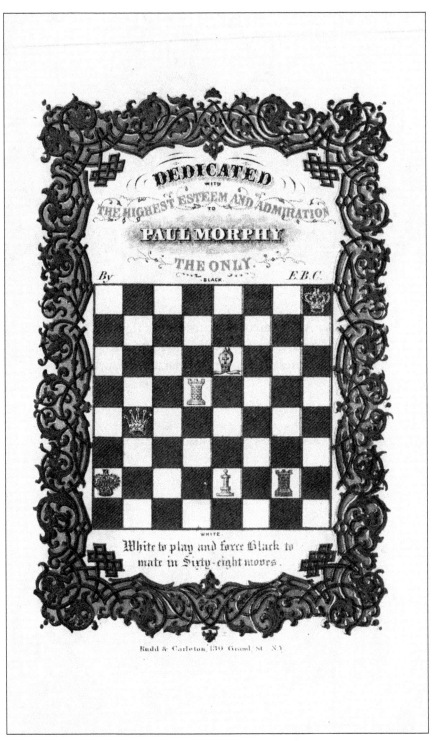

Frontispiece for the First American Chess Congress book, 1857.

Paul Morphy's American opponents: (left to right) G. Hammond; T, Loyd; C. D. Mead; D. S. Roberts; H. P. Montgomery; C. H. Stanley; F. Perrin; James Thompson; N. Marache; W. J. A. Fuller.

Paul Morphy's British opponents.

Paul Morphy photographed by Matthew Brady, 1859.

Paul Morphy in Paris, 1858: blindfold exhibition (above); and challenged by Adolf Anderssen (at right).

Paul Morphy and opponents:
Lewis Elkins in Philadelphia, 1859 (above);
and Johann Lowenthal in London, 1858 (below).

Paul Morphy's chessmen, "the Roman" (above), "the Barbarians" (below).

Watch presented to Paul Morphy, May 25, 1859 (above);
banquet given to honor Paul Morphy, November 21, 1859 (below).

Paul Morphy engraving by D. J. Pound, 1859
(above); with a women, undated (below).

Paul Morphy (clockwise from top left): in New York by Matthew Brady, 1859; in Paris, 1863; in New Orleans, 1870; and in Paris, 1867.

Tomb of Paul Morphy in St. Louis Cemetery #1, New Orleans, La.

CHAPTER 14

"The World Is His Fatherland"

Morphy's formal challenge to the chess players of the world, offering the odds of Pawn and move, was never taken up. Thereafter, however, in his casual games, he almost invariably offered Knight odds. With his friend Rivière, he made a single exception, continuing to play him even.

Morphy had promised a match with Augustus Mongredien, president of the London Chess Club, who, knowing Morphy would have no time for it in London on his way back to America, decided to come to Paris in late February to redeem the promise. The match of eight games was played at Mongredien's hotel, the Hotel du Louvre. It began on February 26 with only St. Amant and Rivière present. Mongredien had no illusions as to what the outcome would be, and the match ended on March 3, Morphy seven, Mongredien zero—the first game having ended in a draw. Apart from these, and three with Lowenthal, one with Boden, and some with Mongredien and Rivière in 1863, Morphy never thereafter played others without giving odds.

As was seen in Chapter 13, after his defeat of Anderssen, Morphy's acclaim seemed to cover all Europe. T. J. Werndly of Holland celebrated him in the January 1859 *Sissa* in a five-stanza poem ending:

> Weep not, O Europe
> Rejoice not, America!
> For genius like his,
> Both lands are too small.
> The World is his Fatherland!

Many such testaments to Paul Morphy have continued to be voiced by great masters down to the present day. Emanuel Lasker (in *Lasker's Chess Magazine* of January 1905) pronounced him

> the greatest chess player that ever lived. Every student of the game, who has delved into the stories of the past, realizes that no one ever was so far superior to the players of his time, or ever defeated his opponents with such ease, and no one ever offered Knight odds to the men who considered themselves his equal.

In *Pablo Morphy,* by V. F. Coria and L. Palau, Capablanca is quoted as saying

> Morphy's principal strength does not rest upon his power of combination but in his position play and his general style. . . . Beginning with La Bourdonnais to the present, and including Lasker, we find that the greatest stylist has been Morphy. Whence the reason, although it might not be the only one, why he is generally considered the greatest of all.

Dr. Max Euwe said, in *"64" Shakhmatny,* June 24, 1937: "Morphy is usually called 'the greatest chess genius of all time.' This formula, to be sure is somewhat broad, but just the same it remains in force even after a more attentive examination of the question."

What with Morphy's decisive victory over Anderssen, and his almost universal acclaim as the greatest chess player, past or present, interest in his games knew no bounds. Max Lange and Jean Dufresne were already preparing a collection of his games. Within about three months, the former issued a collection of 120 Morphy games. Lowenthal in London and Jean Prèti in Paris were pressing Morphy to help in the selection and annotation of 100 games. Edge wrote Fiske on January 6, 1859, that

> Morphy is seriously engaged at the present moment in annotating some 100 of his best games, played in America or Europe. Prèti edits for France and Lowenthal for England. The proposition came from themselves and they are forcing Morphy to work—which the gentle Paul does not like.

The Lowenthal (New York) and Prèti volumes came out much later in the year. The interest in Morphy and his games may be gauged by the fact that altogether some fourteen books and pamphlets on him were published by 1860; one of them (Lowenthal's *Morphy's Games of Chess* in the Bohn edition) was destined to be reprinted many times.

After the Mongredien match, Rivière induced Morphy to collaborate on an analysis of chess openings. However, they had hardly begun before Morphy received an urgent message, delivered by his brother-in-law, John Sybrandt, to return to New Orleans. And four years were to elapse before Morphy was able to resume work with Rivière on the analysis.

As the end of March approached, any thought Morphy may have had of visiting Germany was abandoned, and with the arrival of Sybrandt, Morphy's departure from Paris was hastened. The amateurs of Paris, headed by St. Amant, Lequesne, Rivière, Prèti, Delannoy, Journoud, and others, anticipating Morphy's departure, had planned a chess festival in his honor. The original plan was to hold a preliminary tournament of one hundred amateurs, arranged in five categories according to strength. Then, on the day of the banquet, Morphy was to play the winner of each category, giving to the first the odds of Pawn and move; to the second, Pawn and two moves; to the third, a Knight; to the fourth, a Castle; and to the fifth, a Castle and first move. The public banquet was to follow this simultaneous exhibition.

However, Sybrandt's arrival left no time for all these plans, for Morphy decided he could not wait for the final result of the preliminary tournament. A banquet was therefore hastily arranged in his honor at Pestel's famous restaurant. St. Amant gave an account in *Le Sport* (April 6, 1859), of the Parisians' last evening with Morphy—April 4, 1859:

> After six months sojourn in Paris, Mr. Paul Morphy has just left us. He is already far off. He sails from England for the United States, where the homage and congratulations of his fellow-citizens await him, who long to celebrate his triumphs in Europe, and the share which the superiority of his genius for Chess adds to the glory of the young Republic.
>
> It had been hoped that he could be kept a few days longer, but the hour of his departure rudely sounded, and that before the termination of the Tournament which had been organized at la Régence for the sole purpose of offering him a festival; a brilliant, yet, at the same time, weak manifestation of the pleasure which had been derived from his visit, and homage of the admiration excited by his fine talent in the art illustrated by Philidor and Labourdonnais, who preceded him in having attained, in the chivalrous lists of the Chess-board, the perfection of skill and reputation.
>
> On the first news of his precipitate departure, the Chess players put themselves in motion and promptly organized a banquet, which came off day before yesterday (Monday), in the saloons of the Pestel-restaurant. At six o'clock more than forty amateurs of Chess, with M. de St. Amant as their chairman, crowded around a board splendidly provided. Here are the names of some of the guests:—Messrs. Morphy and his brother-in-law, Lequesne, Arnous de Riviere, Journoud, Sasias, Delannoy, Panseron (Professor at the Conservatory of Music, who was acquainted with Richér, brother-in-law of Philidor), Commandant Cheret, Dubail, Van der Huys, Pfeiffer, Bodin, Gillet, Chausson, Pasquier, Moret, Mariage, father and son,

Budzinsky, Gautier, Lamouroux, Pagonkine, &c., &c.

At the dessert, the part was assigned to Mr. Delannoy to propose the health of Mr. Paul Morphy. In a few words, sparkling
and elegantly couched, the orator dwelt upon the various in-
cidents connected with the Sojourn in Paris of the illustrious
American, who has won both the affection and the admiration
of all those who have had the opportunity of knowing him.

With a distinct enunciation, betraying no foreign accent, Mr.
Morphy thanked, with great felicity of expressions, the honorable company for all the evidences of sympathy he was receiving from them, and which were but the crowning of all the kind
attentions with which he had been overwhelmed in the capital
of the civilized world, from which one ever tears oneself away
with regret, and never without the hope of returning, especially
after having been so cordially welcomed. He asked, in concluding, permission to propose a toast: "To M. Saint Amant—so
long devoted to the Chess cause, and who has always so well
served it with the triple talent of his brilliant play, his spoken
and his written word."

M. Saint Amant rose to return thanks. He praised and much
applauded those who, more fortunate than he (prevented by
want of time and leisure), have dared to confront the invincible
American, whose incontestable superiority he disputes still less
than do the vanquished themselves. There had been unanimity
on this point throughout the French School, and not one dis-
senting voice in the nation has mingled with the unison which
now proclaims Morphy the first Chess player in the whole
world. The French School has shown emulation without jeal-
ousy, without regrets, well and justly convinced that one can
fall before an athlete of such superiority without diminution
of reputation and still less of talent, for by contact with light
we are ever illumined by some ray. It is thus that the French
School, which can boast of many youthful *inheritors of Chess
genius*—lately our *hope* but now our *glory*—has grown a step
higher since the presence in its midst of the chief of the great
school.

In conclusion, the Chairman approaching the bust of Morphy,
borne in on a pedestal, said:

"To all the agreeable moments spent with Mr. Morphy are
about to succeed, alas! darkness and silence. This festival,
gentlemen, so full of geniality and fraternity, is unfortunately
a farewell festival. Chequered as are all worldly goods, it is

doomed to have its dark side. To-morrow we shall part with our guest of to-day, and the spirit of our present meeting will only commence with us through the memory of the heart and intellect, as it has just been so happily expressed to you. However, these fleeting and perishable memories failing us, something more durable will remain before our eyes in this striking image of Morphy, sculptured in marble by one of us, in whom the art of playing chess well is the least merit. Honor to the bust of the eminent Chess player, which we owe to the chisel of one of our own brothers in Chess, M. Lequesne, whom it only suffices to name. His young and illustrious model would shrink with his wonted modesty from this crown of immortelles and laurel, which, in your name, I ought properly to place on the seat of so lofty an intellect; but he cannot prevent us, at least, adorning with it the bust which has been legitimately raised to him, and which will dwell among us. Laurels which have never caused a tear to be shed, and which are destined to recall to us the great Chess school, and the illustrious French predecessors whose light and inspiration have been well caught by Paul Morphy! Let us solemnly record his promises not to forget us, and to visit us soon again. May he realize these consolatory words before these very palms shall have had time to wither and dry up.

"Morphy! our friend, our master, you are immortal among us. In truth, to have won, so young, the highest renown of both hemispheres, and to have one's image reproduced by Lequesne, makes immortality doubly sure."

Prolonged applause accompanied the crowning of the bust of Morphy, now deposited in the Chess sanctuary of La Régence.

Different toasts were then proposed by Messrs. Lequesne, Dubail, Pogonkine, to the illustrious dead! to the skillful sculptor! to the memory of Philidor and Labourdonnais; to the absent (among whom most regretted were Messrs. Doazan, Mery, Hermann and Lecrivain), and to our stranger guests. To this last toast replies were made by representatives of Germany and Russia.

The frankest cordiality prevailed throughout this banquet, whence they repaired to the Café de la Régence, there to keep up the genial current. There Mr. Morphy gave new proofs of the facility and disinterested kindness with which he plays against all those who manifest the desire to play with him, to whatever *category* these adversaries may belong.

Saint Amant.

They had wished to crown him—for as Max Lange said in his Morphy book, "Anderssen was formally crowned by the grateful Prussians" upon his return to Germany in 1851—but Morphy would not consent.

It is likely that August Ehrmann, to whom he offered Pawn and two moves on March 31, was the last with whom Morphy contested before leaving Paris.

But time was pressing, and Morphy was ready to leave Paris. However, Edge—as companion, secretary, and valet—was no longer with him. In fact, soon after the Anderssen match, differences developed between them, Edge merely explaining to Fiske as of February 10, 1859, writing from London:

> You will perceive that I have quitted Paris, leaving Paul Morphy alone. The fact is—since his match with Anderssen he has quite forsaken chess and feeling that there was no longer any chance of his playing anyone, I knew I was of no further utility.

Of course, Edge now had much more time to himself. But it would appear that there were other reasons for Edge's leaving Morphy of which the former never spoke. Nowhere in Edge's letters to Fiske or elsewhere is there any satisfactory explanation for Morphy's coolness toward Edge, who had labored so diligently and faithfully for him. In the letter to Fiske of February 10 mentioned above, Edge says that toward the end of January he had begun work on a book about Morphy. Without doubt he wanted primarily to give the world the story of Morphy's trials and triumphs in Europe, such that he knew no one else could furnish.

But Morphy disliked publicity of any sort, especially when it dealt with his chess activity. It is probable that Morphy had seen some of Edge's manuscript and, disliking its treatment of the Staunton affair, had refused to sanction its appearance in book form. And Morphy also apparently objected to Edge's treatment of other matters. When the book was published, an announcement in the July 1859 issue of the *Chess Monthly* stated: "Mr. Morphy expressly disclaims any connection with it [the Edge book] in any way or manner. There are many passages which might well have been omitted; there are many more which might well have been rewritten."

But Edge was determined that the story of Staunton's and Harrwitz's disgraceful conduct should be told, as well as the story of Morphy's chivalry and moments of triumph. By February, when Edge wrote Fiske, the coolness between the former and Morphy had developed into a complete break, and Morphy was unforgiving. A letter to Fiske from W. H. Kent of

Boston dated May 21, 1859, brings out how complete was the break:

> From Dr. Richardson I learned that the publication of Edge's
> book was against Morphy's desire and had not his sanction. I
> also learned why Edge was discharged. I have consequently
> done all I could to stop the sale of the book here. To tell the
> truth, I am disgusted with it myself. No gentleman would have
> written it. I think it places Morphy in a *false position* before the
> public.

The book hardly merits such utter condemnation, and Kent was probably unduly influenced by Morphy's sensitivity in the matter. It is true that
Edge did perhaps take some liberties; for instance, Morphy might well
have taken exception to the following:

> He [Morphy] frightened his adversaries, not by his strength,
> but by his personal appearance. This boy of twenty-one, five
> feet four inches in height, of slim figure, and face like a young
> girl in her teens, positively appalled the chess warriors of the
> old world—Narcissus defying the Titans.

The naming of Narcissus was unfortunate. Nevertheless the book is
for us a source of much information about Morphy and his stay in Europe,
and of course means much more to us today than it could possibly have
meant to those of Morphy's time; and obviously others would not be as
disturbed by its style as was Morphy. Edge finished the book in London,
and it appeared in two editions about three months apart but with some
significant differences between the two. It seems appropriate at this time
to disclose the reasons for the two editions and their differences.

Believing in February that Morphy's chess activities in Europe were
over, Edge ended the first edition of his book with a listing of Morphy's
games (except those at large odds) and a valediction. He called the book
The Exploits and Triumphs in Europe of Paul Morphy, stating that "Paul
Morphy's Late Secretary" was its author, and sent the manuscript to D.
Appleton & Company of New York. Appleton announced publication
three months later in May 1859. Maurian reviewed it favorably in the New
Orleans *Sunday Delta*, June 5, 1859.

However, Morphy did play a few more games in Paris, notably a match
with Mongredien, about which Edge knew, for it had been agreed to
months before. Although Edge was not present during the match, he was
able to include the match results in his first edition, since they were well
publicized and took place soon after he left Paris.

But now Morphy was loath to leave Paris and lingered on until the arrival of Sybrandt, who hastened his departure. He then planned to leave England for America shortly after his arrival there. In fact, he engaged passage, but due to English plans for banquets and blindfold exhibitions, he felt obliged to defer his sailing until April 30, three weeks after his arrival.

Now, with Morphy's renewed activity in exhibitions, etc., Edge had the urge to complete his tale of Morphy in Europe, and wrote an additional chapter describing Morphy's second visit to England, convinced that an English edition that would include Morphy's exciting last weeks would be of great interest. Using exactly the same text he had sent to Appleton, he added a new chapter, quoted freely from Shakespeare for chapter headings, made some minor changes, and submitted the whole to publisher William Lay of London with the title, *Paul Morphy the Chess Champion*, by "An Englishman," without mentioning the earlier American edition that had previously been published.

This London edition was first mentioned by the London *Illustrated News of the World* on July 2, 1859: "'Paul Morphy in Europe' will very shortly make its appearance, being already in the hands of the publisher, Mr. W. Lay, King William-street, Strand." Later that month several London papers, among them *Bell's Life in London* and the *Era*, announced its publication with short reviews in their chess columns. It was also reviewed at length in *The Economist, The Critic, The Literary Gazette*, and elsewhere.

And so we have two editions, both widely accepted and well illustrated with excellent likenesses of English and other great chess players, a frontispiece of Morphy, and an excellent history of English chess clubs.

Both editions have been out of print for over a hundred years, but now *The Exploits and Triumphs in Europe of Paul Morphy*, by Frederick Milne Edge, is available in reprint by Dover Publications of New York, with a new Introduction by this author.*

Now the time had come, and Morphy, accompanied by Sybrandt and Rivière, left Paris for London on April 6, arriving there the next day. But Morphy did not at once announce his arrival.

---

* EDITOR'S NOTE: The Dover edition of Edge's work is still available. The work is also now available in a free online format. See Frederick Milne Edge, *The Exploits and Triumphs in Europe of Paul Morphy* (New York: Dover Publications, 1973), or search Google Books, http://books.google.com/ for *The Exploits and Triumphs in Europe of Paul Morphy*.

CHAPTER 15

Farewell to England

Although Morphy, Sybrandt, and Rivière had arrived in London on April 7, registering at the British Hotel, Morphy's arrival was not formally announced until April 10, presumably because he wished for some days of quiet.

When his presence in London became known, London threw open its doors to him. The St. George's Chess Club and other clubs had planned banquets and ovations for him and perhaps hoped for some further demonstrations of his chess powers. Morphy had secured passage on the *Africa*, which was to leave Liverpool April 16, but two weeks more were to elapse before England would let him go. As will be seen by the following letter, published in the London *Era* of January 9, 1859, plans to receive him had begun on the first of the year:

> Bath, January 1, 1859
>
> To the Editor of the Era,—
>
> Sir,—As I understand that Mr. Morphy contemplates another visit to England before his return to America, will you permit me, through your columns, respectfully to suggest to the Chess community of this country the propriety of offering him a public entertainment, together with some adequate testimonial which may serve to mark our sense of his transcendent ability as a Chess player; and also our appreciation of him as a chivalrous, high-spirited, and honorable man—a character which I hope Englishmen know how to value far more than even any amount of skill at Chess.
>
> Should this proposal take any definite shape, I shall be happy to be allowed to contribute £5 towards its accomplishment.
>
> I am, Sir, your obedient servant
> [Capt.] H. A. Kennedy

It was a hectic week ahead for Morphy, beginning with an entertainment on Monday evening, April 11, given by Mongredien, president of the London Club. On Tuesday afternoon he visited the club and was engaged in a game with Mr. Medley at the odds of Pawn and move. In the evening, he was the guest of Lowenthal at his new club, the St. James'. Here they contested two games, each scoring one.

On Wednesday, April 13, after visiting Lowenthal at his office at the *Era*, the two of them went to the London Chess Club. The Club had asked Morphy if he would give an eight-game blindfold exhibition, to which he had agreed. Play began at 5 p.m., against eight strong players, given as follows in board order: George Walker, F. L. Slous, F. E. Greenaway, F. G. Janssens, A. Mongredien, G. W. Medley, G. Maude, and J. P. Jones. There are indications that Morphy was perhaps tired or lacked enthusiasm for the occasion, although he played rapidly. The exhibition was adjourned at 1 a.m., due to the lateness of the hour, with only three games settled. Morphy won two, while he drew a third with George Walker by the latter's perpetual check. It is probable that Morphy would have won others had play continued.

Among those present as visitors were Lord Arthur Hay, Marmaduke Wyvill, M. P., Barnes, Boden, Rivière, and Lowenthal. The last had been asked to serve as official recorder of the games.

The following day, April 14, Morphy was the guest of honor of the London Chess Club at a banquet at the Ship Hotel, Greenwich. Over forty members with their friends were present. As the *Era* of April 17, 1859, states, Mongredien called attention to the "King of Chess," lauded his ability and courteous demeanor, and concluded by proposing the "Health of the Champion of the Chess World." Morphy returned the compliment by proposing the "Health of the President."

Later, Morphy proposed "The Health of Mr. George Walker," paying him tribute as author and player, and expressing the great pleasure it had afforded him to make his acquaintance. Walker, in responding, expressed his gratification at being mentioned in terms so flattering by a master so distinguished.

On Saturday evening, Morphy again visited Lowenthal at the St. James' Club and had another game with him, which ended in a draw. Lowenthal was now working on a collection of Morphy's games, as has been previously mentioned, and they were probably considering the games to be included. The game score between them since Morphy's return from Paris was now even, quite possibly due to Morphy's having made no determined effort to win against his editor.

Morphy might now have had time for three days of relaxation. However, he had agreed to conduct an eight-game blindfold exhibition on April 20 for the prestigious St. George's Club. This was to be followed by a banquet in his honor. Lowenthal gave the following account in the London *Era* (April 24, 1859) of the exhibition and gala affair at the Wellington Saloon, Picadilly:

ST. GEORGE'S CHESS CLUB
Grand demonstration in Honor of Mr. Morphy

From the moment when it first became known that Mr. Paul Morphy would revisit England *en passant* from the Continent of Europe to that of America, the Chess players of the old country determined to pay a final and worthy tribute of respect to the esteemed and illustrious Champion of the New World. From all parts of the country letters were addressed to London, urging that suitable arrangements should be made for the demonstration; and it is needless to add that the votaries of Caïssa who dwell in the British metropolis—both east and west of the antique boundary of Temple bar—were not less anxious to award the homage due to their renowned friend.

If indeed, Mr. Morphy could have spent a few more weeks in Great Britain, he would have received a series of ovations hardly less brilliant and enthusiastic than that we are about to speak of. But the time our distinguished visitor had already spent on this side of the Atlantic in the severer duties of his art, deprived very many of his admirers of the opportunity of exhibiting their regard for him in the way most congenial to the modern Anglo-Saxon mind. Two public demonstrations were all that he could attend, and the two clubs of the metropolis, each in turn have had the honor of Mr. Morphy's presence at a banquet. Last week we reported the dinner at Greenwich, given to him by the London Chess Club; we now report the demonstration made by the St. George's at the Wellington Saloon, Picadilly, on Tuesday last.

The time was not altogether favorable to the success of a West-end *fete*, but it will be seen that the zeal and enterprise of the promoters of this entertainment were amply compensated by the results.

At two o'clock p.m., the hour appointed for the meeting, the splendid saloon was filled by a body of aristocratic guests. Among the noblemen and gentlemen present were Lord Cremorne, Lord Arthur Hay, Lord Granville, H. Staunton, W. Lewis, S. Boden, G. Medley, A. de Riviere, J. Lowenthal, Esqs., and a host of other gentlemen well known in the chess world. It is, however, but strictly correct to admit that politics had to some extent deprived the assembly of a few of the most notable *habitués* of the clubs, and we dare say, if the truth were told, that not a few members of the House of Commons, and other ardent and noble politicians who were absent, would have been well pleased to have been present, if that had been possible.

Punctually at two o'clock Mr. Morphy commenced his extraordinary feat, eight noblemen and gentlemen being pitted against him in the following order:—

Board No. 1 Lord Cremorne
"   No. 2 Capt. Kennedy
"   No. 3 H. G. Cattley, Esq.
"   No. 4 Lord Arthur Hay
"   No. 5 T. H. Worrall, Esq.
"   No. 6 J. Cunningham, Esq.
"   No. 7 G. Thrupp, Esq.
"   No. 8 T. W. Barnes, Esq.

As is usual in these cases, Mr. Morphy took the first move in every game, M. de Riviere acting as secretary for the occasion, and notifying to the young champion the moves of his opponents. As the play progressed and Mr. Morphy's precision and rapidity became more marvelous, the most anxious interest was expressed in the countenance of every looker-on, and although it is unnecessary to observe that at the very outset the master mind was felt to be there, it was not until a series of moves had been made on each side that Mr. Morphy's preeminent genius was exhibited. His foresight in tracing the designs of his antagonists, his imagination in devising stratagems, and his dexterity in forming combinations only became the more apparent as the demand for their exercise increased, and it was evidently no easy task for the observers to confine their enthusiasm within the limit of etiquette. If such a demonstrative tone had been permitted the lookers-on would probably have broken the continuity of the play by frequent applause. In several of the games he speedily acquired superior positions; in the remainder he maintained his ground throughout. Our space is not adequate to the demands of criticism. We might fill columns with a detailed narrative of the feats performed on this occasion. We can but briefly observe that the play did not consume more than five hours, and when Lord Arthur Hay, the last remaining combatant, proposed a draw which was accepted by Mr. Morphy, there was no longer a motive for concealing the feelings of the assembly. A loud and long protracted round of applause greeted the victor, who accepted this ovation with a degree of modesty that gave him a still higher place in the esteem of his friends. Mr. Morphy, it may also be stated, did not betray any symptoms of fatigue.

We cannot pass from this meeting to a formal report of the speeches delivered at the dinner in the evening without mentioning one significant feature of the demonstration. It will be a source of infinite pleasure to our readers, as it was to those who were happy enough to take part in these festivities, that so many members and representatives of the two leading clubs united in paying a farewell compliment to the American gentleman.

THE DINNER

About sixty noblemen and gentlemen sat down in the splendid dining-room of the building. The banquet was of the most *recherché* description; the viands and wines provided by the establishment were of the choicest kind; and the *chef* of the *cuisine* contributed in no small degree, by a happy selection of names for his dishes in honouring the guest of the evening.

In the absence of the Earl of Eglintoun, the President of the club, Lord Cremorne occupied the chair, being supported on the right by P. Morphy, Esq., and on the left by M. A. de Riviere, the adjoining seats being occupied by the veteran player, W. Lewis, Mr. Medley, the Hon. Sec. of the London Club; Mr. Sybrandt (Mr. Morphy's brother-in-law); Herr Lowenthal, and others. T. Worrall, Esq., now so well known in England as the Mexican Amateur worthily filled the vice-chair; and Lord Arthur Hay and Mr. Hampton, the Hon. Sec. of the St. George's, gave him, on his right and left, the usual support.

After full justice had been done to the bounties of the table, His Lordship proposed the usual loyal toasts, and next proceeded to the toast of the evening, observing that it was never agreeable to say in a gentleman's presence all the flattering things that he could couple with the name of Paul Morphy, that every gentleman present was aware of his skill as a chess player. All had witnessed his modesty, unelated by repeated triumphs, the courtesy that characterized his communion with each and all of his fellow-players; and it was sufficient to give his name merely to ensure for it that hearty reception of which it was so highly deserving.

The proposal of the noble Chairman having been accepted with a burst of cheering such as we have seldom heard given, the young Champion arose, and made the following eloquent response:—

I hardly know, my lord and gentlemen, in what terms to acknowledge the high compliment of which I this day find myself the unworthy object. There are occasions when a language must be spoken, of far more difficult utterance than the ordinary speech obtains among men—moments when the full heart can find no expressions commensurate with the intensity of its feelings—when every word seems cold—when language itself becomes powerless. Of such, I feel, is the present occasion. When I look before and around, and see gathered in my honor so select an assembly of Chess-loving gentlemen, I feel that mere words could never adequately express my deep sense of indebtedness. The only return I can make is to tender to each and every gentleman here present my warm, and I would beg you to believe, my heartfelt acknowledgments. To those gentlemen with whom I have had the honor to contest a few friendly battles over the chequered board, I would also express my profound obligation. Their kindness—their unvarying courtesy—their demeanor, always marked by the most polite attentions—I shall not easily forget. Let me hope that they who, for a few brief hours, were foes in the mimic strife, have become warm personal friends. To have conquered their esteem is my proudest boast. And now, gentlemen, after a sojourn of nearly twelve months in the Old I must again seek my far home in the New World. Gladly would I here remain in company so congenial, but the call of duty must be obeyed. To say that I regret the few months spent in Europe would be saying but little. What may be reserved for me in the future I will not venture to divine, but this I do feel that one of the most delightful episodes of my life is fast vanishing into the past. Come what may—be pleasure or pain my lot hereafter—the remembrance of the golden days passed in your midst will ever be dearly treasured here. Should fortune smile on my future career I shall dwell with delight on the auspicious morn that heralded the bright and happy day; and should adversity—as soon it may—lower around my pathway of life, I shall derive from the remembrance of other and better days a consolation of which nothing shall deprive me.

> Let Fate do her worst; there are relics of joy,
> Bright dreams of the past, that she cannot destroy;
> That come in the night-time of sorrow and care,
> And bring back the features that joy used to wear.

> Long, long be my heart with such memories fill'd!

Like the vase, in which roses have once been distill'd—
You may break, you may shatter the vase if you will,
But the scent of the roses will hang round it still.
                                              [Thomas Moore]

How prophetic were those last words: "and should adversity—as soon it may be—lower around my pathway of life."

It would seem that Morphy had almost no time with Lowenthal on the game collection the latter was compiling. He probably just gave him the same selection that he had chosen with Prèti of Paris. For in the short time before April 20 at Wellington and his free(?) days thereafter, Morphy is known to have played a match of nine games with T. H. Worrall at Knight odds, winning seven and losing two; two games with Mrs. Worrall at Queen's Rook; six games with G. Maude, two at odds of Pawn and two moves, and four at Knight odds; and two games with E. Pindar at Knight odds. Few of these games were ever reported and none were at the time. Morphy also played two more games with Lowenthal, as later disclosed by Jean Dufresne in 1862 in his *Der Schachfreund*.

There now remained one more extraordinary performance expected of Morphy, as was announced by the *Era* of April 24:

> St. James' Chess Club—The Champion, Mr. Morphy, with his wonted kindness, has consented at Mr. Lowenthal's request, to visit this Club on Tuesday evening next, April 26th, and then play four games simultaneously against the following excellent players:—Messrs. Barnes, Boden, De Riviere, and Lowenthal. A most crowded attendance is anticipated.

At the last moment, H. E. Bird asked to be included and so Morphy played all five masters simultaneously. The following Saturday, the *Illustrated News of the World* carried a description of the event:

GREAT MEETING
AT THE ST. JAMES' CHESS CLUB.

A highly interesting assembly met in the splendid saloon of St. James's Hall, on Tuesday evening last [April 26], when Mr. Morphy encountered five of the best players in the metropolis. Among the persons of distinction and great talent present, were Lord Cremorne, W. F. Baring, Esq., T. H. Worrall, Esq. (the well-known Mexican amateur), T. Hampton, Esq. (the honorary secretary of the St. George's Club), F. Healy, Esq., J. G. Campbell, Esq., R. B. Wormald, Esq., R. B. Brien, Esq. (late of Oxford), W. Harris, Esq., of the Richmond Club; H. Foster,

Esq., President of the Cambridge Club; and many others of almost equal reputation. There were, indeed, present players of all shades and grades, and of all parties in this assembly. St. George's and the London Clubs were strongly represented; and the *habitués* of the Cigar Divan, the Philidorian Rooms, and Purssell's, mustered numerously. It is also to be remarked that several of the London *Daily Press* sent members of their reporting staff.

The arrangements of the room were excellent. A portion of the saloon was railed off, and the combatants were thus protected from the pressure of the eager spectators, while, at the same time, peculiar facilities were in this way given for a clear observation by all persons. The first table was occupied by M. de Riviere; the second, by Mr. Boden; the third, by Mr. Barnes; the fourth, by Mr. Bird; and the fifth, by Mr. Lowenthal. Mr. Morphy played all these gentlemen simultaneously, walking from board to board, and making his replies with extraordinary rapidity and decision. Although, we believe, that this is the first performance of the kind by Mr. Morphy, it is a remarkable fact that he lost but one game. Two other games were won by him and two were drawn.

It was afterwards remarked that "Speaking generally, his style of play seems to be rapid and impetuous, and his *coup d'oeil* so perfect that he can master at one glance all the exigencies of the board. More than once in the course of the play his opponents had to call for time, which he conceded with the most good-humored courtesy, chatting in the interim with whoever chanced to stand near him."

Some sixty years later, a casual announcement indicated that Morphy may have received attention from England's royalty during this last visit to London, although there was no inkling of it then or for years thereafter. It was well known at the time that Queen Victoria was fond of chess and played it with Prince Albert, the Queen of the Belgians, and others. The *Hereford Times* of January 1889 reported "that the greatest solace the Empress Victoria has in her widowhood is Chess—a game she frequently played with the Crown Prince when they found themselves with a leisure hour. The Empress generally travels with a Chess board and men." According to Lord Broughton, in his *Recollections of a Long Life,* Queen Victoria knew something of chess before meeting her prince, for Lord Broughton was one of her early chess advisors. In any case, the New York *Sun* of December 9, 1888, carried the following news item:

Queen Victoria a good chess player.

Two Empresses, Victoria, also Queen of England, and the other, her daughter, the wife of the late Emperor Frederick, are at
Windsor together, and spend a great deal of their time playing
chess. Queen Victoria, who was a very celebrated player in the
old days and used easily to beat her husband, the Prince Con-
sort[,] is no match for her daughter, the German Empress who
has made the game a study, and finds in it the only consolation
for her loneliness.

Twenty years later we find in the *American Chess Bulletin* of November 1918 another interesting reference to Queen Victoria and a sheepskin
chessboard. It seems that some years after Paul Morphy's death, Eugene
Morphy came into possession of relics he had owned:

Eugene Morphy, a first cousin of the immortal Paul Morphy,
who greatly resembles the portrait of his illustrious relative, has
many interesting anecdotes to tell of the incomparable master.

Among the numerous and splendid trophies left by the master
was a simple sheepskin, upon which was drawn a chessboard;
no gold lettering, no scroll work, no ornamentation of any kind,
but in the lower right-hand corner the signature of Queen Victoria. It is Mr. Morphy's intention to present this relic to the
British Museum.

Paul Morphy's presence in London in April 1859 could not have escaped the attention of Queen Victoria. It seems likely that either he had
an audience with her, at which time she presented him with the sheepskin,
or that she sent it to him in recognition of his extraordinary chess fame. It
is not known what became of the sheepskin. The British Museum has no
record of having acquired it.

At the time of Morphy's death, it was reported on July 11, 1884, in the
New Orleans *Times-Democrat*, of which Maurian was chess editor, that,
"In a game with the Queen of England he gallantly permitted Her Majesty to win, but with Napoleon III he was less gallant." Nothing further is
known of Morphy's playing with either.

At last, Morphy left London, after some twenty full days of banquets,
exhibitions, and chess playing, which he undertook to gratify his friends
and the curiosity of his admirers. Much of this was probably very wearing
on him.

Samuel S. Boden, in the London *Field* of April 20, 1859, expressed

English esteem for Morphy:

> Often the longest visits seem all too short, and envious Time appears to delight in hurrying on an unwished for parting. As we write, Paul Morphy is departing from amongst us, to set sail, in a few hours, for his native shores. May favoring waves and winds attend the gifted gallant youth! Most heartily do we wish him a prosperous voyage, an enthusiastic greeting among his countrymen, and a joyous reunion with his family.
>
> Truly, transatlantic brethren, you have conquered us at Chess; but let us not be surpassed in candor. We have not a Paul Morphy amongst us, but we acknowledge and admire every whit of his unrivaled powers in our favorite royal game. Your Champion carries with him the best wishes of every English chess-player and friend, and right glad shall we be, next year, or as soon as he pleases, to welcome Morphy in our cities and homes again.

Morphy had planned to leave Liverpool on the *Niagara*, but it was reported in the *Lynn News* of May 11, 1859, that he "had been seized upon forcibly by the Liverpool Chess Club, and compelled to remain their guest" until April 30, at which time he boarded the *Persia*, bound for New York, destined never to return to England.

CHAPTER 16

Testimonials and the Queen's Knight

The *Persia* arrived in New York on the morning of May 11, 1859, and Morphy, accompanied by John Sybrandt, was greeted at the pier by Daniel W. Fiske and others, who escorted him to the St. Nicholas Hotel, where quarters had been prepared for him.

Waiting there to welcome him back to America were Colonel C. D. Mead, president of the New York Chess Club; Frederick Perrin, president of the Brooklyn Chess Club; W. J. A. Fuller; J. Lorimer Graham, Jr.; and many other distinguished friends and admirers.

In the evening Morphy and a small party of friends dined at the Metropolitan Hotel, after which they adjourned to the elegant rooms of the New York Chess Club at New York University, into which the club had moved on the first of May. A large audience had gathered in anticipation of his presence there, and of course he was expected to perform.

Once again, as in 1857, Frederick Perrin was the first to engage him, but now at Knight odds. Out of four games played that night, Morphy won three. Still, Perrin, one of the best New York players, did not believe that any player could give him Knight odds, and he challenged Morphy to a match, the victor to be the first to win five games.

The following day, Morphy, in company with Sybrandt, Lichtenhein, Graham, and Dodge, visited the Morphy Chess Rooms, a recently opened chess divan on Broadway at Fourth Street. Later, Dr. Richardson, president of the Boston Chess Club, extended to him on behalf of that club an invitation to a public dinner planned for him, which invitation Morphy accepted. Two days earlier, Boston had received word that Morphy would be on the *Niagara*, landing there, instead of in New York. A delegation had been sent to meet him at Halifax and accompany him from there to Boston. But Morphy, on arrival at Liverpool, succumbed to the solicitations of the Liverpool Chess Club, it was reported, possibly in error, and left on the *Persia* a few days later.

The evening of May 12, he again visited the New York Chess Club and took up Perrin's challenge for a match at Knight odds. Morphy won the first game of the match. Then, as the New York *Daily News* of May 13, 1859, reported, "at the urgent solicitation of his friends there, he agreed to play no more blindfold games." Nevertheless, six months later at Philadelphia, he was persuaded to play four such games.

At the New York Club, the following notice was posted:

> A member of the New York Chess Club desirous of testing the
> actual strength of the New York players, offers a prize of $100
> to any person connected with the Club, who shall win a major-
> ity of games in a match with Mr. Paul Morphy, at the odds of a
> pawn and move, or of the exchange. The match shall consist of
> not less than five games. Any one wishing to compete for the
> prize will please apply to the Secretary.

No one applied to the secretary regarding the above notice. However,
Morphy offered Knight odds to the club's principal players and won all
matches at those greater odds. Although he engaged in much chess activity
in deference to this friends and admirers, Morphy was somewhat fatigued
from his voyage. Yet he continued to receive a stream of callers at his hotel, and it was reported that "photographers and autograph hunters are not
among the least assiduous and persistent of Mr. Morphy's visitors." He also
received many telegraphic messages from all parts of the Union, requesting information concerning the route he would take on his return to New
Orleans.

It was at first expected, as reported in the following extract from an
article in the New York *Times* of May 13, 1859, that Morphy's stay in the
city might "be prolonged to three or four weeks," for plans had been in the
making for some months for a suitable presentation of testimonials.

> The completed testimonial of the New-York Chess Club will
> be made on or about the 20th inst., after which Mr. Morphy
> visits Boston, where a public dinner has been tendered him by
> several distinguished gentlemen. His headquarters will be in
> this City until his departure for New Orleans. The testimonial
> is nearly complete; the chessmen have been ready for several
> weeks, and have probably never been equaled for costly ele-
> gance and perfection of workmanship. They are composed of
> gold and silver and precious stones. The board will be finished
> by Saturday, and has exhausted the resources of art and skill in
> its production. The splendid American watch, which forms a
> part of the testimonial, will be ready during the present week,
> and will form an unique and specially attractive element in the
> presentation.

On Saturday evening, May 14, Morphy visited the Union Chess Club and won two games each from Messrs. Isidor and Bennecke at Knight odds. Earlier in the day he had played Dr. James W. Stone of Boston at the St. Nicholas Hotel, winning all five games at the same odds.

The following day, Sunday, he visited Hoboken and dined with General Cook and friends. It seemed that every day brought new activities, and Morphy was unable to shake off the fatigue from his voyage. The presentation of testimonials therefore was deferred some days. On Monday evening, May 16, he continued his match with Mr. Perrin, winning the first game, a Sicilian, in three and one half hours; the second game of the evening ended in a draw. That same day, the New York *Courier des États-Unis* mentioned in an article on Morphy that J. E. Saintin was painting a miniature of him. The miniature was shown at the Thirty-Fifth Annual Exhibition of the National Academy of Design in 1860.

May 17, Morphy may have remained at the hotel, for he played two games at Knight odds with Dr. Horace Richardson, winning both.

While little is known of the women in Morphy's life, he seems to have had some attraction for them. Articles in New York papers by women asked why they should not share more of his time and the New York *Evening Post* of May 31 had this item:

> The Mysterious Chess Player.—In a notice of Morphy, the great chess player, a queer incident occurred to him soon after his arrival in New York. A carriage drove to the St. Nicholas, in which was seated a splendidly dressed lady. She sent up a card, and requested an interview with the chess champion. The interview was granted, when the fair visitor demanded the privilege of playing a game with Mr. Morphy. Mr. Morphy looked at the magnificent eyes of the stranger, and said "Yes certainly." The chess table was brought to the window, and Mr. Morphy placed the men. The lady, of course, was permitted the first move. Half a dozen moves on either side and Morphy found himself interested—his visitor promised to prove the most formidable antagonist he had had for a long time. Being absorbed in the game, Morphy directed the servant to admit no one else until it was completed. The game lasted two hours and was *drawn*. The lady was then satisfied, and blushingly took her leave, Morphy himself accompanying her to her carriage. The moment she had gone, Morphy and his friends set at work to ascertain the identity of the beautiful visitor, not doubting that the name upon her card could be found in the directory. This, however, proved to be a mistake, and though every endeavor was made to ascertain precisely who was the visitor, the gentle-

men are as much in the dark as ever. Whoever she may be, she played the best game in which Morphy was ever a contestant, and she probably adopted these means of matching herself with Morphy in order to assure herself of her own skill.

Although it is true that women at that time were quite active in chess, their activity was for the most part restricted to correspondence chess and problems rather than to play in men's clubs. A Mrs. Gilbert, called the "female Morphy," in 1879 announced checkmate against G. H. D. Gossip in thirty-five moves.

On the nineteenth of May, James Thompson met Morphy in a Knight-odds game. Surprised when he lost, Thompson challenged Morphy to a nine-game match at those odds, which the latter had to extend himself to win.

The next day, the New York *Commercial Advertiser* carried a display advertisement of Edge's book, *The Exploits and Triumphs in Europe of Paul Morphy*, published by Appleton, and mentioned that Lowenthal's book *A New and Thorough Treatise on Chess* was in press. Lowenthal's first thought had been to issue a pamphlet on Morphy's games and on the Morphy–Staunton affair for, as he said, he could relate the matter more freely in pamphlet form than in his chess column. Later he decided to issue the above-mentioned *Treatise*, including a discussion of Philidor and others, as well as Morphy. Ultimately, however, he decided to confine himself solely to Morphy and his games.

Morphy resumed match play with Perrin on Saturday, May 21, winning three games and the match within two hours, the final score being Morphy five, Perrin zero, and one game drawn. The following Monday, Morphy played the first match game with Thompson, which the latter won.

The day for the presentation of testimonials had been fixed for Wednesday evening, May 25, at eight o'clock, in the large chapel of New York University. Long before that hour, as the New York *Herald* of May 26, 1859, reported, "every nook and corner of the building was occupied, and even ladies were compelled to stand in the passages so great was the desire to be present on the eventful occasion."

The following series of extracts is taken from an article in the New York *Times* of May 26, 1859, which reported the testimonial proceedings.

> Promptly at the hour a solitary policeman edged his way through the crowd in the right-hand aisle and cleared a passage for Mr. Morphy and his escort. Immediately thereafter

some twenty or thirty gentlemen, among whom were Charles O'Connor, Esq., Judge J. R. Whiting, Baron de Trobriand (and others). Mr. Morphy, leaning upon the arm of Col. Mead, President of the Chess Club, brought up the rear. His appearance was greeted with overwhelming and long continued applause. Gracefully acknowledging it, Mr. Morphy took his seat and Col. Mead arose and spoke as follows:—

Ladies and Gentlemen: The Testimonial Committee has conferred upon me the honor of presiding upon this interesting occasion. You are aware that the object of our assembling to-night is for the purpose of presenting testimonials to our distinguished young countryman, Paul Morphy. He has lately returned from a visit to the *Old World*, where, as in the *New*, he has proven himself to be the master of the checkered field. He has not only acquired for himself undying renown, but has reflected honor and credit upon the land that gave him birth. He had not only been successful in winning in every contest in which he had been engaged, but he has also succeeded in winning the hearts of all who have come in contact with him.

It is not my purpose to refer to the moral and intellectual influences of the science and art of chess. It is sufficient to point to one who may be well considered a living embodiment of its morality and intellectuality.

In view of these considerations, a few of the crowd of his admirers and friends have been desirous of making to him some acknowledgment of his unrivaled powers, as well as a testimonial of their personal regard. For that purpose they have procured the chessmen and board now before you, which they desire to have presented to-night. After this has been done, the members of the Testimonial Committee also intend to present him with an additional token of their esteem.

The presentation of the chessmen and board will now be made. The Hon. John Van Buren has kindly consented to discharge, on behalf of the Committee, that agreeable duty.

After Col. Mead had concluded, John Van Buren came forward. Taking Mr. Morphy by the hand, he introduced him to the audience amid hearty cheers. Silence having been restored, Mr. Van Buren delivered the following address to Mr. Morphy and the audience, Mr. Morphy remaining standing meanwhile.

Mr. Morphy: A number of your friends and admirers have deemed it appropriate to signalize your return to the United States by this reception, and by the presentation to you of a testimonial of their admiration and regard. I am happy to be enrolled among their number, and feel honored at having been selected to convey to you their sentiments, and to offer for your acceptance this beautiful specimen of taste and skill of those to whom its execution was confided. . . . For more than a thousand years [chess] has been played in Europe. 'Like a universal alphabet' as a clever writer has said 'the chessboard is known to all nations. . . .'

Ladies and gentlemen, I ask you to unite with me in welcoming with all the honors, PAUL MORPHY, the Chess Champion of the World.

At one point, Van Buren interrupted his address to read the following letter from Prof. Samuel F. B. Morse:

Poughkeepsie, May 24, 1859

Sir: I have this moment received your polite invitation and ticket, as Chairman of the Testimonial Committee, to witness the "presentation testimonials" to our distinguished countryman, Paul Morphy, Esq., and assigning me a seat on the platform on the occasion. While I regret exceedingly that my engagements will prevent my being present, I would yet take this opportunity to offer through you my humble tribute of admiration not merely to the man of unequaled skill in the time honored game of chess (the most valuable for certain kinds of mental discipline, of all existing games), but to the man of modesty, who can receive such demonstrations of enthusiasm as have been showered upon him without any show of vanity or conceited inflation. I was so fortunate as to be present at Paris, at the Café de Régence, at the marvelous contest of Mr. Morphy with the most skillful European players, when he engaged with them in eight different games at the same time, and without seeing their boards, unaided but by his most extraordinary memory, and unrivaled skill. I witnessed not only his marvelous triumph, but his modest and unassuming bearing in the moment of victory and not the least gratifying part of the scene was the spontaneous outburst of generous and magnanimous applause from his French antagonists that filled the air with shouts as they conducted him in triumph to his carriage. It was a beautiful proof to me that the flame of a high souled chivalry still burned in the hearts of Frenchmen.

In asking that my personal gratulations to Mr. Morphy may be allowed to mingle with yours on this occasion, I remain, Sir, with respect, your most obedient servant.

Samuel F. B. Morse

To S. D. Bradford, Esq., Chairman of the Testimonial Committee.

Mr. Van Buren's address was frequently interrupted by applause. When he concluded his remarks, Mr. Morphy replied:

Mr. President, Ladies and Gentlemen: Twelve months have elapsed since bidding adieu to my Western home. I sought beyond the blue waters the foreign skies of another hemisphere; and again have I returned to the land of my birth and affections. Another year has glided by and once more do I find myself surrounded by the friends whose good wishes and approbation cheered my wandering course. I thank them—I most sincerely thank them for the more than cordial welcome which has greeted my return to the Empire City. Well may they say that they have made their City the verdant spot in my sandy path—the green and ever-blooming oasis of repose where, like the wayworn traveler, I forget the fatigue and exposure of the journey, and gather renewed life and energy for its completion. Not satisfied, however, with showering innumerable attentions upon me, they this night cap the climax of their favors by presenting me, in conjunction with a large number of the citizens of New York, this beautiful piece of workmanship as a superb testimonial of their regard and sympathy. How thankfully received— how dearly prized—mere words cannot portray. I shall proudly take it to my Southern home and preserve it as a precious memento of my friends in New York.

I fear, ladies and gentlemen, that lengthy comments upon the game of chess might prove uninteresting to a large portion of the highly intellectual audience before me. Of my European tour I will only say that it has been pleasant in almost every respect. Of the adversaries encountered in the peaceful jousts of the chequered field, I retain a lively and agreeable recollection. I found them gallant, chivalrous and gentlemanly, as well became true votaries of the kingly pastime.

A word now on the game itself. Chess never has been and never can be aught but a recreation. It should not be indulged in to the detriment of other and more serious avocations—should not absorb the mind or engross the thoughts of those who worship at its shrine; but should be kept in the background and restrained within its proper province. As a mere game, a relaxation from the severer pursuits of life, it is deserving of high commendation. It is not only the most delightful and scientific, but the most moral of amusements. Unlike other games in which lucre is the end and aim of the contestants, it recommends itself to the wise by the fact that its mimic battles are fought for no prize but honor. It is eminently and emphatically the philosopher's game. Let the chess board supercede the card-table, and a great improvement will be visible in the morals of the community. [Great Applause] But, ladies and gentlemen, I need not expiate on the field so ably traversed by the eloquent gentleman who has just addressed you. I thank you from my heart for the very flattering manner in which you have been pleased to receive his too complimentary remarks, and for the numerous attentions received at your hands. I shall leave New York with melancholy sorrow, for I part from friends than whom none truer can be found. Let them rest assured that along with the memory of the chess board I possess the memory of the heart. And now, with a renewal of my sincere thanks for the splendid token of your regard with which you have presented me tonight, and the assurance that I shall cherish in unfading memory the remembrance of my sojourn here, I bid you, ladies and gentlemen, a farewell, which I fondly hope will not prove the last.

Colonel Mead then announced that W. J. A. Fuller would present the watch on behalf of the Testimonial Committee. After this presentation, Morphy responded:

Sir: It has been my good fortune, on a previous visit to your City, to form acquaintances which have ripened into friendships. You are the organ, Sir, of some gentlemen with whom my intercourse has more particularly assumed the character of intimacy. The presentation of the very elegant watch you have handed me must necessarily be less formal than that which has just taken place. Words of learned length or thundering sound would ill become the nature of the occasion. I will simply say that I value this testimonial not less highly than the other. It is friendship's gift—the *vade mecum* that must accompany me wherever I go, to remind me that in whatever section of this broad Republic my abode may be planted, there will be in the far North friends whose anxious gaze will be turned to my home, whose hearts will watch with deep emotion the part I sustain in life's great drama, eager to see me touch the goal of success. Interpreting it in such a manner as a token of the interest felt in my future career by those you represent, I receive this beautiful piece of workmanship with unaffected pleasure. Long may the hands on its dial mark golden hours for my friends, and may no untoward mate ever arrest their course of success on the great chess board of the world.

The watch presented by the committee was made to order by the American Watch Company of Waltham, Massachusetts. The *Testimonial Program* describes the watch:

The stem or pendant is exquisitely carved, so as to represent a King's Crown. It is set round with brilliants, with another large diamond at its top, which answers for a push-piece by which to open the watch. Upon one lid the United States coat of arms is richly carved in relief, and on the other lid, also in relief, the monogram:

P.M.

Instead of the usual Roman numerals on the dial, the hours are represented by the various pieces of chess, finely done in red and black—the Black King standing at twelve, and the Red King at six, the Queens at one and eleven, Bishops at two and ten, Knights at three and nine, Castles at four and eight, and Pawns at five and seven. The cap is engraved with the following inscription:

TO PAUL MORPHY
From the testimonial committee of the New York
Chess Club, as their tribute to his genius
and worth
New York, May, 1859

It was added elsewhere in the *Testimonial Program* that

The movements of this watch were made entirely by machinery, and its interior and exterior presents as elegant a specimen of art as can well be imagined. The whole is highly creditable to the celebrated makers, and to American ingenuity.

Col. Mead then announced that the chess board and men, which were on the platform, would be on exhibition at Tiffany's for several days and the watch at Runnels. The company then separated, to the tune of the Marseillaise.

Charles A. Buck, author of a little pamphlet on Morphy, *Paul Morphy, His Later Life*, written some seventy-five years ago, appears to be responsible for a number of erroneous statements that have been widely accepted. In his pamphlet, Buck mentions an incident that interrupted the testimonial presentation:

> The festivities of this occasion were unhappily marred by a dramatic episode that showed Morphy's growing sensitiveness to the "profession of chess." Colonel Charles D. Mead, president of the American Chess Association, was chairman of the reception committee which greeted Morphy, and in his address of welcome he made an allusion to chess as a profession, and referred to Morphy as its most brilliant exponent. Morphy took exception to being characterized as a professional player, even by implication, and he resented it in such a way as to overwhelm Colonel Mead with confusion. Such was his mortification at this untoward event that Colonel Mead withdrew from further participation in the Morphy demonstration.

No such incident occurred. Contrary to Buck's contentions, Colonel Mead never characterized Morphy as a professional chess player, nor did he use the word "profession" during the proceedings. Mead introduced the speakers, mentioning where the chessmen were to be seen, and closed the proceedings as reported above by the New York *Times*. He was also with Morphy the following evening at another testimonial.

Buck first published *Paul Morphy* in the *Evening Gazette* of Cedar Rapids, Iowa, on December 29, 1900, and it was later reprinted in the *American Chess World* of January 1901. Will H. Lyons published it in pamphlet form in January 1902 and added *His Later Life* to the title. Evidently, Buck did not consult Morphy's *Chess Monthly*, the *Ledger*, or other major sources, for the pamphlet contains numerous errors in addition to that already cited. He apparently just talked to "old-timers" and did little research for his article. The following corrections to false statements in Buck's pamphlet should be especially noted:

- Stanley did *not* win one of his match games with Morphy at the odds of Pawn and move.
- Morphy annotated thirty-five Labourdonnais–M'Donnell games, *not* fifteen as Buck states.
- Morphy attempted to establish a law practice in 1864, *not* in 1859 or 1860 as Buck states.
- Morphy *did* complete his contract with the *Ledger*, although Fuller helped.
- Fiske, in a letter to Will Lyons dated February 5, 1901, says Buck "errs when he states that Mr. Morphy contributed

very little to the *Chess Monthly*."

- There is no evidence that Morphy was rejected by anyone because he was "a mere chess player," even though Frances Parkinson Keyes corroborates Buck in this contention. Keyes's novel about Morphy is more fiction than fact.
- Morphy returned to New Orleans in 1864, *not* 1865 as Buck states.
- He *did* play some chess *after* 1869.
- Zukertort did not meet Morphy in 1882 as Buck states he did, nor is it likely that they ever met. Zukertort first visited New Orleans in 1884.
- Buck mentions an incident concerning a lawyer, a piece of candy, and a remark that he says Morphy made, about all of which nothing whatsoever can be authenticated. It is likely to have as much substance as other statements by Buck called into question here.
- The New York Chess Club *never* acquired Morphy's chessmen as Buck states it did.
- The "apochryphal" game was played between Lowenthal and a Mr. Murphy of London in 1855.
- Morphy was co-editor of the *Chess Monthly* for three years, *not* five.
- It is *not* difficult to determine the first symptoms of his malady. Rumors of a Morphy mental condition started in 1875, *not* 1871 as Buck states. Maurian says he first noticed something was wrong with Morphy in 1875.
- Morphy was taken to the Louisiana Retreat in 1875, *not* in 1882.
- Colonel Mead in his address of welcome at the testimonial reception did *not* refer to chess as a profession. Morphy did not resent anything he said. Mead did *not* retire in confusion and mortification, but remained as chairman throughout the proceedings as previously stated.*

After the testimonial presentation at the New York University Chapel, Morphy was taken to the Century Club, a club frequented by literary gentlemen and artists, and was received by the club's president, Mr. Verplanck, and others. Following a cordial reception and collation he was presented to the members.

---

* EDITOR'S NOTE: Buck's "Paul Morphy: His Later Life" is no longer in print. But its place in the public domain has allowed its reproduction online. See Charles A. Buck, "Paul Morphy: His Later Life," http://en.wikisource.org/wiki/Paul_Morphy:_His_Later_Life.

The Century Club has today a mahogany chess table with the following inscription on a plate:

> This table was used by Paul Morphy at the rooms of the New York Chess Club in 1857. On it he frequently played with Paulsen, Fiske, Marache, Thompson, Mead and other celebrities of that period. The table was presented to the Century Association in 1875 by John Treat Irving.

The public furor over Morphy at this time was such that several New York newspapers devoted most of their front pages the next day to an account of the testimonial presentation given at New York University. One can imagine the excitement Morphy created when one considers that the New York *Daily News* of May 26, 1859, gave its entire first page, except for a portion of its last column, and the New York *Times* used four of its six first-page columns to describe the Morphy testimonial. Few celebrated persons have received such attention from the New York papers.

The following letter also appeared on the first page of the New York *Times* on May 26, 1859:

THE LADIES AFTER PAUL MORPHY

> *To the Editor of the* New-York *Times:*
> Would you not oblige a great many ladies by inviting Mr. Paul Morphy to give a chess matinee, where they could witness his method of playing the Royal game, and make his acquaintance on equal terms with our gentlemen friends. If Mr. Morphy had the slightest idea of the anxiety that prevails among his fair countrywomen to see and do him honor I am sure he could not say them nay.

> M. L. M.

On the day following the New York Chess Club presentation, Morphy was the object of another testimonial, as reported in the New York *Times* of May 27, 1859:

> Last evening the members of the Union Chess Club entertained Mr. Paul Morphy at Buhler's Restaurant, corner of Eighth Street and Broadway, and presented him with the beautiful silver wreath which has attracted crowds of admirers to the windows of Ball, Black & Co. for the last fortnight.

Upwards of seventy gentlemen sat down, among whom we observed Dr. Waterman, Mr. Isidor, President, Col. Mead, Mr. Perrin, D. W. Fiske, James Thompson, Theodore Lichtenhein, and other gentlemen prominently known in the chess world.

At half-past ten o'clock the President addressed the honored guest: Mr. Morphy—Gentlemen: It affords me much pleasure to welcome, in the name and behalf of the Union Chess Club, over which I have the honor to preside, our distinguished guest . . . crowned with the laurels of victory over the acknowledged chess masters of the old world.

Dr. Waterman then arose and addressed Mr. Morphy at the close of which he presented to Mr. Morphy an elegant silver wreath. The wreath was of sterling silver, weighing 12 ounces, handsomely shaped into laurel leaves.

REPLY OF MR. MORPHY

"Mr. President and Gentlemen: I sincerely thank you, and to one and all tender my warm and heartfelt acknowledgements. I feel the more deep the compliment paid me this evening from the fact that it proceeds from a quarter whence it was not reasonably anticipated. You, gentlemen, assembled here in my honor, this evening, are, for the most part, countrymen of that great master of the 'chequered field'—the world renowned Anderssen. [Applause] Leaving aside all feeling of nationality, you have, with the chivalry worthy of the German character, extended the right-hand of friendship to his late antagonist. [Applause] I speak it advisedly, when I say, that were he now within our reach, none would act more heartily in paying him every honor than myself. [Applause] You have spoken, Sir, of some qualities of mine, and to many of which I must say, I can lay no pretensions; nor do I deserve so flattering a testimonial of your regard.

"The present occasion, Mr. President and gentlemen, furnishes a beautiful illustration of the cosmopolitan character of chess. You and I are natives of countries between which there is the space of the great ocean. You speak a different vernacular, and on many subjects probably entertain conflicting opinions, yet we are congregated this night in honor of the same game, and, gentlemen, we worship the same Deity. And now, Mr. President and gentlemen, I hope you will not doubt my sincerity when I say I fully appreciate this token of your regard. Its value is enhanced in my eyes when I think of the motive which has actuated the donors, and long may their Association flourish in undimmed splendor. I propose, in conclusion—'Health and prosperity to the members of the Union Chess Club.'" [Cheers]

The toast was heartily responded to.

The President then gave:

The United States—Proud to claim Paul Morphy as a citizen thereof.

Mr. Dittanhoper responded in an elegant speech, in which he eulogized Mr. Morphy's achievements in Europe.

The next toast—"The Champion of the Chess World Universally Acknowledged"—was responded by Mr. Steen, who delivered an appropriate address.

The American Chess Congress—Forever to be remembered, the brightest star in the horizon of chess.

Mr. Thompson responded, in the absence of Col. Mead who was obliged to leave at an early hour. Mr. Thompson's address was very humorous, and elicited loud cheers.

Late in the evening of the next day, Morphy, accompanied by J. Lorimer Graham, Jr., and other friends, left for Boston. He arrived there Saturday morning and put up at the Revere House. In the afternoon, he was escorted from the Revere House to the Boston Chess Club for a reception held in his honor. That evening he won two games at Knight odds, one with Mr. Broughton and the other with Dr. Richardson. Late that night he was serenaded by the Germania Band. Sunday may have been a day of rest for him. Undoubtedly the quiet was most welcome.

Monday afternoon, May 30, Morphy went sightseeing and visiting. He enjoyed a ride through Cambridge (where he called upon Professor Longfellow), Watertown, and Brighton. When he arrived in Waltham he visited the American Watch Company's factory and was shown through it by the proprietor. Upon returning to Boston, a private dinner was held in his honor at the Park House.

It is likely that Morphy's visit to Waltham was by invitation of the proprietor of the American Watch Company, who probably asked him at the factory if he would be willing to report on his watch's accuracy after a few months. Without doubt the company was immensely pleased to receive the following letter from Morphy some months later (published in the New York *Saturday Press* of October 15, 1859, and later):

New York, Oct. 5th, 1859
Mr. R. E. Robbins, Treas., Am. Watch Company:

Dear Sir:—The American watch, No. 9240, presented me by the New York Chess-Club, has proved to be a most reliable and accurate time-keeper—almost unnecessarily so for ordinary purposes. It is now nearly five moths since it came into my possession, and during that period its variation from standard time has been but a trifle more than half a minute. The following is a record of its performance. It was set June 3d, correctly:

June 15,	fast	4 seconds
July 1,	"	6 "
July 15,	"	10 "
Aug. 1,	"	16 "
Aug. 15,	"	18 "
Sept. 1	"	23 "
Sept. 15,	"	28 "
Oct. 1,	"	32 "

I give you permission to make use of this statement as you may think proper. I am, with respect, yours truly,

Paul Morphy

The watch company received the above "commercial" gratis, although it appeared in the New York *Saturday Press* a number of times. Any suggestion that he be paid for it would have been repugnant to Morphy.

As reported in the Boston *Gazette* of June 4, 1859, the evening of Morphy's visit to Waltham, "a large number of ladies and gentlemen assembled at the rooms of the [Boston] Chess Club to witness Morphy's play." Among those present was Henry Wadsworth Longfellow, who mentions Morphy several times in the second volume of his *Journal and Letters*:

May 30th. In the evening, went to town to see Paul Morphy play, at the Chess Club. A crowd of ladies and gentlemen. Morphy played serenely, and with a delicate nervous touch, as if the chessboard were a musical instrument. A slight youth, pale and quiet. T. [Thomas Appleton, Longfellow's brother-in-law] said he reminded him of Chopin.

> June 1. The Paul Morphy dinner was a brilliant affair. Holm-
> es presided; and of course there were endless speeches. Judge
> Shaw, Sparks, Agassiz, and so forth.

> 2d. Dined with the homeopathic doctors in the armory of Fa-
> neuil Hall. In the morning, Morphy and two handsome youths
> from New York came out and sat an hour. Also Murdoch, the
> tragedian.

It would appear that Morphy was playing chess much more than he
desired. He was now *expected* to play wherever he went—to entertain, to
show off, or to convince others of his superiority. Morphy was an innately
courteous person and therefore seldom expressed his displeasure with being asked to play so often. Only rarely did he disappoint the often unreasonable demands made upon him. However, on the evening of May 30, after winning from Broughton, the Boston *Gazette* of June 4, 1859, reported,
"It was expected that Mr. Morphy would play several games, but fatigue,
incident upon the pleasures of the day, made him unwilling to do so." It
was further noted in the *Gazette* that "Mr. Morphy has thus far played but
three games since his arrival in Boston, all of which he won. It is hoped and
expected that he will, before the close of his visit, give further opportunity
to our players to cope with him." And a letter from J. A. Graham, Jr., of
Boston to Fiske, dated June 1, 1859, mentions complaints made about his
playing so few games there!

The evening of May 31, the Boston Chess Club gave Morphy a complimentary dinner at the Revere House. The occasion was made particularly brilliant by 18 of the 140 invited guests. The Boston *Journal* of June 1,
1859, reported the event as follows:

> At 6 ½ o'clock the company entered the hall to the music of
> a popular march played by the Germania Band. The Auto-
> crat of both Hemispheres, the learned, witty and genial Dr.
> Holmes, presided at the festive board. On his right were Paul
> Morphy, Dr. Horace Richardson, President of the Club, Hon.
> Jared Sparks, Prof. Pearce of Harvard College, Rev. Dr. Hun-
> tington, and Prof. Lowell. On his left sat President Walker of
> Harvard College, Chief Justice Shaw, Hon. Joel Parker, Prof.
> Agassiz, Prof. Longfellow, and Rev. T. Starr King. At another
> table in front of the President were the other invited guests—
> Hon. Henry Wilson, Mayor Lincoln, Hon. Josiah Quincy, Jr.,
> Edwin P. Whipple, Esq., James T. Fields, Esq., and Hon. B. F.
> Thomas.

At 20 minutes of 9 o'clock, the President of the Boston Chess Club, Dr. Richardson, arose and addressed the assembly as follows:

"In behalf of the Boston Chess Club I am very happy to welcome on this occasion our distinguished guest, Mr. Paul Morphy, and the many other eminent guests assembled on this occasion. And they may be assured that the welcome is not less cordial and sincere, although so brief. I now introduce to you the President of the evening, Dr. Oliver Wendell Holmes." [Prolonged applause.]

DR. OLIVER WENDELL HOLMES

"We have met, gentlemen, some of us as members of a local association, some of us as its invited guests, but all of us as if by a spontaneous, unsolicited impulse, to do honor to our young friend who has honored us and all who glory in the name of Americans, as the hero of a long series of bloodless battles, won for our common country. . . . Honor went before him, and Victory followed after. . . .

"I propose the health of PAUL MORPHY, the world's Chess Champion: His peaceful battles have helped to achieve a new revolution; his youthful triumphs have added a new clause to the declaration of American Independence!"

Dr. Holmes's speech was greeted with frequent applause and at its conclusion the band played "Hail Columbia." Morphy, upon rising to respond, was greeted with three times three cheers. As soon as he could be heard he replied:

"*Mr. President and Gentlemen*: I sincerely thank you. To one and all I tender the expression of my warm and heartfelt acknowledgements. But, gentlemen, on such an occasion as the present, unprepared as you know I am, I must be allowed to say, gentlemen, that I rise with peculiar embarrassment and unaffected diffidence in attempting to speak before an intellectual aristocracy such as I have never before witnessed, whose celebrity and literary achievements are a part of our country's history. In such an illustrious presence it would ill become me to make a speech. I can only tender my thanks to the committee, with an expression of my sincere acknowledgements for the pleasure of being surrounded by a company so distinguished."

The President has spoken of chess. He (Mr. Morphy) had taken occasion in New York to say something upon that subject, and he would not weary the patience of the company by adding anything to these remarks. He would merely say that chess could not form an object of life. At best it was but a relaxation. As a discipline of the mind it was worthy of commendation. As a substitute for cards, chess would go far towards improving the morals of our people. [Applause] But he would not detain the company. He thanked the President most sincerely for the very kind and flattering manner in which his name had been proposed, and the other gentlemen present for the manner in which they had received it. In conclusion he begged leave to propose the following:

"*The Literary and Scientific Men of whom Boston is so justly proud*—The stars of the first magnitude that adorn the intellectual firmament of our country."

Six cheers were here proposed and given for Mr. Morphy.

The President then announced the first regular sentiment—

The Commonwealth of Massachusetts—Proud of her own sons and their eminence in intellectual pursuits, she is eager to welcome surpassing excellence in others.

A letter from Hon. Edward Everett was read, as a response to this toast:

                                    Summer Street, 26th May, 1859, Boston
Gentlemen:
I have received your very obliging invitation to the dinner to be given by the Boston Chess Club to Mr. Paul Morphy on the 31st inst. It would have given me great pleasure to join you in this mark of respect to your distinguished guest, who has not only evinced the most marvelous skill in the ancient and noble game which you cultivate—having shown himself to be *facile princepe* among the chess players of the world—but who wears his laurels with a modesty equal to the mastery with which he has won them.

I deeply regret that an engagement to repeat my address on the character of Washington in a neighboring city, on the 31st inst, will put it out of my power to be present on the interesting occasion.

With my best wishes for an agreeable festival, I remain, gentle-men

Very respectfully yours
Edward Everett

Charles R. Cadman, Jacob A. Dresser, John Jeffries, Jr. and others.

Altogether, some eighteen speeches or talks were reported, most of them in the press of Boston and New York. Some papers devoted more than half their first page to the proceedings. James Russell Lowell composed a poem of some one hundred lines for the occasion and the entire evening passed off with great éclat.

Morphy did play one more game before leaving Boston, giving five of the club members an opportunity to meet him in a consultation game—Messrs. Hammond (probably its strongest member), Ware, Rabuski, Stone, and W. Everett. It was played June 2 and won handily by Morphy.

On June 3, Morphy and friends (James A. Graham, Jr., W. J. A. Fuller, and others) left Boston. They arrived in New York on Saturday and put up at the Brevoort House. Morphy resumed his Knight-odds match with Thompson on Monday, losing his second game on June 6 at the Morphy Chess Rooms. Now he roused himself and won the next four games in rapid succession. Thompson won the seventh game of the match, the eighth was drawn, and Morphy then won the ninth game and the match on Friday afternoon, June 17, 1859. If the first Knight-odds games (casual) are counted, the final score stood Morphy six, Thompson three.

Morphy's defeat of Thompson at Knight odds was considered an outstanding feat because Thompson played so-called *close* games throughout the match and was himself accustomed to giving the same odds to comparatively strong players. As Lowenthal wrote to Fiske on February 25, 1860:

> I am decidedly of the opinion that his (Morphy's) winning a match at the large odds of a Knight to a player like Mr. Thompson, is the most marvelous feat which ever a master of his rank has performed. Neither La Bourdonnais, M'Donnell nor Philidor could ever have accomplished a similar task.

The Thompson match had not interfered with Morphy's social life. Sunday, June 12, Morphy had dined with Robert J. Walker and a party of friends. On the day before he won the match he had spent the afternoon and evening in Brooklyn. It had been anticipated that Morphy would engage various players at the Brooklyn Chess Club, for Messrs. Stanley, Thompson, Perrin, Frère, Knott, and Tilton, and other prominent players of New York and Brooklyn were present. As reported in *Frank Leslie's Illustrated Newspaper* of June 25, 1859,

> Mr. Morphy accompanied by Mr. Frère, the secretary, Mr. Fiske and other gentlemen, arrived at the club and, after introductions, was solicited to play a game. Mr. Morphy, with that good sense, which, notwithstanding his youth, has characterized his deportment since he has sojourned among us, declined, observing "it was too hot, he played at chess as little as possible; he had to play the great game of life;" and, with many other observations of a similar character, remained passive. Some members of the club seemed disgusted. They had brought the "lion" there, and why should he not be lionized? Why would he not play—show his teeth? Again and again was he solicited. Again and again did he refuse. Mr. Frère at last came to his rescue. Dinner was ready. Mr. Morphy seemed relieved. Mr. Frère asked him to accompany him home and partake of refreshments, which had been provided for himself and friends. Mr. Morphy gladly complied, and to Mr. Frère's home they went and partook of a right royal dinner. In the evening Mr. Morphy played two games with Mr. Knott and one game with Mr. Marache, in all of which games he gave the large odds of the Queen's Knight, winning all in a dashing style. Not less than five hundred Chess players and visitors attended during the day and evening.

As it has already been observed, Morphy did not always wish to be playing chess. It must have become very boring to him—so many people talking only chess with him as though that were all that interested him. As Edge, who was with him as companion and secretary the whole year he was abroad, said:

> I was almost constantly with him, and certainly no subject was less frequently referred to than chess. I have been amused with the conduct of gentlemen on similar occasions, who seemed to think that no other subject than that could interest him, and after pertinaciously confining the conversation to the game, took it upon themselves to declare that it was the single thought of his life.

On June 22, the Athenaeum Club in New York held a birthday reception for Morphy, for its members had elected him an honorary member. Cards had been issued to announce the event, and a large and brilliant party of guests attended. As the New York *Express* of June 23, 1859, noted, "The whole building was filled with a dense crowd, of which at least one-half was made up of ladies." Morphy's testimonial chessmen were displayed on the second floor of the clubhouse.

Now display advertisements appeared in the Boston and New York papers for "The Morphy Hat"; and "The Morphy Cigar," a special brand ordered from Havana, was copyrighted. Enthusiasts in Brooklyn organized the Morphy Baseball Club, of which he was elected a member. Robert Bonner, the most astute weekly publisher of the period, had become aware of Paul Morphy. As Mary Noel says in *Villains Galore*, a book about the heyday of the "story weekly," "When the chess player Paul Morphy achieved world championship and was banqueted and glorified in the most extravagant fashion, Bonner secured him a year's column for the New York *Ledger*." He had approached Morphy through W. J. A. Fuller a few days after the former's arrival in New York. Sensing Morphy's potential impact on the public, Bonner offered him $3,000 in advance for a weekly chess column. Morphy's reply was published in the New York *Post* of May 28, 1859:

> St. Nicholas Hotel, May 27, 1859
> Robert Bonner, Esq.—
>
> Dear Sir: The offer you made to me to edit a Chess Department in the New York *Ledger* is so exceedingly liberal that I do not feel at liberty to decline it. I will commence my contributions some time during the month of June next, and shall furnish chess matter to no other newspaper.
>
> > Truly yours,
> > Paul Morphy

Edward Everett, who later shared the platform with Abraham Lincoln at Gettysburg, made the following reference to Morphy in a letter to Bonner:

> Boston, 3 June, 1859
>
> My dear Sir
>
> I was much pleased to see that you had engaged Mr. Morphy as a Contributor. His articles will secure you the entire chess-playing Community:—which, taking the Union through, is I

suppose a very large body. . . .

Yours, dear Sir, Sincerely
Edward Everett

In his letter to Bonner, Morphy had promised his first contribution to the *Ledger* in June. However, busy as he was with chess engagements, Morphy did not produce it until August 6, although Bonner placed the following display advertisement in the New York papers on July 25 to announce Morphy's chess column:

The Imperial Chess-Player
PAUL MORPHY
makes his appearance TO-DAY at 1 O'CLOCK
before the largest audience
that ever honored the imperial game.

Apparently, George N. Cheney of Syracuse (who was to be a casualty of Bull Run just two years later) came to New York at this time, for he played two games with Morphy at Knight odds within a day or two of Morphy's birthday, one of which he won. Morphy did not reveal the scores of his games unless pressed for them, and so we only know the game he lost to Cheney, not the one he won.

Many others came to New York to play Morphy, among them the Reverend M. D. Conway of Cincinnati and E. C. Palmer of St. Paul. In his autobiography, Conway describes his encounter with Morphy:

Despite all my freedom there was a curious survival in me up to my twenty-seventh year of the Methodist dread of card-playing. The only indoor game I knew was chess. There was a flourishing Chess Club in Cincinnati, and I entered into the matches with keen interest. For a time I edited a weekly chess column in the "Cincinnati Commercial," and wrote an article on Chess which Lowell published in the "Atlantic Monthly." Whenever in New York I hastened to the Chess Club there, and watched the play of Lichtenhein, Thompson, Perrin, Marache, Fiske (editor of the "Chess Monthly"), and Col. Mead, president of the club. This was at a time when the wonderful Paul Morphy was exciting the world. In July, 1859, I called on him at the Brevoort House, New York. He was a rather small man, with a beardless face that would have been boyish had it not been for the melancholy eyes.

He was gentlemanly and spoke in low tones. It had long been

out of question to play with him on even terms; the first-class players generally received the advantage of a knight, but being a second-class player I was given a rook. In some letter written at the time, I find mention of five games in which I was beaten with these odds, but managed (or was permitted) to draw the sixth. In the same letter I find the following:—

"When one plays with Morphy the sensation is as queer as the first electric shock, or first love, or chloroform, or any entirely novel experience. As you sit down at the board opposite him, a certain sheepishness steals over you, and you cannot rid yourself of an old fable in which a lion's skin plays a part. Then you are sure you have the advantage; you seem to be secure,—you get a rook—you are ahead two pieces! three!! Gently as if wafted by a zephyr the pieces glide about the board; and presently as you are about to win the game a soft voice in your ear kindly insinuates, *Mate*! You are speechless. Again and again you try; again and again you are sure you must win; again and again your prodigal antagonist leaves his pieces at your mercy; but his moves are as the steps of Fate. Then you are charmed all along—so bewitchingly are you beheaded: one had rather be run through by Bayard, you know, than spared by a pretender. On the whole I could only remember the oriental anecdote of one who was taken to the banks of the Euphrates, where by a princely host he was led about the magnificent gardens and bowers, then asked if anything could be more beautiful. 'Yes,' he replied, 'the chess-play of El-Zuli.' So having lately sailed, as I wrote you, down the Hudson, having explored Staten Island, Hoboken, Fort Hamilton, and all the glorious retreats about New York, I shall say forever that one thing is more beautiful than them all,—the chess-play of Paul Morphy."

This was in July, 1859. I had already received a domestic suggestion that it was possible to give too much time to an innocent game, and the hint was reinforced by my experience with Morphy. I concluded that if, after all the time I had given to chess, any man could give a rook and beat me easily, any ambition in that direction might as well be renounced. Thenceforth I played only on vacations or when at sea.

Chapter 17

Morphy and the *Ledger*

Morphy's continuing success—even at the large odds of Queen's Knight—against the first-class American players, which had interested poets and savants such as Longfellow and Agassiz, as well as chess players and others, continued to accelerate the recognition and practice of chess throughout the country. The United States was aflame with Morphy and chess. In Buffalo, H. M. Clay, and in Cincinnati, D. C. Fabronius, published large portraits of Morphy. Newspapers and weeklies met the public's interest with chess columns and articles. Even the *Musical World* felt the need to have a chess column and engaged Sam Loyd to start one in February 1859. By July, the chess column took over the *entire* front page as though it were a chess magazine, sometimes invading page 2!

As Fiske wrote in the *Chess Monthly* of July 1859, "The chess columns of the United States now form a formidable brigade. From as far East as Boston to as far West as San Francisco, from southernmost Texas to northernmost Minnesota."

Even before Morphy had reached New York, a ground swell had set in for him, and in Missouri the St. Louis *Daily Democrat* of December 18, 1858, published the following puzzle based on the Knight's tour:

A KNIGHT'S TOUR TRIBUTE
TO PAUL MORPHY

It is an eight-line tribute to Paul Morphy. The puzzle is to find where to commence and how to arrange the words so as to read the verse. This puzzle beautifully illustrates the moves of the knight in traversing the board, galloping from square to square with a measured tramp, and although apparently without purpose, yet visiting every spot in the field, and visiting each square but once.

The solution beginning at QR1 reads as follows:

> Hail! Morphy, bloodless victor, hail!
> Thou mightier than Napoleon;—
> His triumphs were the price of blood,
> His wars by many generals won,—
> While thou, upon the chequer'd board,

With never-erring certainty,
Alone, unaided, leadest on
Thy troops to glorious victory.

—G. Grundy

BOARD	EST	WERE	IOUS	NEV	THY	MIGHT	TOR
UMPHS	VIC	WITH	ON	THE	HAIL	·ER	TROOPS
LEAD	QUER'D	PRICE	RALS	GLO	IER	VIC	THOU
TO	TRI	THE	MAN	HIS	GENE	TO	ER
CHE	ED	WON	OF	ON	BY	THAN	LESS
HIS	RY	UP	WARS	Y	BLOOD	RING	TY
AID	WHILE	MOR	LE	LONE	TAIN	BLOOD	NA
HAIL	ON	UN	THOU	PHY	PO	A	CER

A Knight's Tour Tribute to Paul Morphy

The London *Lancet* in 1823 had been the first to have a chess column. C. H. Stanley had started the first one in the United States in the New York *Spirit of the Times* in 1845, and now Morphy's column in the New York *Ledger* was anxiously awaited. And so during July, Morphy was engaged in preparing his weekly series of articles for the *Ledger* so that he might have a few weeks' vacation away from New York before returning to New Orleans. As the *Chess Monthly* of August 1859 states, his *Ledger* column was to consist mainly of games of the "celebrated Labourdonnais–M'Donnell contest. The long desired commentary upon these remarkable battles, of the want of which so much has been said and felt, will thus be supplied."

Perhaps Bonner's notice in the *Ledger* of July 25 was his way of prodding Morphy, who was far behind his promised date of June. At last on August 6, 1859, the *Ledger* had the following:

CHESS DEPARTMENT
Conducted by Paul Morphy

Concerning the game of chess little can now be said that would not be a thrice told tale to the great majority of our readers.

We do not, therefore, in the present brief introduction, propose to offer any remarks on the history, antiquity, or fascination of that truly royal pastime, but simply to map out, without preface or preamble, the course it has seemed to us most proper to pursue in this new accession to chess periodical literature.

It will be our endeavor, in the first place, to render this column not only interesting but instructive to the chess student—to make it, not an object of passing curiosity, but a feature possessing a deep and permanent value in the eyes of all who, in the few hurried moments of leisure snatched from the engrossing, and, to some extent, necessarily selfish pursuits of life, delight to turn to a pleasanter field of strife, and fight battles from which cupidity can expect no golden prize. How best to attain such a consummation was the problem presented for our solution. It has occurred to us that an *eminently practical chess column* was a desideratum in American chess literature; and that an attempt to fill up the void might be received with some little degree of favor. Our attention, then, in the conduct of this department of the *Ledger*, will be steadily directed to the plan here indicated. Excluding mere speculation we shall aim at laying before our readers none but purely practical matter. A good problem, remarkable for the ingenuity or nice accuracy which unravels its mazy intricacies—one or two standard games, contested by the acknowledged masters of the chequered field, and accompanied by elaborate notes, critical and analytical, will form the staple of our weekly contribution.

Our readers will not be surprised by the announcement that we *positively decline any correspondence in connection with this department.* The reason is obvious. We could not undertake such a task. From the number of letters that we daily receive, *in our private character*, on the subject of chess, we can well imagine what an increased quantity we would receive in our character of *chess editor.* To answer every epistle would be an impossibility. Besides, correspondents must allow us to suggest that any leading treatise on the game contains all the information generally sought by them.

We present our readers in the present number with the first of the long series of games contested between Labourdonnais and M'Donnell. True, they have been published before; but no satisfactory analysis has, to our knowledge, ever been appended to them. We purpose giving one or two a week, in the order in which they were played, with careful annotations. It is hoped that this attempt to furnish the American public with a clue to the intelligence of these beautiful models of chess strategy, will not prove unacceptable.

> At the request of numerous friends, we will occasionally publish
> some of the games played by us in Europe and in this country.

Morphy then gave as a problem a neat endgame position he had against
Lowenthal, and the first of the Labourdonnais–M'Donnell games. It was in
examining the twenty-sixth game between these two masters that Morphy
characterized the "Evans Gambit" as "that most beautiful of openings." It
was M'Donnell who had offered it and won, Labourdonnais resigning on
his thirty-third move.

As noted above, Morphy had positively declined to have any column
correspondence, which at that time was a very popular feature, occasionally being half the column. Many readers wrote in anyhow, some addressing their letters directly to Robert Bonner. One reader remarked, "What
would the chess column of the *Illustrated London News* be without its correspondence?" while another asked, "How long will they remain pleased?"
Finally Bonner bowed to popular demand and engaged W. J. A. Fuller to
answer correspondents, being careful to state that Fuller would consult
Morphy on all important matters.

Without doubt Morphy's limited interest in chess, which others could
not understand, together with his being perhaps constitutionally unsuited
for any job as such, is what may have led Fuller to say later in the Steinitz–
Zukertort Match Program 1886 that "he was incorrigibly lazy." Also it is
necessary to consider the unsettling situation between North and South at
that time, with those of the South especially affected.

In any case, Morphy's association with Bonner and the *Ledger* ended
in August 1860. However, during the year in which his chess column ran,
Morphy annotated thirty-five of the Labourdonnais–M'Donnell games
and others, including a few of his own, undoubtedly fewer than his readers
would have liked.

After the first few months, Morphy did his editing from New Orleans.
At that time, the South was seething over "free states" and "slave states,"
Louisiana to secede some months later. Lincoln had already said, "A house
divided against itself cannot stand."*

But while Morphy was preparing the first of his *Ledger* articles, he was
facing another challenge. As the Thompson match neared its end, the New
Orleans *Sunday Delta* and other papers mentioned a match in the offing

---

* EDITOR'S NOTE: South Carolina became the first state to secede from the Union
December 20, 1860. From 1789 to 1860, Southerners had dominated the presidency.
No northern president had ever won reelection. Two-thirds of the Speakers of the House
and presidents pro tempore of the Senate had been Southerners. The Supreme Court

with Theodore Lichtenhein, considered a slightly stronger player than Thompson. Certainly Lichtenhein did not believe that Morphy could successfully give *him* odds of a Knight.

Lichtenhein won the first two games as had Thompson, but the final result was Morphy six, Lichtenhein four, and one game drawn. Lichtenhein objected to the presentation of the game between them that appeared in the *Chess Monthly* of that August with Morphy's approval, but witnesses to the games agreed with Morphy about the outcome of the match, although it was not mentioned as a match at the time.

Also during that July of 1859, Morphy was induced to sit for Charles Loring Elliott for a portrait in oil, later exhibited by the National Academy of Design. And at the Eighth Annual Banquet of the Manhattan Chess Club on March 1, 1884, Thomas Frère presented the portrait to the club, on behalf of the Directory, in an address that the club later published.

Four months later according to the Manhattan Chess Club Resolutions, the portrait was "draped in mourning for a period of three months," since which time Morphy has looked down from the walls of the club these many years, upon contests of the world's great and lesser masters. He saw Capablanca make his last move and Robert J. Fischer make his first impressive move in "The Game of the Century."

During that same month of July 1859, *Ballau's Pictorial* devoted its front page to Morphy, illustrated by a large drawing of him by one who was later to be considered one of America's greatest painters—Winslow Homer.

---

had Southern majorities since 1791. And so the election of an antislavery northerner was more than a simple glitch in the traditional, Southern-dominated system. Abraham Lincoln was elected without any Southern votes.

Other states began to fall in line after South Carolina—Mississippi, then Florida, then Alabama, then Georgia, all in the first three weeks of January 1861. Louisiana's first secession meetings came in December 1860, but cooperationists (largely from Morphy's New Orleans) opposed secession on the grounds of the port city's vulnerability and the economically beneficial federal protective tariffs on Louisiana sugar. Amid the fever pitch that was secession, however, those urban voices would be shouted down. The state elected delegates to an official secession convention on January 7, 1861, and the state itself absconded on January 26. Louisiana representatives would be present at the first meetings of the Confederate States of America in November. But the legacy of dissent would remain strong, particularly amongst the urbanites of New Orleans. See Willie Malvin Caskey, *Secession and Restoration of Louisiana* (New York: Da Capo Press, 1970; originally published 1938); John D. Winters, *The Civil War in Louisiana* (Baton Rouge: Louisiana State University Press, 1991); and Arthur W. Bergeron, ed. *The Civil War in Louisiana: The Home Front*, vol. 5, part B, *The Louisiana Purchase Bicentennial Series in Louisiana History* (Lafayette, LA: Center for Louisiana Studies, 2004).

As reported in the New York *Saturday Press* of July 30, 1859, toward the end of July what was described as

> A curious dinner-party came off . . . at the Athanaeum Club, in Fifth Avenue. It consisted of Mr. Morphy, Senator Douglas, Colonel Forney, John Brougham, the Rev. Mr. Milburn, Park Benjamin, and others. A few days before Mr. Morphy dined with Ex. Governor Walker at Hoboken, and a few days later with Mr. Senator Benjamin at the New York Hotel.

Earlier in the month the press reported that Morphy was seriously indisposed and might go to the White Mountains for his health, and he finally decided to do so. In early August he left New York for the White Mountains and Newport. While at Newport, he stayed at the Ocean House, where he met Mrs. Butt and her daughter, Virginia. The latter engaged Morphy over the board and probably won.

A letter from Newport, published in the New York *Albion* of September 3, 1859, stated that

> the ladies wished to put on a set of *Tableaux Vivants* and engage the services of Mr. Morphy, the celebrated chess-player, who is among the temporary lions here. And it was proposed to enact a tableau of the "Game of Life" [Retzsch] with a complimentary variation representing Morphy as the young man *beating the Devil* in the final game. But the characteristic modesty of Mr. Morphy was invincible, and he courteously declined to appear.

As will be described later, an incident did occur in which Morphy played the role of a young man trying to save his soul by winning a game of Satan.

Morphy also visited Niagara Falls and returned to New York to find Judge Meek and W. W. Montgomery sojourning in the city. He was, of course, induced to play chess with them. Thompson, still dissatisfied with the result of his match at the odds of a Knight, asked for further play, and again Morphy won in the same proportion as he had before—Morphy ten, Thompson six—for a total of Morphy sixteen, Thompson nine, and one game drawn at the odds of Knight.

On September 10, at long last, *The First American Chess Congress* book was published. It had originally been promised for the spring of 1858 but the book grew in the hands of Fiske and finally appeared as a volume of 563 pages. It is not only a full report on the Chess Congress of 1857 but contains invaluable chapters on the history of chess, Americans in chess from Benjamin Franklin to Paul Morphy, the Automaton, etc., and all the games of the Grand Tournament, as well as many other Morphy games. As the *Chess Monthly* of October 1859 stated, "The games contained in the lengthy sketch of Mr. Morphy's life are regarded by him as the very best contests he ever played." It also gave the sixty-eight-move solution to Cook's frontispiece problem, which Cook later found he could solve in twenty moves. At this point, games of the Congress, including Morphy's, were made public for the first time, released from the restrictions of the Congress rules.*

In October, the proof sheets of Lowenthal's book on Morphy's games arrived, for the Appleton edition, and Morphy was busy proofreading.

The *Gambit*, a new chess weekly periodical edited by Theodore Lichtenhein, made its appearance on October 22, priced at three cents a copy, and it was the first to publish some of Morphy's games.

While in New York, Morphy had received many earnest solicitations from cities eager to honor him, but time allowed him to visit only those directly on his path toward New Orleans. He planned to visit Philadelphia, Baltimore, and Washington, the last merely for sightseeing. Philadelphia had great plans for his visit, but Morphy, in the following letter, published in the *Charleston Courier* of August 3, 1859, ruled them out:

> Brevoort House, New York, July 21, 1859
> Professor George Allen
>
> My Dear Sir:
>
> In my last communication to you I stated that it was not in my power to specify any period at which to visit your city. My engagements here have been such, that I have, up to this day, found it impossible to determine upon any definite time for the acceptance of your invitation. In view of this fact and for other reasons, which will readily suggest themselves to you, I feel compelled to decline any public reception in Philadelphia.
>
> I shall, however, avail myself of the earliest opportunity to pay a friendly and unceremonious visit to the members of the Athenaeum.
>
> With high regard,
> Paul Morphy.

---

* EDITOR'S NOTE: As previously mentioned, Fiske's *The First American Chess Congress* was republished in 1985 by Edition Olms.

On receipt of the above letter, the Philadelphia Committee of Arrangements held their final meeting and authorized the return of all money to the subscribers, but they did so with resentment, feeling Morphy had slighted them. The resentment increased with time, becoming most noticeable the following year in a case involving a Mr. Deacon, discussed in Chapter 18.

After a hectic four-month period, Morphy's time in New York drew to a close. New York's *Porter's Spirit of the Times* of November 5, 1859, described Morphy's last few days in the city:

> Mr. Morphy's Congé.—Thursday evening, Oct. 27th, was the time appointed for Mr. Morphy to say farewell to the New York Chess-Club, as he is about leaving the city. The Club was crowded to see the great chess-player's last appearance in our own chess-circles. Mr. Morphy played two games, at the odds of the Rook, with Arthur Napoleon, the great pianist winning both games but the young artist showed the possession of very considerable chess-talent, and the games were highly interesting. On Friday evening a supper was given to the Champion, at Jones's Hotel, by several of his friends, members of the chess-club. Mr. Morphy will leave behind him, besides the memory of his many extraordinary victories, reminiscences of his kindly manners and courteous conduct.

During Morphy's stay in New York, two local publishers brought out books about him. Edge's book, *The Exploits and Triumphs in Europe of Paul Morphy*, appeared on May 21, and in August, Charles H. Stanley brought out *Paul Morphy's Match Games*, of which the frontispiece engraving of Morphy is the finest to be had. Its price was thirty-eight cents.

Earlier in the year, Thomas Frère's little book, *Morphy's Games* (not including those with Anderssen), was published. Still earlier a little booklet had been published by M. M. Couvée in 1858 at Gravenhage's, *Twee Merkwaardige Partijen* (*Two Remarkable Games*), containing only two games— one of Morphy's with Barnes and the other Morphy's fourth match with Harrwitz.[*]

Morphy left New York on October 30. The next day, on the way back to New Orleans, he stopped in Philadelphia, and that evening he was introduced by Louis Elkin to the members of the Athenaeum Chess Club. The following day he encountered William G. Thomas at Knight odds and lost

---

[*] EDITOR'S NOTE: As previously mentioned, op cit page 206, Edge's *The Exploits and Triumphs in Europe of Paul Morphy* was republished in 1973, and is also available in a free online edition. Stanley's *Paul Morphy's Match Games*, Frère's *Morphy's Games*, and Couvée's *Twee Merkwaardige Partijen* have not been so lucky.

both games. They then played two games at odds of Pawn and two moves, and Morphy won both. On November 2, Morphy played Dr. Samuel Lewis, B. C. Tilghman, and others at Knight odds, winning all games.

Apparently Morphy received a testimonial gift of sorts the next day, for it was reported in the Pennsylvania *Inquirer* of November 4, 1859, that "the next move Mr. Morphy makes will be to the Brown Stone Clothing Hall of Rockhill & Wilson . . . where he will get himself a new and elegant suit."

On November 7, Morphy and Thomas again contested at Knight odds, but this time Thomas agreed to play open games, answering Morphy's P–K4 with P–K4, with the result that Thomas lost both games. On the following Friday, November 11, Morphy departed from his previously announced intention, giving Philadelphia its first blindfold exhibition for the benefit of the Mount Vernon Fund, as told by the Philadelphia *Evening Bulletin* of November 12, 1859:

> On Mr. Morphy's return from his triumphant foreign campaign, last Spring, it was announced that he had wisely determined to abandon the exercise of his extraordinary gift of blindfold play, regarding it very justly, as injurious in its effects on the brain, and therefore, as we should suppose, likely to weaken the general force of his play.
>
> In departing from this sensible resolution, for a single occasion, and yielding gracefully to the behests of the enthusiastic Vice Regent of the Mount Vernon Association, Mr. Morphy at once testified his practical interest in the noble object of the Association and afforded a rare treat to the chess playing community of Philadelphia.
>
> It was arranged that four blindfold games should be played simultaneously at the Academy of Music. The four gentlemen who offered themselves willingly as victims at the shrines of Caïssa and Mount Vernon were Wm. G. Thomas, Esq., B. C. Tilghman, Esq., Samuel Smyth, Esq., and Samuel Lewis, M.D.
>
> Four of the large Athenaeum chess tables were ranged across the front of the stage, and at a few minutes after six the players seated, and Mr. Morphy was introduced to the audience by Rob't Rogers, M.D., Dean of the University of Pennsylvania, in a very neat and appropriate manner.
>
> Mr. Morphy then took his seat in a comfortable arm-chair, placed in the middle of the stage, where he could be distinctly

seen and heard, and where he could not see the boards.

The games were begun by Mr. Morphy announcing in a clear, smooth voice, which we presume was heard throughout the house, "Pawn to King's Fourth on all the tables." His moves were carefully repeated by R. H. Jones, Esq., who deserves much credit for the careful manner in which he super-intended the four games. It will be observed by an inspection of the games below, that Messrs. Thomas and Tilghman, with much more chivalry than prudence, boldly accepted open games, while their more wary if not more successful comrades, played close defenses.

The progress of the games was watched with breathless interest by the spectators. Chess boards were in operation in various parts of the house, and a battery of opera-glasses were leveled at the battle-field. Mr. Morphy's manner was perfectly quiet and collected—occasionally he paused long over the move, but we were satisfied that he was not engaged in reforming the position before his mind's eye, but in working out his combinations as he would have to do over the board.

The result will be seen below. Mr. Tilghman first, then Dr. Lewis, then Mr. Thomas, and, last of all, Mr. Smyth went down before the irresistible force of Mr. Morphy's lance and each in turn gracefully resigned his seat amid the plaudits of the spectators. The whole four games were concluded at about half-past nine o'clock, and the audience retired highly delighted at this remarkable exhibition, and wondering more than ever over the extraordinary mental powers, whose exercise they had just witnessed.

The following Monday, W. G. Thomas, still doubting that Morphy could give him Knight odds and beat him at any opening, played two more games with Morphy. The first was a draw, but Thomas lost the second. It had been expected that H. P. Montgomery, considered Philadelphia's strongest chess player, would participate in games with Morphy. He did sit down with Morphy, prepared to play, but when Morphy offered odds, Montgomery refused to accept them, and so no play took place between the two men.

It was not unusual at that time for games and matches to be played at varying odds, and while Morphy was in Philadelphia, the New York *Albion* published a challenge to Mr. Montgomery to play a match for $1,000 with Mr. Morphy, consisting of an equal number of games at the odds of the

Knight, Pawn, and two moves; Pawn and move; and even. The indirect reply, as reported in the Philadelphia *Bulletin* of November 19, 1859, was that "Mr. Montgomery has never claimed the ability to play such a match, or any other match, successfully with Mr. Morphy, and therefore is not bound to entertain such a proposition."

Morphy left Philadelphia Thursday morning, November 17, and arrived in Baltimore that afternoon, putting up at Barnum's Hotel, where he was happily greeted by members of the chess clubs of the city, and as chronicled in the Baltimore *Clipper* of November 18, 1859, that night "he visited the Holliday Street Theatre and was quite lionized."

Friday evening he visited the rooms of the Monumental Chess Club, where he met successfully at Knight odds Messrs. Walters, Nicholson, and Gill of the Baltimore Chess Club, and Dr. A. B. Arnold and S. N. Carvalho of the Monumental Chess Club. The next day he visited the Baltimore Chess Club. The large library rooms of the Maryland Historical Society were put in use for the occasion, Morphy offering Knight odds to Messrs. Miller, Zimilini, White, Williams, and Drs. Baer and Cohen. About one hundred persons were present to watch the playing.

Over the weekend Morphy sat for S. N. Carvalho for a portrait in oil that is presently owned by the Maryland Historical Society. On Monday afternoon he visited Chapin B. Harris, an invalid who had expressed a desire to see Morphy, and they also played a game. The Baltimore *Daily Exchange* of November 24, 1859, reported that that evening there was an "entertainment in honor of Paul Morphy by the Chess Amateurs of Baltimore prepared by Guy's House," at which time he announced he would be leaving Baltimore the coming Wednesday.

Morphy arrived in New Orleans the week of December 12, some twenty days after having left Baltimore. Obviously, he had stopped somewhere in the interim. Washington and Richmond have been mentioned as places he may have visited.

His announced intention now was to establish himself in his profession in New Orleans. Morphy had for a time considered taking up residence in New York, but in the end he decided against it. Back home now, he wished to relax and rest on his laurels for a while, and enjoy the comforts and pleasures of private life. However, he did say, as the New Orleans *Sunday Delta* of December 18, 1859, reported, that it was "his intention to visit the amateurs of the Commercial Chess Rooms as soon as he will have entirely recovered from the fatigues of his journey." But Morphy had not come back to play chess, except perhaps with his friend Maurian. And of course at this time he still had his chess editorial responsibilities for the *Ledger* to attend to.

CHAPTER 18

The Deacon Games

Now that he was back in New Orleans, it would seem that at last Morphy could settle down to a normal life. There was even the possibility that Staunton's unkind remarks would now fade away. But it was not to be. Staunton had been working on a new book, and the following announcement of it appeared in the *Illustrated London News* of December 17, 1859:

CHESS IN THE METROPOLIS

The two following games, hitherto unprinted, are extracted from the forthcoming Guide to Chess by Mr. Staunton. This work, so long expected, is on the eve of publication, and will be found to contain the promised new code of chess laws, based upon the treatises of Messrs. Jaenisch, Heyderbrand, and Staunton—a copious analysis, extending over some four hundred pages, of all the improvements in the openings devised since the appearance of the author's "Handbook," and, "in compliance with the expressed wish of very many influential amateurs," a classified collection of Mr. Morphy's games, about one hundred and fifty in number, accompanied by critical and explanatory annotation. The new volume is to be issued by Mr. Bohn, and will be uniform in size, appearance, and price with "The Chessplayer's Handbook."

Then followed "a finely-played Gambit between Mr. Morphy and Mr. F. Deacon," won by the latter, giving checkmate to Morphy in forty-six moves. This was followed by an Evans Gambit between the same players, won by Morphy.

Apparently Morphy did not become aware of the above until well into January 1860, when he sent the following letter to W. J. A. Fuller of New York:

New Orleans, January 19th, 1860

Dear Fuller:

The two games published by Staunton in the *Illustrated London News* of December 17th, were not played by myself with

253

Deacon. I never contested a single game with Deacon, either on even terms or at odds. Had I played at all, I would have given him the Pawn and Move at least, as public estimation does not rank him as a player on an equality with Owen, to whom I yielded those odds successfully. One of the games published in the *Illustrated News*—the Evans Gambit—was shown to me in London by Riviere, as having been played between Deacon and himself. I do not know who Deacon's competitor was in the other game, but must repeat that some one has been guilty of deliberate falsehood in both instances.

Ever yours,
Paul Morphy

The following Sunday, January 22, 1860, the *New Orleans Delta* commented:

The games published in the *London Illustrated News* of the 17th December last, and purporting to have been played between Messrs. Morphy and Deacon, were certainly never played by the former gentleman; indeed, he never played a game with Mr. Deacon. If we did not know who the Chess editor of the *Illustrated News* is, we might suppose he had here committed an error, but being aware that the Chess Department of that paper is under the care of Howard Staunton, we do not hesitate to say that he willfully attributed games of inferior quality to Mr. Morphy, well knowing they had never been played by him. This is in perfect accordance with his course heretofore, but it is needless to say that no one will be gulled by this new dodge of Mr. Staunton, as it will be duly exposed, we hope, by all chess-publishing papers.

Fiske now published "A Card" on February 1, 1860:

A CARD.

HOWARD STAUNTON.

It will be remembered that the *Illustrated News* of London, under date of December 17th, 1859, published, in its chess column, two games purporting to to have been played between Mr. MORPHY and Mr. DEACON. These contests have been extensively copied into the chess journals of this country, and doubtless, by this time, have been reprinted in many of the chess periodicals of Europe. Since their appearance, it has been a matter of surprise, with many, that Mr. MORPHY, in the very full list of his European competitors, which was published by authority in the CHESS MONTHLY, should have omitted the name of Mr. DEACON. The matter is explained by the following extract from a private note, just received from Mr. MORPHY by W. J. A. FULLER, Esq., of New York city.

NEW ORLEANS, January 19th, 1860.

DEAR FULLER:

The two games published by Staunton in the *Illustrated London News* of December 17th, were *not* played by myself with Deacon. I never contested a single game with Deacon, either on even terms or at odds. Had I played at all, I would have given him the Pawn and Move at least, as public estimation does not rank him as a player on an equality with Owen, to whom I yielded those odds successfully. One of the games published in the *Illustrated News*, —the Evans Gambit—was shown to me in London by Rivière, as having been played between Deacon and himself. I do not know who Deacon's competitor was in the other game, but must repeat that some one has been guilty of deliberate falsehood in both instances.

Ever Yours,

PAUL MORPHY.

This hardly needs any comment. The world has long been familiar with the weaknesses of the Chess-Editor of the *Illustrated News*. It has seen him guilty of a thousand misrepresentations, of a thousand prevarications, of a thousand mis-statements. But it could hardly expect to see him originate a gross literary fraud—a fraud which, without any of the genius, exhibits all the moral depravity of a Chatterton, a Macpherson, or an Ireland.

After this, it will hardly be necessary to caution the chess public against Mr. Staunton's new volume, which he styles, it is believed, *Chess Praxis.* It is to contain, as Mr. Staunton says, the games alluded to above, together with many other contests purporting to have been played by Mr. Morphy. How many of these will be spurious, it is impossible, as yet, to state. But it is to be hoped that Mr. Bohn, the publisher, will not run the risk of injuring his large American trade by the encouragement of an imposture so bare-faced as a collection of PAUL MORPHY's games, edited by Howard Staunton, must necessarily be.

New York, February 1st, 1860.

Staunton's book was undoubtedly too far advanced in the press for any possible alterations, and the two games appear therein. Incidentally, Morphy mentions in his letter to Fuller that had he played Deacon he "would have given him the Pawn and Move at least." Morphy may or may not have known that Lowenthal had given those same odds to Deacon successfully on June 2, 1857, and that the game was printed in the *Era* of London on August 2, 1857, for all to see, including, of course, Staunton. Yet Staunton was a staunch defender of Deacon and said that Morphy "condescend[ed] to depreciate" Deacon's skill by suggesting odds (see Appendix, Staunton in *Illustrated London News*, March 31, 1860).

The *Chess Monthly* for March had a short comment on the alleged Morphy–Deacon games:

> We are authorized to state that the games in question are forgeries, and that Mr. Morphy never played any games whatever with Mr. Deacon. Had he contended against that gentleman he would have given him Pawn and move at least, as public estimation does not rank him as a player as high as Mr. Owen, to whom Mr. Morphy successfully yielded these odds.

Philadelphia's *Forney's War Press* of April 27, 1864, also spoke of the games:

> Immediately upon seeing these games Mr. Morphy pronounced them forgeries, asserting that he had never played at all with Deacon. He also stated that one of the games was shown to him in London by the French player, Dr. Riviere, as having been won by him from the Englishman; and in this Mr. Morphy was corroborated by M. De Riviere before his statement had reached Europe. Of course, it was now incumbent upon Mr. Deacon to prove his veracity, but he contented himself with simply affirming the authenticity of the games, in which he was supported in very bitter and abusive language by Mr. Staunton, in the *Illustrated London News* [March 31, 1860].

Fiske's "Card" of February 1, 1860, given above, appeared in the New Orleans *Delta* of February 26, 1860. Mr. Deacon took notice of it in letters to the *Illustrated London News* of March 31, 1860 (see Appendix), and the *Illustrated News of the World* of March 24, 1860, but took no notice of Morphy's statement that the Evans Gambit game was played by Rivière.

There is no reason to believe that Staunton and Deacon acted in concert in any publication of forged games, but it is possible that once Deacon had submitted the games, Staunton willingly accepted and backed them, even though he may have had doubts concerning their authenticity. It is hardly to be considered that Deacon, known as a "game parader" in Mac-Donnell's words, would have kept a successful encounter with Morphy a secret for several months, especially at a time (April 1859) when winning from Morphy on even terms would have meant great publicity and prestige.

As it happened, Rivière had seen the *Illustrated London News* of December 17, 1859, before it reached America, and wrote Staunton that the Evans Gambit was one that he, not Morphy, had played with Deacon. Rivière's recollection of the game was evidently good because he had discussed it with Morphy. On February 18, Staunton published a Rivière–Deacon game, which was identical with the one he had printed as the Morphy–Deacon game up to the ninth move. But Staunton added an opinion, which he said Rivière had offered as a possible explanation for the situation created by Deacon.

Staunton never published Rivière's letter, unfortunately, for he had a reputation of using his chess column arbitrarily, but he added the following note to the game, which might or might not have been in strict accordance with the intent of Rivière's letter:

> Up to this point [ninth move] the moves are identical with a game between Mr. Morphy and Mr. Deacon, printed in our journal of Dec. 17th; and, indeed, M. de Riviere writes to us expressing an opinion that this identity in the opening has led Mr. Deacon into the error of confounding the games. Mr. de Riviere believes that the Evans Gambit in question, published on Dec. 17th, was really played betwixt him and Mr. Deacon, while the present game was that won by Mr. Morphy.

Altogether, a very disagreeable controversy developed in the press, which had its effect on Morphy, who wanted no part in it. Again there was attack and the question of veracity. On April 22 the New Orleans *Sunday Delta* had the following:

> A delay has occurred lately in the forwarding of Mr. Morphy's copy to the *Ledger*, owing to a painful indisposition of that gentleman from the effects of which he is, we are happy to say, almost entirely recovered.

Mr. Deacon's reply to Mr. Morphy's letter, published in this paper, appears in the *News of the World* in March, and in the *London News* of the same date. It is evident that the clever English amateur did not anticipate so prompt and forcible a denunciation of his trick when he forwarded these spurious games to Mr. Staunton, for his reply to Mr. Morphy's card is weak in the extreme; he does not even attempt to prove his assertion, but merely insists that Mr. Morphy is mistaken, and has forgotten, &c. The public would certainly be very glad to learn when these games were played, where they were played, in presence of whom and why. Mr. Morphy's score with Mr. Deacon was not published, whilst that with every other player of note was regularly made known to the public by the weekly chess columns. It is to be hoped that in some future communication Mr. Deacon will throw some light on the subject; indeed he will be required to do so by Mr. Morphy.

We have gathered the following facts from Mr. Morphy.

1st. That he made Mr. Deacon's acquaintance only two weeks before his departure.

2nd. That he did not play with Mr. Deacon in any of the Chess Clubs of London, as their respective members will testify.

3rd. That he once visited Mr. Mongredien in company with Messrs. Deacon, Sybrandt, De Riviere and Maude, but did not play there, except with Mr. Maude at Pawn and 2, as the gentlemen who were present will prove.

4th. That he did not meet Mr. Deacon at chess at the British Hotel, where he (Mr. Morphy) resided during his sojourn in England, as Messrs. Sybrandt and De Riviere, who were constantly with him, will say.

Where then were the games played? How comes it too, that one of the games purporting to have been played with Mr. Morphy is claimed by Mr. De Riviere as his own[?]

Mr. Deacon indirectly replied to the above through his response to a request from the chess editor of the Philadelphia *Evening Bulletin*, who had written to a friend in London rather than to Morphy for information:

> May 9, 1860 3 Hales Place
> South Lambeth

Dear Sir:

In answer to your letter of yesterday, I need hardly say how happy and thankful I am to give the particulars of my playing with Mr. Morphy; to bear out gentlemen who have so fairly, and to their honor, preferred believing in the fallibility of memory, rather than in loathsome—may I not say impossible—crime.

On the night when Mr. Morphy played his blindfold game at the London Chess Club, Mr. Lowenthal and myself accompanied Mr. Morphy and his brother-in-law from the Club, as far as Charing Cross; on leaving them, both Mr. Morphy and his brother-in-law pressed me to call upon them at the "British Hotel." This invitation was repeated a day or two afterwards at the St. James Chess Club, and on the following Monday I called upon them at that hotel. I was accompanied by my cousin, Col. Charles Deacon, and Mr. Morphy received us very courteously, and showed us a game he had played at Paris, and then played two games with me, the first of which he won, and lost the second.

One of the waiters came in the room several times, and my cousin was present while Mr. Morphy played with me. Our visit was made at about half-past ten in the morning, and we left at about two o'clock. On the evening of that day, I took down the games, together with some others, although I only put Mr. Morphy's name to the game I had won of him, and that game my cousin distinctly remembers, with some remarks which were made during and after the play. These games were played exactly as they were published in the *London Illustrated News*.

Col. Deacon is now in Westmoreland, but I will write to him, by to-day's post, and he will give you his corroboration of these circumstances.

Regarding the affair, however, as in truth, only a question of memory, I do hope and trust that Mr. Morphy will be able and will soon make amends for the forgetfulness by a manly and honorable acknowledgement.

May I add, dear sir, these details are to be used as you may think best, for I feel and know full well how unnecessary any information would be to satisfy your mind upon the subject.

Believe me, sincerely yours,
Fred. Deacon.

In the above letter Deacon does give specifics, i.e., time, place, and a witness. But Morphy, on the other hand, names two, Sybrandt and Rivière, the latter an esteemed chess master, willing to testify that no chess games whatsoever took place at the British Hotel between Morphy and Deacon. It may well be, as Deacon says, that he "*called* [italics added] upon them [Morphy and Sybrandt] at that hotel." In the *Delta* of April 22 it is stated that Morphy "did not meet Deacon at chess [playing] at the British Hotel." But this does not rule out Steinitz's explanation of what happened, which will be given later.

Note that Deacon also says, "I only put Mr. Morphy's name on the game I had won of him." It seems very unlikely, even strange, that he would not have put Morphy's name on both games he says he played with him. Of course he knew that in saying he had not put Morphy's name on the Evans Gambit game that evening as he "took down the games" and made notes, it would lend plausibility to Rivière's explanation of a possible mix-up, about which Deacon now knew and was undoubtedly glad to accept.

The *Chess Monthly* of July 1860 printed Deacon's letter of May 9, 1860, "without comment, to our readers, as sufficient time has not elapsed since its publication in this country to enable Mr. Morphy's reply to reach us. His answer will appear in our August number." But Morphy refused to reply, and there was no longer a Frederick Edge to assure a forthright rebuttal. However, the *Illustrated News of the World* of September 1, 1860, quoted J. D. Sybrandt, Morphy's brother-in-law, in defense of Morphy's position:

> J. D. Sybrandt, Swedish and Norwegian Consul in New Or-
> leans, and brother-in-law to Mr. Morphy, was with the lat-
> ter during the whole of his second sojourn in London . . . Mr.
> W. J. A. Fuller authorizes us to state that Mr. Sybrandt used the
> following language in speaking of the Deacon affair to him: "I
> was with Morphy constantly, went with him everywhere, and I
> would *swear* that he did not play a game with Deacon!" To Mr.
> D. W. Fiske he said, "I was at Morphy's elbow continually, and I
> know that he played no games with Deacon."

The following reasons, noted in *Forney's War Press* of April 27, 1864, were also offered as proof of the inauthenticity of the Morphy–Deacon games:

> 1st. The lapse of time between Mr. Morphy's departure from
> England and the publication of the games, eight months were
> suffered to pass, that the memory of Mr. Morphy and his friends
> might become indistinct.

2d. Mr. Morphy's score was repeatedly published in England, but contained no mention of any games with Deacon, yet the latter never opened his lips to say that it was incorrect, as, if he were honest, he ought to have done.

3d. He did not contribute the contests to Lowenthal's edition of Morphy's games, a work published under Mr. Morphy's superintendence; this looks very much as if he knew that Morphy would deny them.

4th. The mistake before noticed about the De Riviere game, which was never satisfactorily explained.

5th. The game asserted to have been won by Deacon is very inferior to Mr. Morphy's usual style of play.

As for Rivière, neither Staunton nor Deacon ever challenged Morphy's call upon Rivière as his witness that Deacon never played a game with Morphy at the British Hotel.

Oddly, neither Deacon nor Staunton ever mentioned or questioned the authenticity of the Evans game published as a Morphy–Deacon game, although Morphy and Rivière both agreed the latter had played it with Deacon. In this letter of May 9, 1860, Deacon said, "These games were played exactly as they were published in the *Illustrated London News*."

Staunton confined himself to a slashing and abusive attack on Morphy in the *Illustrated London News* of March 31, 1860 (see Appendix), the language of which Morphy would not have known how to cope with:

The [Morphy–Deacon] games were published, accompanied by annotations from the pen of the English player, Mr. Deacon, in our paper of December 17, 1859. Upon their reaching America, Mr. Morphy flatly denied that he had ever played a single game with Mr. Deacon. This denial might be pardoned, if expressed in gentlemanly terms on the ground that the American had forgotten, among battles with so many eminent opponents, an encounter with one so little known. But Mr. Morphy, not content with denying ever having played with Mr. Deacon, condescends to depreciate his skill, and asserts, in the most offensive manner, that "some one has been guilty of deliberate falsehood. . . ."

Now, apart from the incredible stupidity and grossness of such a charge, what is most remarkable in the affair (giving Mr. Mor-

phy credit for really having forgotten his play with Mr. Deacon)
is the surpassing vanity of that gentleman. . . . If there has been
any "deliberate falsehood" in the matter, it originated on the
other side of the Atlantic.

Such abusive terms as "offensive manner," "incredible stupidity,"
"grossness," "surpassing vanity," and "deliberate falsehood," do not seem
to apply to Morphy, nor does the bold statement that he did not remember
having played two games with Mr. Deacon eight months before and accus-
ing him of "deliberate falsehood."

Deacon said in his letter of May 9 that "Col. Deacon is now in Westmoreland, but I will write to him, by to-day's post, and he will give you his
corroboration of these circumstances." But this corroboration was a long
time coming; only after being pressed by the chess editor of the Philadelphia *Evening Bulletin*, who appears to have been sympathetic to Staunton
and Deacon, did Colonel Deacon finally write:

> 4, Edwards-square, Kensington, London,
> Jan. 14, 1861
>
> Dear Sirs,—
>
> In reply to your note of December 17, accept my sincere acknowledg-
> ment for your fair and manly defense of my cousin, which we warmly
> appreciate; but the controversy to which you refer has been conducted
> by a portion of the American press in a manner which really precludes
> my entering into it—indeed, in the whole course of my life I have never
> known anything so outrageous and dastardly as the manner in which we
> have been attacked. Under different circumstances however, I should
> have been happy to have given you my testimony, which would have
> fully borne out the statement sent to you some time ago by Mr. Fred
> Deacon; and I must add, from the gentlemanly way in which you have
> put the case, I regret that, for the reason I have mentioned, I cannot give
> you a more complete answer.
>
> I am, dear Sirs, Yours truly
> Chas. Deacon

The letter seems peculiarly evasive. Certainly it is not an outright
statement that the colonel had accompanied Frederick Deacon to the British Hotel and had there witnessed Mr. Morphy playing chess with Mr.
Deacon. He says that "under different circumstances" he *would have given*
supporting testimony. Yet if there was unjust criticism, then one would
imagine there to be all the more reason for his "testimony which would

have fully borne out the statement" of Frederick Deacon.

Staunton published Colonel Deacon's letter of January 14, 1861, in his chess column of March 30, 1861 (see Appendix), together with comments on the behavior of Morphy and others. For him there was no shadow of a doubt about the authenticity of the Morphy–Deacon games. As he noted in that column:

> Mr. Deacon stated in writing [May 9, letter] that the disputed games were played, on a certain day named, at the British Hotel in Cockspur-street, where Mr. Morphy then resided, in the presence of Colonel Charles Deacon. Among gentlemen this explanation would, of course, have been conclusive.

If one is to take Mr. Staunton literally, it should not have been necessary for Mr. Deacon to have named a date, place, or witness, for among gentlemen, his word should have been sufficient without details, and for Mr. Staunton and the Philadelphia *Evening Bulletin* it was sufficient.

Three years later there appeared in the chess column of Philadelphia's *Forney's War Press* on April 27, 1864, a long letter reprinted from the Syracuse *Daily Journal*, to which it had been sent by an American in London:

> London, Jan. 26, 1864

> I called at the St. James Club Rooms to see Lowenthal, and while there was introduced to a person whose name I failed to catch. From his appearance and talk I very soon concluded that he was a very small nobody whose constant effort was to appear a very great somebody ... when—imagine my sensation! someone addressed him as Mr. Deacon! ... Deacon is rather laughed at than disliked. Whenever his name is mentioned, a smile comes up and somebody is pretty sure to say, "poor Deacon."

> A person who dislikes the bottom of Morphy's character, told me that there could, nevertheless, be no doubt that Deacon never played the disputed games with Mr. Morphy. Not satisfied with his success in his first effort at forging games, Deacon made a second display of his talents in the same direction. He published a number of games purporting to have been played between himself and Steinitz.

> The latter declares that these games were never played! A letter of repudiation was written for publication by Steinitz; but Lowenthal prevailed upon him to suppress it. Steinitz was a poor man, and a foreigner, and Lowenthal told him that he could not

afford to make enemies; and that the cause of chess was injured by the constant controversies and bad deeds of chess-players. Another of Deacon's misdeeds was to send old problems—or at least, one old problem—to compete for the prizes offered in connection with the Congress of 1862.

The following note was added to the above letter by Forney: "There can be little question as to the veracity of the writer, who is a gentleman long and favorably known in the American Chess community."

The best proof of the veracity of the above letter was given by Steinitz himself some twenty years later, during a visit to New Orleans in 1883. His words were still later recorded in the New Orleans *Times-Democrat* of September 17, 1911:

> When the Deacon games came up for discussion—"What— Deacon win those parties?" broke in the great Bohemian master. "Nonsense! he has claimed to have won just such a game from me, though I never played any such with him." And then he went on to explain that Deacon had a habit of getting master players to try out certain variations of particular openings with him, testing and re-testing sub-variations innumerable, taking back moves *ad lib*, and the like; and then lo and behold! reproducing some one line of play that had turned in favor of his side of the board as a game won from his distinguished adversary! And Steinitz thumped his stick on the pavement and chuckled grimly, as he imparted the data in relation to the even then somewhat ancient controversy.

Steinitz told of his Deacon experience in greater detail in his *International Chess Magazine* of September 1891:

> I judge that Deacon played on Morphy a trick similar to the one which he practiced upon myself in the following manner. Shortly after I had played my match with him in 1863 he invited my attention on the one occasion when we were both alone in the rooms of the London Chess Club to a new move which he said he had invented in one of the openings. At that time a novelty in the openings was considered quite a revelation, and as I knew little of the books I got interested and consented at his request to examine the variation with him. . . .
>
> In the skittle analysis which followed I demolished his suggested novelty in several main lines of play as well as in sub-

variations which he tried after taking moves back. But at last, probably owing to some thoughtless move which I had adopted in the investigation, he got hold of a better position and then he began to move slowly. But when I wanted to amend my previous play as he had done repeatedly before, he begged of me to go on[,] on the plea that he believed that he would construct a fine position from that point for analytical purposes or perhaps for a problem (for he was also a composer). He then deliberated on each move as if it were a match game, and if anyone had come into the room he must have thought we were playing a real hard fight. After some more moves the position resolved itself into an ending in which he had a decisive advantage and he agreed ultimately not to go further.

On another occasion shortly after that[,] another opening was made the subject of one experiment and the same story almost exactly repeated itself. Great was, however, my surprise when about six months later I saw two games published which were alleged to have been played between Deacon and myself in the Dutch Chess journal *Sissa*. They comprised the opening moves in the two "novelties" which were the subject of our investigation, but almost all the rest (and I am certain about the concluding six or eight moves on each side) was entirely a new and imaginary fabrication. . . .

But some time afterward it also came out that Deacon had played similar tricks on Signor Dubois and also to Mr. Blackburne and the Rev. J. Owen, and especially the latter gentleman threatened to take action against Deacon at the St. George's Chess Club, of which both were members. Deacon then disappeared and retreated to his Belgian refuge. He was never seen in London again, and about a year afterward his death was announced. Judging from that[,] I have no doubt that Morphy was entrapped to answer some analytical questions and to investigate some suggestions of Deacon over the board. What Colonel Deacon saw was nothing more than experimenting, in the course of which Morphy most probably had given back moves, as I did subsequently.

We now come to the final stage of the Morphy–Deacon affair. As Sergeant says in the Preface to his *Morphy Gleanings* on the question of the genuineness of the "Evans" game given on page 65 as a Morphy game, it has been "for very many years relegated to the category of spurious." The Evans game Staunton printed lost all credibility as a Morphy game when

Morphy and Rivière both agreed it belonged to the latter. There has never been any serious consideration of the other game Staunton published, beyond Deacon's *"ipse dixit"* ("he himself said so"), as London's July *Chess World* of 1868 points out:

> Why did not Mr. Deacon hand about among his friends the game he won of Morphy at the time it was played? Or, if he did, why did he not adduce their testimony? I understand that nobody that has played with Mr. Deacon is likely to forget him, and Morphy had an extraordinary power of recollecting trains of play; so, if he was beaten by Mr. Deacon, it is impossible that he could have forgotten either the fact or the games.

In Part II, Section 6 of *Morphy Gleanings*, Sergeant discusses an attempt made by B. Goulding Brown to make a case for Deacon in the matter of the Evans game. Sergeant nevertheless concludes that

> it is difficult to get over the statement in the American Chess Magazine [*Chess Monthly*] of May 1860: "We are authorized to state that the games in question are forgeries, and that Mr. Morphy never played any games whatever with Mr. Deacon." It was pointed out in the New Orleans *Times-Democrat* of September 16 [September 17], 1911, that neither Staunton nor Deacon ever seems to have challenged Morphy's call upon Arnous de Riviere as his witness in the matter.

In the same volume, Sergeant states that Brown said Deacon "gave evidence very fully" when asked for it, providing a date, place, and a witness. But Brown does not mention that Morphy named two reliable witnesses, Rivière and Sybrandt, who would testify that no such meeting ever took place. Nevertheless, Brown is very satisfied with Deacon's "evidence." It would seem from Brown's account of the Morphy–Deacon controversy that he stretched the circumstances of the case in favor of Deacon and Staunton, just as he had slanted the case in Staunton's favor in the earlier Morphy–Staunton controversy (see Chapter 11).

Again, in *Morphy's Gleanings*, Sergeant discusses the manner in which Brown arrived at his seemingly untenable position in defense of Deacon in this matter:

> Now comes [as Brown says] de Riviere's contribution to this mystery. An Evans Gambit was published in *The Illustrated London News*, February 18th, 1860, as won by de Riviere

against Deacon, but de Riviere believed, first, that he had never played this game, and, secondly, that he *was* the winner of the alleged Morphy–Deacon Evans. The games were the same up to White's ninth move, and it was de Riviere's *opinion* that this similarity had caused Deacon to confuse them, and to publish de Riviere's win as Morphy's, and Morphy's win as de Riviere's.

Brown relies greatly upon Rivière, not only on account of Rivière's opinion as reported by Staunton, but also because of the known friendship between Rivière and Morphy. Brown makes the point that Rivière's interpretation

> shows that a witness favorable to Morphy, and in fact the European chess player whom Morphy most liked[,] believed in the bona-fides of Deacon, at any rate to the extent of accepting the fact that Morphy had beaten him.

It is true enough that Rivière was the European chess player whom Morphy liked most. But, if quoted correctly by Staunton, Rivière expressed an opinion about an error Deacon might have made in choosing as a Morphy game the one *he* (Rivière) had played with Morphy, before he (Rivière) knew that Morphy had categorically denied having ever played a game with Deacon and had recognized the Evans game as one Rivière himself had shown him (Morphy) as a game he had won from Deacon.

Rivière could not know that Morphy had never played with Deacon in London before going to Paris. Deacon did not mention the April 1859 date of the game until months later, May 9, 1860. It is not known when Rivière played with Deacon but it has to have been before September 1858, for Rivière lived in Paris and was there when Morphy arrived, and from then on he was with Morphy until the latter left London in April 1859. Rivière's retention of such matters was not equal to Morphy's. About these games he expresses an *opinion*. It is quite probable that the game Staunton printed on February 18 as a Rivière–Deacon game was his also, played perhaps two or more years before. But Rivière had reason to remember the December 17 game as he had shown it to (and talked about it with) Morphy. And so, in writing to Staunton he offered a possible explanation for the confusion created by Deacon. Deacon himself never admitted being confused over the games. In fact, in his letter, as late as May 9, he said, "These games were played exactly as they were published in the *London Illustrated News*." And it may be noted that nowhere in Edge's book, or elsewhere in the chess press going back to 1857, is there mention of Deacon's name.

Brown classed Morphy with those chess players who do not remember about the games they lose. He says:

> If he (Morphy) were certain that he had never won (played) this (Evans) game against Deacon, it may have been easier for him to think that he had never lost the King's Gambit, for it was a commonplace of those times that chess-players were notoriously forgetful of the games they lost.

So Morphy did not remember playing the King's Gambit game because he had lost it, Brown suggests. It is evident that Brown was satisfied that Morphy played two games with Deacon, winning the first and losing the second, as Deacon said. He then wished to seal the case against Morphy by mentioning "strong language," indicating a mental weakness as the explanation for Morphy's repudiation. The only "strong language" Morphy used was that in his letter to Fuller of January 19, 1860, when he declared, "someone has been guilty of deliberate falsehood."

Perhaps Brown thought that Morphy had lost his grip on the game (losing to Deacon) and things in general because he knew of the mental disturbance that began to emerge about fifteen years later in Morphy's life. Obviously no one had reason to think of it at the time, but Brown was delving into the matter some seventy-five years later.

We only need quote Charles A. Gilberg to deny Brown's intimation that Morphy was suffering from a mental debility prior to and during the Deacon controversy. Gilberg, in an article on Morphy for *The Fifth American Chess Congress* book, published in 1881, mentions that in 1865 he was working closely with Morphy almost daily for several weeks, and "it would then have been a freak of the maddest folly to have discredited his complete possession and control of that finely balanced intellectual organism which six years before had carried him triumphantly through his severest ordeals."

In light of the new evidence and information that we now have on the so-called Morphy–Deacon games, it would seem that they should remain, in the words of Philip W. Sergeant, "in the category of the spurious."

CHAPTER 19

Odds Before Even

Morphy was in New Orleans during the first few months of the Deacon controversy, which began after he had enjoyed but one month's rest and relaxation, during which time he is not known to have played any chess in New Orleans or even to have visited the New Orleans Chess Club (though he may have). And except in connection with the Deacon matter, his name rarely appeared in the New Orleans *Sunday Delta* until August, when it was announced that he was leaving for New York. On August 4, undoubtedly to his great relief, his *Ledger* contract came to an end.

But Morphy continued his game annotations for the *Chess Monthly*, a number of which had been prepared before January, including those for the newly discovered Philidor games. He was invited to attend the Western Chess Congress, to be held in St. Louis in April, but declined. In April, the American Chess Association canceled the chess congress to have been held in Philadelphia in 1860, considering, as the New Orleans *Sunday Delta* of April 15, 1860, states, that "it is inexpedient to convene the Congress this year," and it was deferred until 1861. The Deacon affair had been a disturbing factor.

Leaving New Orleans on August 1 by the New Orleans, Jackson & Northern Railroad, Morphy arrived in New York on August 4. During a stay in the city of about a week, he visited the New York Chess Club two or three times, but played no chess. He then visited Saratoga and Newport, spending altogether several weeks before returning to New York early in September.

On September 18 he again encountered James Thompson at Knight odds, losing a fine game in seventy-six moves. A few days later they played three more games at the same odds, all of which Morphy won. He also gave the same odds to Frederick Perrin on October 10, and to Sam Loyd, winning all games.

Louis Paulsen was also in New York at this time, and not by chance. Although at the Chess Congress of 1857 Morphy had a plus score against him of fourteen to one (counting casuals and blindfold games), Paulsen was nevertheless sure he was much stronger than the score indicated. As early as November 1858 he began thinking about a match with Morphy. In a letter to Henry Harrisse he wrote, "Having in view to see Morphy on his return to New York, I am studying chess with such zeal that I don't like to lose five minutes of time."

Early in 1859 Paulsen wrote Harrisse of his intention "to visit Morphy at New Orleans in December, provided he agrees to play me a match on even terms. If I should beat Morphy I will write a complete work on the openings." Morphy's long stay in New York and late arrival in New Orleans may have changed his plans. Also, evidently he had heard from Harrisse that Morphy had no intention of playing except at odds, for Paulsen wrote Harrisse as follows on October 2, 1859:

> As soon as I received your letter I commenced analyzing the pawn and move game. I have not yet finished my work. Should the result prove that in the pawn and move game the advantage is really on the side of the player who receives the odds, as it is supposed to be, I will play a match with Morphy at these odds; and should I beat him he will be obliged to play a match on even terms.

By the autumn of 1860 Paulsen had convinced himself (even if no one else agreed with him) that Pawn odds offered no advantage to the receiver. This decision was undoubtedly influenced by his great desire to play Morphy on even terms. He therefore wrote the following letter:

> New York, Oct. 3, 1860
>
> Paul Morphy, Esq., Dear Sir:
>
> In the hope of promoting the cause of Chess, permit me to invite you to a friendly contest over the board on the following terms:
>
> A match even, consisting only of *open* games, or, to make it more definite, a match of six Evans Gambits, each player to conduct three times the attack and three times the defense; and of twelve Gambits on the King's side, attack and defense to be played alternately by each player throughout the match. I am aware that you have declined playing with our most prominent Chess-players, except at odds of pawn and move. Allow me in reply to express the opinion that the odds of pawn and move is a doubtful advantage, whilst it invariably and necessarily results in a kind of mongrel game, never advancing the cause of Chess and rarely proving interesting to the great majority of Amateurs.
>
> If your high and justly acquired reputation as a Chess-player makes it a matter of necessity on your part never to meet an ad-

versary without imposing the condition of receiving odds, I beg leave to suggest an advantage, which without marring the beauties of our noble game, may still prove acceptable to you, viz:

I shall receive as many games out of the match as in your opinion would make the chances of winning the match perfectly even, or yield your opponent an advantage equal to the pawn and move.

In sincere hope that you will accept the invitation and favor me with a reply, I remain

Very respectfully yours,
Louis Paulsen

Soon thereafter Morphy received the following letter from Harrisse pertaining to the above:

51 Exchange Place, Oct. 6, 1860

Paul Morphy, Esq. Dear Sir,

At the request of Mr. Paulsen, I tried to see you twice on Friday and Wednesday last, at your residence, and not being able to find you left with the clerk of the Hotel a letter from Mr. Paulsen to be handed to you.

The object of this note is to ascertain whether the above communication duly came into your hands.

In the hope of a reply, I remain, Dear Sir,

Your Admirer,
Henry Harrisse

Morphy replied to Harrisse as follows:

New York, Oct. 6th, 1860

H. Harrisse, Esq.

I have received Paulsen's letter, and am quite astonished that he should ask me to play a match with him on even terms, after my repeated declarations that I had not come North to play chess, and would only encounter him, if at all, at odds, and in an occasional game or two at the club. I am getting heartily tired of the subject, and would request you, should you see him before I do (I went to the club yesterday but did not meet him there) to inform him of the resolution I have taken.

Regretting that I was not at the Fifth Avenue Hotel when you called, I remain, Truly yours,

Paul Morphy

As it happened, Morphy and Paulsen never encountered each other during this time (nor ever again), although both visited the New York chess clubs several times, each playing with others. Undoubtedly, D. W. Fiske, Morphy's co-editor at the *Chess Monthly*, was expressing Morphy's thoughts about Paulsen and chess in the following excerpt from an article in the New York *Saturday Press* of October 20, 1860. Paulsen probably read it before leaving New York.

The Reasons for the declension of Mr. Morphy to play a match on even terms with Mr. Paulsen are, as we think, simply these:

1. Mr. Morphy did not come North for the purpose of playing Chess, much less Chess-matches, and has given but a fraction of his time while here to the game in any shape.

2. In a series of games, including an important match, played in 1857, Mr. Paulsen succeeded in securing only one game in twelve, or if we count the blindfold games, only one in fourteen of the contested parties. It seems eminently proper, and Chess-like, therefore that Mr. Paulsen, if a match be played, should be the last person to request that it be an even one.

3. Mr. Morphy has again and again declared—a declaration which, as the acknowledged champion of two continents, he had a perfect right to make—that he would play no more even matches without having been first conquered at odds. If an exception were to be made to this rule, it certainly would not be right to make it in favor of one who has already been proven to be so greatly the inferior of the champion.

4. It has not been said by Mr. Morphy, but it is the general feeling among those who have seen Mr. Paulsen play, even recently[,] that the fatigue of contending in a set match against that gentleman would be such that few persons would willingly undergo it. It is certainly to be regretted that so fine a player should be obliged to evolve his combinations so slowly. We say this in no spirit of censure.

5. Mr. Morphy has said that he would gladly consent to play a few off-hand games with Mr. Paulsen, at the odds of Pawn and Move, an offer which we think all candid persons would

have advised the justly distinguished Western player to accept, if his desire to meet Mr. Morphy be indeed based upon a wish to properly advance the interests of the game.

At every stage of Mr. Morphy's brilliant Chess-career, he has distinctly enunciated the fact, in words of manly utterance which are still ringing in our ears, that his life was not to be the life of a professional Chess-player. He has said that he looked upon the game merely as a highly intellectual pastime, and that the larger portion of his future years would be devoted to graver studies and more serious avocations. It seems to us that, at every step, he displays, steadily but gentlemanly, the consistency of his character in this respect. For, while he is proud of the honors he has received, and the honorable fame which he has acquired, even in the arena of a simple amusement, he still shows himself resolved to make that amusement occupy its proper place in the development of his life. Few persons, at his age, after having achieved such excellence and so great renown as a Chess player, could have brought themselves to form this resolution, and to firmly execute it.

Morphy stayed on in New York a few weeks into October, and he and Paulsen left the city a day apart. Paulsen sailed for Germany via England on October 25, 1860, and Morphy returned to New Orleans. During his last days in New York, Morphy met J. A. Leonard and Otto Michaelis, offering both the Queen's Rook. The New Orleans *Times-Democrat* of December 22, 1889, published a long letter from Michaelis describing his experience with Morphy, drawing some comparisons between Morphy and Steinitz, and giving one of the games they played together.

With the close of the year 1860, the December issue of the *Chess Monthly* published a "Card" in which Daniel W. Fiske stated that he was withdrawing as editor of the magazine. Fiske also added:

I am requested by Mr. Morphy to announce at the same time the withdrawal of his name from the title page. This will scarcely change his position towards the readers of the magazine, for he assures me that his best games, accompanied by his own notes and distinguished by his initials, will still be published in the *Chess Monthly*.

However, the prospects for the coming year were none too good for the *Chess Monthly*, nor Morphy. As for the 1861 Chess Congress, it simply never came into being. As *Wilkes' Spirit of the Times* of June 29, 1861, states:

> We do not see any prospects for the next Chess Congress to
> meet in Philadelphia in Fall, as previously announced. Should
> it be a fact, however, we still believe that Mr. Morphy would
> attend its meetings; and in that case, we should, without doubt,
> have also the presence of Herr Kilisch.

On July 27, 1861, an article in the same newspaper attempted to explain the sudden diminishment of interest in chess in the United States:

> It is very easy to account for the aspect of things to which we
> have alluded at home. The Chess-mania which seized upon the
> whole nation when Morphy's brilliant star first rose on the ho-
> rizon, was violent and exaggerated; and as his star rushed up
> into the zenith of its world-wide renown, and then with equal
> rapidity withdrew itself from the public gaze in the obscurity of
> private life, from which there seems small prospect of its reap-
> pearance, the fever died away with it, and it is not to be won-
> dered at that Chess Clubs and Chess Columns, that owed their
> existence to the excitement of the day, should dwindle away and
> disappear. Added to this sufficient cause, comes the Southern
> rebellion, and by common consent, all other interests sink into
> subservience in the one grand idea of maintaining the Govern-
> ment in its deadly struggle against anarchy and treason.

The times were certainly not propitious for Morphy to embark on his professional life as a lawyer. The law was probably very little on his mind, what with his inner turmoil, related as it undoubtedly was to the political upheaval the country was experiencing. Louisiana had already aligned itself against the Union, and yet darker clouds were on the horizon.

CHAPTER 20

Kolisch, Secession, and Cuba

Morphy's withdrawal from chess activity, together with Fiske's resignation from the *Chess Monthly*, resulted in a great loss of interest in the game in this country. Both had made a large contribution to American chess, and the game had brought them into close collaboration. But now they were to be driven apart by tragic events, to meet but once again after the Civil War.

In the month of December 1860, South Carolina led a disastrous parade of eleven states from the Union by voting an ordinance of secession on December 20, 1860, although the fall of Fort Sumter was yet four months in the future. Louisiana followed, the sixth state to join the seceders, on January 26, 1861.

But these dark rumblings hardly affected the chess scene abroad, where a new chess star was rising, magnitude yet unknown. Earlier, in July 1859, the *Chess Monthly* had noted that "a new player, Mr. Kolisch of Vienna, has just made his appearance at Paris. Of four games with Harrwitz he had won two, lost one and drew one [Harrwitz then got 'sick']." With Rivière his score stood Rivière five, Kolisch five; and he was invited to London, where he was equally successful. So successful was he that he thirsted to challenge Morphy and found a backer in Baron Rothschild. The *Illustrated London News* of March 16, 1861, stated, "We believe it is perfectly true that a wealthy foreign nobleman has offered to back Mr. Kolisch in a match against the American player Morphy for £500 a side, and that a challenge has been duly forwarded to the latter."

On April 13, 1861, the following announcement and correspondence appeared in the New York *Wilkes' Spirit of the Times*, addressed to its chess editor, N. Marache:

MATCH FOR $2500 A SIDE!!
A probability of Morphy being challenged by Kolisch

363 Broadway, New York, April 1

Mr. N. Marache:—Dear Sir: I take the liberty to consult you in reference to a communication just received from London—

the object of which is to ascertain whether or not Paul Morphy would accept a challenge from Herr Kolisch, for a match at Chess, £500 a side. Please ascertain if Mr. Morphy would accept, leaving the arrangements as to time and place for further consideration. I sail myself for England on Saturday, and you would oblige me very much by giving your opinion.

Allow me, then, to call your attention to an extract of a letter, which I received from my brother in London, dated March 16.

Yours respectfully, Edwin Mayall

". . . Could you inquire for me whether Morphy, the great chess player, would be likely to accept a challenge from Herr Kolisch, to play a match for £500 (five hundred pounds) a side; the winner of the first 11 (eleven) games to be declared the victor, and entitled to the stakes; and whether Mr. Morphy would come out here on being challenged? If not, would he play if Mr. Kolisch went to New York?

"It is said here that Mr. Morphy would neither come here to play the match, nor play if Kolisch went to New York. Nothing certain is known as to this point. If you could make inquiry either at the New York Chess Club, or ascertain from a responsible person, it would save a great deal of unnecessary correspondence.

"The question is: Would Mr. Morphy be likely to accept the challenge?

"Yours truly   John Mayall"

P.S.—Mr. Marache, if you will kindly write to Mr. Morphy for me, and send his reply, addressed as follows, I shall be under a deep obligation to you.

Edwin Mayall, 224 Regent Street, London

Office of Wilkes' Spirit of the Times
New York, April 4, 1861

Mr. E. Mayall:—Dear Sir: I will be most happy to fulfill your wishes, and will immediately write to Mr. Morphy concerning the matter referred to in your note. Whatever information I may receive as to the contemplated match, I will transmit to you at the earliest convenience.

Yours truly,   N. Marache.

On June 8, 1861, *Wilkes' Spirit of the Times* published the following letter from Morphy. It had been delayed, as Marache said, "Owing to both irregularities of the mails [Louisiana had voted itself out of the Union] and our ignorance of Mr. Morphy's address direct, his letter only reached us in time for this week's issue."

New Orleans, May 5, 1861

N. Marache, Esq.:—Dear Sir: Your letter has come to hand, together with the accompanying paper. Both would have reached me much sooner, if addressed "Care of Sybrandt & Co.," but of that you were probably not aware. With regard to the object of your communication, my answer may be readily anticipated. It is now nearly three years since I visited Europe, and during my trans-Atlantic sojourn I studiously availed myself of every opportunity to encounter the leading European amateurs. Had I then been afforded the pleasure of meeting Mr. Kolisch, I would cheerfully have accepted the proffered contest. Having now, however, returned to my home, and my attention being turned to more serious matters, I cannot be expected, much as I should be gratified to play with Mr. Kolish, to forsake everything for the purpose of contesting a match with that gentleman. Especially is this impossible at the present time, as a moment's consideration will satisfy you [secession, of course].

All I can promise (and I wish it to be understood as a *special exception* to the rule I have adopted, of playing no matches in future) is so to arrange my time, whenever I may again visit the Old World, as to devote a couple of weeks, or more if necessary, to the contemplated match. I must state, in this connection, that I *positively decline playing for any stake whatever*. The non-acceptance of this clause by Mr. Kolisch will be fatal to the match. In my contests with Messrs. Anderssen and Mongredien, as in nearly all my matches in Europe and America, no stakes whatever were pending. In the cases of Messrs. Lowenthal and Harrwitz, I was prevailed upon by friends to depart from the rule I have prescribed to myself, under the belief that the course pursued was best calculated to promote the immediate commencement of the play. With regard to the contemplated match with Mr. Staunton, the facts are well known to you. Stakes were offered by the New Orleans Chess Club, and the amount subscribed for by the members, without any participation of mine in the premises. To my mind, one of the supreme excellences of Chess, and, to me, the chief source of its attractiveness, is the fact that, being purely intellectual, it exercises over the mind of its votaries a fascination which it can never be necessary to enhance by allurements foreign to its spirit.

A quiet, friendly match attended with no publicity, would afford me much pleasure, as I am sure it would to Mr. Kolisch. I shall with pleasure engage in a contest of that description whenever I may again have the good fortune to cross the ocean. Believe me, dear Sir

Yours truly, Paul Morphy

And so Morphy's letter foreclosed any possibility of a match taking place, at least at that time, although his condition: "I positively decline playing for any stake whatever" might also have doomed the encounter. In any case, it would seem that Kolisch was not in Morphy's class, as evidenced later that year in the former's trials against Paulsen and Anderssen—he lost to both by one game.

Kolisch's match with Anderssen in July is of special significance, for this match ushered in the present method of time control. In *Le Sport* (later reprinted in *Wilkes' Spirit of the Times*, August 31, 1861), St. Amant describes this momentous step forward in chess play:

What particularly pleased us in this match was an innovation, a real progress, without which it is no longer possible to undertake a serious struggle. This innovation, which we have always advocated in the *Palamède*, and still more recently in *Le Sport*, consists in fixing a maximum of time for the moves; for it is necessary that a game should not be interminable, and that the conditions should be equal for both parties, which they were not when one of the players was allowed, by intentional slowness, to weary out the patience and facilities of his antagonist. As long ago as 1836 (see *Palamède*, t.l., p. 189), we ourselves were authorized to propose to the English, in the name of Deschapelles (our illustrious and regretted master), on the occasion of his challenge, to establish a measure of time. The practical means of execution selected was the hourglass of old Saturn, which he borrowed from the mythological deity to recommend it for adoption by our insular neighbors, who take for their device, 'Time is money.' A quarter of a century has elapsed before our idea has prevailed, simple and excellent as it is. The London Chess Club has now adopted the emblem of the fabled god, and we found Kolisch and Anderssen separated by two gigantic clypsedras, or rather sandglasses, each made to measure the space of two hours.

While the sand is running through, the player is bound to make

> twenty-four moves, which give an average of five minutes for each; but the player is at liberty to give more or less time to any move he pleases, provided the twenty-four moves are made in 120 minutes. We are happy to state that this first trial was most satisfactory. The two antagonists, though a little moved at first on account of this sword of Damocles suspended over their combinations, soon got used to it, and not the slightest inconvenience was experienced. Seeing that a great many moves, especially at the opening, may be played rapidly, as much as half an hour, or even an hour, may be taken for a decisive move at the close.

As for Morphy, without doubt he was torn between his loyalty to the Union and to the state of Louisiana. If Morphy's 1854 Commencement address is recalled, and Father Kenny's comment on it, it becomes clear that Morphy would have difficulty bringing his sympathies into line with the secessionist cause. The situation certainly was not clear-cut, but as Lincoln put it (see *Abraham Lincoln* by Benjamin P. Thomas), "All they ask, we could readily grant, if we thought slavery right, all we ask, they could as readily grant, if they thought it wrong."* The question of slavery was really what divided the nation.

In South Carolina on April 14, 1861, the first clash of arms took place. Gen. P. G. T. Beauregard of New Orleans, a friend of the Morphy family and now with the Confederacy, had been instructed to take over Fort Sumter, by force if necessary. Some months later, Paul Morphy was to call on him at Richmond.

President Lincoln's response to the fall of Fort Sumter was to call for seventy-five thousand militia for three months' service, and the conflict was on. Paul's brother, Edward, joined the Seventh Regiment of New Orleans. Although Paul was not of the same mind, he finally decided that perhaps he could serve his state in some nonbelligerent capacity, and in October 1861 we find him in Richmond, as mentioned by the Richmond *Dispatch* of October 24:

> Paul Morphy—This distinguished gentleman has been in our city for some days, and has received visits and attentions from a number of our citizens to whom his unassuming dignity and agreeable manners have made his society very pleasant. He is a

---

* EDITOR'S NOTE: This quote comes from the close of Lincoln's address at Cooper Institute, February 27, 1860. See "Address at Cooper Institute, New York City, February 27, 1860," in *Lincoln: Speeches and Writings*, vol. 2, 1859-1865 (New York: Library of America, 1989), 111-129.

fine specimen of the Southern gentleman. From a notice in another column, it appears that he is expected to visit the rooms of the Richmond Chess Club this evening.

In another column in the same issue, the following announcement appeared:

RICHMOND CHESS CLUB—A meeting of the members of the Club will be held at their Room over J. P. Duval's Drug Store, THIS EVENING (Thursday,) 24th inst. At 8 o'clock.

Mr. Morphy has kindly consented to be present.

It is known that Morphy played at least ten games of chess while in Richmond, winning eight of them at Knight odds. While nothing definite is known about the reason for Morphy's visit to Richmond, there were press reports that he had offered his services to Beauregard, or that he was being considered for diplomatic service. Frances Parkinson Keyes, in her novel on Paul Morphy, *The Chess Players*, based upon all known facts she could uncover, seized upon the possibility that he was an agent for the Confederacy in Europe, but there is not a shred of evidence indicating that this was so. Morphy waited a year after his visit to Richmond before leaving for Europe, and he returned a year before the war was over.

Undoubtedly Morphy went to Richmond with some thought of being useful, perhaps influenced by other Southern youths who were responding to the call of the South. And it may be that he was on Beauregard's staff for a short while and that he had been seen at Manassas, as had been reported. It would seem that Beauregard sensed that Morphy had little or no enthusiasm for secession and that the general brought it home to Morphy that he was not war material, on or off the battlefield.

We know Morphy was in Richmond for a while, not only from the Richmond *Dispatch*, but also from the memoirs of others who mentioned having met him there. Mrs. Burton Harrison in *Recollections Grave and Gay* writes:

Early in the war Paul Morphy, the celebrated chess player, whom we knew in Richmond, accepted a commission to purchase for me in New Orleans, whither he was returning, a French violette of real black thread lace, the height of my ambition. When the veil arrived, as selected by himself, we voted Mr. Morphy an expert in other arts than chess.

Some years later, Gilbert R. Frith, president of the State Chess Association of Virginia, related in the *Columbia Chess Chronicle* of August 18, 1888, and January 24, 1889, an anecdote concerning Morphy in Richmond. The incident centers around a well-known picture by Retzsch or, it would seem likely, a variation of it. As Frith tells it:

> The arrival of the noted player excited, even at that troublous time, a keen interest among the lovers of the kingly game. An invitation was extended to the champion, and, with himself as the centre, a coterie of notables assembled for an evening's play at the home of Mr. H. (Rev. R. R. Howison). . . . While at supper Morphy's attention was attracted by a picture which hung prominently upon the wall, Mephistopheles playing a game of Chess with a young man for his soul. The Chessmen with which his Satanic majesty plays are the Vices; the pieces of the young man are, or have been, the Virtues—for, alas! he has very few left. In bad case, indeed, is the unhappy youth, for his game, as represented, appears not only desperate but hopeless, and his fate sealed. His adversary gloats in anticipation of the final coup, and the gleaming smile on the face of the latter intensifies the despair which that of the young man shows.

> With the close of the supper, deeply interested, Morphy approached the picture, studied it awhile intently, then turning to his host he said, modestly: "I think I can take the young man's game and win." "Why, impossible!" was the answer; "not even you, Mr. Morphy, can retrieve that game." "Yet I think I can," said Morphy. "Suppose we place the men and try." A board was arranged, and the rest of the company gathered round it, deeply interested in the result. To the surprise of every one, victory was snatched from the devil and the young man saved.

Incidentally, Frith mentions Morphy as being at that time "an officer on Beauregard's staff."

Others have mentioned seeing Morphy in New Orleans. Grace E. King in *New Orleans, The Place and People* mentions, "It was not very long ago that, at opera, theatre, concert, ball, or promenade, or at celebrations at the cathedral, the figure of Paul Morphy was instinctively looked for. Dark-skinned, with brilliant black eyes, black hair; slight and graceful, with the hands and smile of a woman, his personality held the eye with a charm that appeared to the imagination akin to mystery."

George Haven Putnam, in *Memories of a Publisher*, adds to our picture of Morphy in New Orleans at this time. Putnam was stationed in New Orleans for part of 1862, after its capture by Farragut in April and its occupation by General Butler and his troops. A chess player himself, Putnam mentions that he carried a book of Morphy's games in his haversack:

> My regiment happened to be among those that took part in
> 1862 in the occupation of Louisiana, and I had occasion dur-
> ing two years of the campaigns in Louisiana to be in and out of
> New Orleans. A friend in one of the New England regiments,
> also a chess player, pointed out to me one day crossing Caron-
> delet Street the figure of Morphy. This must have been in 1862.
> Morphy was walking with the lagging step of an ill man. . . .
>
> There was also, however, upon him a special pressure of trou-
> ble. While a loyal citizen of Louisiana, he was opposed to seces-
> sion. He did not believe that the Republic ought to be broken
> up. The men of the good families in New Orleans, a group to
> which young Morphy certainly belonged, were nearly all mem-
> bers of the "Louisiana Tigers," the Seventh Regiment of New
> Orleans.
>
> Morphy had refused to join with these old-time associates in
> the attempt to over-throw the Republic. This brought him into
> social isolation. The girls were said to have scoffed at him. He
> ought, of course, to have done what other Southerners, object-
> ing to secession, did. He should have made a home for himself
> in Paris, or somewhere in England.

As will soon be seen, Morphy did exactly that, but for the time being
he was still in troubled New Orleans and much troubled himself.

In February of 1862 the British Chess Association issued a "Preliminary Programme for a Grand International Chess Congress and Tournament" to be held in June in London. The "Program" mentioned "the ad-
vent of Morphy" and noted that "a limitation of time in moving will be
enforced. Two-thirds of the Players agreeing, may compel Pawn to King's
fourth to be played on each side every game. In the meantime, special invitations have been sent to Messrs. Morphy, Anderssen, etc." Morphy felt
obliged to decline this invitation.

At last, for whatever reason, Morphy decided he must leave New Orleans. The city had been occupied by Union troops since April. His mother
and sister Helena had left some months before for Paris, but now in October of 1862 it was not easy to book passage out. However, about the tenth
of October, taking with him his testimonial gifts received in New York,
he boarded the Spanish man-of-war *Blasco de Garay* incognito, bound for
Havana. He was accompanied by Charles Maurian, and together they de-
barked there and put up at the Hotel America, keeping much to themselves.

However, after four or five days, Morphy's presence became known, and on October 16, 1862, *La Gaceta de la Habana* and *El Siglo* blazoned forth the news, and a committee of chess players and other prominent Cubans, Srs. D. Blas Du Bouchet, D. Vicente, D. Aureliano Medina, and D. Felix Sicre, called on him at the hotel.

From then on his presence was the subject of much publicity, and he was honored by banquets and private invitations. In turn he gratified his hosts with sessions at the chess table, among them some blindfold games. Among others with whom he played were Messrs. Medina, Fesser, F. Sicre, Toscano, and J. M. Sicre, the latter a very good chess player and a slave of Felix Sicre. Maurian also engaged in a few games. Morphy and Maurian departed on October 31 on the mail steamer for Cadiz, Spain, following a final grand banquet given by Don Eduardo Fesser at the French inn L'Hermitage, at which Morphy's health was toasted. He in turn made a toast "to the prosperity of Cuba."

CHAPTER 21
Paris and Petroff

After arriving in Cadiz, Morphy traveled by train to Paris, where he was reunited with his mother and sister Helena in December 1862. Fiske, in a letter to his parents from Vienna dated January 15, 1863, tells of Morphy's arrival in Paris and of his difficulties in getting there: "Morphy, as I learned from the papers, is in Paris, but has not yet played, owing to the 'unfortunate condition of his country, and the fatigues of his escape from the South through the blockading squadron, and the ocean voyage.'"

An American correspondent for the New York *Times* in Paris wrote in December:

> Since my arrival, I have met with Mr. Paul Morphy, the famous chess player, about whose doings and whereabouts such contradictory reports have been circulated in the United States. Mr. Morphy has not been on any rebel general's staff, nor has he taken any part in the war. He left New Orleans long after the capture of the city by the Federal forces, and went to Havana, taking passage thence to Cadiz, and reached Paris a few days ago. Kolisch[,] the eminent Hungarian player, is also here, and chess amateurs are making efforts to bring about a meeting between the greatest chess genius of the world and another star not unworthy to encounter the master. Morphy, however, assures me that he has renounced chess altogether, and the unhappy state of affairs at home will not permit him to bring to the task of meeting a great player the calmness and coolness which are essential to success. He has also matters of more importance to occupy his mind, and seems to be in feeble health.

The remark in the last sentence about "matters of more importance" would seem to be Morphy's way of saying that he did not want to be bothered about chess, although he played privately with friends—Rivière and Maurian, as well as people he had met in Paris, such as St. Leon. We have a record of a few games he engaged in at this time at Doazan's and Rivière's homes; one of them, with Rivière, was played at Doazan's house on January 7.

Morphy enjoyed some social life apart from his mother and Helena, who had the company of Paul's sister Malvina, who was married to Sybrandt and was living in Paris. Occasionally there was something of a party, such as one in early February at the house of the Countess de Colbert, at which were present Rivière, Prèti, and others. The Countess herself was a very good chess player. At the time of the 1867 Emperor's Tournament in Paris, the Countess, in consultation with Mme. Regnauet de St. Jean D'Angély, the Princess Anna Murat, and the Duchess de la Trémoille, won two games from Rivière and G. R. Neumann, who were also in consultation. All the above women had, at one time or another, contested with Morphy.

Without doubt his presence in Paris increased that city's chess and social activity. As Delannoy said years later in *Brentano's Chess Monthly* of May 1881, "His name, during his sojourn in Paris, made a great noise; it even fills it now." And Howard Staunton made the following comment on May 2, 1863, in the *Illustrated London News*:

> The game has invaded even the salons of the noble Fauberg and the Chaussée d'Antin. In the most aristocratic circles there are weekly reunions, presided over by the amiable mistresses of the mansions, and attended by the most celebrated amateurs of chess. Two of the most fashionable of these private salons are those of the Duchess de la Trémoille and Mme. De Colbert. At these reunions all except actual players of chess are rigorously excluded. Even the husbands of the fair patronesses form no exception to the rule, since, if not initiated, the doors of the sanctuary are pitilessly closed against them.

Although isolating himself from public chess, Morphy was not to be free of it entirely. Ignatz Kolisch took advantage of Morphy's presence in Paris to endeavor again to arrange a match. He wrote the following letter to Morphy dated February 14, 1863, Paris (published in *La Nouvelle Régence*, March 1863):

> Sir,—The distinguished reputation which you have acquired at chess has long since excited in me an ambition—presumptuous, perhaps, but very ardent—to have the honor of encountering you at that game. You will remember that two years since my friends endeavored to bring us together, and transmitted to you a proposal, to which you replied by a promise equivalent to a formal engagement in case you should ever return to Europe—a promise which was made public in the American journal *Wilkes' Spirit of the Times*, and which has been registered in *La Nouvelle Régence*. On the faith of this engagement I left England when I heard of your arrival in Paris to put my-

self at your disposal. Knowing, however, that at the beginning of your visit certain private considerations withheld you from playing chess, I abstained from communicating my resolution. But now, Sir, that you have resumed a recreation in which you so much excel, and daily play the game with various adversaries, the time appears to have arrived when I may recall to you your former promise.

I am sure, Sir, that I shall not appeal to your courtesy in vain; and I believe you will think it reasonable that I should exercise the same liberty which you used when you first came and threw down the gauntlet to the chief players of Europe.

Justified both by your promise and by your example, I have the honor to propose to you a chess match. The conditions, if you please, shall be the same as those which were first proposed to you in the letter of the secretary of the St. George's Club— namely, that whichever of us wins the first *eleven games* shall be pronounced the conqueror.

Awaiting your reply, I beg you to accept the assurance of my consideration, &C.

Ignatz Kolisch

Morphy replied in a note to Kolisch to the effect that he had already expressed his determination to separate himself from the chess arena and declined the request for a match. He then wrote to *La Régence* asking it to publish an addition to the reply he had already sent Kolisch, and the following appeared in its pages in April:

Mr. Morphy has requested us to add a few lines to complete the answer which he has addressed to Mr. Kolisch and which clearly show the reasons of his refusal—"I could have believed at the time when hearing of your successes that you are superior to the other players whom I had encountered in Europe; but since, as you are well aware, the result of your matches with Messrs. Anderssen and Paulsen had not been favorable to you, there is now no reason why I should make an exception in your case, having decided not again to engage in such matches, an infringement of my rules which I should be obliged to extend to others, &C, &C."

Paul Morphy

It will be recalled that on his previous visit to Paris, Morphy and Rivière planned a *Treatise on Chess Openings*, mentioned in the *Chess Monthly* of May 1859. That Morphy was serious about the treatise will be seen from one of his notes for the Greenaway game, published in the July 1859 *Chess Monthly*, in which he said that he would publish a complete analysis of it (the Evans Gambit) in his forthcoming treatise. Rivière and Morphy now resumed work on it, beginning with Philidor's Defense, which they completed as given in *La Régence*, December 1863 through February 1864. But apparently Morphy was unwilling to do more, since nothing further was published.

On February 4, 1863, Morphy replied to a letter from Fiske bearing an invitation from the Vienna Chess Club:

> My dear Fiske,
>
> Pray, do not be too prompt in condemning the tardiness of my reply, for in this case at least, it can be justified. I have purposely abstained from returning an immediate answer to your favor, in the hope of being enabled to take a trip to Vienna, not for the sake of chess playing, but activated by the very natural desire to see you after such a lapse of time as has gone by since my last visit to New York, and inquire about old friends and associations made doubly dear by the sad events that are transpiring in our distracted America. Much as I would enjoy a visit to Germany for these and other reasons, I am sorry to say that it will not be in my power to leave Paris at present. I am here with my brother-in-law and part of my family, the remainder being in New Orleans. We are all following with intense anxiety the fortunes of the tremendous conflict now raging beyond the Atlantic, for upon the issue depends our all in life. Under such circumstances you will readily understand that I should feel little disposed to engage in the objectless strife of the chess board. Besides you will remember that as far back as two years ago I stated to you in New York my firm determination to abandon chess altogether. I am more strongly confirmed than ever in the belief that the time devoted to chess is literally frittered away. It is, to be sure, a most exhilarating sport, but it is only a sport; and it is not to be wondered at that such as have been passionately addicted to the charming pastime, should one day ask themselves whether sober reason does not advise its utter dereliction. I have, for my own part, resolved not to be moved from my purpose of not engaging in chess hereafter. The few games that I have played here have been altogether private and *sans façon*.
>
> I never patronize the Café de la Régence; it is a low, and, to borrow a Gallicism, *ill frequented* establishment.

Hoping that you will excuse my dilatoriness, and wishing you health and happiness,

I remain, Yours truly
Paul Morphy

P.S.—Sybrandt begs to be kindly remembered to you.

In his hour of distress, Morphy was thinking of some very disagreeable moments he had at La Régence with Harrwitz; otherwise, his was the respect and adulation of its frequenters. And again it would have been the same had he chosen to meet Petroff or others there. And there still hangs on the wall of the Café de La Régence these many decades later his likeness, as he gave Paris its sensation of 1858, as he conquered without seeing. Of one of the games, George Walker wrote that it was "worthy of being written in letters of gold on the walls of the London Chess Club." Later Fiske mentioned Morphy's letter in writing to Professor George Allen:

> Did I write you that I had received a letter from Morphy? He answered one which I wrote him (to my great surprise) about his coming to Vienna at the invitation of the Club. . . . Sybrandt, his brother-in-law, who met a friend of mine in Rome, says that P.M. is as lazy as ever, and will not do anything. My offer to him on the part of the Schachgesellscheft was 1500 francs for a two weeks' visit, and his expenses could not have exceeded five or six hundred.

Morphy's "laziness" at this time might well be attributed to the "intense anxiety" mentioned in his letter to Fiske, which probably had a numbing effect; but it might also have been due to something more personal than worries over the outcome of the Civil War. Due to the war, the Morphy family's pecuniary condition was much reduced. Yet Paul was unwilling to profit from his chess skill—*that* he associated with professionalism and gambling—as his refusal to consider the profitable Vienna Chess Club invitation proves.

However, he had a watch and chain valued at over two hundred dollars which he placed with Rivière as collateral for a large loan. The watch was never redeemed. We next hear of it in 1886, two years after Morphy's death, when Rivière showed it to W. J. A. Fuller at La Régence. Upon seeing it, Fuller said (*European Correspondence* of November 13, 1886), "I have seen this before, for it was I who had the honor to make the speech on the occasion of the presentation of this watch and chain to Morphy, a quarter of a century ago." In 1921, the watch was offered at 6,000 francs to A. W. Mongredien, the son of August Mongredien, with whom Morphy had played his last match in France. At the present time, someone unknown has the watch, minus its red and black Caïssan countenance, which noted the passing hours with Kings and Queens each having their Castles, Bishops, Knights and lowly pawns.

Some practical person, upon acquiring the watch, substituted more readily understood symbols for the time of day, and ultimately the dial became a part of the Dr. Barclay Stephens Horology Collection at the Academy of Science, San Francisco, where it is to be seen on display in its glass case.

One of Morphy's more pleasant and interesting experiences during this period in Paris was his meeting with Alexander D. Petroff, the "Northern Philidor" and the first great Russian chess master.

Petroff had written to Morphy in 1859, expressing his admiration and enclosing a problem he had dedicated to him. Both were printed in the July issue of the *Chess Monthly* of that year. The problem, dedicated to Morphy in the form of an "M," can also be found in J. M. Linder's biography of Petroff.

In *A. D. Petroff*, Linder mentions that Prince Urusoff also wrote Morphy at the same time, and in an article in *Shakhmatny Listok* of December 1859 the Prince wrote:

> I consider it absolutely necessary to call our Russian players out of obscurity because we Russians in my opinion have outstripped the foreigners in the art of chess. I have decided to get Petroff and myself the chance to measure ourselves with the strongest player of our time, Morphy. If Morphy comes to Russia and accepts my challenge then after me undoubtedly Petroff will also come to grips with him; he [Petroff] has already mentioned before many witnesses his willingness to play.

Urusoff said that he was ready to pay all the expenses of the match, and beyond that, expressed his confidence that many of his countrymen would bet on Petroff. As Linder quotes him, Urusoff said, "My letter to Morphy in which I challenged him to a match has already been mailed to him." Nothing further is known about the challenge or the correspondence. Urusoff also said, "Petroff is tireless, and that is a great virtue; he is not nervous like Harrwitz and he does not yawn like Anderssen [Anderssen did not yawn while playing Morphy]. He is like Morphy in everything but has an advantage over him in years." In 1859 Petroff was sixty-five years old.

On Petroff's arrival in Paris there were great hopes and expectations that a public chess contest might take place between him and Morphy. *La Nouvelle Régence* of July 1863 observed: "We have heard talk about the coming encounter between Morphy and Petroff. This will truly be one of the most remarkable battles which has ever taken place. This will be a splendid day for chess."

Staunton commented in his chess column in *The Illustrated London News* of November 7, 1863:

> One of the oldest and most accomplished chess masters, Mr. Petroff (now 69 years old), has lately enlivened the Chess circles of Paris by his presence. His stay, for the moment, was a brief one; but he intends, it is said, to return to the French capital in a few weeks and make it his home for the winter. Should he do so, expectations are entertained that Mr. Morphy, who is still in Paris, will be tempted to break a lance with the Nestor of Russian chess. In that case we may anticipate the pleasure of recording some of the finest games which have been played since the great combats of twenty or five and twenty years ago. During his recent sojourn in Paris, Mr. Petroff was a frequent visitor to the Café de la Régence [and played with Journoud and others].

Petroff himself was a willing adversary. As Linder quotes him, "I never refused and I never will refuse to play all comers. As far as a match with Morphy is concerned, then why not play? And I am ready to play whenever they will back me." This he said in 1859, but there is no doubt it was equally true in 1863. As we know, Morphy had no time for additional matches in 1859 after his brother-in-law came for him, nor was he well enough to travel to Russia at that time. A public match between Petroff and Morphy then or in 1863 would have been an historic meeting.

However, an encounter of some sort did occur between Morphy and Petroff in 1863. Of this meeting with Morphy, Petroff wrote Mikhailov, editor of *Shakhmatny Listok*, "I visited Morphy twice and he visited me. Doazan says that he has absolutely given up the game." It is likely, nevertheless, that some chess, their great common interest, took place between them at these meetings, although nothing is known.

During 1863 Morphy also played a few games with St. Leon and Mongredien, and a good many with Rivière. But he and his family were getting restless for New Orleans. Perhaps they had a sense of what the inevitable ending of the war between the states would be. The South was fast being drained of its manhood and its hope. Morphy planned to return and salvage all possible, and he left Paris at the end of January 1864.

CHAPTER 22

Paul Morphy, Attorney at Law

On the morning of February 16, 1864, *El Siglo* of Havana announced:

> Morphy:—Today, should arrive at this city this celebrated chess
> player from New Orleans, who visits us for the second time.
> He arrived at Santiago de Cuba in the steamship from Europe
> "without having found anyone who could beat him." According
> to a newspaper in Cuba, he should continue his trip to Havana
> in the steamer "Aguila," that is expected at any time now.

Morphy did arrive at Havana that day, February 16, and since he had
been expected, Francisco Fesser had planned in advance an elaborate reception banquet for him. As it happened, Morphy's stay this time was only
two days, and he left on the eighteenth for New Orleans. In those two days
he played a number of games with the Cuban champion Celso Golmayo,
and others, always giving odds of the Knight. The Havana *El Tiempo* of
February 18 reported the banquet evening:

> The rich banker, Mr. Francisco Fesser, gave a sumptuous ban-
> quet on Tuesday in honor of the celebrated chess player Mr.
> Morphy; who should be leaving today for New Orleans. Nat-
> urally the greater part of the invited guests were enthusiasts
> of the noble game in which Mr. Morphy recognizes no rival,
> but this was no reason why we could not count many and very
> beautiful ladies of our high society. Before the dinner he played
> a game with Mr. Sicre, giving him a Knight. Later he played
> alternately several games with Messrs. Dominguez, Golmayo
> and Sicre, by memory, while carrying on at the same time an
> animated conversation with the estimable family of Mr. Fesser.
> On all the games he came out winner, being applauded each
> time that his fatigued opponents gave up their games and asked
> for grace. . . . Among the invited guests we could count Messrs.
> Villergas, Golmayo, Sicre, Dominguez and Palmer, very well
> known because of their affection for the difficult game, and the
> Messrs. Valdes, Cespedes, La Calle, Diaz, Albertini and oth-
> ers.

Years later, in the Charleston *Chess Chronicle* of April 1888, Celso Golmayo recalled playing with Morphy, comparing him to Steinitz: "In many games with Morphy at the odds of a Knight, I became hopelessly bewildered by the brilliancy and intricacy of his combinations, but when I sit down with Steinitz on even terms I feel as though I had a very respectable chance to win."

But the fact remains that out of five games between them, Golmayo won three to Morphy's two. Always quick to compliment his winning opponent, Morphy gave him full credit, to the great satisfaction of Golmayo's compatriots, as reported by *El Moro Muza*:

> Mr. Morphy having played several times with Señor Golmayo, to whom he gave a Knight, has come to confess frankly that Señor Golmayo is too strong to receive a Knight from him and that the most he could give him would be a Pawn and two moves, a declaration that places Señor Golmayo at a very high level amongst Chess players.

Morphy arrived in New Orleans during the last week of February 1864. Presumably he was allowed to use the family home on Royal Street, but little is known of him until November. Although the city was occupied by Union troops, the citizens of New Orleans enjoyed much freedom of speech and movement. The *Daily Picayune* of November 5, 1864, for instance, devoted half its front page to war news, referring to the Union Army as the enemy and conceding no sign of defeat for the Confederacy. Also, its front page carried a "Proclamation" by Jefferson Davis, President of the Confederate States of America, which ended by calling on Almighty God for victory.

Now, at last, Morphy decided to set up his law office. Elsewhere it is stated erroneously that he opened a law office soon after his return in 1859, but this was his first time to establish himself at his profession, even if he says below "having resumed," and the same *Picayune* of November 5 displayed on its front page, under "BUSINESS CARDS," the following short notice:

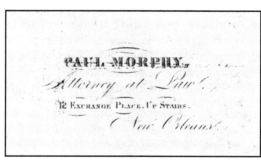

At the same time, Morphy had 5 x 8 circulars printed, mentioning the special service and facilities offered (see in the Appendix). The above notice in the *Picayune* was continued for some weeks.

It is not known to what extent, if any, Morphy profited from his profession. It is almost certain that his success at the chessboard worked against his success at the bar. As learned as Morphy was, and in the best tradition of the Southern gentleman, he was recognized first and foremost as a celebrated chess player. No wonder he liked Paris. There at least his company was sought for all of himself.

Another factor militated strongly against him in New Orleans at this time. After the outbreak of the Civil War, the Bar of Public Opinion questioned his loyalty to the Confederacy; clearly he had no time to set up a law office. And then it would be remembered that during her need the South did not have his help. But at any rate, he was the great chess player before whom the world bowed, and when people came to see him this latter fact blotted out all mundane matters.

To what extent was Morphy fitted for the bar, for the role of advocate pleading before judge and jury? One wonders. Presumably he had chosen the legal profession with his father's example before him, and perhaps at his suggestion. Perhaps he had more than the legal requirements, a fine classical background and other intangibles, but was he temperamentally and psychologically suited? Again one wonders, even if chess and the time were not against him, whether he would have done as well in later life as attorney at law as he did as Portia in *The Merchant of Venice*, that Commencement of 1852 at Spring Hill College.

However, with the odds against him, Morphy now, in 1864, endeavored to put all chess behind him, and to retrieve his fortune through his profession, for the Morphys were now in reduced circumstances.

New York papers soon heard of Morphy and his law office, and *Wilkes' Spirit of the Times*, on December 3, 1864, printed his circular with the following comment:

> The gentleman who handed us the circular is one of our leading citizens bearing an irreproachable character, and advocating the strongest Union sentiments. He emphatically denied any rebel proclivities which had been assigned to Paul Morphy. Coming from such a source, and without having in the least broached the subject with the gentleman, we can but say, to use his own earnest and strong expressions, that Paul Morphy is no "rebel or traitor," as willfully published as such in some few

journals, to our knowledge. Thus, lies will ever recoil upon the slanderer!

Now, with the silencing of the guns after Grant and Lee met at Appomattox Court House on April 9, 1865, Morphy had a plan. He would edit a book of all his games, but to get the book published he would have to go North. He reached New York about July 25 and saw Fiske and Marache at once. *Wilkes' Spirit of the Times*, of which Napoleon Marache was chess editor, reported on August 5, 1865:

> PAUL MORPHY—We learn from authentic sources that the visit of this gifted Chess genius to this metropolis is likely to be one of very great importance and interest to the Chess-loving community. One of his specialties in coming North is to make arrangements with one of the leading New York publishers (either Appleton or the Harpers) to publish in book form the whole of his games, carefully annotated by himself. Such a publication, from the pen of the greatest Chess phenomenon the world ever saw, would indeed be a valuable prize, both for the lovers of Chess and publishers. We will joyfully hail the appearance of the work.

With Marache acting as secretary and Charles A. Gilberg working closely with Morphy, the three set to work collecting and annotating all games to be found. Gustave Reichhelm of Philadelphia, who had started collecting Morphy games in 1863 and continued indefatigably doing so down to the 1880s, was able to contribute some not generally known. The work went on for weeks, and Gilberg says in *The Fifth American Chess Congress* that "it was the writer's privilege during that period to be in almost daily intercourse with Mr. Morphy. He took a lively interest in the chess news of the day, analyzed games and unraveled the intricacies of chess puzzles with an avidity and swiftness that was astonishing."

Morphy himself wrote out his plan and expectations, presumably for the press:

> Mr. Morphy, who has been engaged for several years in the practice of his profession (the law) in New Orleans, and is now in New York on professional business, devotes his leisure time to the preparation of a chess work which his friends here and elsewhere have often urged him to publish. It is a complete collection of every recorded game of his, played both in Europe and America, with full variations, annotations, etc. The book will probably be the standard work on the subject and will, no

doubt, supercede Lowenthal's and Staunton's collections, the analyses of which will be carefully reviewed in the forthcoming volume.

Confident of publication, Morphy was doomed to disappointment, and not just as explained by Gilberg in the *Fifth American Chess Congress*, who wrote that Morphy

> spent several weeks in New York with the avowed purpose of preparing and bequeathing to the chess world a complete and extensively annotated edition of his games; but the financial depression which resulted from the long national struggle had seriously affected the trade of literature, and publishers were found unwilling to place a work of its character upon the market at a cost that would have warranted him in devoting the necessary time and labor to its completing, and the project was, in consequence, ultimately abandoned.

Morphy's plan was excellent as far as it went, but publishers asked that he enrich the collection (mentioned by Reichhelm in *Chess in Philadelphia*) with new games. This Morphy would not do. He refused to enter tournaments, play matches or casual games in public, even though it meant abandonment of the project. He refused to reenter the chess arena. No longer would he be a chess player as far as the public was concerned. On his first return from Europe, undoubtedly he and his mother had agreed that now chess would be put aside, except for leisure hours. He had accomplished his purpose with chess, to test his strength against the world, and now was ready for his profession. Chess was no career for a gentleman at that time in history. Yet the question remains, could he have turned the intuitive insight he had used in chess as successfully in other directions?

Not much of the work on that Morphy game book remains. A few diagrams that Gilberg had prepared for the first games (usually more than one diagram for Games I, II, III, etc.) are all that is left.

Morphy left New York in mid-October and arrived in New Orleans about the first week of November. He continued to show some interest in the game, and the chess players of the city reorganized the chess club, electing Paul Morphy its president and Charles A. Maurian secretary. Inauguration of the officers took place on November 14, 1865. The New Orleans *Star* was the first to publish three of Morphy's games—two with Maurian and the third a blindfold game. Two of these games are unknown to the chess world. The blindfold game adds a new name to the list of Morphy's opponents, Paul Capdevielle, and reveals that soon after Morphy's arrival in New Orleans, in May, he had taken on four players blindfolded simultaneously. About this same time Whitelaw Reid toured the South, and he gives us a glimpse of a gentleman's evening in the New Orleans of that time in *After the War: A Southern Tour*. He describes in this book an evening at the home of Christian Roselius, Professor of Civil Law and Dean of the Faculty at the University of Louisiana, who conferred the degree of L.L.B. on Paul Morphy in 1857:

> One noticed here, as at most of the formal dinner parties given during our stay, and at my subsequent visits to the city, the absence of all ladies save those of the host's household. Indeed, except in peculiar cases like this, the prevailing idea of a dinner in New Orleans seems to have for its leading feature copious libations of a great many kinds of the choicest wines—to be licensed by the earliest possible retiracy of the hostess.
>
> Among Mr. Roselius's guests that evening was a modest-looking little gentleman, of retiring manners, and with apparently very little to say, though the keen eyes and well-shaped head sufficiently showed the silence to be no mask for poverty of intellect. It was Mr. Paul Morphy, the foremost chess-player of the world, now a lawyer, but, alas! by no means the foremost young lawyer of this his native city. "If he were only as good in his profession as he is at chess-playing!" said one of the legal gentlemen, with a shrug of his shoulders, as he spoke in an undertone of the abilities of the elder Morphy, and the hopes that had long been cherished of the son. They evidently looked upon the young chess-player as a prosperous banker does upon his only boy, who persists in neglecting his desk in the bank parlor and becoming a vagabond artist.

Whatever activity Morphy engaged in other than chess during the years 1865 through 1866, we know not. Nothing is known of his legal work for clients, if he engaged in any. But we do know of private games Morphy played with Maurian in both years, as the latter disclosed in his notebooks. It would appear that time passed for Morphy without other outside interests, except the opera, of which he was a confirmed lover, and his mother grew concerned about his monotonous and melancholy life. Maurian says that Morphy's mother, knowing what Paris meant to him, decided that a sojourn there might be good for all of them, and by July 1867, Paul, Helena, and herself were en route for Paris.

CHAPTER 23

Paris, Frustration, and Obsessions

In the Paris of July 1867, a Grand International Chess Congress was in progress. There had been rumors even before Morphy left for France that he might enter. In March, the Paris correspondent of the Springfield, Massachusetts, *Republican* had reported, "Paul Morphy, whom the French journals speak of as 'the handsome young man who plays blindfold,' is to represent America. Morphy is spoken of with genuine admiration by all good Chess-players, and it is evidently feared that he will carry off the laurels."

However, Morphy had had no thought of competing, or of playing chess with anyone. In fact, although he was in Paris during the tournament, in which his friends Rivière, Eugène Rousseau, and others he knew were participating, he never once visited the tournament hall nor is he known to have played Rivière or anyone else during this, his last and longest stay in Paris.

He occasionally visited Rivière, but not to play chess. Some insight into Morphy's life in Paris at this time is given by Sheriff W. C. Spens in the Glasgow *Weekly Herald* of July, 1884:

> Morphy returned to Paris, where he had a married sister living. Events had proved disastrous to his parents [the Civil War], and also blighted his own prospects, which had such a depressing influence on his over-wrought mind, that it perfectly paralysed his energies. He lost his taste for chess entirely, and Neumann told us in 1867 that he never could prevail upon Morphy to play a game. They frequently met at De Riviere's house, and Morphy would occasionally condescend to look on at some variations, when the Paris Congress book was being prepared for press. We recollect his coming once as far as the door of the Régence to make some inquiries, but he would not enter, in spite of M. Lequesne's entreaties.

But in America in 1867, there was one voice not in harmony with others there and abroad, who held Morphy in slight esteem. This was the "literary" chess editor—so called by a contemporary editor—of the Philadelphia *Evening Bulletin*. The *Bulletin's* chess column had started in 1858, edited by Francis Wells and Dr. Samuel Lewis. Dr. Lewis, it appears, left the *Bulletin*, and Gustavus C. Reichhelm took his place in 1861. Colonel Forney of *Forney's War Press* said in the August 24, 1864 issue, that "it is Mr. Reichhelm upon whom the labor of preparing the chess column of the *Bulletin* almost entirely falls, while the credit of it is usurped by another." Apparently Reichhelm, the Morphy-game collector mentioned in Chapter 22, who stayed in the background during the first years of the *Bulletin's* chess column, was not the "literary" editor referred to by "Contemporary" as "decidedly against Morphy," the one who had chosen to believe in Deacon rather than Morphy.

This "literary voice" of the *Bulletin* said of Morphy and his presence in Paris, "We understand that Mr. Paul Morphy is now in Paris, but that he refuses to play with any of the eminent players there, unless at odds. We can hardly credit this, silly as Mr. Morphy has shown himself to be on many occasions." At other times the literary chess editor used the *Bulletin* columns for snide remarks, and it is very likely that Morphy became aware of them, and that they accumulated against him and had their effect on his sensitive nature.

About Morphy's fifteen months in Paris, almost nothing is known. However, from one of his letters it is known that he accepted an invitation to a costume ball for the twenty-seventh of March 1868, given by Colonel and Madame Norton, which probably indicates the kind of life he was leading.

About a month before this, *Wilkes' Spirit of the Times* reported:

> It gives us much pleasure to announce that the Champion of the World, Mr. Paul Morphy, has emerged from his retirement. Rumor says that he has played four games with Mr. Steinitz, losing one and drawing three. It is impossible that he will remain satisfied with that result with a player who was beaten by Mr. Kolisch at the Paris Tournament; therefore we confidently expect to see him contest a series of games either with Mr. Steinitz, or some other chess champion of equal strength, without fear that the laurels which he earned will be wrested from him.

Unfortunately for the chess world, they had not met, nor did they until 1883 during Steinitz's visit to New Orleans. About this time, 1863, Steinitz had several games with a Mr. Murphy of London, and evidently someone, finding Steinitz's opponent rather vaguely described, thought it was Morphy. This mistake was made even though Steinitz was conceding odds of Pawn and move to his opponent, which should have canceled the possibility that the opponent was Morphy. Some of these games were published in 1863 in the *Chess Players Magazine*.

In September 1868, Morphy was in New York on his way back to New Orleans. He put up at the New York Hotel for a few days but did not visit the New York Chess Club, a fact upon which the newspapers of the city commented.

Years later it was revealed that during the following year, he and Maurian met frequently for a game of chess. In fact, Maurian said they played, in particular, four series of games, all at Knight odds, the result being:

First Series	—	Morphy 6, Maurian 3 Drawn 2
Second Series	—	Morphy 3, Maurian 3
Third Series	—	Morphy 7, Maurian 10
Fourth Series	—	Morphy 0, Maurian 4, Drawn 1

It was Reichhelm who succeeded in getting these results and many of the game scores from James Wibray of New Orleans, who evidently had gotten them from Maurian. The results indicate Maurian's growing strength. After the conclusion of the Fourth Series in December 1869, Morphy told Maurian that he was now too strong to receive the odds of Knight and that hereafter he would allow him the odds of Pawn and two moves only.

The Second American Chess Congress, now ten years later than originally planned, was set for December 1871 at Cleveland. The divisiveness of the Civil War affected entries and prize money, but the *Prospectus* was able to offer one hundred dollars for First Prize. It had been hoped that Morphy would attend, but he declined the invitation.

From meager reports, Morphy was now living quietly in New Orleans. In March of 1873 the Dubuque *Chess Journal* reported, "Mr. Paul Morphy has just entered the great banking house of Seligman, Hellman & Co. of New Orleans, but in what capacity we have not learned."

In this same month and year, on March 15, a letter from Charles J. Woodbury to the Hartford *Times* disclosed that Morphy still played chess, but only on special occasions and in privacy, although this time it was a "numerous" privacy, so to speak. Woodbury's interview letter is for the most part taken up with the story of and comments on Morphy's life. Morphy greeted him in French and Woodbury replied in the same, and, knowing something of the family circumstances, may have mentioned that chess could do a lot for him. As Woodbury reveals, if there was one thing that enraged Morphy, it was constant talk of chess with strangers and the suggestion that he use his skills at the game for profit:

> A flight of stairs leads up to the dwelling-rooms. I had never
> seen Paul Morphy, but I knew the moment he stood quietly be-
> fore me, simply dressed, slight, smooth and melancholy-faced,
> with a head and brow overhanging with their own weight. So
> full of dignity, so empty of self-consciousness, was his pres-
> ence, that I was almost prepared by it for the quick answer he
> made me that he was but an amateur, and was averse to noto-
> riety. But the passion of the Creole eyes overspoke the tutored
> voice at a remark I made about the contrast between what he
> said and what he had done. My imperfect French added to the
> embarrassment of the moment, and his thin self-control gave
> way to one of those sudden paroxysms of passion to which I
> have since learned he is constantly subject. Happily, the com-
> ing of his mother soon divested him of the strange suspicion
> that I thought him to be a professional gambler; and, after-
> wards, through Mons. C. A. Maurian, an intimate friend and
> the best public player today in New Orleans, all of these misun-
> derstandings were removed. . . .
>
> Once in a while, the solitary athlete can be induced to show
> that his power is only in abeyance. I saw him at a private séance,
> just before I left, beat simultaneously, in 1 ¾ hours, sixteen of
> the most accomplished amateurs in New Orleans. His strength
> had never been fully tested, and will probably never be fully de-
> veloped.
>
> Paul Morphy is poor. Unlike a Yankee, he finds it impossible
> to live on his talent. Opportunities there are in abundance,—
> rich offers for public exhibitions of himself as delicate as those
> grasped at by men who would pretend to more honor. He stead-
> fastly refuses them. He was morbidly sensitive to misjudgment,
> lest he be taken for one who "travels on his muscle," and, on
> all his journeys, defrayed his own expenses, and always played
> in the presence only of select companies, to which no money
> could gain access. There seems to me to be a certain attraction
> in this fine delicacy, which one would encounter not elsewhere
> among us than in the half-foreign society of New Orleans, amid
> which Mr. Morphy was reared. It is dearer to him than wealth
> or reknown, or the strange gift by which he must get his daily
> bread or go without it. Some there are who do not live by bread
> alone.

About this same time (ca. 1872) Morphy made another attempt to enter the legal profession by joining in partnership with E. T. Fellowes, who

was already well established. Cards were prepared and the office advertised as "Fellowes & Morphy, Attorneys and Counsellors at Law."

It is not known whether friendship entered into the reasons for their partnership, or whether Fellowes thought that the Morphy name would bring clients. In either case, failure for Morphy seemed inevitable. He could not escape his chess reputation, especially in New Orleans. If anyone came to the law office because of him, the subject of chess was certain to be introduced. And if there was one thing Morphy did not want to talk about, it was chess. Furthermore, at the office he was a "sitting duck" for anyone who might want to see or talk to him, whether they had business with him or not, and there were many not easily deterred who thought they flattered him by mentioning his great days of the past. Even if Morphy desired daily work at this time, about which there seems some question, chess was forcing itself between him and his profession. Chess hounded him, and his growing morbidity, extreme sensitivity, and increasing suspiciousness of those around him culminated in an imbalance that deprived him of practically all company except that of his immediate family. Undoubtedly there were scenes at the office, such as occurred during Woodbury's visit. Morphy's partnership with Fellowes lasted for some time into 1874, but his active share in it, if any, is unknown. It might have happened before, but at this point in his life, in the wake of all that had happened, one finds it difficult to visualize Morphy hard at work on any case.

Gradually, as these experiences continued and piled up, frustrated and thwarted at every turn, unable to overcome the odds against him and now lacking a meaningful interest in life, his mind turned inward, begetting its own poison. He began to think of evil intentions where there were none.

About this time Morphy began to show some evidence of the effects of his years of frustration, of lasting bitterness from some experiences, and of a very solitary existence. All this welled up in him and darkened his days, and now, confined to the bursting point, began to show in little irrationalities. He had an obsession about professionalism in chess which in any case was not for him. For him it was the same as gambling and such suggestions infuriated him. His irrationalities increased, and for a while he would eat nothing unless prepared by or under the watchful eyes of his sister Helena or his mother.

His present circumstances suggested to him that his brother-in-law Sybrandt, the administrator of his father's estate, had defrauded him or mismanaged the estate, and so Morphy started an absurd lawsuit against him which came to nothing—he had probably spent most of his available patrimony before his second trip to Europe, one reason why he had taken a large loan on his watch while there.

It appears that before Woodbury's visit, and indeed into 1875, Morphy lived a quiet and uneventful life. He had given up the law office he had established in 1864 after two or three months and also his partnership with Fellowes; otherwise his daily activities consisted of a promenade on Canal Street, a visit to the lobby of the St. Louis Hotel to read his newspaper, attending Mass at the St. Louis Cathedral, and an occasional game of chess, as had been witnessed by Woodbury. And he may have been otherwise engaged. He had been invited to participate in the 1874 Chicago Chess Congress, but had declined, and he defended himself against unwanted chess by pleading that he had matters of importance requiring his attention. He had done this in New York in 1865, professing to be there on legal matters, merely using his leisure time on his contemplated book.

It was in 1875 that Maurian first began to notice some strange talk by Morphy, as mentioned in his letter below. Soon after, Morphy's imbalance reached a climax when he suspected a barber of being in collusion with one of his friends, Mr. Binder, whom he attacked, actually trying to provoke a duel (Maurian said he was a good swordsman), believing the friend had wronged him. This raised the question of mental competence. As a consequence of the attack, thinking it might be the prelude to further violence against himself or others, his family considered putting him in an institution for care and treatment, the "Louisiana Retreat," run by an order of the Catholic Church. So one day all the family took a ride, and he was brought in. Upon realizing the situation, Morphy so expounded the law applying to his case that the nuns refused to accept him, and his mother and the others realized he needed no such constraint.

It was this attack upon Mr. Binder that brought public attention to his condition and North, South and all of Europe took it up, of course exaggerating the whole incident. There were inquiries about Morphy's condition and Maurian answered some of them. It was frequently questioned whether the condition might not have resulted from Morphy's extraordinary (as it was thought) mental strain induced by his chess playing.

Maurian felt obliged to answer inquiries from Captain George H. Mackenzie, the American chess champion, and Jean Prèti of Paris (see Appendix), among others. The following letter from Maurian, published in the Watertown, New York, *Re-Union* of December 1875, is quite informative:

New Orleans, Dec. 5, 1875

My Dear Sir:

It is unfortunately too true that Mr. Morphy's mind has been deranged of late but not to the extent that the New York *Sun* would have us believe; for I fervently hope that the kind attention of his family will in time result in a complete cure. I noticed some time ago some extraordinary statements he made of petty persecutions directed against him by unknown persons, that there was something wrong about him, but after a while he openly accused some well known persons of being the authors of the persecutions, and insisted upon their giving him proper satisfaction by arms. Thus it is that the matter was noised about. Outside of the persecution question, he remains what his friends and acquaintances have always known him to be, the same highly educated and pleasing conversationalist.

An attempt was made to induce him to remain in the "Louisiana Retreat," an institution for the treatment of insane persons, but he objected and expounded to all concerned the law that governed his case and drew certain conclusions with such irrefutable logic that his mother thought, and in my opinion very properly, that his case did not demand such extreme measures as depriving him of his liberty, and took him home.

He has been very quiet of late and seems to have been impressed with the remark of some good friends about his "persecution mania." I met him some days ago and the objectionable subject not having been broached, he was as rational and pleasant in his conversation as anybody else.

Since somewhere about 1864 or 65 Mr. Morphy has had a certain aversion for chess. (Indeed he never was, strange as it will seem, an enthusiast.) This was caused, no doubt, by his being constantly bored to death by all sorts of persons who thought it a nice thing to play a game with the champion of the world, or to ask him in how many moves he could force mate in a game, or what was the best way to open the game, or to be kind enough to solve this or that problem &c, to say nothing of the mountains of stupid letters he was called upon to read. At that time he told me very frankly that he was going to abandon completely everything in the shape of public chess. But he consented to play with me as often as I should like. After this he went to Europe and on his return, observing that he played with me only to please me, I ceased to impose this species of penance on him. Our last games were in 1869 in the month of December.

It is an error to suppose that Mr. Morphy is an idler. He is engaged upon no particular business, it is true, but he is fond of literature, an enlightened admirer of the fine arts, a great lover of books and he loves study. He is rather of sedentary habits (a great deal too much so), his tastes and habits are eminently refined, and his deportment is always gentlemanly; I may say aristocratic. He was a regular frequenter of opera, that is, when our city was right enough to support one, and he was able to appreciate the beauties of music and to understand and feel and profit by the elevating influences of the works of Mozart, Rossini and Meyerbeer and other great masters. I assure you, my dear sir, it will be a pity indeed if disease impairs permanently such a powerful brain, such a splendid mental organization, one so well stocked, too, with learning and varied information.

Very truly yours, Charles A. Maurian

It is evident from Maurian's letter of December 5 that while Morphy had a persecution complex that sometimes reigned out of control, in general, he was his usual self; in fact, a strong but unsuccessful effort was made to get him to participate in the 1876 International Chess Congress at Philadelphia.

Morphy's fame had not dimmed. As a part of the First Centennial Celebration of the country, R. M. Devens had written *Our First Century*, in which he devoted one chapter to Paul Morphy as one of the "One Hundred Great and Memorable Events in the History of Our Country."

The persecution complex mentioned above seems not to have lasted very long for Maurian took issue with a paragraph in the New York *Sun* of April 24, 1877, and his letter in the *Sun* of May 2, 1877, indicates that Morphy had recovered his mental stability:

New Orleans, April 28, 1877

The *Sun* of the 24th inst. contains a repetition of that oft-told lie about the insanity of Paul Morphy—that he had not played chess for a long time, and so forth, *ad nauseam*. Will you have the kindness to publish the following, which contains all of the facts concerning Paul Morphy with which the public have anything to do?

He is now practicing law in this city, and has never been insane, or spoken of in that relation by his family or friends.

As to chess, he is unquestionably to-day the best chess player in the world, although he does not play often enough to keep himself in thorough practice. He gives the odds of a knight to our strongest players, and is seldom beaten, perhaps never when he cares to win.

His disappearance from public view as a chess player has just this explanation—no more, no less.

The publicity and lionizing which attached to him for a time, both in this country and Europe, were always distasteful to his family, and especially so to his mother.

On his return from his European triumphs, he entered into an engagement with his mother never again to play for a money or other stake; never to play a public game or a game in a public place, and never again to encourage or countenance any publication of any sort whatever in connection with his name.

This last clause in the agreement has heretofore been so strictly construed as to prevent any denial by him or his family of the numerous silly publications that have been made concerning him. It is now time, however, that the thing should be stopped.

Will you have the kindness to inform the public at large, and newspaper paragraphers in particular, that Paul Morphy is engaged in a strict attendance upon his own affairs, and that his family and friends do not at present adjudge him in need of any assistance therein?

Very respectfully, Chas. A. Maurian.

Maurian indicates that Morphy was still playing chess in 1877. He also mentions Morphy's "agreement" with his mother in 1859 "never again to encourage or countenance any publication of any sort whatever in connection with his name." It would seem (judging from the many public activities Morphy subsequently engaged in with reference to chess) that this agreement was nothing more than a mutual understanding rather than a promise. For during his visits to Cuba in 1862 and 1864, Morphy's chess games were hardly played in private and were immediately published in Cuba, Europe, and America, with attendant publicity. A large lithograph was published in *El Moro Muza* in October 1862, showing him playing the Cuban amateurs. He even resumed work with Rivière on their Openings treatise in 1863. None of this would have happened had Morphy expressed a desire that publicity be withheld.

Apparently no promise to his mother was responsible for his abstention from public chess, contrary to what has often been contended. Even as late in his life as 1878, Morphy was being asked to participate in public chess. In the Philadelphia *Sunday Times* of June 30, 1889, Bird said, "We hoped to have him play in the Continental tournament of 1878, but were doomed to disappointment." At this time, A. Rosenbaum of London was completing a painting of prominent English chess players, and he included a most delightful portrait of Paul Morphy as in his debonair days.

About the beginning of 1879, Morphy developed symptoms of a mild form of illusion. Dr. L. P. Meredith, who visited New Orleans that year, reported his observations of Morphy in a letter dated April 16, 1879, in the Cincinnati *Commercial*. (The complete letter appears in the Appendix.)

> On the street in New Orleans, last month, I frequently saw Mr. Morphy, but I was longer in his presence, and had a better opportunity of studying him at the old Spanish Cathedral on Easter Sunday than elsewhere. He paid devout attention to the services, and appeared thoroughly familiar with all of the ceremonies, always assuming the kneeling posture, and moving his head and lips responsively at the right time, without apparently taking the cue from any of the worshipping throng. . . .

> I have spoken of his imagined salutations, and his pleasant bow and smile, and graceful wave of the hand, in response. This must have occurred twenty or thirty times as he stood behind a massive column for a few minutes, in a position in which it was impossible for any one to see him from the direction in which he looked. In the speculations regarding his mental derangement it has been natural to attribute it in a great measure, to an over-exertion of brain power in his wonderful feats at chess, but nothing has ever been found to establish positively such a conclusion. His astonishing achievements appeared to cost him no effort. Analyses that would require weeks of laborious study on the part of the greatest masters, he would make as rapidly as his eyes could look over the squares. His eight or ten blindfold games, played simultaneously against strong players, appeared to require no more attention than the perusal of a book or paper. With rare exceptions, he appeared to know intuitively the strongest moves that could be made. His uncle, Ernest Morphy, during his visit to Cincinnati many years ago, told me how Paul, when a child, would suddenly drop his knife and fork at the table and set up on the checkered table-cloth a problem that had suddenly sprung into his head, using the cruets, salt-cellers and napkin-rings for pieces. I asked him if his nephew was remarkable for anything else than his peculiar aptitude for chess,

and I recollect that he stated, among other things, that, after his
return from a strange opera, he could hum or whistle it from
beginning to end. . . .

It is unquestionably an instance of a brain excessively developed
at the expense of the physical man, having the mind expanded
to the utmost bounds of sanity, and ready to wander outside its
limits on the occurrence of some peculiarly exciting circumstance; and this happened, probably, in the sudden realization
that what he had considered a competency was expended, and
that he had become, for the present at least, dependent. After
this he was in no condition to reason—to see that he had lived
extravagantly while abroad and after his return, and that his expenditures were in excess of his share of his father's estate. He
imagined that he had been defrauded, intentionally or through
mismanagement. . . .

Gradually, Morphy's imbalance advanced to a point where he occasionally believed that he was in great need and would approach a friend
for a loan of $200. His condition was well understood, and his request
was never refused, but upon being assured that the money was available
he would feel relieved and invariably say he would call for it on the morrow, which he never did. One such occasion, reported in the *Turf, Field and
Farm* of October 21, 1881, is of interest:

On a recent occasion Mr. Morphy hastily entered the office of
a well-known resident of New Orleans, and made known his
need of two hundred dollars to save himself from impending
disaster, and requested a loan of that amount. His friend resolved on an experiment which would test the relative strength
of the hold upon Morphy's mind of this delusion, and the other—his aversion to chess, and assuming a serious tone, he said:
"You want this money very much, it seems." "Yes," said Morphy, "I must have it—it is absolutely necessary." "Well," replied
the other, "I'll tell you what I will do: if you will play a game of
chess with me, I will make it two hundred and fifty dollars."
Morphy's countenance betrayed the internal struggle between
the conflicting emotions aroused by this offer. He paused, in
thought, for some moments, and then in a tone expressive of his
sense of the hardship inflicted upon him by the condition, and
also, of a quiet exultation over the anticipated success of a plan
he had formed, he accepted the terms; chess-board and men
were produced in an inner office, and Morphy played his latest
game of chess. With a disdainful curl of the lip, and a mani-

fest repugnance, Morphy moved in such a way that his friend mated him in a very few moves, whereupon Morphy exclaimed, "There! I have done what you require: but the next time I play chess with you, I will give you the Queen!" and already oblivious of his pecuniary necessities, he was going away, when his friend reminded him that he was forgetting his reward. "I will come for it tomorrow!" was his reply, as he left the apartment.

The necessity of a 200-dollar loan did not last very long, but Morphy still felt the need to be on his guard, as brought out by a young barber and published in the *Turf, Field and Farm* of April 22, 1881. It should be noted that the barber's story was written by a reporter who probably exercised some license in describing Morphy's condition, about which the papers were prone to exaggerate, as mentioned by Maurian:

In a Broadway print shop a picture of Paul Morphy, the once famous monarch of chess players, is on view. It is a pastel drawing, with a good deal of life and vigor about it. The artist is Paul Schoeff, a barber, who recently came to this city from New Orleans to study art on his savings. To our reporter, Schoeff told a curious story of the original of his picture.

"Mr. Morphy is crazy," he said, "and lives with his mother and a servant. He is harmless, and no one ever has any trouble with him. His manias are very peculiar ones, and it is to one of them I owe my acquaintance with him. He is possessed of a belief that the barbers are in a vast conspiracy, suborned by his enemies, to cut his throat. There are only one or two shops in New Orleans he will enter, and when a strange barber, or even an old one, operates on him, he watches him closely, on the alert always for a suspicious movement. Often he springs from his chair and rushes into the street, half shaved, lathered and with his towel about his neck, screaming murder. Everybody knows and likes him, however, and though he is a nuisance they pity him too much to refuse to shave him.

"You might wonder that he gets shaved at all, or at least does not shave himself, but here another of his manias comes in. He is a confirmed fop, and sometimes changes his clothes as often as a dozen times a day, each time going out for a walk, saluting all sorts of imaginary acquaintances as he trips along, and returning to get himself up over again. Of course he must be as immaculate in his hair-dressing as in that of his person, and nobody but a barber can do him justice.

"I worked for a man named Schmidt, to whose shop Mr. Morphy used to come to get shaved. I was the boy of the shop, and was just learning to use the razor. One day Mr. Morphy came in, looked around and beckoned to me to shave him. The boss and the barbers winked at each other, as much as to say: 'Well, he is crazy, sure enough,' but no one interfered, for you must always let Mr. Morphy have his own way. Well, I lathered and shaved him, fortunately without a cut, though I was so excited at shaving a lunatic that it is a wonder I did not really cut his throat. From that time forth he never had any one else tend to him.

"I was practicing drawing then, and the boss used to let me work in the back of the shop when there was nothing else to do. Mr. Morphy noticed my drawings, and one day, without a word, he sat down on a chair, pointed to himself and to my drawing board and nodded. I knew what he wanted, and went to work and made a picture of him. He sat to me every afternoon for a week. When the picture was done I presented it to him. Next day, when he came in, he gave me a little bundle. It contained a handsome silk handkerchief, a scarf and a fine scarf pin. Poor Mr. Morphy had given me his pet finery, for they were things he was very fond of wearing himself. The picture I brought on with me is one I drew from the first sketch of the old one, and it is a good deal the better of the two. I wear his presents with my Sunday suit."

Among all the reports on and letters about Morphy in his latter years, nowhere else is there any suggestion of his many daily changes of attire and nowhere else is it mentioned that he sometimes rushed into the street screaming. The same *Turf, Field and Farm* that published the above story about Morphy also published the following statement in his defense in its May 9, 1879, issue:

Another base rumor that was amplified in print represented him as a silly fop, intoxicated with vanity, parading the fashionable streets of New Orleans, ogling the ladies, and impertinently saluting them with bows and grimaces. This report is false and cruel.

Regina Morphy-Voitier, Paul's niece, relates in *The Life of Paul Morphy* that he was "always neatly attired and never without his monocle and his small walking stick" for his afternoon walk on Canal Street, and she goes so far as to say that on those walks he gave "feminine charms an admiring glance, but later sometimes stopped and stared." She also mentions that sometimes, in his later years, he would walk on the verandah overlooking the garden declaiming in a low voice, "Il plantera la bannière de Castille sur les murs de Madrid au cri de ville gagnée, et le petit Roi s'en ira tout penaud." (He will plant the banner of Castile upon the walls of Madrid, amidst the cries of the conquered city, and the little king will go away looking very sheepish.) The significance of this statement is obscure.

Regina's booklet conveys very little new information about Morphy, and much of it is inaccurate. She was a young girl during this period in Morphy's life, and offers little firsthand knowledge of her subject.

CHAPTER 24

Psychoanalysts and Paul Morphy

During the last years of his life, Morphy's mental condition was marked by distrust, obsessions, and delusions, and his somewhat erratic behavior has attracted the attention of many in the psychiatric and psychoanalytic professions. In his time there were those who believed they could help him, but he would have no help, satisfied he needed none. Some believed that a return to chess would have stabilized him and relieved his tensions, but he would have none of it.

The mental disorder which descended upon him, incidentally seeming to clear up in the last year or two of his life, during which he occupied himself with his reading, daily walks, and visits to his brother's house, has been the subject of much psychoanalytic discussion. While some of the discussion of Morphy's illness has been superficial, much of it has been serious and extensive, mainly that by Dr. Ernest Jones, the eminent English psychoanalyst, who made a comprehensive study as reported in "The Problem of Paul Morphy," published in the *International Journal of Psycho-Analysis* of June 1931. Dr. Reuben Fine also dealt with Morphy's problem.*

However, due to their sources, both were obliged to proceed on the basis of a good deal of misinformation. The many errors to be found in the booklet by C. A. Buck, *Paul Morphy, His Later Life*, have been noted in Chapter 16, nor is Regina Morphy-Voitier's pamphlet free of them; and since both Jones and Fine relied upon these sources to some extent, this may have resulted in some ill-founded assumptions and conclusions.

Dr. Jones observed in "The Problem of Paul Morphy" that "the slightest acquaintance with chess shows one that it is a play-substitute for the art of war." But he then goes considerably further, claiming that "the unconscious motive actuating the players is not the mere love of pugnacity characteristic of all competitive games, but the grimmer one of father-murder."

---

* EDITOR'S NOTE: Jones's article, "The Problem of Paul Morphy: A Contribution to the Psycho-Analysis of Chess," is still available through the *International Journal of Psycho-Analysis*, but it has also been reprinted in many collections and is available in online formats from distributors such as Psychoanalytic Electronic Publishing. See http://www.pep-web.org/document.php?id=IJP.012.0001A. As Lawson notes later in the chapter, Reuben Fine's *The Psychology of the Chess Player* is still available from Dover, originally reprinted in 1956.

He then says, "In Morphy's mind chess must have signified a fully adult activity," and so it was with Labourdonnais, Steinitz, Capablanca, Alekhine, and other great players. However, while Morphy accepted the game as an adult recreational activity, he resolutely refused from the beginning to consider it as a profession.

Dr. Jones also says, "He [Morphy] knew, as though it was a simple fact of nature, that he was bound to win [Capablanca thought the same until he met Alekhine] and he quietly acted on that knowledge." And, Jones adds, "It is not surprising that endowed with such confidence in his powers his play was marked by a boldness and even audacity." S. S. Boden seemed to agree, for he said from firsthand knowledge (*Chess Life-Pictures* by G. A. MacDonnell) that Morphy had a truly gigantic capacity for chess that was never fully called forth, and that his play "was rather over hazardous."

Calling on Freud in this same article, Dr. Jones goes on to ask, was Morphy one of "those wrecked by success," his meaning being best expressed by a line that he quotes from Browning's "Pictor Ignotus": "The thought of success grew frightful, t'was so wildly dear!" However, it does not appear that Morphy was ever driven by anxieties to succeed; as has been noted, Jones himself suggests Morphy "knew, as though it was a simple fact of nature, that he was bound to win." Perhaps he was wrecked by success, but not in the sense Freud intended. It can be said that Morphy's chess success was largely the cause of his failure in his professional career. *

Morphy's acclamation in the United States and abroad was such as would have turned the heads of most, and not only great chess players like Anderssen, St. Amant, Lowenthal and others, but also such as Oliver Wendell Holmes and Samuel F. B. Morse. Henry Wadsworth Longfellow made a trip to Boston to see him, as he records in his "Journal and Letters." But instead of being elated by his success, Morphy expressed dissatisfaction. As Dr. Jones says, "On his return home, far from being flushed with pride, he remarked that he had not done so well as he should have." There is no evidence that Morphy ever succumbed to adulation: instead he was apparently embarrassed and put out by it, for he retained the unassuming modesty of a gentleman throughout his life.

---

* EDITOR'S NOTE: As shall be seen, Lawson does not agree with Jones' Freudianism, but an even more strident critique came later from Robert Philipson, who argues that Jones's work was "predictably Oedipal" and overly simplisitic in its focus on father murder and queenly power. See his "Chess and Sex in Le Devoir Du Violence." *Callaloo* 38 (Winter 1989): 216-232, included in the annotated bibliography following Lawson's text.

Dr. Jones makes much of Morphy's failure to get Staunton to meet him in a match, and without doubt Morphy was greatly disappointed by it. Of Staunton's treatment of Morphy in his chess column, Dr. Jones remarks, "It is hardly an exaggeration to call it scurrilous." It was not so much Staunton's refusal to play as it was his "scurrilous" (to use Jones's word) conduct over a period of months that seared Morphy's soul and left a lasting scar that without doubt was a contributing factor to his later condition.

Also, Dr. Jones overlooks the added significance of the refusal to Morphy of a diplomatic or other appointment during the Civil War, and Morphy's inactivity for the Confederacy when every young Southerner was expected to do his "duty." Had not these factors combined against him, together with others mentioned, Morphy might well have established a law practice of some kind.

Morphy did not wait to be "in the safety of his New Orleans home" as Dr. Jones states, before challenging the world at Pawn and move odds, for this was announced while he was in Paris in 1859. In view of Morphy's overwhelming success here and abroad against the masters of his time and the opinions of such masters as Anderssen, Lowenthal, St. Amant and others, it is difficult to understand how Dr. Jones could feel qualified to make the statement that Morphy was "probably overestimating his power" in so challenging the world. None accepted his challenge and, none accepting, Dr. Jones may well ask, "Did he withdraw from the world with the disdainful consolation?" As in Browning—"At least no merchant traffics in my heart."

The following statement by Dr. Slater pertinent to the above discussion appeared in the *British Chess Magazine* of February 1952. It is preceded by a short summation of Dr. Jones's article, "The Problem of Paul Morphy."

> Your columns, Sir, are obviously not the place for debate on matters of psychiatric theory. Nevertheless, your readers are entitled to know whether Dr. Jones' views would be generally accepted in a circle of his colleagues. This is not so. Psychoanalysis is repudiated by a majority of psychiatrists, and, indeed, in the opinion of many of us is a body of dogma more than a scientific theory. To the non-analytic psychiatrists Morphy's paranoia is an illness whose main cause is constitutional, determined by hereditary predisposition, and can be regarded as an accident of nature. In any case it did not come on till many years after his withdrawal from chess.
>
> The psychoanalytic theory of the psychology of chess pre-

sented by Dr. Jones must also be received with skepticism. It is a main motif of psychoanalysis to explain all human activities, even the highest, in terms of sex and hate, and to ignore all other drives. However, man, like all the higher animals, takes delight in the use of his powers to the fullest extent. To explain the enthusiasm of the chess player, particularly that of such a supreme player as Morphy, one need not go beyond this, and the father-murder motive is superfluous. Not only does psychoanalysis make no allowance for the pleasures we obtain from successful mental effort, it is also powerless to explain the aesthetic beauties of interaction and interference which appear, often with surprising unexpectedness, in the unfolding development of a game of chess. It is a matter for remark that Dr. Jones should ignore these aspects, for he is himself an accomplished and enthusiastic player.

Yours faithfully, E. T. O. Slater,

Senior Lecturer, Institute of Psychiatry, London University

Dr. Reuben Fine, one of America's great chess players, is another psychoanalyst who has devoted some thought to the problem of Paul Morphy, among others, in the *Psychoanalysis Journal*, Number 3, 1956, which has been reprinted by Dover Publications as *The Psychology of the Chess Player*. With one prime exception, he is in agreement with Dr. Jones, but he has taken some liberties with his subject that the latter did not.

Dr. Fine appears to be on firmer ground than Dr. Jones with reference to the significance of Morphy's failure to get Staunton to meet him over the chessboard. As Fine suggests, originally the chess match with Staunton was Morphy's great objective, but as time dragged on and he could get no starting date, the meeting itself became of less and less importance to Morphy. Later, the match with Anderssen assumed a great deal more meaning for him, and was of vastly greater import than any match with Staunton could have been.

Certainly there may be reason to believe Dr. Fine's statement that "more importance must be attached to Morphy's repeated declaration that he was not a professional" chess player, but Dr. Fine enlarges upon this by declaring that Morphy's refusal to accept chess "was followed by his refusal to embrace any profession."

Actually, Morphy made two earnest attempts to establish a law practice. Due mainly to the Civil War, he was over twenty-seven (not twenty-one as stated by Fine) when in November 1864 he opened a law office, advertised for four weeks in the New Orleans *Picayune*, but had no choice than to close up after two or three months, for reasons already discussed.

Seven or eight years later he entered into partnership with E. T. Fellowes, which association did not flourish for the same reasons that the earlier attempt did not. That Morphy was a victim of his chess, as he told Steinitz years later, is undoubtedly true: "He [Morphy] said, 'people think I am nothing but a chess player, and that I know nothing about law.'" One must also note that between his two attempts to establish a law practice, he was also engaged, in some capacity, with the banking house of Seligman, Hellman & Co. of New Orleans. He may also have been engaged with others at times.

Fred Reinfeld observed in his *Chess Prodigies* that Morphy "possessed to an astounding degree that uncanny quality of the child prodigy which consists in by-passing all the years of training and study that go into the making of a great practitioner of some art or science." The significance of this seems to have escaped Dr. Fine's notice, who says, "Throughout his adolescence Morphy must have spent a major portion of his time playing chess." This appears not to be so. In fact Maurian wrote that Morphy "may be said to have virtually abandoned chess during his collegiate career" (1850–1857). He even remarked in a letter of 1875, given above, that Morphy "never was, strange as it will seem, an enthusiast" about chess.

Dr. Fine mentions Morphy's sex life, about which nothing is known except what little Steinitz revealed (about which more in the next chapter). Regina Morphy-Voitier writes that on opera nights, "he would call upon some of his lady friends," while Edge and various letters bring out that he led an active social life in Paris during his three sojourns there. His company was sought by women of the French nobility, but Morphy left behind no such intimate notes as the one Benjamin Franklin sent to a Madame Brillon (see *The Writings of Benjamin Franklin*, by A. H. Smyth), in which he importunes, "Never hereafter shall I consent to begin a game in your boudoir. Can you forgive me this indiscretion?"

On his first visit to Paris, about which we know most, he was the idol of society. Over twenty years later, in *Brentano's Chess Monthly* of May 1881, Delannoy wrote, "His name, during his sojourn in Paris, made a great noise; it even fills it now." It is known that during 1868 he was an invited guest to society's soirées and enjoyed the society of the elite. Anything beyond this can only be surmised.

Dr. Fine is in error when he states that Morphy played only fifty-five serious games, i.e., match and tournament. As has been listed elsewhere, the number of his match and tournament games totals ninety-five. And one must also ask, are all of Morphy's blindfold and casual games to be taken lightly? Some are considered brilliant. As George Walker has been quoted as saying, one of them is "a gem of excellence, worthy of being written in letters of gold on the walls of the London Chess Club."

As for Morphy's casual games, which Dr. Fine rather dismisses as unimportant, "in the days before tournament play almost every casual game had an importance far greater than the casual games of today. And these were not casual games in the true sense, for a stake and indeed reputations were involved." So say the authors of *Howard Staunton*, Raymond D. Keene and R. N. Coles. Sergeant says, "if we took only the friendly games recorded against such players as Barnes, Bird, Boden, Arnous de Rivière, Owen[,] etc., we should probably be justified in saying that Morphy's marvelous powers are nowhere better shown than when he played, for the love of the game merely, against a high-class opponent." And there are nearly one hundred such casual games (excluding match and tournament) if games with Anderssen, Paulsen, Stanley, and others are added.

Unlike some others, Morphy was not careful about choosing his blindfold opponents: in fact, he often requested the very strongest players to take boards against him. And as with Anderssen's "Immortal" and "Evergreen" casual games, some of Morphy's casual games have found themselves on "brilliant" lists.

Dr. Fine asks why so many of Morphy's casual games were recorded. Probably it was because Staunton, Lowenthal, Walker, Lange, Falkbeer, Boden, and other chess editors were always eager to publish them. The chess columns of the day were almost completely dominated by Morphy's games. Most of his European games printed in this country came from Staunton's column, the most widely circulated. Even Fiske used Staunton's column as a source for his column in the *Chess Monthly*. Morphy himself kept no record of his games, except in his head.

During and before Morphy's time, most games were played informally, and there were not dozens of tournaments a year as there are today. After 1851, no tournaments occurred until 1857.

Dr. Fine states, "Morphy was active in chess for a period of a little over a year (1857–1858), a period in which the development of chess was most rudimentary," presumably including the years before which gave us beautiful and significant games by Philidor, Labourdonnais, Anderssen, and others, and his remarks would seem unduly disparaging.

A story that has had wide circulation in recent years about Morphy and shoes would seem to have little substance in fact. As Dr. Fine tells it, Morphy had an "eccentric habit of arranging women's shoes in a semi-circle in his room. When asked why he liked to arrange shoes in this way he said: 'I like to look at them.'" Regina Morphy, Paul's little niece, appears to have been in Morphy's room more than once, and in all likelihood is the prime source for this story. She describes the room in her pamphlet, *The Life of Paul Morphy*:

> This room had a peculiar aspect and at once struck the visitor as such, for Morphy had a dozen or more pairs of shoes of all kinds which he insisted in keeping arranged in a semi-circle in the middle of the room, explaining with his sarcastic smile that in this way, he could at once lay his hands on the particular pair he desired to wear.

It seems strange that Regina's description of the shoes and Morphy's explanation should have become so changed as to fall into the account given by Dr. Fine, and the story has grown.

Abnormal as were Morphy's actions at times, he retained until the end of his life all his keenness on chess and other subjects. As late as March 1883, Steinitz said in the New York *Tribune*, "Morphy is a most interesting man to talk to."

According to Lombroso in *Men of Genius*, Schopenhauer apparently had a mental condition similar to, but more pronounced than, Morphy's. Like Morphy, he feared a razor and would not trust a barber. He walked the streets of Frankfort "gesticulating and talking aloud to himself," but later the condition passed. Dr. Fine mentions that Steinitz, too, had strange delusions, and the former mentions in *The Psychology of the Chess Player* one story about Steinitz's last year, when he believed "that he could give God Pawn and move."

CHAPTER 25

The Pride and Sorrow of Chess

In July 1882, the New Orleans French newspaper *l'Abeille* announced plans for a biographical work on Famous Louisianans and proposed to include Paul Morphy as "the most celebrated chess-player in the World." Morphy immediately wrote an indignant letter, which he asked them to publish, and it appeared in *l'Abeille* the following day, August 1, 1882:

> New Orleans, July 31, 1882
>
> Editors of *The Bee*:
>
> I read in yesterday's *Bee* "that Mr. Meyiner, Editor of the 'Louisiana Biographies' will begin tomorrow the publication of the first part or section, that of the 'Governors of the State' and 'that following those biographies the reader will find that of Paul Morphy, the most celebrated chess player of the world, and that of Jean Lafitte." [Lafitte, the pirate who fought side-by-side with Andrew Jackson in the defense of New Orleans.]
>
> My father, Judge Alonzo Morphy, of the Supreme Court, at his death having left a fortune (the inventory of the succession made in December, 1856, which can be seen at the office of Theodore Guyol, Esq., Notary Public, amounts to $146,162.54) (one hundred and forty-six thousand and one hundred and sixty-two dollars and fifty-four cents), and the share of each heir being ample enough to allow him to decently defray all his expenses I have followed no calling, and have given no cause for a biography. I have received a diploma as a lawyer.
>
> I am ignorant of the spirit in which the "Louisiana Biographies" are conceived, but Louisianan by birth and in heart, son of a father who acquired a reputation of juris-consult at the Louisiana Bar, who was a member of the Legislature, Attorney-General and Judge of the Supreme Court, grandson of a grandfather who had the honor of representing Spain in New Orleans during a part of the first quarter of this century, I could but approve of a work that would bring to light the services, recent or of old, rendered to our Louisiana.
>
> I have the honor, Messrs. Editors, of presenting you with my

most distinguished sentiments.

Paul Charles Morphy

When displeased, Morphy usually added his middle name to his signature. It seemed that this time his only eccentricity or obsession was to mention or repeat to friends the sum that his father's estate had amounted to.

Perhaps some misrepresentation arose abroad from *l'Abeille's* mention of a Paul Morphy biography, for some time later in 1882, English and other papers were commenting on his demise at forty-five years of age. Sheriff Walter C. Spens, chess editor of the Glasgow *Weekly Herald*, quoted an announcement about it in his chess column of November 25, 1882, and added a five-stanza sonnet. It is owing to Sheriff Spens that we have "The Pride and Sorrow of Chess."

C. A. Buck, in his booklet *Paul Morphy, His Later Life*, states that J. H. Zukertort met Paul Morphy in New Orleans in 1882, and according to that account they had met before in Paris. Zukertort was not in New Orleans in 1882. He first visited there in 1884 from April 15 to May 21, but in the ample coverage of his visit in the American press and in his own magazine, the *Chess Monthly*, there is no suggestion of his meeting Morphy.

Morphy died in July 1884, seven weeks after Zukertort's visit, and Zukertort and his co-editor of the *Chess Monthly* designated the August issue of the magazine, "The Morphy Number," saying:

> It is our duty to give expression to the high admiration we have always entertained for the phenomenal genius of the greatest master that ever lived. As a slight mark of this estimation we devote the present number to the memory of the Chess-Achilles.

Without doubt, Zukertort would have added to the long obituary some comment on his having met Morphy just two months before, if in fact he had.

The year 1883 was uneventful for Morphy except for his meeting with Steinitz, who was in New Orleans for a month's engagement with the New Orleans Chess, Checker & Whist Club. He had arrived on December 28, 1882, and soon made inquiry about Morphy, whom he was most anxious to meet. On being told of Steinitz's presence, Morphy said, "I know it," and then added, "his gambit is not good." Morphy could not help disclosing that he was au courant on chess news and developments.

Failing to get a response from Morphy by writing, mutual friends arranged that they should meet as if by chance. The New York *Tribune* of

March 22, 1883, has a most interesting account of that meeting, of what Morphy had to say to Steinitz and of what Steinitz had heard about Morphy. As Steinitz told it:

> "The first time I met him in the street I stopped him and presented him with my card. He took it and read it, giving me a wild, questioning look for the moment. Immediately recovering himself he shook hands with me, saying that my name was well known to him, and then he entered into conversation with me. Twice after that I met him, and on each occasion, he was exceedingly pleasant and agreeable. As a crowd collected round us on each occasion, he excused himself on the score of pressing legal engagements. I am very angry with that crowd still for interrupting us; Morphy is a most interesting man to talk to. He is shrewd and practical and apparently in excellent health. . . .
>
> I took the opportunity of remonstrating with him [about his lawsuit; actually there was no lawsuit]. I told him he had a number of legal friends; if he would allow them they would thoroughly investigate his business matters, and if he had a chance to recover his property, would tell him so. 'Though,' I added, 'even Morphy may be mistaken, and you may not have taken a correct legal view.' 'That is it,' he answered; 'people think I am nothing but a chess-player, and that I know nothing about law.'"
>
> "Will Morphy ever play chess again, Mr. Steinitz?"
>
> "Probably, if his friends go to work in the right way. At present he will not look at a board and never visits his club, under the apprehension that they will make him play . . . What I said to the men at New Orleans was: Do not ask Morphy to play; let him sit and watch you play, perhaps one of his own games . . . !"
>
> "Why does the loss of his money affect him so much?"
>
> "That is another curious thing. Morphy wants to get married. He is perpetually having 'love affairs.' All the people in New Orleans know it and humor him a little. Mind you, he is the most chivalrous soul alive. He is a thorough gentleman. But if he sees a strange face in the street that pleases him, you will see him lift his hat and give a bow . . He regrets his loss (money) because he wishes to be married, and the cure is, I think, to play chess again determinedly."

Evidently there was no talk of chess between Morphy and Steinitz for

Steinitz would surely have mentioned it during the *Tribune* interview.

On Thursday morning, July 10, 1884, Paul Morphy dressed meticulously as always for his noonday walk, but meeting friends, returned a little later than usual. The weather was very warm, and he went immediately to his bath, which he ordinarily took at one o'clock, and lingered over. But this day his mother thought he was a very long time and finally knocked at the door to inquire. When she received no answer, she opened the door to see his head resting on the side of the bathtub, to which his hands were clinging. He was apparently unconscious.

His mother called out for help, and Dr. Meux, who happened to be passing by the house at the moment, came in and tried in vain to restore him to consciousness. Paul Morphy was pronounced dead at 2:30 p.m., July 10, 1884, from congestion of the brain brought on by entering the cold water while very warm after his walk.

The funeral took place the following day at 5 p.m. from the family residence at 89 Royal Street. The ceremony was performed by the Reverend Father Mignot of the St. Louis Cathedral, after which internment took place in the family tomb at the old St. Louis Cemetery.

The pallbearers were his brother, Edward, his cousin Captain E. A. Morphy, Charles A. Maurian, Edgar Hincks, Leonard J. Percy, and Henry F. Percy.

The news of Morphy's passing spread rapidly here and abroad. Sheriff Spens announced receipt of a special telegram on July 11, and the Glasgow *Weekly Herald* of July 19, 1884, eulogized Paul Morphy in a five-stanza poem by the Sheriff, given in part below:

PAUL MORPHY

> He played a glorious game: in open field,
> Whate'er the opening was, he met the attack,
> And almost always hurled it grandly back;
> And when he did his rival's fate was sealed.
> 'Tis wrongly said the greatest art's concealed
> Behind art, for he never strove to hide
> His forte to see beyond the opposing side!
> And deadly mesnes many a time revealed
> To his surprised and quite defenseless foe
> That move of ten moves back a master-coup,
> Who vainly deemed it lost at any rate.
> Most dreaded was he when he seemed to throw
> Piece after piece away, for then all knew
> Swiftly approached the inevitable mate.

The Manhattan Chess Club, which only three months before had acquired the oil painting of Morphy by Charles Loring Elliott, called a special meeting for July 15, 1884, when it was

> Resolved that the Portrait of Paul Morphy in the rooms of this Club be draped in mourning for a period of three months, and that a full record of these proceedings be entered upon the minutes of this club, and that an engrossed copy thereof, attested by the officers of the Club, be transmitted to the family of the deceased.

> Whereas, the Manhattan Chess Club have learned with deepest regret of the death of Paul Morphy and desire to express their sorrow at the loss of one who, by his matchless skill in their noble game earned for himself the FIRST PLACE in the roll of chess-masters, and by his true modesty and worth gained the esteem and respect of all who knew him.

And Mrs. Telcide Morphy received the following:

Manhattan Chess Club
104 East 14th St.

New York, August 13th 1884

Dear Madam,

I have the honor of transmitting you herewith a copy of the Resolutions passed by the Manhattan Chess Club at a Special Meeting held July 15th, on receiving the sad intelligence of the sudden death of your son, and which we beg you will accept as a slight token of the esteem in which Paul Morphy was held by the members of our Club.

Trusting that the knowledge of the high place he occupied in the hearts of all whose fortune it was to know him personally, and of the respect and admiration he gained of those who knew him through his achievements in the game of Chess alone, may serve, in a small measure to lessen the grief which we know you to feel in your bereavement,

I remain, dear Madam,
Your's very respectfully
W. M. De Visser
Corresponding Sect'y M.C.C.

Mrs. T. Morphy
89 Royal St.
New Orleans

To this his mother replied:

> New Orleans, August 20, 1884
> 89 Royal Street
>
> To the Manhattan Chess Club
>
> Very Honorable Gentlemen,
> The homage which you have rendered to my dear son, and your
> just appreciation of his talent and of his qualities, have, for an
> instant, softened my grief. I am deeply grateful in thinking that
> there are superior minds who have not forgotten him, in this
> world where every thing disappears so rapidly.
>
> I beg of you to accept my cordial thanks, you who have given a
> thought to that which was the glory of the son and the everlast-
> ing grief of the mother.
>
> Receive Gentlemen, the expression of my respect.
>
> Telcide Morphy.

The little household, now composed of Morphy's mother and her
daughter Helena, was stricken and deeply affected by Paul's passing, the
one for whom they had lived and looked after for years. For long years,
Helena and her mother had helped provide for the family by giving music
lessons. On January 11, 1885, Telcide Morphy also died. Apparently, Dr.
Max Lange had written to Helena previously, asking for information about
Morphy, for he received a letter from her dated January 17, 1885:

> . . . I have experienced the intense grief of losing my poor
> mother whose health had been fatally impaired by her son's
> loss. . . . We possess the first and second edition of my brother's
> biography written by you; and as to the information you desire
> I am very sorry to say we had no letters, in fact not the least
> paper from our dear Paul. For years preceding his death, he
> was averse to any social intercourse and confined himself to a
> gloomy retirement apart from his former friends. It pains me
> etc.
>
> Helena Morphy

The magic of Paul Morphy called forth from I. O. Howard Taylor of
England a tribute to his mother, to be found in the Appendix.

But another, F. F. Beechey, had feared the worst in 1882, and sorrowed
for Morphy when the rumors of his death reached England. The below appeared in the *British Chess Magazine* of that October:

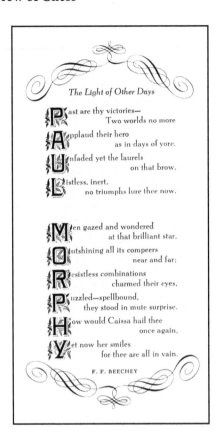

The Light of Other Days

Past are thy victories—
      Two worlds no more

Applaud their hero
      as in days of yore.

Unfaded yet the laurels
      on that brow.

Listless, inert,
      no triumphs lure thee now.

Men gazed and wondered
      at that brilliant star.

Outshining all its compeers
      near and far;

Resistless combinations
      charmed their eyes.

Puzzled—spellbound,
      they stood in mute surprise.

How would Caissa hail thee
      once again,

Yet now her smiles
      for thee are all in vain.

F. F. BEECHEY

Some paid their homage to Morphy in prose, others in verse and music. In Italy, Professor Ottolenghi penned a sonnet, and Giuseppe Liberali composed an elegy for the piano, dedicating it to the American chess players.

The auction of Morphy's trophies, together with other items of the estate, now took place, and soon after, on September 8, 1886, Helena Morphy followed her mother to the grave. There now remained of the Morphy family but the brother, Edward, and the sister Malvina (Mrs. J. D. Sybrandt). The Sybrandt family took over and occupied the house at 89 Royal Street for a short time and then, forty-five years after its purchase by Alonzo Morphy, it was occupied by strangers. But the memory of Paul Morphy still lingers round that house, now known as the Morphy House.

> 'Tis all a Chequer-board of Nights and Days
> Where Destiny with Men for Pieces plays:
> Hither and thither moves, and mates, and slays,
> And one by one back in the Closet lays.
>
> Omar Khayyam

CHAPTER 26

Trophies and Authenticity*

New Orleans without Morphy was different. During his last years, the chess amateurs seemed to lose spirit. However, in the early 1880s an effort was made to reorganize, and the chess players united with others to found the New Orleans Chess, Checkers & Whist Club. It was this club that invited Steinitz in 1883 and Zukertort in 1884 to the city, and both of them for their match in 1886.

With Morphy gone, no longer living his solitary existence and insisting on being left alone by the press, he once again came into his own. No longer was he thought of as an obsessed and ailing man. His idiosyncrasies were forgotten. Now he was again proclaimed Paul Morphy, "The Incomparable," as Kolisch had called him.

The Chess, Checkers & Whist Club now flourished with some seven hundred members, a valuable chess library, and many relics, including a replica of Lequesne's bust of Morphy, considered by both Fiske and Maurian as the best likeness of him. On the night of January 22, 1890, fire broke out below the club, which occupied the second, third, and fourth floors of the building, and the morning of January 23 saw the building, including all the club's possessions, reduced to ashes.

With a good amount in its treasury, the club soon found suitable quarters elsewhere and immediately commissioned Sr. Perelli, an accomplished sculptor, to "bring Morphy back," and on April 15, 1891, a life-size plaster bust was put on view for all to see. The bust has never been recast or reproduced and is presently possessed by Cletus G. Fleming.**

Of the whereabouts or fate of Morphy's testimonial chessmen and board, nothing is presently known. The chessmen were first noticed by Fiske in the window of the renowned Tiffany & Company at 550 Broadway, below Houston Street in New York City. He mentioned them in the January 1858 *Chess Monthly*: "Tiffany & Co. have for sale a splendid set of

---

* EDITOR'S NOTE: Some of the pictures Lawson included in this chapter, originally titled "Trophies, Authenticity, and Morphy Pictures," are included in the image gallery of this volume, while others have been eliminated.

** EDITOR'S NOTE: The whereabouts of the bust are now unknown, but are presumably still in the family of Fleming.

gold and silver Chessmen. The price demanded for them is fifteen hundred dollars." He did not known at the time that they were destined for Morphy.

Later, when the chessmen were considered for presentation, Tiffany also wished to be a contributor to Morphy's testimonial, and, when asked about them, wrote the Committee of Management of the First American Chess Congress on March 21, 1859, that

> the set of chess cost us $800 besides the case but we propose to offer them to the members of the Club (including a board to cost us $150.) at whatever price they may suggest and we hereby authorize you to submit this proposition. The difference between the price you may conclude upon and $800 we would prefer added to the subscription list in our name.

And so, at an impressive ceremony on May 25, 1859, they were presented to Morphy. He took his chessmen with him both times he went to Europe and brought them back with him. One year after his decease, his brother Edward offered them to the St. George's Chess Club of London for £1,000. Presumably they had been first offered to American Clubs, but apparently they had been overpriced. Steinitz expressed the hope that means would be found to retain them in the United States.

On July 24, 1886, the chessmen and board, together with Morphy's other trophies, were put up for auction by Mather & Homes. The chessmen were auctioned first, and were acquired by Walter Denegre for $1,550. The silver laurel crown brought $250, and the silver service set $400. The latter was Morphy's First Prize at the 1857 National Chess Congress. Both the crown and the service were acquired by Mr. J. Samory, one of Paul Morphy's intimate friends.

At the auction, Mr. Denegre had acted for an unknown party in acquiring the chessmen, and not until many years later did the true owner become known. C. A. Buck, in his booklet *Paul Morphy, His Later Life*, is in error when he states that Denegre had acted for the Manhattan Chess Club, for that club never owned them.

Years later, as given in an article in the *British Chess Magazine* of May 1929, John Keeble translated from the French magazine *Les Cahiers de L'Échiquier* the following mention of the chessmen by Count Gasquet in response to a questioner:

> Morphy's chessmen used to be in my family following a transaction between the family of the famous player and M. de Gas-

quet living at New Orleans. The pieces represent the Gaelic and Roman armies, in gold and silver, very cleverly worked on bases of rose colored stone. The rooks are represented by four elephants with rubies as eyes. Unfortunately I do not know what has become of these pieces. The board is at my home at Dinard. It bears a silver plate on which is inscribed the names of the donors (Sic.). The board is in ebony and the squares in mother of pearl (nacre). If one day I find the pieces I will let you know.

So apparently for years, W. A. Gasquet, a Morphy friend and member of the New Orleans Chess Club, had possessed them. Evidently on his death or return to France, the chessmen eventually came into the possession of the Count. Nothing more is known of the whereabouts of the chessmen and board. It is likely that due to war conditions the chessmen were melted down for the metal; as for the board, nothing is known.

Mr. J. Samory left the silver service set to Judge Edward Bermudez in his will. It was later acquired by the Claiborne family of New Orleans, descendants of Louisiana's first governor, and it is presently in that family's possession. It might be of interest to mention that a copy of Eugene Lequesne's bust of Paul Morphy, published by W. Lay of London in 1858, and the life cast of Morphy's right hand taken by Lequesne are possessed by the author, together with other Morphy memorabilia.*

Paul Morphy was memorialized at Spring Hill College on April 27, 1957, when a plaque and monument presented by E. Forry Laucks were unveiled by the Mayor of Mobile, Henry R. Luscher, with an honor guard from the Spring Hill ROTC.

It would seem that Paul Morphy should now come into his own and be recognized as the first official world chess champion, for he was the first to meet and defeat the several strongest players of his time in formal matches, and in addition he was recognized as world champion in public ceremonies in both hemispheres and in the press of the world.

William Steinitz has been generally mentioned as the first official world chess champion, because he was the first to claim to be such. As Al Horowitz says in his recent book, *The World Chess Championship*, in 1886, "the world championship was at stake because both players [Steinitz and Zukertort] said so," however "official" that might have made it. And

---

* EDITOR'S NOTE: As previously mentioned, Lawson's Morphy collection went to Dale Brandreth, who keeps much of its contents.

true enough, the first article of the "Contract between the Players" reads: "Agreement made this twenty-ninth day of December, 1885, by and between William Steinitz of New York, and J. H. Zuckertort, of London, to play a match at Chess for the Championship of the World and a stake of Two Thousand Dollars a side." At that time neither claimed to be world champion.

For various reasons, a number of games have been falsely ascribed to Paul Morphy. A hydra-headed game appeared in the first edition of *Morphy's Games of Chess* by P. W. Sergeant (GAME CCXCIV) but it was never played by Paul Morphy. The game was played by Ernest Morphy against P. Shaub in 1862 and it was published in the *Dubuque Chess Journal* of 1873. However, it got into *Brentano's Chess Monthly* in 1880 as a Paul Morphy game, from which Sergeant may have taken it. It would appear that two others at least, G. Reichhelm and W. Steinitz, have played the same game move by move, but Steinitz is given credit for having first played and published it. Sergeant replaced it with another when his attention was called to it by J. H. Blake, who reviewed Sergeant's book in the *British Chess Magazine* of February 1916.

It has been shown in Chapter 2 that GAME XCVII in Sergeant's *Morphy's Games of Chess* was played by Ernest Morphy against Dr. A. P. Ford, and that it should not appear in any collection of Paul Morphy's games.

And it would seem that the Deacon games, associated with Morphy by Staunton, have been thoroughly discredited in Chapter 18 as having been played by Morphy. Maróczy in his 1909 collection of 407 Morphy games, including endings, listed the Deacon games and one each by F. H. Lewis, G. Medley and T. Barnes as doubtful Morphy games, but he excluded all of them in his revised 1925 edition.

Of the F. H. Lewis game it may be said that there is no evidence that Lewis ever played with Morphy. His name never appeared on any list of Morphy games, and he never suggested that he had played with Morphy.

The doubtful Medley game first appeared in the London *Era* of January 2, 1859, as a Medley–M game. Very evidently the "M" stood for Mongredien and not for Morphy, for Mongredien was mentioned in the notes to the game, and it never appeared on any list of Morphy games at the time.

The Thomas W. Barnes game falls into a different category. This game was first published in the Stuttgart magazine *Vom Fels zum Meer* in October 1881 and was published elsewhere without question until James Mason annotated it for the *British Chess Magazine* for August 1893, preceding the game with a questioning of its authenticity. But it is to be noted in comparing the game score in both magazines that the game, as Mason presents it, varies from that originally published, as will be seen on inspection. *Brentano's Chess Monthly*, in which it appeared in December 1881, copied the game exactly as given in *Vom Fels zum Meer*, and added the accompanying remarks:

> Among the many interesting games which Paul Morphy, the greatest Chess-player of recent times, has played, there are but few excellent examples which have not yet become generally known by publication. Through the kindness of Dr. Lange we are able to produce one of those few games, played between the American and an English master of the first rank in 1878. [The date was 1858; Barnes died in 1874.]

"J.G.C." examined the game a month after Mason in much greater detail in the same magazine, and agreed with Mason's discrediting of the game. He called it "The Pseudo Barnes v. Morphy game," possibly "made in Germany," and comments:

> Let me put on record one fact which to my mind completely confirms Mr. Mason's contention. The game first "went the rounds" about twelve years ago, but in its journey it took more than one shape. It was originally given to the world in the *Stuttgart Magazine*, and from that periodical it was copied into the *Turf, Field and Farm*, and thence into *Brentano*, where it will be found on pages 382-3, in the number for December, 1881. But before appearing there the editorial pen had evidently been at work, for moves were transposed, as if an attempt had been made to "doctor" the game up. The game given in the *B.C.M.* is the original version, and to enable your readers to see the amount of "doctoring" effected, I subjoin the two versions:—

The Original Version
Re-published in *B.C.M.*,
Aug. 1893.

The Revised Version
Re-published in *Brentano*,
Dec. 1881.

The first ten moves of each version are then given, and a diagram is added, but neither version arrives at the position diagramed.

"J.G.C." then proceeds to take the game apart, and adds, "A fair inference from a comparison of the two series of moves is that the later version [*Brentano's*] was an attempt at emendation with the intention of concealing Black's [Morphy's] weak play." Also, both Mason and "J.G.C." make the point that their "original" ends with move twenty-six "and Black forces mate in five moves."

Obviously neither Mason nor "J.G.C." had actually seen the game in *Vom Fels zum Meer*, although "J.G.C." writes as though he had seen it there, for the game score in *Brentano's* is precisely that given in *Vom Fels zum Meer*, and furthermore both give the thirty moves to mate.

Mason makes one favorable comment on Black's move twelve—N-K4, "This is something like Morphy, certainly." In *The Chess Player's Scrap Book* of January 1907, Emanuel Lasker says of the move, "A combination of rare originality, which has several interesting variations."

P. W. Sergeant states in including the game as originally given in his *Morphy's Games of Chess* (CLXXXVIII), that "although this game is put in the Appendix by M. L. [Max Lange] and Maróczy, it seems reasonable to accept its genuineness." It was undoubtedly played in 1858 and is one of the twenty-six games Morphy is known to have played with Barnes at that time, of which only seven were previously known, and eighteen are still unknown.

The *British Chess Magazine* for May 1898, in "The B.C.M. Guide to the Openings," gives the game in its *original* form in illustration of "The Ruy Lopez Knight's Game," but does not mention Morphy's opponent.

In 1889, Andrés Fernandez Pozo came into possession of a game which he believed Morphy had played with Lowenthal, in which Morphy received the odds of Pawn and two moves, and he communicated with J. J. Machado of Havana, editor of *La Revista de Ajedrez*:

Gijon, Feb. 18, 1889

My much esteemed Friend—I have the pleasure of forwarding you for publication in your interesting journal, if you think proper, the score of a game of the great Paul Morphy, played in the year 1850 in New Orleans, when he was only thirteen years old, against the already famous master, Mr. Lowenthal. It is the only recorded game, in which our immortal chessist appears as receiving odds, and it is not to be found published in any magazine, nor in any collection of his games.

Becoming possessor of this curious gem, which came to my hands through a fortunate occurrence, in order to satisfy myself that it was authentic, I forwarded it to the learned Dr. Max Lange, of Leipzig, asking him about it, and he replied to me that it was really genuine, and that the fact that it was not to be found in any collection or magazine was owing to an agreement entered into by both players not to publish, during their lives, the games they had played at that period; but that Morphy having died, this game had become the property of the chess world, and could, and should be published. Finally, that this game, without any doubt, must be one of the three to which Mr. Lowenthal referred in the *Book of the New York Congress* in 1857, page 394.

I have then, the greatest pleasure in forwarding it to you, in order that our country should have the glory of having published it for the first time in your *Review*, the only one that sees the light in the language of Cervantes.

Remaining as ever, your affectionate friend, etc.
                                             Andres Fernandez Pozo

The above translation of the letter appeared in the New Orleans *Times-Democrat* of January 10, 1892, which continues with a refutation by Maurian:

Along with this letter, there appears in the same magazine [*Havana Chess Review*] a game at the odds of Pawn and Two Moves, in which Morphy, receiver of the odds, administers mate to Lowenthal on the forty-seventh move.

In *El Pablo Morphy* (for November, 1891), a monthly chess review, now conducted with much talent by Sr. Andres Clemente Vasquez, in the city of Havana, a similar letter and the same game are recently published.

Unquestionably, a game by Paul Morphy, even at the odds of Pawn and two, must be accounted a most interesting and valuable chess relic, were it only for the reason, as stated in the letter, that it is the sole game on record where Morphy appears in the role of odds receiver, and especially, we would add, in view of the fact that it affords the first intimation that Morphy, whose chess career has been so often dilated upon by chess writers and is so well known to persons still living, ever at any time received any odds from any known player.

To the writer, who for years lived with him in daily companionship, who played chess with him almost daily, who talked chess with him almost constantly and heard from his own lips many a time all the details of this self-same encounter with Lowenthal in 1850;—to the writer, this game at odds is startling news indeed! I would, however, have had nothing to say, but for the fact that the question, being an historical one, assumes considerable importance to chess players, and, being thoroughly convinced that Mr. Pozo is entirely in error, and has been led astray by whomsoever gave him the information, I think the subject worthy of study with a view to its elucidation.

Maurian then goes on for several pages of examination and elaboration of all circumstances bearing on its authenticity as a Paul Morphy game so convincingly that the game has never since been considered or even referred to as a possible Morphy game. He concludes by saying:

I am convinced that the game was never played by Morphy, and that the editor of the review or magazine, whether English or American, in which Mr. Pozo saw the game about 1865 or 1867, was imposed upon, or that his informant was himself made the victim of a 1st of April hoax.

Yours very truly, Chas. A. Maurian

As it happens, convincing as Maurian was in demonstrating that Morphy never received odds from Lowenthal, the mystery of the odds game has been completely solved by finding the game in which Lowenthal conceded the odds of Pawn and two moves. The game was played in 1855 before a Mr. Murphy went to China. The following appeared in Lowenthal's chess column in the London Era, February 17, 1861:

Mr. Murphy in London

This gentleman, who must be well-known to our readers on account of the many interesting games which he played in London previous to his departure for China, has returned to his native land, and has paid a short visit to London. We are glad to find that he has still the same enthusiasm for Chess. The following is one of the games which the Editor had the pleasure of playing with him:—

P and two moves.   (Remove Black's K.B.P.)
White (Mr. M.)   Black (Mr. L.)

Then followed the game, the score of which Mr. Pozo and Dr. Lange had thought of as a Paul Morphy game. Apparently, someone seeing the game as played between M. and L. had assumed it to be a Paul Morphy game. The game was reprinted in the Philadelphia *Evening Bulletin* September 26, 1863, but this time as a game between a Mr. Murphy and Mr. Lowenthal.

Another game of questionable authenticity has come to light in relatively recent years, and has been a subject of some discussion. The game first came to public attention in June 1935, when W. H. Watts inserted it as a last page in some copies of *Morphy Gleanings* by Sergeant:

A NEW MORPHY GAME

In the lengthy research conducted in America, on the Continent and in this country by Mr. P. W. Sergeant or on his behalf to collect new matter for inclusion in *Morphy Gleanings*, only three new games came to light. By great good fortune another new game which bears every evidence of being genuine has recently been discovered in America.

The circumstances of its discovery are themselves interesting. Mr. Joseph P. Beck, of Brooklyn, purchased a second-hand copy of Lowenthal's "Morphy," and on the flyleaf was a statement in the handwriting of Mr. G. B. Ruggles as follows:—

"Mr. Morphy was in poor health when I visited him, and it was with great reluctance that he consented to play a game of Chess with me, the score of which will be found among my effects."

The book and the game were both autographed by Paul Morphy himself. The book has been sold to a collector of Morphiana, but the score in the handwriting of Mr. John Ruggles was found in the book and a facsimile reproduction appears overleaf. As this may be a little difficult to follow, the game and the footnote are repeated here.

The footnote reads: "The game was broken off here. Mr. Morphy has the best of it—it was never resumed. Played at New Orleans on March 24, 1869. Score recorded by John Ruggles."

In answer to an inquiry, J. F. S. Rumble supplied the game score to the *British Chess Magazine*, which published it for March 1969 and quoted some of the information accompanying the game in 1935. The following month, in the same magazine, Bruce Hayden discussed the game and under what circumstances it might have been played, if it had been played. As Hayden was careful to say, all was "based first on the assumption that the score and Morphy's signature [on the score] are authentic."

There is no way of knowing whether a John Ruggles wrote the score of the game, but the Morphy signature is an obviously labored forgery as may be judged by comparison with those of Morphy. The game may be dismissed as the fabrication of one wishing to associate himself with Morphy.

Franz Gutmayer has a section on Morphy and his games in many of the chess books he authored. The *Deutsche Schachzeitung* of September 1897 had the following notice about him:

> A new chess society under the name of the "Morphy Chess So-
> ciety" has just been formed. The principal object of the Society
> is the collection and publication of all previously unknown or
> unpublished games, letters or other significant material on Paul
> Morphy's life and work. The leader of the Society is Franz Gut-
> mayer of Berlin. Any chess lovers or sponsors in the world may
> become members. Annual dues (which may be paid quarterly)
> 12 marks. We doubt that it will be possible for Dr. Max Lange to
> unearth something noteworthy about Paul Morphy.

It is not known to what extent the society was successful in its collection of new games or information about Morphy, but it is possible that it
was helpful to Géza Maróczy in his first edition of Paul Morphy in 1909,
in which Maróczy gave a total of 407 games, some published for the first
time.

The following problem by E. B. Cook has often been falsely ascribed
to Paul Morphy. It was first published under the initials "E.B.C." by C. H.
Stanley on October 23, 1852, in the New York *Albion*. Dr. H. Keidanz published it as number 15 in *The Chess Compositions of E. B. Cook*.

Black

White
White mates in eight moves

To correct an erroneous statement by C. A. Buck in *Paul Morphy, His Later Life* that Paul Morphy "did very little of the work" on the *Chess Monthly*, D. W. Fiske prepared from notes on his copies of the magazine a list of the games Morphy had annotated. He sent the list, dated April 15, 1901, to James D. Seguin, chess editor of the New Orleans *Times-Democrat*, and mentioned other work Morphy had done for the *Chess Monthly* while editor. The following is a list of those games:

> Volume II (1858)—Games 84–98; 99–107; 109–112; 121–129; 133–135; 144–147; 152–153; 163–164; 169; 173–174; 180–181.
>
> Volume III (1859)—Games 182–198; 200–237; 239; 257; 262–266; 272–275.
>
> Volume IV (1860)—Games 283–286; 291–294; 299–302; 309; 348; 354–355.
>
> Volume V (1861)—Games 1–2.

Fiske did not list the two games in Volume 5, but Morphy initialed the notes. In three other instances, Fiske failed to list the games exactly, but they are identified elsewhere.

H. E. Bird mentions in *Modern Chess* that Morphy provided the notes for games 49 and 50 with Harrwitz and Rivière as given in his (Bird's) volume.

In his New York *Ledger* column, Morphy annotated a total of fifty-seven games, of which thirty-five were Labourdonnais–M'Donnell games, while fourteen were his own. Games with his notes also appeared in the New Orleans *Sunday Delta*, the New York *Clipper*, the New York *Sunday Press*, and other newspapers. He provided the notes for all his games in *The First American Chess Congress* and played more match games than are generally known or credited to him, as will be seen in the following table and summation. (The London Match with Worrall was mentioned in the *Chess Monthly* of August 1859.)

TOURNAMENT AND MATCH GAMES

DATE	PLACE	OPPONENT	WON	LOST	DRAWN	TOTAL	GAME SCORES KNOWN	ODDS GIVEN
1857	New York Tournament	Thompson	3	0	0	3	3	
1857	New York Tournament	Meek	3	0	0	3	3	
1857	New York Tournament	Lichtenhein	3	0	1	4	4	
1857	New York Tournament	Paulsen	5	1	2	8	8	
1857	New York Match	Stanley	4	0	1	5	3	Pawn and Move
1858	London Match	Lowenthal	9	3	2	14	14	
1858	London Match	Owen	5	0	2	7	7	Pawn and Move
1858	Paris Match	Harrwitz	5	2	1	8	8	
1858	Paris Match	Anderssen	7	2	2	11	11	
1859	Paris Match	Mongredien	7	0	1	8	8	
1859	London Match	Worrall	7	2	0	9	4	Queen's Knight
1859	New York Match	Perrin	5	0	1	6	1	Queen's Knight
1859	New York Match	Thompson	5	3	1	9	8	Queen's Knight
		TOTALS	68	13	14	95	82	

TOTAL KNOWN RECORDED GAMES

Played at even	200
Played blindfold	54
Played simultaneous	5
Played at odds of Queen's Knight	128
Played at odds of Queen's Rook	27
Played at other odds	50
	464

63. Tournament, Match, and Recorded Games

APPENDIX

TABLE OF CONTENTS

1.

Michael Morphy's Letter to Thomas Jefferson of June 30, 1793

Malaga, 30th June 1793

Sir,

I received the 20th instant by the Schooner Fredericksburg Packet of Philadelphia, Atkinson Anderson, Master, the honor of your letter dated the 2nd March, and also that of the Commission granted by the President and Senate as Consul of the United States of America at Malaga, and a copy of the Laws thereto appertaining which with that of a circular letter written to the Consuls and Vice Consuls the 26th August 1790, shall serve as my Standing Instructions.

After returning my most grateful thanks to the President, Senate, and you, Sir, for this mark of distinction, I must beg leave to offer that I shall pay due regard to it by exercising the functions of my post with such circumspection and application to the Duties thereof, as will be necessary to promote the Interest of the trading Subjects of the United States in their Navigation and trade to this continent, guided by my experience and long residence in Spain of forty years, and for which purpose I forwarded my said Commission the 25th instant to William Carmichael, Esq., Chargé des Affaires from the States at the Court of Madrid for obtaining His Catholic Majesty's exequator of approbation thereto for without it no Consul is allowed to act officially in the Sea Ports:

I am extremely happy Sir, to learn the strict neutrality that is likely to be kept by the United States during the present disturbances in Europe, on which account it is to be hoped that we shall be the carriers to and from those nations that are at War, except to the Eastward of Malaga on account of the great risk of meeting the Algereen Runners [pirates] that keep hovering on the coast of Spain, two of which captured on the 9th of last month the Schooner Lark of Marble Head, John Pattin, Master, coming from Cartagane [sic] and bound to this Port, he was met about 29 Leagues to the Eastward and had the good luck to escape with his crew in the boat and landed at Aora, the Vessel had of us barrels of Beef and about one thousand Dollars on board which fell a prize with the Vessel.

I beg leave to suggest that if a small naval force from America were to appear in the Mediterranean during these troublesome times for protecting their trade, that it might contribute much to bring about a speedier and easier Settlement with the States on the African Coast.

The Portuguese Squadron Stationed at Gibraltar proves very Servicable [sic] to those powers in war with the Algereens, for there is no instance of any of their Cruisers passing to the Westward of the Straights since the former laid the plan of keeping a naval force at that Port to cruise in the Straights.

I have the pleasure to assure you Sir, that notwithstanding no Commercial treaty is known to have taken place between the United States and Spain, that the former Vessels, as well as Subjects sailing therein are received in the ports on this Continent with the same hospitality, privileges and regulations *as are shown* to those of other favored powers, and I beg leave to add that I shall make it my ardent duty to maintain the Same and to follow Strictly such instructions as you may honor me with and that may tend hereafter to the Publick Service.

The trade of the Beligerant [sic] Powers against the french nation, is feeling the hardships of war, and must continue so until a peace is happily brought about, the continued Successes of the Arms employed against france. It is expected, will soon put an end to the Contests especially as its Subjects are now divided and the party of the royalists becoming formidable—Lord Hood with the British fleet sailed from Gibraltar up the Mediterranean the 27th instant, inclosed [sic] gives a correct list of the forces under his command; His Lordship is to join the Spanish fleet composed of twenty six sail of the Line besides several frigates Armed Vessels and Gun boats which are at sea aloft: what the operations of so formidable a force will be, only time can tell. The King of Sardinia only waits their arrival for commencing his operations with an Army of 80 [80,000] men—the Spanish Armys are making a great progress in the french territory near the frontier and will in all appearance be soon masters of all Rosellon:

It is to be hoped that Congress will prescribe some Special dues on the trade for the support of the Consular Offices and that they will take into consideration that such employments in foreign countrys must create an expense to the holder to maintain the dignity of the post especially in Spain.

I am informed that by the late navigation act made the last Session that Consuls are allowed to own Vessels under American Colours: I will be much obliged to you for this Act and any other that may be proper to have lodged in my Office, and also that you may number such letters as you may find needful to write to it—to communicate thereto hereafter.

In the communications which you are pleased to direct shall be given by my office to your department every six months, which is also to comprehend the cargoes outward and inward—do you mean Sir, the quality of the goods only, or is it the contents—If it is to be the latter, I beg leave to offer, that it would be better for the Masters of Vessels to sign a report of these homeward cargoes before me to present to the custom house, for I cannot see what use it will be to furnish such intelligence at so late a period as six months.

I have the honor to be with great truth and regard:

Sir

Your Most Obedient
Humble Servant
Michael Morphy

Thomas Jefferson, Esq., etc.

2.

Michael Morphy's Letter to Thomas Jefferson of July 30, 1793

Malaga the 30th July 1793

Sir,

I had the honor of addressing you the 30th June by the American Schooner Fredericksburg packet, Anderson bound to Philadelphia—having now to confirm what I then mentioned about the interruption continued to be given by Algereen States to the American trading Vessels in the Mediterranean especially to the Eastward of this Port, and more so since the Spaniards gave up the Port and fortress of Oran on the Coast of Mascara to the Moors, the situation thereof and proximity to this Continent has encouraged a number of small privateers to be fitted out there which are become very destructive to all powers with whom they are at war, and particularly to our American Colours as none will venture to pass Malaga from the fear that threatens the Subjects of becoming Slaves, and on this account we are deprived of conveying our products to parts aloft where they are most wanted and thereby deprived of the great benefits which otherwise would fall to our lot—the Schooner Madison, James Parrock from Philadelphia with flower and tobacco for Marseilles, and the Brigantine Fox, Robert Miller from New York with wheat for Barcelona have been obliged to stop and sell their cargoes at Malaga. I beg leave Sir, to report that there is no remedy to this evil but the sending of a naval force from America to repel the force of these barbarians and to protect its trade while measures are not arranged for our having a free navigation in this part of the World, and I have reason to think that such a resolution on the part of the States would contribute in great measure to settle this point.

I have also to lay before you, that great abuses are committing by the American and British seamen aboard by changing their allegiance as it suits their fancy or interest when brought before the Consuls of said powers or in the presence of the Magistrates of the Countries they are in to settle their disputes. I have a very recent proof of it of the crew of the Ship Neptune of Boston in this port, the greater part whereof having quarreled with the Captain Edward Preble they called themselves British Subjects although well known to be Americans for the sake of leaving the ship to go on board an English Man of War that lay here[,] however I found meant to keep them quiet—to prevent similar cases in future happening and the consequences attending such disputes, I beg Sir, you will use such measures as may be necessary for our Ships to have their men enrolled in a separate Document before they clear out on a foreign voyage which every man should sign and declare his Vassalage of the Country he belongs to by which means our American subjects may be prevented from giving a deal of trouble to the Masters of Vessels and distressing them in foreign ports where they often cannot replace them with other Mariners. . . .

I have the honor to be with great truth and regards

Sir

Your Most Obedient
Humble Servant
Michael Morphy

Thomas Jefferson, Esq., etc.

3.

DON DIEGO MORPHY

Last Will and Testament—August 27, 1813

In the City of New Orleans, on the 27th day of August of the year 1813, and 36 of the Independence of the United States of America, before me Pedro Peceschaux, Notary Public of the State of Louisiana, and of the undersigned, Don Diego Morphy, Consul for the Catholic Majesty, says: that finding himself sick in bed but in the perfect exercise of his mental faculties, fearing death, natural to all creatures, and its time also uncertain, and foreseeing his, he wants to make his testament and order his last will, for which reason he dictates literally as follows:

In the first place I declare my name and surname to be Don Diego Morphy, a native of the city of Malaga, legitimate child of Don Miguel Morphy and Doña Maria Porro: the first of them being now dead.

Item: I declare to be a catholic, apostolic, roman Christian, and as such I commend my soul to God, praying that it may find rest with the selected ones; I bequeath my body to the earth from which it was formed, to be placed whenever I should die, where by testamentary executors may decide, as I leave to their discretion my funeral and burial.

Item: I order that three masses for the dead be said in praying for the rest of my soul.

Item: I declare to have been married in first nuptials to Doña Maria Creagh, from which marriage I have three children, named: Don Diego, 23 years of age; Doña Elena Diego, 17 years; and Doña Matilde Morphy, 18 years of age.

Item: I declare to have been married in second nuptials to Doña Luisa Peire, from which marriage I have 5 children, named: Don Alonzo, 15 years of age; Don Tomas Augusto [Ernest], 6 years; Doña Ana Esmeralda, 3 years; Doña Magdalena Antonietta, 15 months; and one girl of two months who has not yet been named, because she has not yet been baptized [Emma, who married D. O'Hinks, collector of the Port of New Orleans]; and all of them I declare to be my legitimate children and of my above mentioned wife.

Item: I appoint and name for guardian of my minor children my above mentioned wife; and for curator *ad litem* Don Pablo Francisco Gallion Preval; relieving them from giving security.

Item: I appoint and name as my testamentary executors and trustees the above mentioned Don Pablo Francisco Gallion Preval and Doña Luisa Peire, my wife, to whom I confer and grant all power as may be required in law to the end that after my death and without any intervention of any court and obligation to give security, they proceed to administer my properties, making an inventory and valuation of them, appointing appraisers, forming the account of the testamentary executors and that of division of properties, and finally, doing all that may be necessary for the liquidation and winding up of my estate, till presenting the whole to the proper court for its approbation; for all which I extend the one year of testamentary execution to the time that they may need; as this is my express and last will.

Item: I order that my mentioned testamentary executors proceed to make separately and in the presence of a Notary Public the Inventory of the papers and other documents belonging to the Spanish Government, which are put aside in a desk, and that having done so, they remit them to the Spanish Minister. I omit all recommendation on the exactitude of this inventory, as I have full confidence in their sufficiency.

Item: I appoint and name as my sole and universal heirs my above mentioned 8 children: Don Diego, Doña Elena, Doña Matilde, Don Alonso, Don Tomas Augusto, Doña Ana Esmeralda Ciriaca, Doña Magdalena Antonieta Morphy, and the girl that is not yet baptized; so that after my death, they may have and inherit my properties in equal shares to use them as their own, with God's blessing and mine also, and that is my will.

Finally, I repeal and annul any other testaments, codicils, powers or testamentary dispositions that I may have made previously, verbally or in writing, as I invalidate them, granting in their stead in the most legal form, this expression of my last will.

I the Notary having read this writing to the testator, in high and intelligible voice in the presence of documentary witnesses, he states that he affirms and ratifies its contents, as it is well and faithfully written in the same words in which he dictated it; and signed it with the three witnesses, who are Don Joseph Rufinaco, Don Pedro Collet and Don Juan Longrre, present neighbors.

(Signed) Diego Morphy   J. Longrre
              P. Collette   Jose Rufiniaco
        Pierre Pedeschaux Vre
Dated in New Orleans, August 30th 1813
        Pierre Pedeschaux, N.P.
Will Book No. 2, 1817
Pages No. 55 to No. 56
        Don Diego Morphy

(Taken from *The Good Companion*, vol. 8, p. 179-182).

4.

The "M.A." Letter
in *Bell's Life in London*—October 17, 1858

Trinity College, Cambridge, Oct. 9, 1858

Mr. Editor: If you enter any chess circle just now, the questions sure to be asked are, How about the Staunton and Morphy match? Will it come off? Suspect Staunton wants to shirk it? Now to these questions it is not always easy to give an answer, and yet they ought to be answered, so as to allow of no possible misconstruction amongst either friends or foes. There is one insinuation which may be very briefly disposed of, namely, that Mr. Staunton wishes to avoid playing. Every one who knows him is perfectly aware that he is only too ready to play at all times, and that at every disadvantage, rather than incur even the faintest suspicion of showing the white feather.

For the benefit of those who have not the pleasure of knowing him, or whose memories are not over tenacious, I may cite as an example that in 1844, after vanquishing St. Amant, upon a hint in the French papers that his opponent had expressed a wish to have his revenge, Mr. Staunton at once started for Paris once more, and challenged him to the field; that from 1840 to 1848 Mr. Staunton played with every antagonist, foreign and English, that could be brought against him; and at the Chess Congress, in 1851, he rose superior to all personal considerations, and did not shrink from risking his hardly-earned reputation, when the state of his health was such that he felt he could not do himself justice; and all this solely that the tournament might not want the *éclat* which his presence could confer upon it. But, sir, I would submit that this is not simply a question between Mr. Staunton and Mr. Morphy. We are all interested in it. Mr. Staunton is the representative of English chess, and must not be allowed to risk the national honor in an *unequal contest*, to gratify either the promptings of his own chivalrous disposition or the vanity of an antagonist. "Oh! then you admit that Morphy is the better player?" No such thing. The question is, not as to which is the better player, but whether, if they meet now, they can do so on equal terms.

Now, I call it an *unequal contest* when one player, in tiptop practice, with nothing to distract his attention, engages another who is quite out of play, and whose mind is harassed by the unceasing pressure of other and more important avocations. This is precisely Mr. Staunton's case. He is engaged, in addition to his customary occupations, upon a literary work of great responsibility and magnitude, which leaves him scarcely a moment for any other pursuit; certainly not for chess practice. Indeed, were it merely a question of time it would be almost impossible for Mr. Staunton to play a match at the present moment; but this is a matter of small importance compared with the mental strain which accompanies such incessant labor.

There is nothing which requires more concentration of thought than chess. One moment of relaxed attention, and the fruits of the most profound combination are scattered to the winds. Real chess between two great players is no mere recreation, but a severe study, and should never be attempted when there is anything else to claim the least share of that attention which alone can insure [sic] success. If Mr. Staunton can steal a few months from business, and devote himself wholly to chess, by all means let him do so, and then meet Mr. Morphy when and where he pleases, and I for one should have no fear for the result. If he cannot do this, I trust he will have moral courage to say "No." If not, his friends should say it for him. He is at least "Pawn and two" below his force of ten years back; and I repeat that he owes it to the English chess world, whose representative he is, not to meet Mr. Morphy at such odds, when he has every thing to lose and nothing to gain. In the present instance, moreover, he is under not the slightest obligation to play, as Mr. Morphy gave him no intimation that he was coming over at this particular time, and I believe Mr. Staunton was not aware of his intention of so doing till he was actually *en route*; and it is certainly rather a heavy price to pay for the position which Mr. Staunton justly occupies if he is to be held bound to enter the lists with every young adventurer who has nothing else to do; and who happens to envy him the laurels so fairly won in many hundreds of encounters with nearly all the greatest players of the day. The result of any match which he might now play with Mr. Morphy would prove literally nothing as to their relative chess powers, and I am very unwilling to believe that the American would at all value a victory snatched under such circumstances.

Yours obediently, M.A.

P.S. Since writing the above my attention has been drawn to a letter in *Bell's Life* addressed to Mr. Staunton by Mr. Morphy, in which the latter tries to assume the character of a much-injured and ill-used man. Now, how stands the case. From the time when he made his sudden appearance here to the present moment Mr. Morphy has been fully aware that the delay in the proposed contest did not depend upon Mr. Staunton, who, so far as he is personally concerned, was, and is, prepared to play; though it does not speak for that man's sense of honor who would ever think of forcing on a contest when the inequality is so immense as it is between Mr. Morphy's position and that of Mr. Staunton—the one with literally nothing to do but to go where he lists to play chess, the other with scarcely time for sleep and meals, with his brain in a constant whirl with the strain upon it; the one in the very zenith of his skill, after ten years of incessant practice, the other utterly out of practice for that very period.

Now, let any one read the reply of Mr. Staunton to the preposterous proposal on the part of Mr. Morphy's friends, that he (Mr. Staunton) should go over to New Orleans, and then say whether Mr. Morphy, after publicly announcing in the American papers his inability, from family engagements, to visit England before 1859, and then choosing to come over without a moment's warning, has anybody but himself to blame if he finds there is considerable difficulty in inducing a man with family cares, and immersed in professional engagements, to sacrifice all for the sake of engaging, upon the most unfair and unequal terms, in a match at chess? If Mr. Morphy does not see the force of what I have advanced, perhaps the following analogous case may bring conviction home to him.

Let us suppose some ten or fifteen years have elapsed, and that Mr. Morphy, no longer a chess knight-errant, eager to do battle against all comers, has settled down into a steady-going professional man, (the bar, I believe, is his destination,) and with bewildered brain is endeavoring to unravel the intricacies of some half-dozen lawsuits put into his hands by clients, each of whom, in virtue of his fee, is profoundly impressed with the belief that Mr. Morphy belongs, body and soul, to him. Presently comes a rap at the door, and in walks a young man, fresh from school or college, and at once proceeds to explain the object of his visit, with:—"Mr. Morphy, I come to challenge you to a match at chess. I am aware that you are quite out of practice, while I am in full swing. I freely admit that you may have forgotten more than I am ever likely to know; that you have not a moment you can call your own, whilst I have just now nothing in the world to occupy my attention but chess. *N'importe*. Every dog has his day. I expect you to play me at all costs. My seconds will wait upon you at once; and if you decline I shall placard you a craven through the length and breadth of the Union."

How would Mr. Morphy reply to such a challenge? Very much, I suspect, as Mr. Staunton now replies to his:—"I have no apprehension of your skill; I am quite willing to meet you when I can, but I must choose my own time. I cannot put aside my professional engagements, to say nothing of the loss of emolument entailed by such a course, and risk my reputation as a chess-player at a moment's notice, just to gratify your ambition." In giving such an answer Mr. Morphy would do perfectly right, and this is precisely the answer which Mr. Staunton now gives to him. And why Mr. Morphy should feel himself aggrieved I cannot possibly imagine. There is one other point which I think deserves mention, namely that four years ago, on the occasion of his being challenged in a similar manner, Mr. Staunton put forth a final proposal to play any player in the world, and to pay his expenses for coming to England. This defi remained open for six months, and he announced that if not taken up in that time he should hold himself exonerated in refusing any future challenges. I now leave the question in the hands of the public, who will, I doubt not, arrive at a correct appreciation of its merits.

                                                                    M.A.

5.

The "Fair Play" Letter—October 17, 1858

To the Editor of Bell's Life:

Mr. Editor,—It is a pity chess-players will not "wash their dirty linen at home." Among a few frivolous noodles to whom chess forms the staple of life, Mr. Morphy's jeremiads may assume an air of importance, but to sensible men they sound ineffably absurd, while to those who take the trouble of looking a little below the surface they appear something worse. For what are the plain facts of the case? Mr. Morphy started for England, not to play a match with Mr. Staunton, for he was told that that gentleman was too deeply immersed in business to undertake one, but to take part in a general tourney to be held in Birmingham. Upon arriving here he duly inscribed his name on the list of combatants, and paid his entrance fee.

On hearing this, Mr. Staunton, in a spirit of what some may call chivalry, but which, looking at his utterly unprepared state for an encounter of this kind, ought more properly to be termed Quixotism, entered his name also. Well, what happened? On the mustering of the belligerents, Mr. Morphy, who had come six thousand miles to run a tilt in this tournament, *was not present*. In his place came a note to say particular business prevented his attendance. A message was dispatched, intimating that his absence would be a great disappointment, &c., &c. His reply was, that, understanding neither Mr. Staunton nor any other of the leading players would take the field, he declined to do so. A second message was forwarded, to the effect that Mr. Staunton was then in Birmingham expressly to meet Mr. Morphy, and that he and several of the best players were awaiting Mr. Morphy's arrival to begin the combats. To this came a final answer, to the effect that the length of time that the tourney would last prevented Mr. Morphy from joining in it, but he would run down in two or three days. Passing over the exquisite taste of this proceeding, and the disappointment and murmurs it occasioned, I would simply ask, If Mr. Morphy thought himself justified in withdrawing from a contest which he had come thousands of miles to take part, and to which he was in a manner pledged, upon pretences so vague and flimsy, what right has he to complain if the English player choose to withdraw from one to which he is in no respect bound, and against which he may be enabled to offer the most solid and unanswerable objections? In asking this, I beg to disclaim all intention of provoking a chess players' controversy, a thing in which the public takes not the slightest interest, and for which I individually entertain supreme contempt. I am moved to it only by the spirit of

Fair Play

Birmingham

6.

Edge's Letter in *Bell's Life in London*
—October 24, 1858

Hotel Breteuil, Paris, Oct. 20, 1858

To the Editor of Bell's Life in London:

Sir,—Two letters appeared in your paper of last Sunday, one with the signature of "M.A.," the other of "Fair Play." In justice to fact, those communications must not remain unanswered, as the misstatements they contain might perchance mislead some as to the good faith of Mr. Morphy. It is in no improper spirit that I appear before your readers under my own name, but simply because, as I intend replying to your anonymous correspondents with facts, not with hypotheses, I think I am bound in honor to hold myself responsible for what I advance. The chess players of London and Birmingham are not ignorant of the intimacy with which Mr. Morphy has honored me during his visit to Europe, and they will permit me to state, that no one is better conversant with the facts bearing on the case in point than your subscriber. Were it not that Paul Morphy positively refused to reply to any attack upon himself, preferring that his actions should be the sole witness to his faith, I should not have troubled you or the public with this communication.

On the 4th of last February, the New Orleans Chess Club challenged Mr. Staunton to visit the Crescent City, "to meet Mr. Paul Morphy in a chess match." On the 3d of April the former gentleman replied to this *defi* in the *Illustrated London News*, in the following language:—"The terms of this cartel are distinguished by extreme courtesy, and, with one notable exception, by extreme liberality also. The exception in question, however, (we refer to the clause which stipulates that the combat shall take place in New Orleans!) appears to us utterly fatal to the match; and we must confess our astonishment that the intelligent gentlemen who drew up the conditions did not themselves discover this. Could it possibly escape their penetration, that if Mr. Paul Morphy, a young gentleman without family ties or professional claims upon his attention, finds it inconvenient to anticipate by a few months an intended visit to Europe, his proposed antagonist, who is well known for years to have been compelled, by laborious literary occupation, to abandon the practice of chess beyond the indulgence of an occasional game, must find it not merely inconvenient, but positively impracticable, to cast aside all engagements, and undertake a journey of many thousand miles for the sake of a chess encounter. Surely the idea of such a sacrifice is not admissible for a single moment. If Mr. Morphy—for whose skill we entertain the liveliest admiration—be desirous to win his spurs among the chess chivalry of Europe, he must take advantage of his proposed visit next year; he will then meet in this country, in France, in Germany, and in Russia, many champions whose names must be as household words to him, ready to test and do honor to his prowess."

No one would regard the above observations as tantamount to aught else than "If you will come to Europe I will play you;" but we are relieved from the difficulty of discovering Mr. Staunton's real meaning by his reiterated declarations that he would play Mr. Morphy. Within a few days of the latter's arrival in London, the English player stated his intention of accepting the match, but postponed the commencement of it for a month, on the plea of requiring preparation. In the month of July the acceptance of the challenge was announced in the *Illustrated London News*. Before the expiration of the time demanded in the first instance, Mr. Staunton requested that the contest should not take place until after the Birmingham meeting. At Birmingham he again declared his intention of playing the match, and fixed the date for the first week in November, in the presence of numerous witnesses. Mr. Morphy may have erred in believing that his antagonist intended to act as his words led him to suppose, but it was an error shared in common by everyone then present, and particularly by Lord Lyttelton, the President of the British Chess Association, who recognized the true position of the case in his speech to the association, stating that he "wished him (Mr. Morphy) most cordially success in his encounters with the celebrated players of Europe, whom he had gallantly left home to meet; he should be pleased to hear that he vanquished all—except one; but that one—Mr. Staunton—he must forgive him, as an Englishman, for saying he hoped he would conquer him."— (Report of Birmingham meeting, *Illustrated London News*, Sept. 18, 1858.)

So firmly convinced were the members of Mr. Staunton's own club, the St. George's, that he had accepted the challenge, that a committee was formed, and funds raised to back him. What those gentlemen must now think of Mr. Staunton's evasion of the match can easily be understood; but so strong was the conviction in other chess circles that he would not play, that large odds were offered to that effect.

"M.A.'s" reasons for not playing, or "M.A.'s" reasons for Mr. Staunton's not playing—a distinction without a difference, as we shall hereafter show—is that "he is engaged upon a literary work of great responsibility and magnitude." Did not this reason exist prior to Mr. Morphy's arrival in June? And if so, why were Mr. Morphy, the English public, and the chess community generally, led into the belief that the challenge was accepted? And what did Mr. Staunton mean by stating at Birmingham, in the presence of Lord Lyttelton, Mr. Avery, and myself, that if the delay until November were granted him, he could in the mean while supply his publishers with sufficient matter, so as to devote himself subsequently to the match?

Mr. Staunton's (I mean "M.A.'s") remark in the letter under review, "I (Staunton or "M.A." indifferently) have no apprehension of your skill," is hardly consonant with the previous observation, that "he (Staunton) is at least pawn and two below his force," unless the "English-chess-world-representative" wishes it to be understood that he could offer those odds to Paul Morphy. Nor is it consonant with the fact that he has never consented to play Mr. Morphy a single game, though asked to do so, and when frequently meeting him at St. George's. Of course the two consultation games played by him, in alliance with "Alter," against Messrs. Barnes and Morphy count for nothing, as they were gained by the latter; a result due, doubtless, to "Alter" alone.

Mr. Morphy, in the eyes of the chess world, can have nothing to gain from a contest with this gentleman. When Mr. Staunton has met even players such as Anderssen, Heyderbrandt, and Lowenthal, he has succumbed; whilst his youthful antagonist can cite a roll of victories unparalleled since Labourdonnais. And herein is the true reason for "M.A.'s" saying, Staunton must not be allowed to risk the national honor (?) in an unequal contest.

In wishing "M.A." adieu, I would state that his style of composition is so like Mr. Staunton's that no one could detect the difference. And no one but Mr. Staunton himself would ever set up such a defense as "M.A.'s"—that of inferiority, "Pawn and two below his strength," &c. &c. And no one but Mr. Staunton could have such intimate knowledge of his own thoughts as we find in the following verbatim quotations from "M.A.'s" letter: "The state of his health was such that he felt he could not do himself justice"—"his mind harassed"—"the other (Staunton) with scarcely time for sleep and meals, with his brain in a constant whirl with the strain upon it." In the language of Holy Writ: "No man can know the spirit of man, but the spirit of man which is in him."

Served up in a mess of foul language, the letter signed "Fair Play," contains an obviously untrue assertion, namely, Mr. Morphy started for Europe, not to play a match with Mr. Staunton. This is rather outrageous in the face of the challenge from the New Orleans Chess Club, and with Mr. Staunton's reply in the *Illustrated London News* of April 3d. So much was it Mr. Morphy's desire to play him, and so little his intention to engage in the Birmingham Tournament, that he informed the secretary he did not regard such a contest as any true test of skill.

To sum up the whole matter, I will state the naked facts.
1. Mr. Morphy came to Europe to play Mr. Staunton.
2. Mr. Staunton made everybody believe he had accepted the challenge from Mr. Morphy.
3. Mr. Staunton allowed the St. George's Chess Club to raise the money to back him.
4. Mr. Staunton asked for a delay of one month, in order to brush up his openings and endings.
5. Mr. Staunton requested a postponement until after the Birmingham meeting.
6. Mr. Staunton fixed the beginning of November for the commencement of the match.

If all this do not mean "I will play," then is here no meaning in language. I beg to subscribe myself, Mr. Editor, most respectfully yours.

Frederick Milne Edge.

7.

The "Pawn and Two" Letter in the London *Field*
—November 13, 1858

Mr. Staunton and Mr. Morphy

Sir,—I am desirous, with your permission, of saying a few words upon the relative position now occupied by Messrs. Staunton and Morphy, whose proposed encounter has been brought to such an unfortunate, though not unforseen [*sic*], termination. Now I am well acquainted with Mr. Staunton. I have been concerned on his behalf in the arrangement of one of his (proposed) matches, with a player whom he has never ceased to vituperate since that period when I endeavored so strenuously to bring them together. I have fought Mr. Staunton's battles for him by pen and by word of mouth on sundry occasions. I wish, indeed, I could do so now; for, as a chess player, and as a laborer in the field of chess literature, I place him on the very highest pinnacle. Since the time of M'Donnell, I believe that no player in this country—not to say Europe—has ever reached so high a standard as was attained by our English champion when he did battle with St. Amant. Since that time he has been the rather concerned in editorial duties, and in intimating to real or imaginary correspondents in the *Chess Players' Chronicle*, (now defunct) and in the *Illustrated London News*, (full of vitality,) what he could do on the chequered field, if those who dreamed of approaching him could but muster sufficient money to meet his terms, or what other and peculiar restrictions (owing to delicate health and "nervous irritability") he should impose upon any adversary with whom he engaged himself.

From what I have seen of Mr. Staunton, I should think the term "delicate" thoroughly inapplicable to his condition, but that he is highly irritable, and nervously susceptible of all antagonistic impressions, no one who knows him can for a moment doubt.

> How easy 'tis, when destiny proves kind,
> With full-spread sails to run before the wind.

So sings the poet. Destiny *did* prove kind to Mr. Staunton when he played his match in Paris with St. Amant. The Englishman made the most of it, and achieved a splendid triumph. At the great Chess Tournament in 1851 destiny was not quite so obliging. The champion from whom we expected so much had a head-wind against him, and he was beaten. I saw much of Mr. Staunton at that time. I believe—in all justice let it be said—that he was thoroughly unnerved, that he was utterly unequal to an arduous contest, and that his great merits ought not to be gauged by his play upon the occasion alluded to. He deserved (he did not receive, for he had never given the same to others) every sympathy under circumstances which were intensely mortifying to himself personally, and to us nationally.

Since 1851 it has been pretty generally understood that Mr. Staunton's irritability has not diminished, and that his literary responsibilities have the rather multiplied. Consequently we had no right to expect, nationally, that he would again be our champion, and contend with the young American, whose reputation ran before him to Europe, and has accompanied him ever since his arrival from the United States. We had no right, I say, to expect this, *but for one reason.* That reason is to be found in the chess department of the *Illustrated London News*, of which Mr. S. is the acknowledged editor. It has been there constantly implied— nay, it has been over and over again unequivocally stated—during the last eight years, that the vanquisher of St. Amant is still the English champion; that as such he has a right to dictate his own terms, and that if any one is prepared to accede to those terms, he (Mr. Staunton) is prepared for the encounter. It matters not whether the correspondents to whom these implications are made are real or (as is generally supposed) imaginary. It is sufficient that certain statements are made with the intention of conveying a false impression to the public as regards Mr. Staunton's desire to play and capability of playing. This is where he is so greatly to blame; this is the point on which he has alienated from himself during the last few years so many of his warmest friends. No one blames Mr. Staunton for not playing with Mr. Morphy; but every one has a right to blame Mr. Staunton if, week after week, he implies in his own organ that there is a chance of a match, if all that time he knows that there is no chance of a match whatever. This, I affirm deliberately, and with great pain, is what Mr. Staunton has done. It has been done times out of number, and this in ways which have been hardly noticed. If the editor of the chess department of the *Illustrated London News* merely states as a piece of news that Mr. Morphy is coming to England from America to arrange a match at chess with Mr. Staunton, and Mr. Staunton (being that editor himself, and being burdened with literary responsibilities which he knows to be so great as to prevent his playing an arduous contest) fails to append to such statement another, to the effect that he has given up public chess, and has no intention of again renewing it, he is not acting in a straightforward and honorable manner. But much more than this has been effected. So solicitous has Mr. Staunton been to trade as long as possible upon his past reputation, that it has been written in the *Illustrated London News* since Mr. Morphy's arrival in this country, that he (Mr. M.) is not prepared with the necessary stakes for an encounter with Mr. Staunton. What truth there was in such averment may be gathered from the admirable letter in your impression of last Saturday from the young American to Lord Lyttelton. Why is not Mr. Staunton content to say (what those who like him best would be glad to be authorized to say for him): "I have done much for the cause of chess, but I am not equal to what I once was; and I am hampered by engagements which do not admit of my playing matches now. I cannot risk my reputation under such manifest disadvantages as would surround me in a contest with Mr. Morphy." The public at large would then respect Mr. Staunton's candor, and have a larger appreciation than they now have of his great merits. It is true that Mr. Staunton has said this at last; but he has been forced to say with a bad grace what ought long ago to have been said voluntarily with a good one.

These unpleasant (not to use a harsher term) circumstances are the more to be deplored at present because of the frank, courteous, and unassuming conduct of Mr. Morphy upon every occasion since he set foot in Europe. I have seen him play in London and in Paris; and I have noted those obliging and unobtrusive manners which secure to him the good-will of everybody, and surround him by troops of friends. How is it that Mr. Staunton is not surrounded by troops of friends likewise? Is he not a scholar and a gentleman? Has he not many qualifications for the distinguished literary position he now fills? Undoubtedly he has, But he has never been able to merge the personal in the general—to regard his own individuality as other than the first consideration. Brought into contact many years ago with players who were not refined gentlemen, an antagonism was immediately established between the two parties. Unhappily for the chess world, literary opportunities were afforded in the columns of rival newspapers for the indulgences of malevolent feelings on both sides. To this warfare there has never been a cessation. So notorious is the fact of its existence that it is impossible to rely, in one paper, upon any statement having reference to the London Chess Club; it is equally impossible to rely, in the other, upon any statement affecting the St. George's Club. Ladies who are devoted to "Caïssa," and write to the *Illustrated London News*, are not aware of these things. Imaginary correspondents, of course, are utterly ignorant of them. But we who live in and about London, who have been behind the scenes at both theatres, know how much reliance is to be placed upon a certain kind of chess intelligence with which two rival journals regale their correspondents and the general public every week. Look even at the *Illustrated London News* of last Saturday, and you will see a letter professing to come from Birmingham, (I think it is a misprint for Billingsgate,) which is absolutely disgraceful. Why should Mr. Staunton try to bolster up his reputation (which is European) with sentiments and language of a purely (I mean impurely) local character? Why is one player always to be cried up at the expense of another? Why are ungenerous and ungentlemanly insinuations to be made against a youth whose conduct has been characterized by so much unobtrusiveness and so much good feeling as that of Mr. Morphy? Why is Mr. Harrwitz always to be run down in the *Illustrated London News*? Why are Mr. Lowenthal and Mr. Brien, quondam editorial protégés, now never spoken of but in terms of disparagement? Why should Mr. Staunton call upon the *cercle* at Paris to insist upon Mr. Harrwitz progressing with his match with Mr. Morphy at a more rapid pace, when the German had pleaded ill health as the cause of the delay? Who has drawn so largely upon the patience of the British public, on the score of ill health and "palpitations of the heart," *et hoc genus omne*, as the generous and sympathizing writer who thus stabs a rival player when he is down? It is time, sire, that these things should cease. We are all weary of them. What better opportunity for crying a truce to these mean and petty warfares of the pen than the one which now presents itself? Mr. Staunton is our champion no longer. We must turn to some one else to uphold the national flag upon that field where Labourdonnais and M'Donnell fought and struggled. So anxious am I that good feeling should be restored, and that we should be united as I see chess players united in other countries, that I have put together hurriedly these reflections, which, however imperfect they may be, are true and just. And because I have observed that the chess department of *The Field*, which you so ably edit, is peculiarly free from personalities and remarkably authentic in its information, I ask you to help me in the good cause by giving publicity to this letter. I am not ashamed of what I have written, nor do I desire to shrink from the responsibility of revealing my name, if it is necessary. I enclose my card, as a guarantee, and prefer, if it meets your views, to appear only under the name of—

Pawn-and-Two

8.

Dinner Address of
OLIVER WENDELL HOLMES
at Banquet for
PAUL MORPHY
Revere House, Boston May 31, 1859

We have met, gentlemen, some of us as members of a local association, some of us as invited guests, but all of us as if by a spontaneous, unsolicited impulse, to do honor to our young friend who has honored us and all who glory in the name of Americans, as the hero of a long series of bloodless battles, won for our common country.

His career is known to you all. There are many corners of our land which the truly royal game of kings and conquerors has not yet reached, where if an hour is given to pastime, it is only in an honest match of checquers played with red and white kernels of corn, probably enough upon the top of the housewife's bellows. But there is no gap in the forest, there is no fresh trodden waste in the prairie, which has not heard the name of the New Orleans boy, who left the nursery of his youth, like one of those fabulous heroes of whom our childhood loved to read, and came back bearing with him the spoils of giants whom he had slain, after overthrowing their castles and appropriating the allegiance of their queens.

I need not therefore tell his story; it is so long that it takes a volume to tell it. It is so brief that one sentence may embrace it all. Honor went before him, and Victory followed after.

You know the potential significance and the historical dignity of that remarkable intellectual pursuit, which although it wears the look of an amusement and its student uses toy-like instruments, as did the great inventor of logarithms, Napier of Merchiston, in the well known ivory *bones or rods* by which he performed many calculations, has yet all the characters of a science, say rather of a science mingled with a variable human element, so that the perfect chess player would unite the combining powers of Newton with the audacity of Leverrier, and the shrewd insight of Talleyrand. You know who of the world's masters have been chess players; happy for the world, had some of them been nothing worse than chess players! You know who have celebrated the praises of the art in prose and verse. Among them the classic Italian remembered in those lines of Pope:

> Immortal Vida on whose honored brow
> The poet's bays, and critic's ivy grow,—

Who wrote one poem on the Heavenly Teacher, one on the art of Poetry, and one on the game of Chess.

That you know all this may be taken for granted: I need not say that there is something very different from, something far deeper than, the pride which belongs to the professed amateurs or the outside admirers of this particular game, noble as it is, famous as it is, which brings us together.

No, gentlemen: This seemingly gracious and pleasing occasion is far more than it seems. Through these lips of ours, as through those which have spoken before us and shall speak after us, the words of welcome to our young friend, there flows the warm breath of that true American feeling which makes us all one in the moment of every great triumph achieved by a child of the Great Republic.

We who look upon the sun while the old world sleeps, are after all but colonists and provincials, in the eye of the ancient civilizations. There are Europeans enough, otherwise intelligent, who, if we may trust the stories of travelers, would be puzzled to say whether a native American of the highest race, caught in one of our streets, would be white, or black, or red; it cannot be disguised that we have been subject to the presumption of inferiority as a new people, and that nothing has been granted us except what we have taken at the cannon's mouth, at the point of the bayonet or in that close Indian hug of peaceful but desperate competition in which, sooner or later, must crack the loins of the civilization belonging to one or the other of the two hemispheres.

It would be tedious and ungenial to show in all its details how the American has had to make his way against these obstacles to the position he now holds before the nations. It took the revolutionary war to disprove the assertion that a British officer with a few regiments could march through the length and breadth of our land, in the face of its disorderly rebels. Once more we had to argue the question over with our dear obstinate old parents, and it was only after lugging in a dozen of his sea bulldogs by the ears that we succeeded in satisfying him that we could reason yard-arm to yard-arm as convincingly as we had argued bayonet to bayonet. You are not old enough, my young friend, to remember the eighth of January, 1815 but you may have heard of a great discussion which took place on that day near your native city of New Orleans. The same question was debated. If the logic of Mr. Andrew Jackson had failed to convince the opposite party, and Mr. Pakenham's syllogism as to provincial inferiority had been followed out in its corollary of sword and fire, your little game of life, sir, might never have been played, which would have been a great misfortune to us and all the world— except perhaps the late champion of England, Mr. Howard Staunton.*

We love our British cousins too well to repeat all the sharp things they have said of us. Reviewers, tourists, philosophers like Coleridge and Carlyle, nay, some

---

* AUTHOR'S NOTE: Mr. Staunton, British chess-champion, who evaded a meeting with Morphy.

who have lived among us until their flesh and blood had become American, and their very bones were made over again out of our earth, have all had their fling at the Colonists and Provincials. Such tricks are catching, and have reappeared on the other side of the channel. After all the noble words spoken of our land and its institutions by writers like De Tocqueville and Chevalier, M. Jules Janin could not let the Queen of tragedy visit us without warning her against the barbarians of the new world, *so terrible did we seem to the smooth, round coop-fed* feuilletoniste of the Parisian cockneys.

Now, gentlemen, there are two ways of meeting this prejudice so natural to the good people of the over-ripe half of the planet. We can confess the fact of our green immaturity,—but argue from the history of the past that we may yet come to something. We can show that all mankind are colonists and provincials with reference to some point or points from which they started; that England herself is but a settlement formed by a band of invading robbers, crossed upon a mob of emigrant squatters. We can show that the children of nations have often lived to feed, to teach, and when necessary to chastise their parents. We can remind our old-country friends that Macedonia, the kingdom of the world's conqueror, and the home of the world's philosopher, was but a rough province, speaking a language hardly understood at Athens; and that the great epic, the great poem, the great work of antiquity was written, or spoken, or sung, not in the phrase familiar to Attic ears, but in the liquid dialect of remote provincial Ionia.

That is the first way of arguing the matter. The second course is much shorter and more satisfactory. It consists in administering what in the dialect of our Yankee Ionia is called "a good licking," of course in the most polite and friendly way, to the other party in discussion, whenever we get a chance. And that chance has of late years been afforded us pretty often.

Let us look very briefly at the experiments we have tried in this direction. The first was to take the rod of iron with which we were ruled,—namely, a ramrod with a ball-cartridge at the end of it—and break it over the backs of those who had abused it. This lesson, as we said, had to be repeated, and we trust that costly way of teaching will never have to be tried again with our sturdy old parent. And thus the great and beneficent era of competition in the arts of peace was at last inaugurated. Now it is not fair to ask everything at once of a young and growing civilization. When our back-woodsmen have just made a clearing, we do not expect them to begin rearing Grecian temples; but was not and is not the settler's log cabin good of its kind—better than Irish shanties and English hovels? As larger wants unfolded, we have had a fair opportunity of showing what we could do. The first great work of civilized men everywhere is to tame nature. And some of her wild creatures are never yet wholly tamed, though the old world has been at work at them for thousands of years. There is the earth,—that huge dumb servant, out of whose sturdy strength, by goading and scourging and scarifying, we wring the slow secret toil that fills his brown arms with food for our necessities. There is the sleepless, restless complaining monster, that overlaps two-thirds of our globe with his imbricated scales: the great ocean,—architect and destroyer of continents. There is man's noblest servant among the unreasoning tribes of being, of whom the oldest and grandest of books says, that "his neck is clothed with thunder," whose nature the classic fable blended with that of man himself to make the centaur, rival of demigods.

Who has tamed the earth, gentlemen, like the Americans, whose instruments of husbandry so far surpassed all others in the day of trial that they reaped not only all the grain before them, but all the honors and all the prizes, without leaving anything for the gleaners? Who has tamed the ocean like the American shipbuilder, whose keels have ploughed the furrows in which all the navies of the world may follow at their leisure? Who has so merited that noble Homeric name of horse-subduer, the proud title of heroes, as the American enchanter, whose triumphs have never been approached before since Bucephalus trembled and stood still at the voice of Alexander. It is time for the men of the old world to find out that they have to do with a people which, if we may borrow an expression from one of its earliest and greatest friends, "tramples upon impossibilities."

Let me give you proofs from one department of applied science. In the book before me (London, 1852) Mr. Ross, the great English optician, says that 135 degrees is the largest angular pencil of light that can be passed through a microscopic object-glass. On the cover of the object-glass before me, a glass made by Charles A. Spencer, then of Canastota, in the "backwoods" of New York, as they got it in London, is marked 146 degrees, which impossible angle he has since opened, as all the microscopic world knows, to the thrice impossible extent of 170 degrees and upwards.

I mention this exceptionally to illustrate the audacity of democratic ingenuity in a department remote from the wants of common life. But it is to supply these common wants that the American brain has been chiefly taxed. Here it has known no equal. One other example is enough. It took a locksmith trained among the guessing Americans to pick the locks of the world's artificers and defy them all to push back the bolts of his own. So much, then, we have made thoroughly and triumphantly ours; the breast of the earth to feed us, the back of the ocean to bear us, the strength of the horse to toil for us, and the lock of the cunning artisan to protect the fruits of our labor from the rogues the old world sends us! We have had first to make life possible, then tolerable, then comfortable, and at last beautiful with all that intellect can lend it!

And when the old world gets impatient that we will not do everything in the best way at once, when it is not contented with our material triumphs, and that greatest of all triumphs, the self-government of thirty empires, not contented that we should move on as the great tide-wave moves—one broad-breasted billow, and not a host of special narrow currents; when the old world, filled with those experts, who have often gained their skill for want of nobler objects, like the prisoners who carve cunning devices in their cells, becomes impatient, we must send over sometimes a man and sometimes a boy, to try conclusions with its people in some peaceful contest of intelligence. And this young gentleman at my right, looking as tranquil and breathing as calmly as if he were not half-smothered in his laurels, is one of the boys we sent. No! I am wrong. The thoughtful mothers of America would have cried out against us with one voice if *we* had sent this immature youth, his frame not yet knit together in perfect manhood, to task his growing brain in those tremendous conflicts which made the huge

Père Morel, the veteran of the Café de la Régence, strike his broad forehead and beg to be released from the very thought of following the frightful complexity of their bewildering combinations. No! the men, with their ambition and proud confidence in his strength, might have been willing to send him, but the women, with their tender love as mothers and sisters and well-wishers, would have said, "He shall not go!"

He went. It was not we that sent him,—it was Honor! And when we meet to welcome his triumphant return, we know what his victories mean. We have had one more squeeze at the great dynamometer which measures the strength of the strongest of the race. There it lies in the central capital of Europe. The boy has squeezed it, and it is not now the index that moves, but the very springs that are broken.

The test is as true a one of cerebral powers as if a hundred thousand men lay dead upon the field where the question was decided,—as if a score of line-of-battle-ships were swinging, blackened wrecks, upon the water after a game between two mighty admirals. Where there is a given maximum there is always a corresponding average, and there is not one of us who does not think better of the head he carries upon his own shoulders, since he finds what a battery it is that lies beneath the smooth forehead of this young brother American.

As I stretch my hand above this youthful brow, it seems to me that I bear in it the welcome, not of a town or a province, but of a whole people. One smile, one glow of pride and pleasure runs over all the land, from the shore which the sun first greets to that which looks upon the ocean where he lets fall the blazing clasp of his dissolving girdle,—from the realm of our Northern sister who looks down from her throne upon the unmelted snows of Katahdin, to hers of the broad river and the still bayou who sits fanning herself among the fullblown roses and listening to the praises of her child as they come wafted to her on every perfumed breeze.

I propose the health of PAUL MORPHY, the world's chess champion: his peaceful battles have helped to achieve a new revolution; his youthful triumphs have added a new clause to the declaration of American Independence!

At the end of the evening Dr. Holmes exclaimed: "Gentlemen, I am the automaton chess player, and I now cry *check*. But before we part, there is one toast in which I am sure you will all cordially join—*The Boston Chess Club*." The sentiment was received with great enthusiasm and Professor Agassiz proposed three cheers for the Boston Chess Club, which were heartily given. Soon after, Dr. Holmes pronounced, *checkmate*, and shortly before one o'clock the company dispersed.

(From The Boston *Journal*, June 1, 1859.)

9.

Howard Staunton in the *Illustrated London News*—March 31, 1860 (with a Letter from Frederick Deacon)

M.D.—"Disgraceful," indeed! The recklessness of imputation and utter disregard of all decency which characterize the lower members of the press in the United States is absolutely revolting. The plain facts are these. Some months since we received two very good games from a well-known English amateur, which were played between him and Mr. Morphy, the American chessplayer, of which each won one. The games were published, accompanied by annotations from the pen of the English player, Mr. Deacon, in our paper of December 17, 1859. Upon their reaching America, Mr. Morphy flatly denied that he had ever played a single game with Mr. Deacon. This denial might be pardoned, if expressed in gentlemanly terms on the ground that the American had forgotten, among battles with so many eminent opponents, an encounter with one so little known. But Mr. Morphy, not content with denying ever having played with Mr. Deacon, condescends to depreciate his skill, and asserts, in the most offensive manner, that "some one has been guilty of deliberate falsehood."

Upon this, with a yell of execration, up spring all that very small fry which, not being very literary, keep a feeble hold on the skirts of literature, and boldly denounce the games as "forgeries," "spurious," "fabrications," a base attempt to sully the star-spangled banner, &c. Now, apart from the incredible stupidity and grossness of such a charge, what is most remarkable in the affair (giving Mr. Morphy credit for really having forgotten his play with Mr. Deacon) is the surpassing vanity of that gentleman and his friends in believing that his fame as a chessplayer is of sufficient importance to move sundry Englishmen, ourselves among the number, to the commission of a shameful fraud, the publication of games as his which he never played. And for what? For the paltry purpose of making it appear that he had won one less game than he had accounted for! Below is a note from the young and clever player to whom we are indebted for the game; and we have no hesitation in asserting, from what we know of him, that, if there has been any "deliberate falsehood" in the matter, it originated on the other side of the Atlantic.

To the Editor of the *Illustrated London News*.

My attention has been called to a paragraph in an American paper, purporting to be a denial from Mr. Morphy of his having played chess with me. The fact of my having won a game of Mr. Morphy, upon even terms, is, I sincerely believe, attributable more to chance than to skill on my part; but I am pained and surprised that the publication of that game should have been met by a deplorable and reckless imputation which cannot but bring discredit upon its originators. Had Mr. Morphy or his friends simply required evidence to recall his playing with me to his mind I would gladly have given it, but I shrink from inquiring into

the motive of an assertion as erroneous as it is heedless, and feel an equal repugnance to a discussion in the spirit of the paragraph I have referred to. A regard for
truth, however, compels me to expose what I hardly know how to characterize.

Believe me, Sir, faithfully yours,

Fred Deacon

3 Hales-Place, South Lambeth
London, March 27, 1860

10.

Howard Staunton in the *Illustrated London News*—March 30, 1861 (with a Letter from Charles Deacon)

The Morphy–Deacon Controversy

It will be in the recollection of our chess readers that towards the end of
1859 we printed two games played between Messrs. Morphy and Deacon, and
that upon the arrival of our paper in America Mr. Morphy addressed a letter to
one of his companions in New York declaring in the most emphatic terms that he
had "never contested a single game with Deacon, on even terms or at odds." Mr.
Morphy was modestly pleased to add that had he played at all with Mr. Deacon
he should have given him at least the odds of pawn and move, as Mr. Deacon was
not accounted so strong a player as the amateur, "Alter," to whom Mr. Morphy
had successfully yielded that advantage.

Directly upon the appearance of this disclaimer we were assailed on all sides
from the "chess organs" of the United States with a torrent of the most disgusting
and savage personalities, some even going so far in malevolence and absurdity
as to accuse us of having fabricated the games for the purpose of damaging their
champion's reputation! It will be further remembered that Mr. Deacon, from
whom we received the games, wrote to us a letter expressing his astonishment at
the behavior of Mr. Morphy and his friends, and added that if those persons had
simply asked for evidence as to when and where the games were played he should
gladly have given it. A few weeks afterwards it appears that, in reply to a communication from some gentleman connected with the Philadelphia *Evening Bulletin*—a paper, it is right to say, which, throughout the controversy, has exhibited
an impartiality and forebearance [*sic*] in the highest degree commendable—Mr.
Deacon stated in writing that the disputed games were played, on a certain day
named, at the British Hotel in Cockspur-street, where Mr. Morphy then resided,
in the presence of Colonel Charles Deacon. Among gentlemen this explanation
would, of course, have been accepted as conclusive: how it was received by Mr.
Morphy and his partisans let the *Evening Bulletin* relate:—

> Immediately upon the publication of this letter an assault was made
> upon the writer and all others in any way connected with it on the part
> of certain Chess papers in New York, aided by a paper then conducted
> in this city. This assault was marked throughout with a savage ferocity

which ignored every rule of decorum and decency, and descended to depths of vituperation and abuse quite unprecedented in all the history of chess. We had our own theory of the purpose of all this, and therefore quietly held on our way, determined, if possible, to fathom the subject to the bottom, without fear or favor.

The Chess Monthly published Mr. Deacon's second letter, and promised a reply from Mr. Morphy in the next number, which reply, however never appeared. Meanwhile we were repeatedly called upon to furnish the proffered testimony of Col. Charles Deacon, and, recognizing the justice of such a demand, while repudiating the temper in which it was generally made, we pledged ourselves to procure it, or to admit that Mr. Deacon had failed to establish his case. Upon application for the testimony, however, we were not surprised to find that the style in which the controversy had been conducted on the part of Mr. Morphy's leading advocates interposed an insuperable obstacle in our way. Few gentlemen in England or elsewhere would agree to be put upon the witness-stand in a case whose advocates had already lavished such vulgar abuse upon them and their relatives and friends. We have at length overcome this most natural repugnance in some measure, and have just received the following letter from Lieutenant-Colonel Charles C. Deacon, C.B., which speaks for itself:—

4, Edwards-square, Kensington, London, Jan. 14, 1861

Dear Sirs,—

In reply to your note of December 17, accept my sincere acknowledgements for your fair and manly defense of my cousin, which we warmly appreciate; but the controversy to which you refer has been conducted by a portion of the American press in a manner which really precludes my entering into it—indeed, in the whole course of my life I have never known anything so outrageous and dastardly as the manner in which we have been attacked. Under different circumstances, however, I should have been happy to have given you my testimony, which would have fully borne out the statement sent to you some time ago by Mr. Fred Deacon; and I must add, from the gentlemanly way in which you have put the case, I regret that, for the reason I have mentioned, I cannot give you a more complete answer.

I am, dear Sirs,

Yours truly

Chas. Deacon

To the
Chess Editors of the Philadelphia *Evening Bulletin.*

11.

Morphy Announcement of Law Office

New Orleans, La.,

(12 Exchange Place, up stairs.)

November 4th 1864

The undersigned, having resumed the practice of his Profession. will attend to the

COLLECTION OF CLAIMS

IN THE UNITED STATES AND STATE COURTS.

His connection with a leading member of the Bar affords him exceptional facilities for a satisfactory adjustment of business confided to his charge

PAUL MORPHY.

12.

Letter to J. E. Orchard from "D"

Mr. J. E. Orchard, Columbia, S.C.

New Orleans, December 5, 1875

Dear Sir—Your letter asking for information as to the mental condition of Mr. Morphy is just at hand. I am sorry to say that the reports concerning him have *some* foundation in fact, but they have been grossly exaggerated in the newspapers. He is not in any sense a lunatic though his mind is affected somewhat. The statement that he is hopelessly insane is far from the truth, for we all have confidence that in time he will be all right again. The fact that his mind was not right was observed by his intimate friends some months ago when he was labouring under the delusion that unknown persons were circulating calumnies about him, and imagined that he was the victim of petty persecutions, the aim of which was to drive him from the country. This idea constantly haunted him and drove him at last to the point where he publicly accused several individuals with being concerned in persecuting him. The thing grew upon him until finally he challenged the supposed authors of the imaginary calumnies to mortal combat with deadly weapons. After this, of course, the whole matter was made public. This is all there was to it.

On all other subjects his mind is apparently sound, and when in company with persons of his liking he converses as rationally as any one. He is not in a lunatic asylum, but walks the streets of our city without restraint and his behavior is as gentlemanly there as it is everywhere else.

It is true that his relatives tried to prevail on him to enter an asylum for the insane, for treatment; and it is also true that he did visit such an institution with some friends, but as he positively objected to staying there and coolly expounded the law governing his case to the Nuns who conduct the institution and so clearly demonstrated that they had no right to deprive him of his liberty without going through certain legal formalities, which he detailed, that his mother intervened, and he was permitted to depart.

On his return from Europe in 1868, and for a long time previous, he had abandoned chess, and rather disliked to converse about it, as he had been bored to death on the subject by indiscreet persons who acted on the supposition that he knew nothing but chess, and wanted to talk of nothing but chess. But notwithstanding the constant boring to which he was subjected, we never found him loath to chat about the game at the proper time and under proper circumstances. If he attended an opera and somebody should be continually dinging chess into his ears, we presume he might show his dislike to talk on the subject and that is about all there is to it. The last games he ever played, so far as the writer knows, was with the well known chess player of this city, C. A. Maurian, Esq. to whom Morphy gave the odds of Knight (not Springer), in the latter part of December, 1866. The story about his being a drunkard is absurd, as he has never taken liquor in his life. His habits and conduct are eminently refined and gentlemanly, and his bearing and ideas rather border on the aristocratic. We believe the foregoing covers the entire ground, and you may rely upon its being strictly true.

Mr. D.

(Published in the *Hartford Times*, December 1875.)

13.

Charles Maurian's Letter to Captain Mackenzie

106, Esplanade Street
New Orleans, Dec. 8, 1875

Captain George H. Mackenzie
New York
My dear Captain,

I am extremely sorry to say that the report that Mr. Morphy's mind has been somewhat deranged of late, is true. The facts, however, have been greatly exaggerated. He believes that he has many enemies who are attempting to drive him from New Orleans by a system of petty persecutions, etc. This idea has led him to behave on one or two occasions in an extravagant manner, but on all subjects not connected with his particular mania, his mind is apparently as sound as it can be. This leads his family and friends to hope that his case is not so hopeless as the Journals would have us believe. Should you think proper to publish these facts, I desire particularly that my name should not be mentioned in connection therewith, for my relations with the family are intimate, and although my present object is merely to correct these erroneous impressions created by the reports in the public prints, I am apprehensive that my motives will be wrongly interpreted. I assure you that this misfortune of Morphy's is very painful to me.

Very truly yours,
Chas. A. Maurian
(Taken from *Life of Paul Morphy* by Regina Morphy-Voitier.)

14.
Charles Maurian's Letter to Jean Prèti

January 15, 1876

My dear Mr. Prèti:

In a letter that I received from you some days ago, you beg me to inform you if it is true that certain rumours about Paul Morphy are true that he may not be right mentally.

I am sorry to have to reply to you that these rumours are only too well founded. I must hasten to add, however, that some of the American papers have greatly exaggerated the facts, especially when they represent this case as absolutely beyond help. Mr. Morphy thinks himself the object of the animosity of certain persons who, he claims, are trying to injure him and render life intolerable to him by a regular system of calumnies and petty persecutions. There is no way of persuading him on this point, but on any other subject he is quite reasonable.

The fixed idea which possesses him has led him on certain occasions to conduct himself in a somewhat extravagant manner. Thus, about two months ago he strove hard to provoke to a duel a gentleman whom he imagined to be one of his persecutors. Since then he seems more tranquil, and it has not been considered necessary to put him into an asylum, as some of the papers have said.

All his friends hope that in time, with care and above all with a change in his mode of life, he will completely recover.

As for the causes which have produced in Mr. Morphy this derangement of his faculties, it is difficult to assign them, and I do not know what the doctors think. I have reason to believe, however, that in their opinion chess has nothing to do with it; for one of them, I am told, has recommended chess as a means of distraction and a change of thoughts. You know, too, that for ten or twelve years Mr. Morphy has completely abandoned chess, and that he never indulged in the game to excess.

For my part, without wishing to hazard an opinion on a question which is beyond me, I cannot help thinking that the sedentary life, devoid of distractions and amusements, which Mr. Morphy has led for some years, must have had a bad influence on his whole system.

Agreez etc.

Ch. A. Maurian

(Translation from *La Stratègie*, February 15, 1876, pages 33-34.)

15.
Dr. L. P. Meredith's Letter in the Cincinnati *Commercial*

New Orleans April 16, 1879.

TO THE CHESS EDITOR OF THE COMMERCIAL:

During my brief visit to the South, after seeing the sights of the Crescent City I was seized by a desire to inform myself in regard to its chess affairs—to see or meet Morphy, or learn full particulars about him. Having satisfied my curiosity in these respects, I have thought that the relation of what I have learned may be interesting to others and sufficiently respond to your suggestions in reference to a letter about chess.

My anxiety to learn all I could about Paul Morphy led me to examine the Directory and wander to the place designated as his residence, No. 89 Royal Street, a plain house of the old style, with a broad double door, without step or vestibule, opening right to the sidewalk. The establishment of a jeweler takes up all of the lower front except the entrance-door. I made some preliminary inquiries of a neighbor, who told me that Mr. Morphy was at home, in good health and able to see people; he had been afflicted mentally, but was better; he walked out a good deal. In answer to a ring at the bell, a negro female appeared, who told me about the same things, and added that he was in, and that I could see him. She went away to announce me, leaving me to observe the broad hall with cemented floor and walls, and look through the archway at the end into a flowering court beyond. The colored damsel returned saying that she was mistaken; that Mr. Morphy had gone out with his mother, but that I could see him at another time. I have since came to regard it as a very fortunate circumstance that I failed to see him while misunderstanding the true state of affairs.

I learn from undeniable authority that he utterly repudiates chess; that when addressed on the subject he either flies into a passion or denies that he knows or ever did know anything of the game. Occasionally, I hear, he admits that he used to play chess some, but not enough to justify persons in attaching notoriety to him. He professes to be a lawyer of prominence, and, although he has no office, no clients, and spends hours promenading Canal St. daily, he imagines himself so pressed with business that he can not release himself for the briefest time. The great case that absorbs nearly all of his attention is an imaginary one against parties who had charge of an estate left by his father. He demands a detailed, explicit account of everything connected with their administration for a number of years, and they pay no attention to his demand and repeated suits, because it is supposed, of the trouble, and because everybody else interested is satisfied and knows that there is nothing coming to him, he already having expended more than his expectancy.

At certain hours every day Paul Morphy is as sure to be walking on Canal Street, as Canal Street is sure to be there to walk on. People shun him for the reason that the least encouragement will result in being compelled to listen for hours to the same old story that everybody knows by heart—that relating to his father's estate. He talks of nothing else, and apparently thinks of nothing else.

His personal appearance is not at all striking, and were it not for his singularity of manner he would rarely be noticed in a thorough-fare. He is of less than medium height and thin in body; his face is yellow and careworn, showing every day of his forty-two years of age, and destitute of beard except an effort at a moustache on a thick upper lip; his eyes are dark gray, large and intelligent. He is always, while on the street, either moving his lips in soliloquy, removing and replacing his eye-glasses, or smiling or bowing in response to imaginary salutations. His scrupulously neat dress renders him a much more agreeable object of curiosity than he would be if he were negligent in his attire.

Physicians regard him as a very peculiar case, amenable to treatment, possibly, if placed under their care; but no opportunity is afforded, as he regards himself as sane as any man, is harmless to society, and is well cared for by willing relatives. Medical experts who have made mental phenomena a study, also say that his chess strength is probably not at all impaired, possibly increased from long rest, and that if he were so inclined he could astonish the world with his wonderful powers more than ever. Judging, however, from his long retirement from the chess arena, and from his persistent devotion to his insane idea, it is only a reasonable inference that Paul Morphy is forever lost to the chess world, and that he will continue to keep buried those talents that would benefit the world and gain honor for himself, together with the wealth he wants and needs, and which he is striving for so energetically in a way that is visionary and hopeless.

On the street in New Orleans, last month, I frequently saw Mr. Morphy but I was longer in his presence, and had a better opportunity of studying him at the old Spanish Cathedral on Easter Sunday than elsewhere. He paid devout attention to the services, and appeared thoroughly familiar with all of the ceremonies, always assuming the kneeling posture, and moving his head and lips responsively at the right time, without apparently taking the cue from any of the worshiping throng. At one time an untidy person brushed against his back, and he seemed stressed for some moments with the idea that his coat had been soiled, endeavoring to brush it with his handkerchief. I caught an inquiring look from his eye, and my glance must have satisfied him that his coat presented a proper appearance, as he immediately composed himself and resumed his attentive air, even spreading his handkerchief in the aisle and kneeling upon it.

I have spoken of his imagined salutations, and his pleasant bow and smile, and graceful wave of the hand, in response. This must have occurred twenty or thirty times, as he stood behind a massive column for a few minutes, in a position in which it was impossible for any one to see him from the direction in which he looked. In the speculations regarding his mental derangement it has been natural to attribute it, in a great measure, to an over-exertion of brain power in his wonderful feats at chess, but nothing has ever been found to establish positively such a conclusion. His astonishing achievements appeared to cost him no effort. Analyses that would require weeks of laborious study on the part of the greatest masters, he would make as rapidly as his eyes could look over the squares. His eight or ten blindfold games, played simultaneously against strong players, appeared to require no more attention than the perusal of a book or paper. With rare exceptions, he appeared to know intuitively the strongest moves that could be made. His uncle, Ernest Morphy, during his visit to Cincinnati many years ago, told me how Paul, when a child, would suddenly drop his knife and fork at the table and set up on the checkered table-cloth a problem that had suddenly sprung into his head, using the cruets, salt-cellars and napkin-rings for pieces. I asked him if his nephew was remarkable for anything else than his peculiar aptitude for chess, and I recollect that he stated, among other things, that, after his return from a strange opera, he could hum or whistle it from beginning to end.

At school, and afterward at college, Paul Morphy was always criticized for his continuous study and aversion to youthful sports, he never taking any part in outdoor games or athletic exercises. So it seems that chess is not to blame for his present singular condition, except as it represents a portion of the mental operations in which his brain was constantly employed.

It is unquestionably an instance of a brain excessively developed at the expense of the physical man, having the mind expanded to the utmost bounds of sanity, and ready to wander outside its limits on the occurrence of some peculiarly exciting circumstance; and this happened, probably, in the sudden realization that what he had considered a competency was expended, and that he had become, for the present at least, dependent. After this he was in no condition to reason—to see that he had lived extravagantly while abroad and after his return, and that his expenditures were in excess of his share of his father's estate. He imagined that he had been defrauded, intentionally or through mismanagement; hence the litigious course he has pursued. Possibly his aversion to chess came through associating it with his misfortunes, his heaviest expenditures having occurred while away on his victorious tour through Europe. Some have thought a complete restoration of his normal mental condition might follow a rendering of the particularized account he demands from trustees or administrators, for he is wonderfully acute at figures, and might be convinced if incontrovertible calculations were placed before him. Why it is not done is not known; whether on account of an impossibility, the amount of labor and trouble, or because of an indifference that is thought justified through the entire satisfaction of other interested parties. I understand that he has a right to demand such an account, and that he could enforce it, probably, if he were not regarded as insane, or if others would join his cause for the sake of humoring him. It is said, to the reproach of certain lawyers, that they would advise and encourage him in his hopeless case as long as he had money to fee them, but that now they will not give him a hearing.

Suggestions in reference to medical treatment amount to nothing, because he acknowledges no ailment. Efforts have been made to induce him to travel, that his physical health might be benefited, and that his mind might be diverted from its absorbing subject; but he regards this as playing into the hands of his enemies, says his absence from New Orleans is just what they are scheming for, and avows his intention of remaining to defeat them on their own ground.

It is distressing to admit that Paul Morphy is hopelessly lost to the intellectual world. Must that superhuman mind be forever devoted to the pursuance of such a petty, insignificant object, when it is capable of exerting such wondrous power? The gratitude of all mankind awaits him who can devise some means for giving flesh and strength to that attenuated body, and restoring the equilibrium of that disturbed brain, thus replacing this shining star in the brilliant galaxy from which it has fallen.

Dr. L. P. Meredith

16.
Dr. R. A. Proctor on Morphy

The Human Mind
The Wonderful Powers of Paul Morphy
Dr. Richard A. Proctor 1887

Oct. 16, 1887

The power of forming and retaining mental pictures is one of great value and great promise; though it is not capable of explaining feats of rapid calculation. Probably this faculty alone may suffice to explain the feats of blindfold chessplay, though some great players who are skillful over the unseen board assert that they form no mental pictures. Blackburne, for example, states that from the mere recording of the moves he is able to recognize the strength and weakness of the resulting positions, and the command of the several pieces over the board. This, however, is by no means the general experience. I have myself often played two games simultaneously without seeing the board; and were it worth while to give much time to such matters have no doubt I could play five or six. In every case I see a definite picture of the board and men. It seems to me so natural to do this, in thinking over a past game, that I wonder blindfold play began so late in the history of chess. Glanvill, in his "Vanity of Dopmatizing," written in 1661, speaks of a blind man managing a game of chess much as one might speak of a gorilla speaking Greek; yet he was himself well acquainted with the game.

The feats of the greatest chess genius that ever lived (let Steinitz argue as he may), Paul Morphy, associate blindfold chess play in some degree with precocity. I doubt if among all the records of boy chess players any case can be found more marvelous than that of Morphy, who, at the very beginning of his career, when he was little more than a child, beat his uncle Ernest Morphy, a strong player, and Lowenthal, the Hungarian champion, when only thirteen years old. Many of the stories of precocity at chess relate to boy players who beat those who were not, indeed, boys, but neither were they players; but Paul Morphy beating Lowenthal was quite another affair. Even when Morphy crossed the Atlantic to challenge and defeat all the finest players of Europe, he was barely out of his teens. One after another they met him and retired discomfited, or like our English Staunton, they compared his chess strength with their own by proxy, as it were, and retired without meeting him.

Now Morphy at the age of thirteen played a strong chess game without sight of the board. Rising step by step to two games, to three, to four, and so on we find him while still in his teens playing twelve games simultaneously blindfold, and against players to whom the champions of the day could not give more than a pawn and move with safety in a set match. More surprising even than the number of games which Morphy could thus play blindfold at one sitting, was the nature of his play under these seemingly difficult conditions. The brilliancy of the combinations was in most cases matched by their soundness and often by their depth—in the sense of the number of moves over which with lightning rapidity he carried his analysis. A veteran player told me of one of these games which he had carefully examined after it was finished; because he believed that a certain brilliant stroke could be more successfully met than it had been in actual play. "Along every line," he said, "but one I found Morphy's strategy sound; but along that line there seemed to me a safe though difficult defense, resulting in eventual victory over him. I passed an hour or two every evening for a week analyzing the game along this line; and having satisfied myself it was sound, I mentioned the point to Morphy when next I met him. I was for setting up the board to show him what I meant; but he would not suffer me. 'I remember the game perfectly,' he said. 'Your defense is not sound, though it is the best available; you have overlooked a mate in three following the sacrifice of my king bishop after the fifth move of your defense.' My veteran friend looked over the position the same evening and found the case was as Morphy had stated."

Imagine the abnormal brain development in some special, though unknown way, which enabled a boy chess player, ten days after playing a game, which was one of twelve [he played only eight] played blindfold, to correct in an instant, and without setting up the position, the result, of ten or twelve hours of analysis of the game by a strong and veteran player!

Dr. Richard A. Proctor

The above is a portion of an article, "The Human Mind. Some Strange Mental Pictures Described—Blindfold Chess Play. The Wonderful Powers of Paul Morphy, the Precocious Genius." (Written for the Louisville *Courier-Journal*, October 16, 1887.)

17.
Testimonial to Paul Morphy

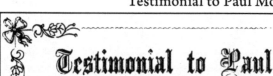

Testimonial to Paul Morphy.

UNIVERSITY HALL, NEW YORK CITY,

Wednesday Evening, May 25th, 1859.

PRESENTATION CEREMONIES.

MUSIC.

ENTRANCE OF THE NEW YORK CHESS CLUB, OFFICERS, INVITED GUESTS, ORATORS,

AND

PAUL MORPHY.

MUSIC—"SEE, THE CONQUERING HERO COMES."

DESCRIPTION OF TESTIMONIALS.

Testimonial furnished by Tiffany & Co.

The Chess-men, which are the conspicuous objects of the "Morphy Testimonial," are of the purest Gold and Silver, and—with the exception of their cornelian pedestals—of those materials alone. In design and execution, as well as in intrinsic value, the set is, so far as we are informed, unequa'ed—the celebrated establishment in the possession of Queen Victoria, though of similar design, being of inferior proportions. The connoisseur will especially remark the exquisite details of the artist's conception. As Chess is a royal game, the pieces in this superb set are appropriately modeled after a study of one of the grandest historic episodes—the contest between Christianity and Barbarism. "The Reds," or the Gold pieces, are highly finished statuettes, indicating the components of an imperial array in the days when Kings and Queens went forth with their armies, and Bishops, exchanging mitre and crosier for battle-axe and sword, transferred the war of proselytism from the sanctuary to the field. The "Whites," or the Silver pieces, in happy contrast, represent the Northern horde which disputed the domination of Theodosius, or, at a later period, for a while withstood the march of Clovis and Clothilde. That the latter page of history is a favorite theme for German study, may be seen in the romances of Fouqué and others' as well as in many of the finest works in Iron and Bronze, which have distinguished the artists of Berlin and Munich.

In detail, the pieces are as follows: The Gold King is a statuette, four inches in height, and weighing three ounces, royal robes gracefully falling over his armor, the Imperial globe upon his martially defended head, the crown and sceptre at his feet, by his side an elegant shield, and in his right hand the sword of Empire. The Queen, arrayed in character, is of proportions slightly inferior to those of her Lord. The Bishops, in the full panoply of warriors, three and a half inches in height, stand perceptibly inclined forward, grasping drawn swords with blades advanced, and are spirited illustrations of the fierce Prelates who anticipated the Higher Law conflicts of the Pulpit and Press by good cut and thrust argumentation hand-to-hand. The Knights, on both sides, are admirably sculptured chargers, prancing nearly upright, and ruby-eyed. In the Rooks, or Castles, the Artist has adopted the Chinese design, and flanked the rear lines by stately Elephants, each bearing an Eastern houda, upon which an elegantly wrought Eagle is spreading his pinions, as if to pounce upon his prey. The eyes of both bird and beast are brilliant rubies. The finish of this piece is especially admirable, the artist having achieved a manifest triumph in the contrast which his fine *chasing* has effected between the coarse hide of the elephant and the tiger-skin mantle of the houda. This elaborate piece is three and three-quarter inches in height, and weighs eighty dollars, o.—more appreciably—five ounces.

The Silver King is a happy counterpart to his Golden adversary. As a leader of the Barbarians, his covering is of bull's hide, and only distinguished from that of his followers by the finer dressing it has received. Disputing the Empire with the leader of the opposing host, he, too, wears the Imperial globe upon which rest those emblematic wings with which the Norsemen and the Goths adorned their helmets. The royal emblems lie at his feet, while on his left arm depends a shield inscribed with the defiant motto— *Liberty*—and in his right hand he grasps a warlike brand. His Queen is arrayed in proper character. The Bishops wear winged helmets, and drawn swords considerably longer than the Roman falchions of their Christian adversaries, their panoply otherwise according with that of their posts. In proportion and weight, these pieces correspond with those of the other side.

The Gold Pawns are statuettes two and a half inches in height, weighing two ounces. In this piece the artist has elaborated the Roman soldier—the helmet, buckler, and straight, double-edged sword being exact copies of those borne by a man-at-arms of the Western Empire. The Silver Pawn is similar in proportion and a correspondingly exact sculpture of the old Visigoth, wearing upon his body the hide and upon his head the horns which he has torn from the wild bull of the Germanian forest. His single weapon is a huge and knotty club, promising a rough encounter for the short blade of his adversary.

The pedestal of each piece is polished Cornelian—for the Pawns, a circle of one inch in diameter—for the leading pieces, an oval one inch and a half in diameter. The value of material worked up amounts to nearly $800, and the entire cost of material and labor is but little less than $1500. In the elaborate finish of the historic study, the statuesque proportion, and the exquisite mechanical execution of each piece, the resources of Art have contributed most liberally for the honor of Genius.

The Board upon which the Gold and Silver Chess-men are to stand, likewise manufactured by Tiffany & Co., is a square of twenty-six inches. The body of the Board is of Rosewood, the Squares being of Ebony and choice Mother of Pearl. A slightly raised edge, ornamented by a single delicate line of inlaid Silver, surrounds the Board. Just within this edge another similarly fine line, and a third more heavy, form an agreeable contrast with the rich color of the wood. Three inches from the edge, four tournament lances, in Silver, inclose the checquered field—a square of twenty inches. In each exterior angle formed by the overlapping of the lances, circled by a laurel wreath of Gold, exquisitely inlaid, are the letters P. M. in decorated cipher. Midway of the border, from which Mr. Morphy is supposed to play, an inlaid oval plate of Silver, surrounded by a trophy composed of the standards of those nations whose subjects have been obliged to recognize the sovereignty of a Republican Champion, bears the subjoined inscription :—

TO

PAUL MORPHY,

A RECOGNITION OF HIS GENIUS AND A TOKEN OF REGARD

FROM

HIS FRIENDS AND ADMIRERS IN

NEW YORK AND BROOKLYN,

NEW YORK, 1859.

Surmounting this plate is a laurel crown in Silver, and beneath it a riband of the same metal is inscribed with—

" Proeliis ex sanguinatis facile princeps."

In the opposite border another plate, oval in inlaid Silver, and edged by a trophy of lances, battle axes, spears, and pieces of armor, incloses an engraved Sphynx, around which are grouped the names of the Committee of Presentation, as follows :—

CHARLES D. MEAD,	JOHN VAN BUREN,	THOS. ADDIS EMMETT,
W. J. A. FULLER,	JAMES L. GRAHAM, Jr.,	REGIS DE TROBRIAND,
JAMES R. WHITING,	SAM. D. BRADFORD, Jr.,	JOHN S. DUNNING,
DANIEL W. FISKE,	JAMES THOMPSON,	H. FOSTER HIGGINS,
NAP'N MARACHE,	H. R. WORTHINGTON,	WM. WALTON,
THEOD. LICHTENHEIM,	FREDERICK PERRIN,	T. FRERE.

Similarly situated, in the left hand border, a third Silver plate, circular, supported by Sphynxes, ornamented with the armorial bearings of the City of New York. In the opposite border a fourth plate, of the same metal, emblematically delineates the Pyramids, three in number, likewise supported by Sphynxes. The center pyramid, in sections, commemorates the Chess-Champions of all ages, that of the last and greatest filling the apex, as follows :

MORPHY.

LABOURDONNAIS. M'DONNELL.

LOPEZ. **PHILLIDOR.** SALVIO.

VON DERLASA. HANSTEIN. ANDERSSEN. BILGUER.

LÜWENTHAL. SZEN. PETROFF. KIESERITZKY. LANGE.

The Board is so paneled and dove-tailed in construction, that no influence of climate or position can possibly affect the integrity of the squares. As a specimen of workmanship, in addition to the felicity of its design, the fact that the most skilful artisans consumed six weeks in its manufacture, and another week in polishing it, is pertinent proof of its superlative excellence. Its cost is not far from $300.

The Testimonial, as furnished by Messrs. Tiffany & Co., includes, besides the Chess-men and Board, a case of Rosewood, fitted with artistically shaped, velvet-lined niches, for the reception of the set when not in use.

INTRODUCTORY REMARKS of Col. CHAS. D. MEAD, President of the New York Chess Club.

Address and Presentation of Testimonial,

BY HON. JOHN VAN BUREN.

REPLY BY PAUL MORPHY.

MUSIC.

DESCRIPTION OF WATCH,

PRESENTED BY THE INDIVIDUAL MEMBERS OF THE TESTIMONIAL COMMITTEE, AND FURNISHED BY THE AMERICAN WATCH COMPANY, WALTHAM, MASS.

THE AMERICAN WATCH,

PRESENTED BY THE COMMITTEE,

Was made to order by the Company at WALTHAM, MASS., and is a

SUPERB SPECIMEN OF THE ART.

The Stem or Pendant is exquisitely carved, so as to represent a KING's CROWN. It is set round with Brilliants, with another large DIAMOND at its top, which answers for a push-piece by which to open the watch. Upon one lid the

United States Coat of Arms

is richly carved in relief, and on the other lid, also in relief, the monogram—

P. M.

Instead of the usual Roman numerals on the dial, the hours are represented by the various pieces of chess, finely done in red and black—the Black King standing at twelve, and the Red King at six, the Queens at one and eleven, Bishops at two and ten, Knights at three and nine, Castles at four and eight, and Pawns at five and seven. The cap is engraved with the following inscription :

To Paul Morphy:

FROM THE TESTIMONIAL COMMITTEE OF THE NEW YORK CHESS CLUB, AS THEIR

TRIBUTE TO HIS GENIUS AND WORTH.

NEW YORK, *May*, 1859.

THE MOVEMENTS OF THIS WATCH WERE MADE ENTIRELY BY MACHINERY,

AND ITS

INTERIOR AND EXTERIOR

PRESENT AS ELEGANT A SPECIMEN OF ART AS CAN WELL BE IMAGINED.

THE WHOLE IS HIGHLY CREDITABLE TO THE

CELEBRATED MAKERS AND TO AMERICAN INGENUITY.

PRESENTATION OF THE TESTIMONIAL OF THE INDIVIDUAL COMMITTEE.

ADDRESS BY W. J. A. FULLER, ESQ.

REPLY BY PAUL MORPHY.

MUSIC.

Wynkoop, Hallenbeck & Thomas, Printers, 113 Fulton Street, N. Y.

18.
List of Poems Written to Paul Morphy

TITLE	SOURCE	FIRST LINE	AUTHOR
1. To Paul Morphy	*Chess Monthly*, December 1857	In days of old with sword and lance	Edwin J. Weller
2. Paul Morphy	*St. Louis Daily Democrat*, December 11, 1858	Hail! Morphy, bloodless victor, Hail!	G. Grundy
3. The Hero of the West	*Chess Monthly*, November 1858	Ring out, O bells, a merry peal	F. H. Norton
4. Morphy	*Sissa*, January 1859	There stands the numerous band of heroes,	T. J. Werndly
5. To Paul Morphy	*New York Evening Post*, June 1, 1859	Illustrious monarch of the chequered field	A. H. D.
6. To the Chess King	*New York's Porter's Spirit*, November 12, 1859	Bold fighter over bloodless fields,	N. Marache
7. Paul Morphy	*New York Evening Express*, June 2, 1859	As I rise, Mr. Autocrat, grim with despair	James R. Lowell
8. Paul Morphy	*New York Evening Express*, June 2, 1859	There's a certain young man of most dignified air	G. W. Pettis
9. A Fight Between Redskins and Pioneers	Book by G. Timme, 1860	De Roodhuid is in't veld (Dutch)	G. Timme
10. Morphy	*Chess Player's Chronicle*, November 1861	Mightiest of masters of the checkered board	C. V. Grinfeld
11. To Morphy	*El Moro Muza*, November 2, 1862	Brendas en prosa liviana	*El Moro Muza*
12. The Triumphs of Morphy	*Forney's War Press*, May 18, 1864	Morphy's praise demands my song,	"A Contributor"
13. The Chess Player's Dream	*London Era*, January 23, 1870	I dreamt that I played a match at Chess,	*Westminster Magazine*
14. Chess Sonnet	*Huddersfield College Magazine*, September 1875	Problems you term the poetry of Chess,	W. C. Spens
15. Paul Morphy	*Glasgow Weekly Herald*, November 25, 1882	By the bright winter fire I lightly read	W. C. Spens
16. The Light of Other Days	*British Chess Magazine*, October 1882	Past are thy victories—Two worlds no more	F. F. Beechey
17. Paul Morphy	*Glasgow Weekly Herald*, July 19, 1884	He came to Europe: English Sages smiled	W. C. Spens
18. In Memoriam	*British Chess Magazine*, August 1884	Harp of the Chessic Bard,	J. A. Miles
19. Paul Morphy	*Chess Fruits*, 1884	Paled e'er that light once bright	Mrs. T. B. Rowland
20. On the Death of Paul Morphy	*Nuova Rev. Degli Scacchi*, September 1884	The immortal Chess player of the New World	G. Ottolenghi
21. To the Memory of Morphy's Mother	*New Orleans Times-Democrat*, May 10, 1885	Mother of Morphy! what a fate was thine,	I. O. Howard Taylor
22. He Cannot Die	*Staten Islander*, December 21, 1910	Smith is my name not strikingly adept	C. F. Simonson
23. An Paul Morphy	*Der Weg Zur Meister*, 1919	Buonoparte der Schachkunst	F. Gutmayer
24. Paul Morphy	*American Chess Bulletin*, January 1930	Fold up the board, the hour is late	H. T. Houston
25. Grosskonig Morphy	*Du "Armer" Schacher*, 1931	Grosskonig Morphy	E. H. Berlemann
26. Paul Morphy	*Deutsche Schachblatter*, June 1, 1937	Overcome by the magic of a noble game	H. Berkenbusch

19.

To The Memory of Morphy's Mother

Mother of Morphy! what a fate was thine;
So loving-living only for thy son;
Granted brief tip-touch of his triumphs won,
Ere dashed with wormwood all life's sparkling wine!
The mind that such transcendent marvels wrought—
Like blooming rose, the cherished garden gem,
Heart-bit, hangs listless on the blackened stem—
Sinks, walled in dim, damp cell of lovely thought.
Earth's greatest, wisest, brightest, best of men,
Owe most to mothers; nor is genius loath
To own the debt; our Morphy's mother, then,
Who warmed and watered all that beauteous growth—
Fading, still watched! Shall keep true union, when,
Chess lays her deathless chaplet on the grave of *both*!

—I. O. Howard Taylor

20.

Paul Morphy and Robert J. Fischer

Certainly comparisons between Paul Morphy and Robert J. Fischer, the only Americans ever to dominate the world chess arena, come to mind. Both were prodigies and both were early in their lives convinced of their superiority as chess players. Both early played spectacular Queen Sacrifice games, Morphy against Paulsen, and Fischer against Donald Byrne. Oddly, Morphy's Queen captured Paulsen's Bishop while Byrne's Bishop captured Fischer's Queen, both Queens being captured by White on his 18th move.

As it happened, the author was with Bobby and his mother the night of his Queen Sacrifice game at the Manhattan Chess Club, and the three of them left together after the game to celebrate at a restaurant. Not much was said that evening at the club about the game, the significance of "The Game of the Century," as it was later dubbed, being scarcely appreciated at the time. These two sacrifice games of Bobby's and Paul's, both winning as Black, are now considered among their most interesting games.

Both Morphy and Fischer were early convinced they would become the world's foremost player, at the earliest opportunity, but Fischer had to wait longer due to FIDE Rules and Regulations. Both believed that only matches, not tournaments, determined relative strength, and that draws should not count.

There are also differences between them, not only in early circumstances, but also in their approach to the game. At thirteen years of age, Paul had never opened a chess book, while Bobby at that age had devoured everything on the game he could lay his hands on, and that was a lot in the 1950s, compared with the 1850s!

Morphy was practically isolated from good players until he was twenty (by 1850 Rousseau would no longer play with him and Uncle Ernest soon went North), while the young Bobby was in contact with the best players of the country and played in tournaments.

Fischer lives for chess. Maurian said Morphy "never was, strange as it will seem, an enthusiast" and, at the age of twenty-three, he refused to play in public.

It would seem that the contrasting personalities of Morphy and Fischer have drawn their chess careers to a similar ending for the time being and perhaps for longer. Morphy practically repudiated public chess almost as soon as he was universally accepted as World Champion. Although apparently he would have accepted a challenge soon after the Anderssen match, at which time he offered Pawn and move to any who wished to challenge his supremacy, no one came forth to take up his offer. Fischer resigned the title almost as quickly as had Morphy, but without making any attempt at further play.

It remains to be seen whether Fischer, having achieved his goal, as did Morphy, will, like the latter, abjure public chess, and whether his chess success will also recoil upon him. But it may be that his great interest in the game will rekindle his desire to reenter the public chess arena and save him from the lonely road taken by Morphy, and from a similar imbalance.*

---

* EDITOR'S NOTE: Alas, that interest did not rekindle Fischer's desire. In 1992, he returned from seclusion to play a rematch with Boris Spassky, from whom he had taken the World Championship in 1972. The two played in UN-sanctioned Yugoslavia, putting Fischer at odds with the American government. He publicly spit on the U.S. order that he not attend the Yugoslavian match. Fischer then resubmerged into obscurity, living in Hungary, the Philippines, and Japan. Fischer's anti-Semitism had been present before his World Championship, but it only became more pronounced at the onset of his seclusion. Like Morphy, his persecution paranoia began to dominate his personality. Arrest warrants in the United States stemming from his Yugoslavian play extended his paranoia toward his home country. Inflammatory public statements following the September 11, 2001, terrorist attacks only grew his infamy. After an arrest in Japan for using an expired passport, Fischer was granted citizenship in Iceland, home to his original 1972 encounter with Spassky.

He died of renal failure on January 17, 2008. In the myriad obituaries of Fischer following his death, Paul Morphy's name was often invoked. Both were American World Champions, both suffered from a form of debilitating mental paranoia, leading to their voluntary withdrawal from chess. But as Lawson's biography demonstrates, Morphy's illness was far less public, far less broad or treasonous. It was not willfully angry and retributive toward people, religions, or nations. It did not revel in death. Still, such distinctions seem much like angels dancing on the head of a pin in bulleted newspaper accounts chronicling Fischer's life and death. The image of the diseased, reclusive, American chess champion will forever embed the metaphor in public perception—though it shouldn't.

But both Morphy and Fischer shook the world of chess to its foundations with their games, their personalities, and their genius.

---

* EDITOR'S NOTE (continued from previous page): For a strong recent biography of Fischer, emphasizing specifically his 1972 championship, but also providing analysis of his later life, see David Edmonds and John Edinow, *Bobby Fischer Goes to War: How a Lone American Star Defeated the Soviet Chess Machine* (New York: Faber & Faber, 2004). For more biography, see Hans Bohm and Kees Jongkind, *Bobby Fischer: The Wandering King* (New York: Batsford, 2005); and Frank Brady, *Bobby Fischer: Profile of a Prodigy* (New York: Dover Publications, 1989). For examples of Fischer obituary, see any major American or European newspaper, January 18, 2008.

AUTHOR'S BIBLIOGRAPHY

This bibliography is divided into five parts. The first consists mostly of sources devoted almost exclusively to Morphy. Many of these sources have been of much usefulness to the author in preparing this biography, others are of interest merely because they reflect the enthusiasm generated by Morphy during the height of his chess career and thereafter. The subject of and inspiration for many poems (listed in the Appendix), Paul Morphy has also had two novels written about him. The first by Frances Parkinson Keyes, *The Chess Players*, appeared in 1960. The second, written in Russian by E. Zagoryansky, was started in 1946 in *Chess in the U.S.S.R.* as *A Tale of Paul Morphy*, but was completed and published in book form in 1962.

During the early years of Morphy's chess activity (1858–1860) a dozen publications were issued about him and his games, of which one has been reprinted many times down to the present while others have appeared in different languages. If anything, interest and understanding of Morphy appear on the increase, for since 1960 ten books about Morphy or on his games have been published or reprinted in Swedish, Russian, French, German, Yugoslavian, and English.

The first part of this bibliography does not include such books as Staunton's *Chess Praxis*, published in 1860, which will be found in the second part of the bibliography. This second part lists books having an entire chapter or important sections on Morphy, while the third part—books—and the fourth and fifth parts—magazines and newspapers, respectively—have contributed the greater portion of the essential information for this biography. The many mentions of Edge refer to his books on Morphy, even if not so stated, or to his letters, some possessed by the author, and other quotes are similarly possessed or available.

Part One

Couvee, M. M. *Two Remarkable Games*. (Dutch) 'S Gravenhage: M. M. Couvee, 1858.

Doazan, G. E. *Labourdonnais-Morphy*. Paris: L. Tinterlin et Cie., 1859.

Dufresne, Jean. *Paul Morphy's Schachwettkampfe*. Berlin: Carl Heymann, 1859.

_____. *Der Schachfreund*. Berlin: Carl Heymann, 1862.

Edge, Frederick M. *The Exploits and Triumphs in Europe of Paul Morphy*. New York: D. Appleton & Co., 1859.

_____. *Paul Morphy the Chess Champion*. London: William Lay: 1859.

Falkbeer, E. *Paul Morphy, A Sketch from the Chess World*. London: J. H. Starie, 1860.

Fiske, D. W. *Prospectus of the National Chess Congress*. New York: T. W. Strong, 1857.

_____. *The First American Chess Congress*. New York: Rudd & Carleton, 1859.

Frère, Thomas. *Morphy's Games of Chess*. New York: Robert M. De Witt, 1859.

Gottschall, H. von. *Adolf Anderssen*. Leipzig: Veit & Co., 1912.

Jones, Ernest. *Essays in Applied Psychoanalysis*, vol. 1. London: Hogarth Press, 1951.

Keyes, Frances P. *The Chess Players*. New York: Farrar, Straus & Cudahy, 1960.

Lange, Dr. Max. *Paul Morphy, Skizze aus der Schachwelt*. Leipzig: Veit & Co., 1859.

_____. *Paul Morphy, Skizze aus der Schachwelt*. Zweiter Theil. Leipzig: Veit & Co., 1859.

_____. *Paul Morphy, Skizze aus der Schachwelt.* Zweiter Theil. Leipzig: Veit & Co., 1881.

_____. *Paul Morphy, Sein Leben und Schaffen.* Dritte auflage. Leipzig: Veit & Co., 1894.

Lowenthal, J. *Morphy's Games.* New York: D. Appleton & Co., 1859.

_____. *Morphy's Games of Chess.* London: Henry G. Bohn, 1860.

Maróczy, Géza. *Paul Morphy.* Leipzig: Veit & Co., 1909.

_____. *Paul Morphy.* Zweite auflage. Berlin: Walter de Gruyter & Co., 1925.

Morphy-Voiter, Regina. *Life of Paul Morphy in the Vieux Carré of New Orleans and Abroad.* New Orleans: privately printed, 1926.

New York Daily News. *Testimonials to Paul Morphy.* New York: J. W. Bell, 1859.

Ovadija, J. M. *Brilliant Combinations of Paul Morphy.* Beograd, 1925.

Petrovic, S. *Morphy.* Zagreb: Sahooska Naklada, 1971.

Prèti, Jean. *Choix des Parties Jouées par Paul Morphy.* Paris: J. Prèti, 1859.

Rask, Bertil. *Paul Morphy.* Stockholm: F. Englunds Forlag, 1915.

Sanz, Jose. *Morphy La estrella fugaz del ajedrez.* Madrid: R. Aguilera, ca., 1950.

Sergeant, P. W. *Morphy's Games of Chess.* London: G. Bell & Sons, Ltd., 1916.

_____. *Morphy Gleanings.* London: Printing-Craft Ltd., 1932.

Smyth, A. H. *The Writings of Benjamin Franklin.* 10 vols. New York: Macmillan Co., 1905-7.

Stanley, C. H. *Paul Morphy's Match Games.* New York: Robert M. De Witt, 1859.

Tchelebi, E. J. *Le Secret de Morphy.* Limoges: Touron & Fils, 1960.

Vasquez, A. C. *La Odisea de Pablo Morphy.* Havana: La Propaganda Litoraria, 1893.

Zagoryansky, E. *Paul Morphy, a Tale.* Moscow: Foreign Languages Publishing House, 1962.

Part Two

Conway, Moncure D. *Autobiography.* 2 vols. Boston: Houghton Mifflin & Co., 1904.

Devens, R. M. *Our First Century.* Springfield, Mass.: G. A. Nichols & Co., 1877.

Drawing Room Portrait Gallery of Eminent Personages. 1859 Second Series. London, 1859.

Dufresne, Jean. *Anthology der Sachachaufgaben.* Berlin: Louis Gerschel, 1864.

Fine, Dr. Reuben. *The Psychology of the Chess Player.* New York: Dover Publications, Inc., 1967.

Fiske, D. W. *Chess Tales & Chess Miscellanies.* New York: Longmans, Green, and Co., 1912.

Frère, Thomas. *Address on the Portrait of Paul Morphy.* New York: Manhattan Chess Club, 1884.

Gilberg, C. A. *Fifth American Chess Congress.* New York: Brentano's Literary Emporium, 1881.

Gutmayer, F. *Der Weg zur Meisterschaft.* Berlin: Walter de Gruyter & Co., 1919.

Kenny, M., S. J. *The Torch on the Hill.* New York: The American Press, 1931.

Linder, I. M. *A. D. Petroff.* (Russian) Moscow, 1952.

Locket, A. M. *Chess Players of New Orleans.* New Orleans: privately printed, 1935.

MacDonnell, G. A. *Chess Life-Pictures.* London: Kelly & Co., 1883

Maróczy, Géza. *Paul Morphy.* (Russian translation) Leningrad, 1929.

Prèti, Jean. *Paul Morphy, Selected Games.* (Russian translation) St. Petersburg, 1884.

Rand, Clayton. *Stars in Their Eyes.* Gulfport, Miss.: The Dixie Press, 1953.

Reichhelm, G. C. *Chess in Philadelphia*. Philadelphia: Billstein & Son Co., 1898.
Reinfeld, Fred. *The Human Side of Chess*. New York: Pelllegrini & Cudahy, 1952.
_____. *Great Games by Chess Prodigies*. New York: Macmillan Co., 1967.
Staunton, H. *The Chess Tournament*. London: Henry G. Bohn, 1852.
_____. *Chess Praxis*. London: Henry G. Bohn, 1860.
Steinitz, W. *Steinitz and Zukertort Match Programme*. W. Steinitz, 1886.
_____. *The Modern Chess Instructor*. New York: G. P. Putnam's Sons, 1889.
Usigli, E. C. *Degli Scacchi: Miscellanea sal giuoco*. Napoli: E. C. Usigli, 1861.

Part Three

Buck, C. A. *Paul Morphy. His Later Life*. Newport, Ky.: Will H. Lyons, 1902.
Coria, V. F., and Palau, L. *Pablo Morphy*. Buenos Aires: Sopena Argentina, 1955.
Cunnington, E.C. *Half Hours with Morphy*. 3rd ed. London: George Rutledge & Sons, 1902.
Harrison, Mrs. Burton. *Recollections Grave and Gay*. New York: Charles Scribner's Sons, 1911.
Hayden, Bruce. *Cabbage Heads and Chess Kings*. London: Arco Publications, 1960.
Horberg, B., and Westberg, J. *Paul Morphy*. Stockholm: Bokforlaget Forum, 1961.
Horowitz, Al. *The World Chess Championship, A History*. New York: Macmillan Co., 1973.
King, Grace E. *New Orleans, the Place and the People*. New York: Macmillan & Co., 1895.
Morphy, L. A. *Stray Leaves*. New Orleans: Louisiana Printing Co., 1925.
Orsini, E. *I Finali*. Livorno-Pisa: G. Meucci, 1879.
Putnam, George H. *Memories of a Publisher*. New York: G. P. Putnam's Sons, 1915.
Reid, Whitelaw. *After the War: A Southern Tour*. New York: Moore, Wilstoch & Baldwin, 1866.
Sandoval, A. *Medias Horas con Morphy*. Mexico: A. Sandoval, 1917.
Selkirk, G. H. *Book of Chess*. London: Houlston & Sons, 1868.
Sergeant, P. W. *A Century of British Chess*. Philadelphia: David McKay Co., 1934.
Timme, G. *Een Gevecht, Rooduiden en Pionniers*. Duurstede: J. G. Andriessen, 1860.
White, H. S. *Willard Fiske: Life and Correspondence*. New York: Oxford University Press, 1925.
_____. *Memorials of Willard Fiske*. 3 vols. Boston: Richard G. Badger, 1922.
Wildhagen, E. *Morphy and Paulsen*. Hamburg: E. Wildhagen, 1967.

Part Four

While most of the magazines of Morphy's time and later have been researched, the following have been of special value:

American Chess Bulletin
American Chess Magazine
Brentano's Chess Monthly
British Chess Magazine
Brooklyn Chess Chronicle
Chess Life

Chess Monthly (Morphy and Fiske, Editors)
Chess Monthly (Hoffer and Zukertort, Editors)
Chess Player's Chronicle
Chess Record
Good Companion Chess Magazine
Harvard Graduates Magazine
International Chess Magazine
International Journal of Psycho-Analysis
Psychoanalysis Journal (number 3)
La Régence
Schachzeitung
Shakhmaty Listok
Sissa
"64"

Part Five

The following is a list of the newspapers—daily and weekly—most frequently consulted:

New Orleans *Sunday Delta*
New Orleans *Picayune*
New Orleans *Times-Democrat*
New York *Clipper*
New York *Frank Leslie's Illustrated Newspaper*
New York *Porter's Spirit of the Times*
New York *Wilkes' Spirit of the Times*
New York *Saturday Press*
New York *Herald*
New York *Express*
New York *Tribune*
New York *Times*
New York *Ledger*
New York *Turf, Field and Farm*
Philadelphia *Evening Bulletin*
Boston *Journal*
Quincy *Whig*
London *Field*
Bell's Life in London
Illustrated London News
London *Era*

EDITOR'S SELECTED ANNOTATED BIBLIOGRAPHY

This brief bibliography contains a selection of work chronicling or critiquing the life and work of Paul Morphy since David Lawson's biography appeared in 1976. It does not include the myriad comparisons to the late Bobby Fischer (1943–2008), whose paranoia, anti-Semitism, and increasingly bizarre behavior from the early 1970s until his death gave credence to Luzhinesque descriptions of chess-player behavior. Charles Krauthammer's 2005 "Did Chess Make Him Crazy?" provides a convenient example of such coverage. "Fischer is the poster boy for the mad chess genius," wrote Krauthammer, "a species with a pedigree going back at least to Paul Morphy, who after his triumphal 1858–59 tour of Europe returned to the U.S., abruptly quit the game and is said to have wandered the streets of New Orleans talking to himself." Krauthammer—like many others—uses Morphy as a tertiary analogy, a foil against which Fischer can be judged. Such instances only intensified after Fischer's death on January 17, 2008. Unlike Lawson's treatment, however, similar mentions never surpass such mundane statements. They serve as quick examples rather than points of significant analysis. For further examples of such comparisons, see any global newspaper dated January 18, 2008.

The bibliography will also ignore Morphy sources published prior to 1976 that went uncited by Lawson, assuming that the breadth of Lawson's research trumped their ability to provide any significant new information. For example, Charles Davy's 1965 *Words in the Mind* includes an appendix describing the Morphy tragedy as a response to pattern recognition in continual chess play—the prototype Luzhin analysis. But Davy's is a work of poetic analysis, not chess biography, and therefore provides no revelatory information to supplement his mundane appended thesis.

Finally, the bibliography will also omit works dedicated to game analysis, instead keeping its focus on biography. Books such as Chris Ward's 1997 *The Genius of Paul Morphy* are thus excluded. Thus what follows is brief selection of post-1976 Morphy books and articles that treat the biographical subject in more than a passing, ancillary manner.

Books

Beim, Valeri. *Paul Morphy: A Modern Perspective*. Milford, CT: Russell Enterprises, 2005.

> Beim's work is largely a work detailing Morphy's games, and the "modern perspective" of the title refers to chess analysis. The work does contain a substantial biographical section, but it provides little in the way of new analysis of Morphy's life.

Dizikes, John. *Sportsmen and Gamesmen*. Boston: Houghton Mifflin, 1981.

> Dizikes places Morphy's 1858 European tour in the context of mid-nineteenth century American challenges to British sports superiori-

ty. It accompanies accounts of the 1860 John C. Heenan–Tom Sayres
boxing match, the 1851 yacht race featuring the boat "America," and
a series of mid-1850s horse races.

Friedrich, Otto. *Glenn Gould: A Life and Variations*. New York: Random House, 1989.

Friedrich includes a brief three-page account of Morphy, in aid of
contextualizing the musical mind of composer Glenn Gould. The
account provides no new revelations about Morphy, but does demonstrate Morphy's invocation as a comparative model for a non-chess
player.

Hillyer, Martin Frere. *Thomas Frere and the Brotherhood of Chess: A History of 19th Century Chess In New York City*. Jefferson, NC: McFarland, 2006.

Hillyer's work chronicles the evolution of chess in New York during the nineteenth century, viewed through the lens of chess author
Thomas Frere. He traces the development of chess into a public phenomenon, particularly in relation to other available board games in
the first half of the century. This discussion leads to a discussion of
the First American Chess Congress and Morphy's role in the growing popularity of the game. Hillyer then continues by chronicling
the rest of the century. In this account, Morphy's success (and resulting celebrity) plays a pivotal role in the preeminent rise of New York
chess.

Shenk, David. *The Immortal Game: A History of Chess*. New York: Doubleday, 2006.

Shenk's history includes a chapter titled "Into Its Vertiginous Depths:
Chess and the Shattered Mind," which chronicles chess manias
through history. He contextualizes Morphy's illness not as a unique
devolution, but rather one in a long series of chess-related mental dis-
orders, from Robert Burton's 1621 exhortation that chess "is a game
too troublesome for some men's brains," to representations of chess-
related mental problems in the television show *Seinfeld*. He also includes a cogent summary of the psychological theories attempting to
explain the phenomenon.

Shibut, Macon. *Paul Morphy and the Evolution of Chess Theory*. New York: Dover Books,
1992.

While Shibut's book is mostly a work of chess analysis, it merits a
place here for its cogent writing on Morphy's pension for early development of pieces, finding his place amongst Anderssen, Steinitz,
and others. This sort of comparative approach leads necessarily to
biographical discussion of both Morphy and his chess age, demonstrating the transformation of chess thinking after Morphy's aggres-
sive appearance.

Winter, E. G. *World Chess Champions*. London: Pergamon Press, 1981.

> The book includes a chapter on Paul Morphy written by Lawson.
> Though it treats its subject in considerable depth, the article is essen-
> tially a condensed version of Lawson's book-length treatment.

Articles

"American Chess Prodigy of the 1850s." *American History Illustrated* 22 (March 1987):
    50-51.

> The article presents a brief and ultimately elementary biography of
> Morphy, emphasizing his early success, his world championship, and
> his status as a lawyer.

Beegan, Gerry. "The Mechanization of the Image: Facsimile, Photography, and Frag-
    mentation in Nineteenth-Century Wood Engraving." *Journal of Design History*
    8 (No. 4 1995): 257-274.

> Beegan analyzes woodcuts by the European Dalziel Brothers, featur-
> ing Morphy and other chess players on his 1858 trip to Europe. Here
> Morphy's image, rather than his game or other constituent elements
> of his biography, is analyzed.

Bisguier, Arthur. "Morphy Versus Fischer: The Inevitable Comparison." *Chess Life* 42
    (September 1987): 32-35.

> Bisguier compares the talents of Morphy and Fischer, evaluating their
> game play in relation to their childhood potential, their study of the
> game, and their different eras and historical contexts. Interestingly,
> he sublimates the discussion of their mental problems. "Although
> only time will tell with Fischer, one can argue that he is destined for
> the telling appellation applied to *Morphy: The Pride and Sorrow of
> Chess*. Still, so what?" Bisguier sticks to an evaluation of their play,
> eventually concluding that a match between the two would end in
> a draw.

Caverlee, William. "The Unenthusiastic Chess Champion of the World." *Oxford Ameri-
    can* (The Sports Issue 2007): 70-71.

> Caverlee rehearses the general Morphy biography, arguing that the
> chess champion remains an enigmatic figure. He cites Lawson's work
> as being the most complete available source, but laments that Law-
> son "cannot quite trace a satisfying outline of the man" through "424
> slow-moving pages."

Hambrick, Keith S. "Morphy, Paul Charles." In *Dictionary of Louisiana Biography*, ed.
    Glenn R. Conrad (New Orleans: Louisiana Historical Association, 1988),
    I:583.

Brief biographical entry based on secondary sources, clearly dependent upon Lawson's text.

Elley, Frank. "America Remembers Paul Morphy." *Chess Life* 39 (June 1984): 19-22.

Elley's account is sourced entirely with secondary material and even takes as its main source an early article from Lawson, "The Life of Paul Morphy," originally published in *Chessworld* magazine. Interestingly, Elley does not use Lawson's monograph, instead turning readers looking for a fuller biography to Lawson's Morphy chapter in E. G. Winter's 1981 *World Chess Champions*.

Ewart, Bradley. "The Devil and Paul Morphy." *Chess Life* 39 (June 1984): 23-25.

Ewart's article provides an extended rumination on Morphy's attempt to replay the match between the Devil and a young man, presented on a Richmond wall. The story itself is recounted in Lawson's text, whereby a traveling Morphy (in Richmond during the Civil War, ostensibly as a service to P.G.T. Beauregard) sees an allegorical picture and wows an audience by playing the position successfully. The great difficulty in validating the tale, notes Ewart, is the representative nature of each piece, and the possible moves that could be derived from different interpretations that might allow for a victory. There is more than one interpretation, as might be imagined, and Ewart examines their viability and uses his examination to speculate about the workings of that specific Morphy episode.

Glickman, Mark E. "Parameter Estimation in Large Dynamic Paired Comparison Experiments." *Applied Statistics* 48 (No. 3 1999): 377-394.

Glickman uses the determination of chess greatness through statistical analysis of select data sets as an example of parameter estimation in large dynamic paired comparison experiments. Lasker, Capablanca, Fischer, Alekhine, and Kasparov comprise the top five according to peak posterior mean strength. Morphy's place on the list varies by analyst, as fewer games hurt his evaluation on one list. One study places him at the eighth position, another at twenty-seven.

Hoffman, Paul. "A Chess Player Realizes the Game Controls His Life." *Smithsonian* 18 (July 1987): 1129-135.

Hoffman uses Morphy's mental illness—in particular his paranoia about being poisoned—to discuss contemporary chess manias in players like Gary Kasparov and Anatoly Karpov. The article emphasizes the 1978 world championship between Karpov and Korchnoi, evaluating their attempts to unnerve one another off the chessboard.

Kurtz, Michael L. "Paul Morphy: Louisiana's Chess Champion." *Louisiana History* 34 (Spring 1993): 175-199.

Kurtz provides a general overview of Morphy's life, with particular reference to his time in Louisiana. Though the article appears in a scholarly journal, it provides little new information and is heavily dependent upon Lawson's work and sources. Kurtz does spend more time on Morphy's Louisiana exploits, entering into more detail about his game with Winfield Scott, for example. "Flustered by the two defeats," he notes, "Scott rose from the table and indignantly left the room without even congratulating the child." Such intimate nuance does provide a level of personal understanding largely unavailable in a five-hundred page work.

McCrary, Robert. "Paul Morphy: The Man, the Myth, and the Misconceptions." *Chess Life* 42 (September 1987): 36-37.

"In honor of the 150th anniversary of Paul Morphy's birth in 1837," writes Robert McCrary, "*Chess Life* debunks several misconceptions without destroying the magic surrounding that memorable master, Paul Morphy." Still, McCrary's lone secondary source is Lawson's book, and the article simply repeats truisms known to any reader of *Paul Morphy: The Pride and Sorrow of Chess*.

Philipson, Robert. "Chess and Sex in Le Devoir Du Violence." *Callaloo* 38 (Winter 1989): 216-232.

Philipson critiques the work of Ernest Jones as "predictably Oedipal" in its focus on father murder and queenly power. Though Philipson's analysis is brief, it clearly finds Jones's evaluation of Morphy's trauma overly simplistic, imprisoned by the dominant Freudian theory of the early century.

Soltis, Andy, and Gene McCormick. "Chess Life: The Morphy Defense." *Chess Life* 39 (August 1984): 26-27.

Soltis and McCormick evaluate Morphy's relationship with Charles Henry Stanley and Eugène Rousseau in an effort to discover the actual genesis of the opening position known as "the Morphy defense." They conclude that the move wasn't original to Morphy.

Torchia, Robert Wilson. "The Chess Players by Thomas Eakins." *Winterthur Portfolio* 26 (Winter 1991): 267-276.

Torchia uses the work of Thomas Eakins to trace a brief history of representations of chess in art, featuring Winslow Homer's sketch of Paul Morphy. He describes the torrent of celebration from the world of American letters following Morphy's 1859 return from Europe, all the while providing an adequate history of Morphy's life in chess.

Williams, David R. "Paul Morphy: The Pride and Sorrow of Chess." *Library Journal*, 1 August 1976, 1653.

Williams writes a brief review of Lawson's biography. It is very favorable, using for comparison Philip W. Sergeant's *Morphy's Games of Chess*, which emphasizes game play over biography.

Fiction

Sheola, Noah. *Paul Morphy*. 2006.

> Sheola's play debuted in Portsmouth, New Hampshire, in November 2006. It chronicles the bulk of the Staunton controversy, with Morphy unsuccessfully hunting the presumed English chess champion. The play is unpublished.

Sitewell, Jason K. "What I Discovered About 'Poop' Glover." *Saturday Evening Post* 248 (September 1976): 14-16, 26, 84-85.

> Sitewell creates a fictional twelve-year-old chess prodigy, Paul Glover, named after Morphy and claiming to be his great grandson. The story posits that Glover's great grandmother would bring Morphy his food and medication, whereby he fell in love with her. Her husband was killed in the Civil War, and yet she bore a child, Glover's grandfather, who was particularly adept at chess.

Index

Thomas Aiello is an assistant professor of history at Valdosta State University. He is the editor of *Dan Burley's Jive* (Northern Illinois University Press, 2009) and the author of the forthcoming *Bayou Classic: The Grambling-Southern Football Rivalry* (LSU Press, 2010) and *The Kings of Casino Park: Race and Race Baseball in the Lost Season of 1932* (University of Alabama Press, 2011).